CORPORATE STRATEGY AND PRODUCT INNOVATION

CORPORATE STRATEGY AND PRODUCT INNOVATION

Second Edition

Edited by

Robert R. Rothberg

THE FREE PRESS
A Division of Macmillan Publishing Co., Inc.
NEW YORK

Collier Macmillan Publishers
LONDON

The Free Press
A Division of Macmillan Publishing Co., Inc.
866 Third Avenue, New York, N.Y. 10022

Collier Macmillan Canada, Ltd.

Library of Congress Catalog Card Number: 80–1857

Printed in the United States of America

printing number

1 2 3 4 5 6 7 8 9 10

Library of Congress Cataloging in Publication Data

Main entry under title:

Corporate strategy and product innovation.

   Bibliography: p.
   Includes index.
   1. New products—Addresses, essays, lectures.
2. Product management—Addresses, essays, lectures.
I. Rothberg, Robert R.
HD69.N4C67 1981   658.5'75   80-1857
ISBN 0-02-927520-2

To Abra, Joan
and the Velvet Shadow

*To Abra, Joan
and the Velvet Shadow*

Contents

PART III   Concept Generation and Evaluation

A. *Idea Generation*

B. *Analysis of New Product Proposals*

PART IV   **Development, Testing, and Commercialization**

A. *Development and Testing*

B. *Commercialization*

Preface to the Second Edition

THIS SECOND EDITION CONTAINS a number of changes. They reflect new realities in the socio-economic and technological environment as well as the availability of significant new material. While a good deal of the content differs from the first edition, the basic organizing principles remain the same.

One change in the second edition is the new emphasis given to the role of law and government as a stimulus and barrier to innovation. Hollomon *et al.* catalog and discuss the various forms and points of impact, while Bennigson addresses the more specialized topic of product liability. A second change in this edition is the far greater emphasis given to product-planning matrices. Conley's classic paper, linking experience curves to the matrix, is now accompanied by papers by Day and Robinson *et al.*, which deepen and extend our understanding of this approach. Day questions the assumptions underlying this technique, while Robinson *et al.* show how a nine-cell version can be used in new ways in a highly competitive industrial setting.

The third major change in this edition is a series of seven new papers on concept generation and evaluation. If these papers can be said to have a common theme, it is that new problems also present new opportunities. Brown, Leaf, Keegan, and von Hippel all deal with opportunity identification—Brown, for instance, in terms of life-cycle costing, and Leaf in terms of analyzing competitor strategy and tactics. Green and Wind, Herbert and Bisio, and Souder, on the other hand, focus on newer or clearer approaches to concept evaluation. Souder, for example, compares eight different methods for screening new product proposals.

The fourth and final change of emphasis in this edition has to do with the internal dynamics of the innovation process within the firm. Abernathy and Utterback relate the nature of the innovation pursued to product/market maturity. Roberts examines the innovation process from the standpoint of the kinds of people required to make it function both efficiently and effectively. Vanderwicken looks at the process as practiced by Procter & Gamble, long regarded as one of the best-managed consumer goods companies in the country. In different ways, all three of these papers note that while it may be possible to institutionalize change, those in charge cannot afford to abdicate their responsibility for overall direction and control.

In the preparation of this edition I have once again relied upon the valuable assistance rendered by others. I would especially like to thank

Ben Barak of Rutgers University College, Merle Crawford of Michigan, David Furse of Vanderbilt, David Hopkins of The Conference Board, Burton Marcus of USC, and Mike Pessemier of Purdue for their advice and suggestions. A considerable debt is also owed to Barbara Amodeo, Natalie Henderson, Russ Nascondiglio, Dorothy Stalma and Willa Troutman for their assistance in collecting, copying, and preparing the source materials. Above all, I would like to thank my wife and daughter for their support and encouragement.

R. R. R.
Hillside, New Jersey

Preface to the First Edition

THIS VOLUME IS A PRODUCT of more than three years of course development work at Rutgers Graduate School of Business Administration. It was undertaken in response to a long-felt need for a book that could integrate strategic planning with new product development and, more importantly, could analyze both from an interdisciplinary perspective.

Product innovation has long been considered to be an important component of corporate strategy for survival or growth. Today it is vital. The squeeze on profits from current products, the need for higher profit margins, and the unceasing search for growth have turned corporated planners single-mindedly towards the objective of successful development and commercialization of new products. Corporate strategy is now inextricably bound up with the planning, structuring, and execution of new product programs.

The approach taken here recognizes that the process of strategic planning and new product development is inherently interdisciplinary in character. Successful management of this process requires the close cooperation of many specialists from diverse fields. These specialists, however, function under a severe handicap which can and does repeatedly undermine their efforts. This handicap is the almost total lack of understanding of any discipline other than their own. This book integrates diverse methodologies while extending reader comprehension and skills in dealing with issues of strategic planning and new product development. The discussion embraces consumer and industrial product-markets and is carried forward at a level appropriate to the thoughtful business student, be he a tyro or experienced executive.

The book itself is organized in four parts. Part I is entitled *The Importance of Innovation*. As its title implies, it is intended to convey the significance of new products to corporate survival and growth. Part II, *Strategy and Planning*, deals with the formulation of strategy and policy at corporate and marketing levels and with the organization of the new product function. Strategic planning provides the direction and discipline necessary for the efficient management of the process. Part III, *Concept Generation and Evaluation*, is concerned with the identification of promising new product ideas and their assessment from a development standpoint. Two points are stressed: first, that the quality of new product proposals is a function of both the number of ideas generated and the diversity of their points of origin, and second, that probabilistic concepts should be employed more frequently to help decide which projects should be put into development. Part IV, *Development, Testing, and Commercialization* refers to those activities that take place after a decision has been made to translate the concept into a tangible market offering. Special emphasis is given to techniques that managers might find useful for decision-making and to concepts that may help them appreciate how potential buyers might respond to their new product initiatives.

"New" is not necessarily "better" in books as well as other product offerings. Classic articles are included in this collection regardless of their date of original publication.

No preface would be complete without acknowledging the valuable assistance rendered by others. I would like to thank David Aaker of Berkeley, David Luck of Southern Illinois, Stanley Shapiro of McGill, and David Wilemon of Syracuse for their helpful comments and advice. A debt of gratitude is also owed to Florence Adams, Michael Bucci, Stuart Gelbord, Howard Schwartz, Willa Troutman, and Arleen Troy for their considerable help in collecting, copying, and preparing the source materials. Above all, I would like to thank my wife for her personal and professional encouragement in the preparation of this book.

Robert R. Rothberg
Hillside, New Jersey

I

THE IMPORTANCE OF
INNOVATION

MOST COMPANIES now recognize that the key to their future survival and growth rests in a continuous flow of new and improved products. The five articles in this section provide important insights into some of the more dynamic elements of the innovation process.

Rothberg defines product innovation and explains how it has come to be an integral part of corporate strategy and planning. Marquis uses the findings of his classic National Science Foundation study on innovation to illustrate how a firm should go about identifying and taking advantage of its new product opportunities in an effective manner. Clifford outlines the product life cycle concept and shows how the diagnosis of incipient product line weaknesses can also be used to help set research priorities.

The last two papers in this section provide some insights as to why Murphy's Law* is so often thought to prevail in matters pertaining to new product development. Schon investigates the fear that innovation efforts frequently encounter within the firm. He notes that because fear is a function more of uncertainty than of risk, resistance to change can be expected to diminish as the project moves forward. Hollomon et al. conclude this section with an examination of the role of government in the innovation process. They also look at the experience of several other industrialized countries and propose a number of legislative and regulatory initiatives to stimulate technological innovation in the United States.

* Murphy's Law: If anything can go wrong, it will—and at the worst possible time!

1

1. Product Innovation in Perspective

Robert R. Rothberg

OVER THE PAST several decades business has come increasingly to the realization that new and improved products may hold the key to their future survival and growth. A host of environmental forces, including changes in consumer and competitor behavior, technology, and government policy have combined to make product innovation a vital element in the formulation of corporate strategy and planning.

The development of new products, however, remains an exceedingly difficult and challenging undertaking. It is difficult because the process of innovation is inherently complex, requiring the close coordination and control of a multitude of vastly different tasks. It is challenging because important decisions, often involving the very survival of the enterprise, must be made on the basis of very limited information.

This introduction has three purposes. First, it will define product innovation. Second, it will show how external forces have caused product innovation to become an increasingly important part of corporate strategy and planning. Third, and most important, it will outline a number of ways in which new products might be developed more efficiently and effectively.

Product Innovation Defined

"Product innovation," like "product" can be defined in several different ways. A product can refer to a physical entity or a cluster of anticipated customer benefits depending on whether the perspective adopted is that of the business or that of the market.

From a business perspective, therefore, a product innovation can be said to represent a change in, or an addition to, the physical entities that comprise its product line. From a market perspective, however, the term

3

refers to a new or revised set of customer perceptions concerning a particular benefits cluster.

That which is considered a product innovation by a business enterprise may not be recognized as such by its customers. Thus, the soap companies frequently change the chemical formulation of their detergents without publicizing the fact. The change may not be consciously recognized by the user. Conversely, a product innovation in the eyes of prospective customers may not be regarded as such by the business. An otherwise unchanged product, for example, may be repositioned in the minds of prospective customers through major changes in advertising, distribution, and pricing designed to attract new users and stimulate new uses. If, after repositioning, a majority of customers perceives this product to be a new benefits cluster, it is, by definition, a product innovation, or new product, from their point of view.

A business perspective is adopted here. Except where otherwise specified, a product innovation shall be defined as a change in, or addition to, the physical entities that comprise the firm's product line.[1]

Environmental Forces Affecting Product Innovation

The importance of new products to a company can be assessed in various ways. Their contribution to growth, for example, might be measured in terms of the proportion of increased company sales or profits that can be attributed to them over a given period of time. Consider Hewlett-Packard's successful line of pocket calculators. These accounted for roughly half of the average increase in H-P sales and roughly two-thirds of the average increase in H-P pretax earnings in the first three years following their original introduction.[2] While they no longer contribute nearly as much to corporate coffers, the funds they did generate have fueled the development and commercialization of a wide range of other H-P offerings. Moreover, their contribution to H-P's reputation for high-quality, technologically advanced products has also opened new avenues of market opportunity to the firm that otherwise would have remained foreclosed.

To assess the contribution of new products to business survival one must speculate on what would have happened if these offerings had not been introduced. The business landscape is littered with the wreckage of once-successful companies that neglected to develop new products while they still had the capacity to do so.

---

[1] A company develops new products for one of two reasons: a) to replace or supplement its existing offerings in their present markets; b) to serve new markets defined in terms of customer benefits or geography. It can develop new markets without new products by making appropriate adjustments in the pricing, promotion and/or distribution policies associated with an existing offering.

[2] Hewlett-Packard Company, 1974 Annual Report, p. 5.

Product innovation has become a vital element in corporate strategy and planning for a number of reasons outside the control of any single company. These include changes in consumer and competitor behavior, technology, and government policy.[3]

Consumer and Competitor Behavior

Two trends in the marketplace have been of major importance in stimulating product innovation: the increasing instability of consumer preferences and the growing intensity and sophistication of competition.

Consumer purchasing patterns have become increasingly less predictable over time as the result of rising discretionary incomes and expanding assortments of purchase alternatives. Rising incomes, of course, have contributed mightily to the absolute growth of virtually all markets over the past several decades. Growing markets not only attract new entrants with their own new offerings but force established firms in these markets to adjust or broaden their product lines in an effort to maintain or expand their sales.

Rising discretionary incomes also stimulate the development of new products in a second way, by encouraging prospective buyers to modify the weights they attach to various purchase criteria. Historically, low price has dominated the purchase decision. Rising incomes, however, allow consumers the luxury of spending more to buy products that more precisely fit their needs. This, in turn, stimulates the development of new products to meet the special requirements of particular market segments or product applications. New products stimulate other innovations. As the focus of competition shifts from price to product design, buying patterns become increasingly less stable or predictable, forcing business to continuously seek out new product and new market opportunities to further the realization of their own objectives.

Product innovation is also stimulated by the growing aggressiveness and sophistication of competition. This is a function not only of changing marketing and technological opportunities, but of the influx of professionally trained managers and the institutionalization of growth as a corporate objective.

Professionally trained managers are equipped to look at business problems and opportunities more objectively than managers whose perspective is limited by their experience in one particular field of endeavor. The professional is less likely to be influenced by emotion and precedent and more likely to try new ideas based upon a dispassionate appraisal of their merits.

---

[3] The forces discussed here represent trends in the business environment of relatively long duration. Speculations concerning the effects of more recent economic developments are deferred to *A Final Comment*.

Growth, measured in financial terms, has also become an end in itself over the past several decades, for reasons that range from the presence of attractive opportunities to the needs of a healthy organizational climate. Professional managers frequently see superior growth opportunities in the development of new products and new markets compared to more intensive efforts to improve financial returns within established product-markets. Competitors affected by these new initiatives are forced to respond in kind if they are to maintain any degree of control over their own destinies.

Changes in Technology

Changes in consumer and competitor behavior are not the only external forces affecting product innovation. Technological advances can have an equally profound effect, often leading to radical changes in the size and character of established product-markets.

Consider the development of large-scale integrated circuits (LSIs) and their use in pocket calculators. This has not only created a major new market for personal computational devices but has dealt a body blow to the market for conventional calculators based upon older electromechanical principles among industrial and institutional users. Rapidly growing calculator sales have also stimulated important improvements in the production of LSIs which in turn have led to dramatic price reductions and still further expansion of the pocket calculator market.

Improvements in product and process technology are often introduced to a wide variety of product-markets simultaneously. LSIs, for example, are used extensively in areas as diverse as computers and television sets, cash registers and automatic sensing devices. They offer a broad range of benefits to prospective users, including increased reliability and lower power requirements as well as smaller size and an expanded range of new performance capabilities.

This is the kind of competition that counts. Schumpeter referred to it as "the gale of creative destruction." [4] A common technological base sets limits to the intensity of interfirm competition within a given product-market, and when this commonality is broken the very survival of the disadvantaged firms may be threatened. The latter have no choice but to respond in kind if they are to maintain or regain their former marketplace position.

NCR, for example, has all but abandoned its traditional approach to cash register design and production in favor of electronics. Zenith, after trumpeting the merits of a hand-wired color television chassis for many

---

[4] Joseph Schumpeter, *Capitalism, Socialism, and Democracy,* 3rd Ed. (New York: Harper & Row, 1950), pp. 83–84.

years, quietly switched over to printed circuit boards and plug-in components. In both instances their response was dictated by the successful technological initiatives of their competitors.

Some forms of technological change have a more pervasive effect upon innovation than others. Consider improvements in the technology of communications and logistics. These break down the spatial barriers among markets and bring new competitive pressures to bear in previously protected regions and localities. The new and larger markets that emerge allow business to take advantage of economies of scale in the production and distribution of a wide range of new offerings.

Technological change has an important effect on product innovation not only because of the opportunity it creates for new products in a wide range of markets but because these in turn create conditions under which competitors must respond in kind if they are to continue to survive and prosper.[5]

Changes in Government Policy

The contribution of government to product innovation traditionally has been equated to its policy of directly subsidizing research in areas deemed vital to the national interest. Research and development grants to military and aerospace suppliers are a case in point. Commercial spinoffs of these research results range from laser technology to synthesized protein. Government policies also take the form of regulatory constraints on innovation, such as the Food and Drug Administration requirements for extensive documentation of clinical research before granting approval for the production and sale of ethical drugs.

To an increasing degree, however, new government standards and regulations are expressed in performance terms that stimulate rather than retard the development of new products and processes. Clean air and water standards, for example, have led to major advances in pollution measurement and control. Safety standards similarly have forced the redesign of product offerings ranging from medicine containers and aerosols to automobiles and machine tools. With this shift to performance-oriented criteria, government can be said to mandate innovation if affected companies wish to remain in business.[6]

---

[5] Not mentioned here, of course, are the opportunities created for new product and service complements to these first and second-round innovations. Raytheon's Radar Range, for example, requires special cookingware for proper use, and Polaroid cameras have helped to create important new markets for photo-identification services.

[6] For fuller treatment of this important topic see J. Herbert Hollomon *et al.,* "Government and the Innovation Process," in this book, and William Abernathy and Balaji Chakravarthy, "Government Intervention and Innovation in Industry: A Policy Framework," *Sloan Management Review* 20 (Spring, 1979), pp. 3–18.

Improving the Process of Product Innovation

Product innovation is a Scylla and Charybdis proposition for most business enterprises today. The environmental factors discussed above force business to press forward with new and improved products or risk the loss of markets to present and potential competitors. When a business does so, however, it must of necessity make important decisions under conditions of uncertainty and thus risk failure for technical and/or commercial reasons. The cost of failure can be enormous and, in itself, may constitute a threat to the continued viability of the enterprise.

New Product Failures

Estimates of new product failure rates vary enormously with the sample of firms studied and the definition of success (or failure) employed. They also vary with the care taken by the researcher to minimize the naturally biased answers of respondents. The most widely cited statistics on new product failure rates are those reported by Booz, Allen & Hamilton in the *Management of New Products.*[7] Their research indicates that it takes a company an average of 58 new product ideas to come up with one successful new product. Only seven of these ideas ever reach the point of actual development where significant commitments of resources begin to be made, and of the seven, six are eliminated in the process of development or in the subsequent stages of testing or commercialization. Two relatively recent studies suggest that roughly one-third of those products that are fully commercialized fail to meet the objectives set for them by their sponsoring firms.[8]

It should be obvious that there is a great deal of wasted time and effort in new product development. If business could reduce this waste even slightly it could multiply severalfold the effective utilization of resources on successful projects.[9] What is required is good strategic planning, proper management controls, and healthy organizational attitudes. These are discussed below.

[7] See Booz, Allen & Hamilton, "A Program for New Product Evolution," in this book.

[8] C. Merle Crawford, "New Product Failure Rates—Facts and Fallacies," *Research Management,* 22 (September, 1979), pp. 9–13, and David S. Hopkins, *New-Product Winners and Losers,* Research Report No. 773, (New York: The Conference Board, 1980).

[9] There is, of course, another kind of new product failure, the rejection of new product proposals that should have been accepted on the basis of their merits. See Robert R. Rothberg, "Playing It Safe in New Product Development," *Advanced Management Journal,* 40 (Fall, 1975).

Strategic Planning

Strategic planning refers to the specification of company objectives and goals and the development of a time-phased plan of action for their attainment. It provides a business with a sense of *direction* for identifying and evaluating new opportunities, *structure* for mobilizing and allocating resources, and *system* for monitoring and controlling plans as they are put into effect.

Without strategic planning, one of two things may happen. First, the company may continue to pursue a strategy which at one time may have been responsible for its success but has long since been outmoded by events. In this situation, means are frequently confused with ends, such as railroads and transportation, movies and entertainment, and so on. Strategic planning is needed here to help the firm anticipate and plan for change. Second, the company may recognize the need for change but dissipate its energies on a host of ill-conceived and poorly implemented ventures. Just because an electronic components firm can build a computer does not mean it should do so, or if it does, that it should try to compete head to head with IBM. Thus, strategic planning is also necessary to help the firm identify and evaluate promising courses of action and, once decisions are made, to be sure that plans are carried out as efficiently and as effectively as possible. The process of strategic planning is examined in detail elsewhere in this book, most notably by Cohen and Cyert, who view it from the perspective of top management, and Ansoff and Stewart, who pay special attention to the needs of high-technology businesses.

Management Control

Product innovation moves forward within the framework established by strategic planning. Given that the new product is to be developed internally, the process of innovation is normally conceptualized as a series of six phases: concept generation, screening, business analysis, development, testing, and commercialization. Each stage provides management with the opportunity to make a go/no-go decision on a project as additional information is accumulated. Good control of this process, in the sense of both stimulating the flow of good proposals and monitoring their progress, can greatly improve the effectiveness with which resources are employed in the new products sector.

Stimulating Good Proposals. Every successful new product starts out as an idea. The best ideas frequently represent answers to pressing strategic or tactical problems. All other things equal, the greater the number of ideas generated and the more diverse their points of origin, the better those ideas are likely to be that are selected for possible commercialization.

The main problem with concept generation, including subsequent efforts to refine or enhance the original ideas, is that this activity is neither planned nor administered in any coherent fashion. In general, business tends to be a passive receiver rather than an active solicitor of new product ideas. Moreover, those ideas it does receive are so poorly handled that it is frequently a matter of chance as to whether they will obtain a full and fair hearing from the standpoint of their possible commercialization. What is needed is a well planned idea-generating system, aimed at improving both the quantity and quality of new product proposals for managerial consideration.

Many companies now delegate specific responsibility for generating new product proposals to a single department within each of its operating units. These departments—which generally control or coordinate the full spectrum of new product activity—disseminate information concerning the kinds of new product ideas that are sought and the procedures to be used in making proposals. They also act as focal points for incoming ideas, rerouting some for further elaboration and scheduling others for formal consideration. The same groups often take a more active role in stimulating proposals by funding exploratory research activities, creativity-enrichment sessions, and the like.

If the efforts described above have one limitation, it is that they tend to encourage proposals that are closely related to current product technologies and existing company markets. To overcome this problem a good many firms in recent years have adopted the venture group approach to complement and extend their other efforts.[10] These groups, small in size and distinctly interdisciplinary and entrepreneurial in character, are detached from their regular duties for extended periods of time in order to identify and evaluate major new business opportunities for their sponsor firms. Companies ranging from Colgate-Palmolive and Pillsbury to 3M and Exxon have found venture groups to be a valuable means for pursuing their diversification objectives.[11]

Regardless of its structure, the main objective of a good concept-generating system is to develop a broad assortment of proposed solutions to an assigned strategic or tactical problem. Its main challenge is to reconcile the discipline needed for the efficient production of promising proposals within these boundaries with the imagination and flexibility needed to recognize and pursue outstanding ideas that fall outside these limits.

Monitoring Results. Given a flow of promising new product proposals the firm must next decide which to discard and which to investigate

---

[10] See David L. Wilemon and Porter L. Hulett, "A Systems Approach to Corporate Development," in this book.

[11] For a contrasting view, see Norman Fast, "A Visit to the New Venture Graveyard," *Research Management,"* 22 (March, 1979), pp. 18–22.

further. Because of the uncertainties involved, the best approach is often compared to a series of filters, each succeeding filter having a finer mesh than its predecessor. Each time a proposal passes through one of these filters, a signal is given to spend additional funds on its appraisal and development. The information thus obtained is then incorporated into its evaluation at the next decision point. Proposals that fail to pass a given filter are either remanded for more study or eliminated from further consideration.

Because successively heavier expenditures of funds usually are made between each succeeding filter, this elimination process allows a company, at least in theory, to conserve the bulk of its resources for those projects which appear to have the most promise. Sometimes, however, this elimination process fails to operate. It is not unknown, for example, for a project to take on a life of its own because of the sizeable funds already invested in its development or because it appears to be a pet project of top management.

The Cost and Value of Additional Information. Apart from the malfunctioning of the new product process itself the most challenging problem is assessing the cost and value of gathering additional information at each decision point. Two kinds of mistakes can be made: endorsing projects with poor prospects, and rejecting projects that in fact have substantial merit. The first type of error (Type I) is presumably discovered at the next decision point. Its cost is that of the intervening research. The second type of error (Type II) is generally buried with the decision to eliminate the project. Its cost is the incremental profits that would have been obtained had the project been commercialized.

To a large degree, the decision problem is a function of what is already known. Uncertainty can be said to dominate the early phases of new product development while risk can be said to characterize its later stages. In the early phases it is virtually impossible to identify the various possible decision outcomes, let alone to estimate the likelihood of their occurrence. The decision resists analysis. In these circumstances, perhaps the best advice for early stage decision-makers is to invest more "front money" in marginal proposals before eliminating them from any further consideration. Thus, if consumer acceptance of a radically new product concept is the chief issue at stake, additional concept tests might be carried out before rendering a decision. The cost of this additional research is not likely to be great, and it may help to reduce the number of Type II errors discussed above.

Risk, on the other hand, refers to a situation in which the various possible outcomes of the decision and their respective likelihoods of occurrence can be estimated with a much greater degree of confidence (at least subjectively). The decision can be analyzed. In the later stages of new product development a variety of probabilistic techniques available to help the firm make decisions in the face of incomplete information. Risk analysis, for example, can be used to help make hard choices among competing new product projects; critical path analysis can be used to help schedule project activities and minimize the time and/or cost required for project completion; and Bayesian statistics can be used to help assess the cost and value of further product testing or marketing research.[12] In all instances management must be willing to take the time and effort necessary to structure its decision problems properly if it is to realize the full potential of these analytical tools. The power of these techniques is such, however, that even when informally applied, they can help the manager to organize his own thoughts and assumptions and to make better decisions than would otherwise be the case.[13]

Organization Attitudes

There are two attitudinal prerequisites for a successful program of product innovation: a top management which is open to new ideas and suggestions and subordinates who are motivated to make new product proposals and see them through to successful conclusions. Objectivity, confidence, and enthusiasm all are vital elements of this process.

Many companies are so obsessed with improving the efficiency of their current operations that they create an atmosphere in which product innovation is all but impossible. They are excessively preoccupied with short-term financial performance. They avoid financial commitments with intermediate or long-term payoff potentials. These companies structure their incentives to encourage short-term accomplishments. Their patience with new product projects is short and they try to eliminate potential failures as rapidly as possible. Top management may give lip service to innovation in these situations, but company policies create an atmosphere in which subordinates find it more in their interest to avoid failure rather than to pursue success. Whatever new products are developed in this environment tend to be relatively certain of success and also relatively small contributors to corporate profits.

Companies with long and successful records of product innovation, by contrast, try to take the longer view. Consider Procter & Gamble, Hewlett-Packard, 3M, and Texas Instruments. They may differ greatly in style of operations, but they also have a number of features in common which

---

[12] See, for example, V. H. Herbert Jr. and Attilio Bisio, "Proposal Development: Analyzing the Risks and the Benefits"; Franz Edelman and Joel Greenberg, "Venture Analysis: "The Assessment of Uncertainty and Risk"; and Paul E. Green, "Bayesian Statistics and Product Decisions," in this book.

[13] A "good" decision in this context is one that is consistent with the goals and decision-criteria employed by the manager and with the assumptions he makes about the magnitudes and likelihoods of the various possible inputs to or outcomes of his decision.

strongly influence their ability to pursue new product programs successfully.

All four companies, for example, are run by top managements that
have historically enjoyed unusually long terms of office. These executives
have the luxury of being able to plan for the future of their companies
in terms that extend beyond next year's operating statements. All four
are heavily committed to research and development, with marketing as ‒
well as technical personnel having a strong influence over project selection
and execution. The development efforts of these companies appear to be
designed more to deliver important new user benefits than to practice
technical virtuosity for its own sake. Most importantly, all four try to create
an atmosphere in which employees are both willing and able to propose
new product ideas. While their individual methods may vary in this regard,
they all offer several forums in which new product ideas can be assured
of a hearing. They also offer meaningful incentives in the form of career
advancement opportunities to those whose suggestions are adopted. There
are penalties for project failure, of course, but these companies go to considerable pains to distinguish between failures attributable to incompetence
and those beyond the individual's influence or power to control.

Healthy attitudes and expectations are essential to the success of any
program of product innovation. They are conditioned by the philosophy
the company adopts with respect to its external environment as well as
by its internal policies and procedures. A positive atmosphere for innovation is a matter of balancing a series of opposites: service and self-interest,
short-term and long-term goals, and objectivity and enthusiasm.

In summary, there are three vital corporate elements required for successful product innovation. Strategic planning shapes the thrust of the
product innovation effort by providing direction and control. Management
executes the new products program by adopting a framework of systems
and procedures as well as marshalling and allocating resources. Finally,
an organizational environment that fosters attitudes of objectivity, confidence, and enthusiasm on the part of individuals charged with implementation of the product innovation effort is crucial. These three elements
are not only important individually, but are mutually interdependent and
thus are *all* necessary for the attainment of the ultimate strategic goals of
corporate survival and growth.

2. The Anatomy of Successful Innovations

Donald G. Marquis

What characteristics make a significant technical advance a success?
Marquis analyzes more than 500 innovations of the nuts-and-bolts kind
and reports his conclusions.

WHENEVER I hear someone begin talking about innovation, I immediately try to answer two questions: Does he understand the distinction between innovation and invention? If so, what *kind* of innovation is he talking about?

The answers are important, for without them it's difficult to make sense out of such discourse. Take the matter of definitions. People tend to use the words innovation and invention interchangeably when, in fact, they are different though related terms.

I shall use the distinction drawn by the economist Jacob Schmookler: "Every invention is (a) a new combination of (b) pre-existing knowledge which (c) satisfies some want."

Innovation is a more subtle concept, but Schmookler's articulation of it is clear and useful:

"When an enterprise produces a good or service or uses a method or input that is new to it, it makes a technical change. The first enterprise to make a given technical change is an innovator. Its action is innova-

Innovation magazine (November, 1969). © 1969 by Technology Communication, Inc. Reprinted by permission of the publisher from *Managing Advancing Technology,* Volume I, pp. 35–48. © 1972 by American Management Associations, Inc.

Donald Marquis, at the time of writing, was Professor of Management at M.I.T. and Director of the Sloan School Program in the Management of Science and Technology.

tion." He goes on to add, "Another enterprise making the same technical change is presumably an imitator and its action, imitation."

Thus an innovation can be thought of as the unit of technological change; an invention—if present—is part of the process of innovation.

The small exception I want to make to Schmookler's concept of innovation is to wash away his distinction between true innovation (a technical change new to both the enterprise and the economy) and imitation (a change that has diffused into the economy, but is picked up and used by the firm).

I do this simply because many enterprises have been profoundly changed by innovations from other organizations and even from other fields (textile firms influenced by synthetic fibers, or typesetting firms changed by computers, for example). Thus to insist on too narrow a conception of innovation would mean ignoring important industry transformations, as well as a vital mechanism for change—imitation or adoption of a technical idea.

Now I must come back to that second question: What *kind* of innovation am I going to talk about?

As we look over the panorama of technological change since, say, the turn of the century, it seems to me that we can discern three distinct types of innovation:

First, there is the complex system, such as communications networks, weapons systems, or moon missions, that take many years and many millions of dollars to accomplish.

Such innovation is characterized by thorough, long-range planning that assures that the requisite technologies will be available and that they will all fit together when the final development stage is reached. Success tends to turn on the skill of managers to sort out good approaches from bad ones on a very large scale indeed. It is not a common type of innovation in most industrial firms as yet, simply because few enterprises, by themselves, face the kind of systems problem that requires it.

Then there is the kind of innovation represented by the major, radical breakthrough in technology that turns out to change the whole character of an industry. The jet engine, stereophonic sound, xerography, and the oxygen converter would be typical examples. Such innovation is quite rare and unpredictable, and is predominantly the product of independent inventors or of research by firms outside the industry ultimately influenced by it.

The reason that, by and large, innovation of this type comes from the outside is simply that technical people within an industry are apt to be preoccupied with short-term concerns. They see their problems as essentially those of product improvement, cost cutting, quality control, expanding the product line, and the like—all of them problems which they can cope with quite naturally through their own technical competence.

This is, in fact, the third kind of innovation—what I call "nuts and bolts" innovation. Modest as it is, such innovation is absolutely essential for the average firm's survival. So long as your competitors do it, so must you. If your competitor comes out with a better product, you must make a technical change in your own—innovate—to get around the advance in his. Thus, this sort of innovation is more intimately paced by economic factors than is innovation of the systems type or of the breakthrough type.

This article is concerned with the third kind of innovation—the ordinary, everyday, within-the-firm kind of technological change without which industrial firms can, and do, perish. In what follows, I shall be attempting to answer the question: What are the characteristics of successful innovations in this category? The answer turns out to be a complex mosaic of factors, but within it you may be able to discern a pattern against which you can measure the innovativeness (or non-innovativeness) of your own organization.

In answering the question posed above, I shall be drawing on the results of a rather interesting study of actual innovations that Sumner Myers and I conducted for the National Science Foundation. Our exploration covered more than 500 innovations in products or processes that occurred in the last five to ten years in 121 companies whose interests encompassed five manufacturing industries—railroad companies, railroad suppliers, housing suppliers, computer manufacturers, and computer suppliers. The innovations studied were judged by responsible executives as most important in their companies and so, presumably, commercially significant. Hence the emphasis in my remarks here is on the characteristics of *successful* innovations.

Model of the Process of Innovation

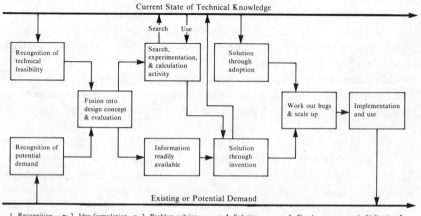

1. Recognition ──▶ 2. Idea formulation ──▶ 3. Problem solving ──▶ 4. Solution ──▶ 5. Development ──▶ 6. Utilization & diffusion

Innovation—the nuts-and-bolts type I'm speaking of—may be carried out from conception to implementation within a single organization. But more commonly it draws on contributions from other sources at different times and places. Thus in the illustration you see two broad arrows representing the major sources of inputs for the process, which is shown taking place schematically between them. Beneath everything I have put a temporal scale which shows the principal stages in the process. The events in these stages will not, of course, always occur in the linear sequence implied by the sketch. Now let's examine these stages a bit more closely.

Successful innovation begins with a new idea which involves the *recognition* of both technical feasibility and demand. At this point in time, there exists a current state of the art, or inventory of technical knowledge, of which the innovator is more or less aware, and on which his estimate of technical feasibility is based. This is the topmost broad arrow. At the same time, represented by the bottom arrow, there is a current state of social and economic utilization in which the innovator can recognize an existing or potential demand.

That word "or" is vitally important, because there's a great difference between recognizing an existing demand and recognizing a potential demand. A company may try stimulating a demand, if it feels that there's a potential one lurking there, by advertising, promotion, and demonstration. But many inventions are ahead of their time, since demand depends on the customer's judgments of the value of a new item in relation to its cost.

A classic example is the reluctance of the railroads to adopt diesel locomotives because of the heavy commitment already made to steam. General Motors had to stimulate demand, in the end, by lending a diesel to a railroad for use in its switching yard. With this successful demonstration, railroads eventually bought diesels for yard use and, later on, for long-haul trains—but only when replacement by the new technology appeared to offer economic advantages.

The next stage is *idea formulation,* which consists of the fusion of a recognized demand and a recognized technical feasibility into a design concept. This is truly a creative act in which the association of both elements is essential. If a technical advance alone is considered, it may or may not result in a solution for which there will be a demand. Similarly, a search for a response to a recognized demand may or may not be successful, depending on the technical feasibility in the current state of technical knowledge.

Part of the stage of innovation I've called idea formulation is really evaluation. It naturally comes after fusion of demand recognition and feasibility recognition into the design concept. Evaluation will recur, of course, all along the line as the process of innovation is managed. But a strong judgmental input must be made here so that the firm can decide whether to commit resources to the next stage.

The design concept is only the identification and formulation of a problem worth committing resources to work on. Then comes the *problem-solving* stage. In some happy instances, the information necessary for the solution is readily at hand in the state of the art; in others, R&D and inventive activity are called for. Unanticipated problems usually arise along the way, and new solutions and trade-offs are sought. And, in many instances, the obstacles are so great that a solution cannot be found, and work is terminated or deferred.

If problem-solving activity is successful, a *solution*—often in the form of an invention—is found, and this knowledge passes into the state of the art once patent protection is assured. Alternatively, the problem may be solved by the adoption of an invention or other input from this pool of technical art. In this case the ultimate technical change becomes, simply, an innovation by adoption—or, in Schmookler's phrase, by imitation.

Whether the solution—invented or adopted—verifies the technical feasibility and demand which were originally recognized, or focuses on a modified problem with somewhat different objectives, uncertainty still remains. Here is where the *development* stage comes in. The innovator attempts to resolve uncertainties with respect to market demand and the problems of scaling up production. Innovation is never really achieved until the item is introduced into the actual market or production process, and sales or cost reductions are achieved.

Finally, we come to the stage in the process where the solution is first *utilized and diffused* in the marketplace. As anyone who has been through it can tell you, this stage is by no means guaranteed. Only one or two new products out of five achieve sales whose profits provide a break-even return on the investment in the innovation. The dollars seep away quickly at this point, too, since the costs of manufacturing start-up, market promotion, and distribution commonly far exceed the costs of achieving the solution. To be sure, some of the uncertainties present at the design-concept stage have been reduced, but the risks—in terms of investment—have increased. In the case of the adopted innovation, the uncertainties are less and the risks can be more accurately evaluated, which, of course, accounts for the popularity of this form of innovation.

Now, with this model before us, let's go back to that question I raised earlier concerning what factors make for successful nuts-and-bolts innovations. To answer the question, I shall cite four examples. This will solidify what I mean by this type of innovation and, I believe make the overall results more vivid. The names used, of course, are fictitious.

The first innovation comes from the housing supply industry, and was but one of nearly 200 technical advances we examined in more than 50 companies therein.

The Janske Asbestos Company wanted to expand its position in the home supply field and began looking for ways to improve its product line. It looked as though a better windowsill had a good market potential, since conventional ones made of wood or cement either required too much maintenance or were too expensive. A different material might solve both problems, but the company wanted to use a material and a method which would not require a significant change in its manufacturing processes.

Janske decided to tackle the problem by extruding windowsills out of asbestos cement. This process and others like it were already widely used in the industry for other products. Janske itself was not unfamiliar with the process, having recently begun to extrude asbestos-cement pipe for commercial use. It proved relatively easy to adapt the process to make the required windowsill cross section, and the total cost of the innovation was less than $100,000.

A simple story, yet one replete with experiences that recurred over and over in our broad sample of innovations in this industry and the four others we explored.

Take the matter of cost. Many companies shrink from innovating out of fear that coming up with a sound technical change in their product or process means investing an enormous sum of money. That certainly may be true for the big breakthrough or the systems type of innovation, but for the incremental type I'm talking about here, it's patent nonsense, as you can see if you glance at table 1. Here are summarized the costs of all of the innovations we looked at. Fully three-quarters of them cost less to accomplish than what Janske Asbestos spent to develop its new windowsill.

TABLE 1. Cost of Innovations

Cost of Innovation	No. of cases	%	
Less than $25,000	187	33	2/3 cost less
$25,000-$100,000	180	32	than $100,000
$100,000-$1,000,000	132	23	
More than $1,000,000	68	12	
	567	100	

Innovations aren't as expensive as you think. Of the 567 innovations examined by the author, two-thirds cost less than $100,000 each and fully one-third cost less than $25,000 each.

Not shown in the table, but revealed by our more detailed analysis, were the following characteristics of the successful innovations we studied: One-fourth of them required little or no adaptation of information readily obtainable from some source, and one-third were modifications of existing products or processes rather than new items. Almost half of the innovations required little or no change in the firm's production processes.

What all this adds up to is what I'll call Lesson No. 1: *Small, incremental innovations contribute significantly to commercial success.* I conclude, therefore, that management ought to back sustained support for innovative activities so as to maintain the competence, experience, and personal contacts of its professional technical staff.

There are some other lessons, so let me turn to the second of my four examples.

Industrial engineers at Mid-North Railroad Co. found that the water coolers the company was required, by union rules, to have in each of its locomotive cabs were costing far too much to maintain. Upon learning of this, the head of the locomotive equipment department asked the director of Rail Lab Inc., the company's wholly owned R&D subsidiary, to find a water cooler that would stand up better under the shock and vibration in a locomotive cab. The director assigned a group to the problem, but none of the alternative designs could stand the gaff.

Impasse.

Then one of the group's engineers remembered his school days. Why not, he suggested, use a modification of the Hilch-Ranque tube? (This is a laboratory curiosity that uses a vortex of compressed air to separate "cold" gas molecules from "hot" gas molecules in a fluid stream. The idea is about 40 years old and is commonly used to demonstrate the theory of Maxwell's demon in physics and engineering classes.)

This engineer worked with the tube, raising its cooling efficiency from 4 percent to about 26 percent. Applied to the water cooler problem after a few months' work, the tube idea produced a new cooler, with no moving parts, which could function in the locomotive cab without breaking down. The only power it required was compressed air, and that was readily available on the engine. Christened the *Whirl-Cool,* the novel cooler saved the railroad company nearly $250,000 per year—the maintenance cost of the old-style coolers on some 2,000 locomotives. In addition, the device was offered for sale to other users.

The key point about this innovation is the fact that it was initiated (stage 1 in our model) by the recognition of a need, rather than by the recognition of the potential of a technical idea. This came later, during design-concept formulation (stage 2). The need came out of a prosaic maintenance situation.

In our analysis of the whole set of 567 innovations, we found that the vast majority of them—three-quarters, in fact, as you can see from table 2—were stimulated by a market demand or a production need. Only

TABLE 2. Sources of Innovations

Innovation initiated by:	No. of cases	%	
Technical feasibility	120	21	
Market demand	257	45	3/4 based on
Production need	169	30	demand or need
Administrative change	21	4	
	567	100	

Spotting technical opportunities plays a surprisingly minor role in sparking innovations. In the author's sample, three-quarters stemmed from recognizing a market potential or a need in a production process.

one-fifth arose from someone saying, aha, maybe we can find a use for *this* technical idea.

This brings me straight to Lesson No 2: *Recognition of demand is a more frequent factor in successful innovation than recognition of technical potential.* It seems to me, therefore, that management ought to concentrate on any and all ways of analyzing such demands and needs. For example, more effective communication should be established among specialists in sales, marketing, production, and R&D to see that such opportunities are not overlooked. Some companies do this as a matter of course. They are the innovative companies.

My third innovation was found in the railroad supply industry. Here, the production manager of the Miles Engine and Gear Co., a man wise in the ways of spotting out-of-line costs, noted that the material cost of cylinder-head inserts for one of the company's line of V-8 diesel engines was much too high. It turned out that the inserts were made of stainless steel and, according to the company metallurgist, the cheapest grade of stainless steel at that.

Then the metallurgist began to wonder why stainless steel was being used at all. Other engines in the line did not, nor did competitors' engines. Where inserts were used, they were of cast iron. It was a case of the seventh soldier standing at attention (because years ago he held the mule-reins) while the artillery was fired; the reason for stainless inserts was lost in the mists of history.

The upshot was that the production manager ordered that some inserts be cast out of valve-guide material, an inexpensive grade of iron. When several hundred engines were tested with the experimental inserts over a period of a year, no difference in performance could be detected. The changeover saved $200 per day in materials cost, based on the production rate at the time the problem was noted.

Here, again, is an innovation arising from a production need, not a technical potential. But the key information input was the production manager's noting, from his experience, that costs were out of line, and the metallurgist, from his experience, concluding that stainless steel wasn't needed at all.

This influence of the training and experience of the innovator in stimulating successful innovations is clearly shown in table 3, which covers the whole gamut of innovations we analyzed. In the actual study, we looked separately at the primary information inputs which evoked the basic idea and those which led to its solution—stages 2 and 4 of our model of the innovative process. The influences were so similar in both cases that I have combined the data into just one table, as shown.

TABLE 3. Key Information Inputs

Innovator got key input from:	No. of cases	%	
Inside the firm			
Printed materials	9	2	
Personal contracts	25	4	
Own training and experience	230	④①	
Formal courses	1	0	
Experiment or calculation	40	⑦	
	305	⑤④	over ½ from inside sources
Outside the firm			
Printed materials	33	6	
Personal contacts	120	21	
Own training and experience	39	⑦	→ R & D
Formal courses	8	②	
	200	36	over ½ from innovator himself
Multiple sources	62	11	
	567	101*	

*Exceeds 100% because of rounding.

You don't necessarily need to look outside the firm for innovative ideas. Most of the major information inputs which evoked the basic idea or led to its solution came from inside the firm. A healthy half of them arose from the innovator's education and experience. Surprisingly, printed materials and R & D work turned out to be minor information sources.

I've annotated the table to indicate the key results. The main one is that in half the cases, the innovators' training and experience—either on that job or previous ones—provided the key information input. If we add to experience the innovators' personal contacts both in and out of the firm, the percentage rises to fully three-quarters. Note that printed materials and R&D were minor sources of information input.

Thus we come to Lesson No. 3: *The training and experience of the people right in your own firm are the principal sources of information for successful innovations.* Thus it's fair to say that competent people within the firm are an invaluable resource. Management should have as its primary responsibility, therefore, the selection, development, retention, and effective utilization of technical personnel—including the facilitation of personal contacts both inside and outside the firm. Almost a cliché, you may say, but the results drive the point home.

The final innovation I've chosen comes from a company we've met before—Mid-North Railroad—and stems from some trouble they were having with their computer system for keeping track of cars, billing other railroads for their use, and so on.

The situation was this: Car-routing and billing data were handled on IBM cards for local tabulating purposes, but to transmit the data elsewhere the cards were fed into an IBM 047, which converted the Hollerith code on the cards into Baudet teleprinter code punched into paper tape. The paper tape was then used for the transmission over teleprinter lines. At the receiving end, the information was punched into paper tape. This was fed into an IBM 063, which repunched the data into IBM-card form.

An engineer at Mid-North, hired by the president specifically to modernize the railroad's communications, decided to eliminate the cumbersome card-to-tape, tape-to-card conversion process. Although the engineer knew from previous experience that equipment existed which could convert card data into an audio tone code transmittable over voice circuits, the combination was not applicable to teleprinter networks and would have required considerable development to make it so.

He searched among manufacturers of computer peripheral equipment, but could not find a conversion device available of the type needed. So he asked for specifications on what such a code-conversion device should be able to do and began looking around for help. One promising approach envisioned a combination of modular transistorized building blocks, and at a trade show the engineer was impressed with what he saw of modules exhibited by the Navigation Computer Co. After discussion of the problem, Navigation gave him a price for a prototype, which was built and eventually developed into a final model. Mid-North purchased the first 60 code-conversion devices for less than the $300,000 cost of one year's rental of the old card-type conversion equipment and, in the process, got some unusual operating features that need not concern us here.

In this case history, as in the previous three, we see the factors of need and previous experience of the innovator playing important roles. But crucial to the success of the code-conversion innovation was the role played by adoption of a technical idea developed by another organization—the alternative way of solving a problem that I talked about under stage 4 of our model.

Table 4 suggests just how common innovation by adoption is. In 128 of the 567 innovations we studied 23 percent, or nearly one out of every four—the problem was solved by going outside the firm for a key product or process. Adopted innovations proved more likely to be process advances than was the case with original innovations from within the firm, which were usually product advances.

TABLE 4. Original vs. Adopted Innovations

Type of innovation	Original		Adopted		Totals		
	No.	%	No.	%	No.	%	
Product	263	60	65	51	328	58	→ product
Component	83	19	16	13	99	18	innovation
Process	93	21	47	37	140	25	predominant
	439	100	128	100	567	100	

23% adopted
process innovation
more likely

There are some other subtleties about adopted innovations that the limited data here do not reveal. For example, compared with the original innovations, we found that fewer of the adopted ones required a lot of adaptation of the major information input or a major change in the production process of the firm. The cost of implementing adopted innovations was about the same as that of developing original innovations, although the uncertainties were undoubtedly less, as discussed earlier. And, as you might expect, vendors proved to be solid sources leading to adoption of technical advances.

All this leads me to set out Lesson No. 4: *Don't overlook adopted innovations; they, as well as those originated within the firm, contribute significantly to commercial success.* Of course applying this lesson brings management smack up against the not-invented-here sort of resistance to technical change that is widespread in many companies. But since no one firm can perform more than a very small proportion of the worldwide innovative activity in any area of technology, it behooves managers to pay serious attention to technology sources outside the firm. Then a deliberate and intelligent trade-off can be made between advancing by original and adoptive innovation. The management of innovation is a corporatewide task that is too important to be left to any one specialized functional department. The R&D department can make its full contribution to the *total process* of innovation not only by effective problem solving, but also by building its competence, knowledge, and personal contacts so as to contribute to the generation of new ideas and to the evaluation of proposed adoptive innovations. Only in this way can it participate effectively in the overall corporate strategy for technical innovation.

Suggested Reading

Technological Innovation: Its Environment and Management. U.S. Department of Commerce, 1967. Available from the Superintendent of Documents, Washington, D.C.

JACOB SCHMOOKLER, *Invention and Economic Growth* (Cambridge, Mass.: Harvard University Press, 1966).

3. Managing the Product Life Cycle

Donald K. Clifford, Jr.

The product life cycle concept can be a valuable tool for marketing planning if properly understood and applied.

NOT LONG AGO, a leading marketer of consumer packaged goods was building a brand of toilet soap. Growth had been fair but not spectacular. Market tests suggested that an increase in advertising, backed by a change in copy, could enable the new brand to reach the "escape velocity" it needed to become a sales leader. But marketing management, feeling the funds would be better spent in launching a new detergent, vetoed the proposal. The detergent was a moderate success, but the promising soap brand went into a gradual sales decline from which it never recovered. Management had pulled out the props at a critical point in the product's growth period.

A supplier of light industrial equipment felt that his major product was not receiving the sales support it deserved. Unconvinced by the salesmen's claims that it was hard to sell, he developed new presentations and sales kits and persuaded sales management to run special campaigns. At year-end, volume had shown no improvement. In fact, the product had long since passed the zenith of its potential sales and profits, and no amount of additional sales support could have profitably extended its growth. Yet in order to give extra sales support to this problem case, management had cut into the marketing budgets of several highly promising products that were still in their "young" growth phase. In short, management had failed to consider each product's position in its life cycle.

Reprinted from *The Arts of Top Management: A McKinsey Anthology*, Roland Mann (ed.), pp. 216–226. © 1971 by McGraw-Hill Book Co. Used by permission of McGraw-Hill Book Company.

Donald K. Clifford, Jr. is a director of McKinsey & Co., Inc., Management Consultants.

26

As these two cases suggest, the concept of the product life cycle—familiar as it may be to most business executives—seems too frequently forgotten in marketing planning. Yet there appears to be conclusive evidence that companies can make far more effective marketing decisions if they take the time to: (1) find out where each of their products stands in its life cycle; (2) determine the overall mix or balance of life cycles in their product line; and (3) analyze the trends in their life-cycle mix and the long-term profit impact of these trends. Without this information, some products will receive neither their rightful *share* of marketing attention, nor the right *kind* of attention. With it, marketing management has a twofold opportunity:

- To reshape and control the life cycles of individual products.
- To raise long-term corporate profitability by improving the overall mix of life cycles in the company's product line.

The size and profitability of any business depend on the product life cycles that make it up. But while companies may continue to grow in sales and profits, no product escapes eventual maturity and decline. Allocating resources so as to reconcile corporate aims and ambitions with the life cycles of the company's products is the objective of life-cycle management. My purpose here is to show how the classic life-cycle concept can be turned into an active profit-making tool, and to describe an approach to life-cycle analysis that has helped some companies make more profitable marketing decisions.

The Life-cycle Concept

The product life-cycle concept derives from the fact that a product's sales volume follows a typical pattern that can readily be charted as a four-phase cycle. Following its birth, the product passes through a low-volume introduction phase. During the subsequent growth period, volume and profit both rise. Volume stabilizes during maturity, though unit profits typically start to fall off. Eventually, in the stage of obsolescence, sales volume declines.

The length of the life cycle, the duration of each phase, and the shape of the curve vary widely for different products. But in every instance, obsolescence eventually occurs for one of three reasons.

First, the need may disappear. This is what happened to the orange juice squeezer when frozen juice caught on.

Second, a better, cheaper, or more convenient product may be developed to suit the same need. Oil-based paint lost its position in the home to water-based paint; plastics have replaced wood, metal, and paper in product categories ranging from dry-cleaning bags to aircraft parts.

Third, a competitive product may, through superior marketing strategy, suddenly gain a decisive advantage. This happened to competing products when Arthur Godfrey's personal charm got behind Lipton Tea, and again when Procter & Gamble secured the American Dental Association's endorsement of its decay-prevention claims for Crest toothpaste.

As the chart below shows, a product's profit cycle is shaped quite differently from its sales cycle. During introduction, a product may not earn any profit at all because of high initial advertising and promotion costs.

In the growth period, before competition catches up, unit profits typically attain their peak. Then they start declining, though total profits may continue to rise for a time on rising sales volume. In the chemical industry, for example, rapid volume increases often more than offset the effect of price reductions early in the growth phase.

During late growth and early maturity, increasing competition cuts deeply into profit margins and ultimately into total profits. For instance, as a result of drastic price cutting, general-purpose semiconductors, once highly profitable, now return so little unit profit that many companies have left the business.

Finally, in the period of obsolescence, declining volume eventually pushes costs up to a level that eliminates profits entirely.

In recent years, as most marketing men are aware, products have been maturing more rapidly and life cycles growing shorter. Indeed, this trend has been responsible for some of the major problems facing marketers today.

The product life cycle concept

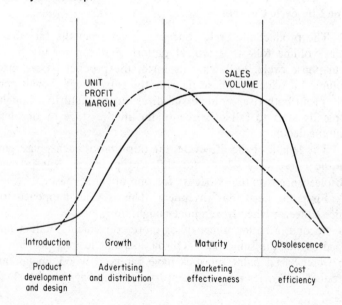

Razor blades are a classic example of accelerated maturity. For decades, with Blue Blades and thin blades, Gillette dominated the market and enjoyed steady growth. Ten years ago, Super Blue Blades arrived—a new product with greatly improved shaving qualities, which could normally have looked forward to a growth period of many years, if not decades. But in less than three years, the stainless steel blade was reintroduced into this country, and the Super Blue Blade started on its way to obsolescence, suddenly shifting from growth to maturity.

The trend to more rapid maturity can be observed in industrial products as well. In chemicals, the competitive advantage afforded by a new product such as nylon once ensured growing sales for a decade or more. But in recent years, the tempo of product innovation and substitution has quickened to the point where some companies, rather than risk heavy research investments on products that may mature within two or three years, now concentrate on exploiting present products and on rapidly copying the products introduced by market leaders.

Not only do products mature more rapidly, but product life cycles generally appear to be growing shorter. For more than 15 years—to cite one conspicuous example—the DC–3 held its place as the leading commercial airliner. But the DC–7, and later the turbo-prop Electra, were rendered obsolete in less than five years by the pure jet DC–8, the 707, and others like them.

The railroads of the United States stand out as a classic example of the first kind of failure, which I call the commodity illusion. For decades they viewed their service as a commodity, a changeless product that would forever meet a changeless transportation need. Only recently have the railroads begun to realize how much ground they have lost—and how much they are still losing—to air, water, and, particularly, over-the-road transportation.

A similar commodity illusion misled the many textile companies that failed to adapt their wool and cotton equipment and marketing capabilities to synthetic fibers in the decade following World War II. In product after product, market after market, companies that had regarded their traditional products as commodities went out of business or were absorbed by more wide-awake competitors.

The second cause of inadequate life-cycle management—neglecting to apply the life-cycle concept—may be illustrated by an electronics company whose products typically have life cycles of two years or less. Too much concerned with present problems, not enough with future opportunities and needs, this company had failed to assess the life-cycle mix of its product line.

As a result, it suddenly found itself with two products late in the growth phase, nine in the maturity or obsolescence phases—and none in introduction or early growth. New and improved products, the lifeblood of any organization in this industry, had simply been allowed to dry up. Had it failed to recognize its predicament in time, the company might 'well have been out of business in another two years. Fortunately, rapid development and acquisition programs were carried out in time to provide the new products it needed for survival.

Failure to Manage the Life cycle

Faced with the challenge of earlier maturity and shortening life cycles, few leading companies have seen the opportunity in life-cycle management, and fewer still have capitalized on it. Most have either (1) failed to recognize that their products have a life cycle, or (2) failed to apply the concept by analyzing the life cycles of their product lines in order to shape marketing strategy.

Such failures by management to fully understand or act on the changing requirements of the company's products and product mix are all too common. And as life cycles grow shorter and products mature more rapidly, the problem for many can only become more acute.

The classic life-cycle concept holds that marketing decisions should be largely determined by a product's position in its cycle, since—as the chart indicates—the critical factors affecting its profitability change with the four phases of its growth and decline.

In the introduction phase, product development and design are considered critical. For industrial goods, where customers have been slow to change from a proven product, technical superiority or demonstrable cost savings will often be needed to open the door. For consumer products, willingness to invest in future volume through heavy initial marketing expenditures may be critical.

During the growth period, consistent, reliable product performance must be regarded as essential to success for most industrial products—and for technically complex consumer products as well. A reputation for quality, backed by adequate production capability, can win a manufacturer the leading market position, as it did for Zenith in black-and-white TV. In contrast, for consumer packaged goods and other non-technical products, effective distribution and advertising have traditionally been the key factors.

The key requirements during maturity, though harder to define, usually come under the heading of "overall marketing effectiveness." Marketing skill may pay off in a variety of ways—for instance, generating incremental profits by reducing price so as to reach additional consumers; finding and promoting new uses for the product; or upgrading distribution channels to reach prime markets more efficiently.

During obsolescence, cost control becomes the key to generating profits. The product of the low-cost producer and distributor often enjoys a profitable "old age" long after its rivals have disappeared from the scene.

Though valid within their limits, the traditional generalizations about management decisions and the product life cycle do not really go far enough. They fail to take into account the all-important fact that *life cycles can be managed.*

The Dimension of Control

Life-cycle management has two basic aspects:

- Controlling the mix of life cycles in the product line by: (1) planned new-product effort and product-line pruning, and (2) planned allocation of money and manpower among existing products and product groups according to the profit opportunity reflected by their respective life-cycle positions.
- Controlling individual product life cycles to generate added profits.

Experience indicates that there may be opportunities at any stage, except for the very end of the line, for marketing management to profitably alter the shape and duration of an individual product's life cycle. The introduction period, for example, can often be shortened by increasing marketing expenditures or securing national distribution more quickly. In the next phase, growth can be speeded and sales and profits ultimately pushed to higher levels by exploiting additional markets, by pricing the product to encourage wider usage, or by more vigorous advertising or sales efforts—in short, by more effectively planned and implemented marketing strategy.

The maturity stage usually offers marketing management the greatest opportunity to change the shape and duration of product life cycles. Has the product really approached obsolescence because of a superior substitute or a fundamental change in consumer needs? Or does obsolescence merely seem near because marketing management has failed to identify and reach the right consumer needs, or because a competitor has done a better marketing job? The question will be crucial, since often the supposed condition of "maturity" is misleading. The challenge may be rather to extend the product's youth by repackaging, physical modifications, repricing, appealing to new users, adding new distribution channels, or some combination of marketing strategy changes. Frequently, as subsequent examples will show, a successfully revitalized product offers a higher return on management time and funds invested than does a new product.

Of course, this will not always be possible. Maturity is forced upon some products by a basic change in consumer habits or the introduction of a greatly superior competitive item. In this event, determining when to cut back the investment of management time and money—and give higher priority to new or more active products—becomes the key marketing decision.

Finally, in obsolescence, marketing effectiveness becomes almost entirely a matter of knowing when to cut short the life of a product which has been demanding more than the small share of management attention that its profit contribution deserves.

Controlling the Life Cycle

The tremendous impact of effective life-cycle management may be demonstrated by the success of several leading companies in directing the progress of both individual product cycles and the overall life-cycle mix. Consider these examples:

- Spurred by rapid technological change and by the trend toward packaging everything—a consequence of our self-service way of life—packaging has been a growth industry for well over a decade. One of the industry leaders has been E. I. du Pont de Nemours & Co. Du Pont has been strongest in cellophane, a product so well known it has become almost a synonym for transparent packaging.

  With the end of World War II, flexible packaging, and cellophane in particular, entered a period of accelerated growth, but in the 1950s new products—notably polyethylene—began to meet certain packaging needs more effectively. Polyethylene film, for example, was less easily ruptured in cold weather—and in time, it also became lower in price. Consequently, cellophane began losing its share of the flexible packaging market. It became clear that sales volume would soon begin falling off unless strong corrective action was taken.

  Faced with the immediate threat of obsolescence in a highly profitable product, Du Pont—followed by the two other cellophane manufacturers—introduced a series of modifications designed to maintain cellophane's growth and prolong its maturity. These included special coatings, new types, and lighter grades at prices more competitive with the newer packaging materials. In all, the customers' choice of cellophane types grew from a handful to well over 100.

  The cumulative effect of these improvements had an impressive impact on cellophane sales. Contrary to widespread predictions of dramatic decline, cellophane maintained the bulk of its sales volume—of which the traditional grades now represent a relatively small fraction. With more than half of a $300 million market, Du Pont has been the primary beneficiary of this reversal of fortunes.

  Further testimony to Du Pont's effectiveness in life-cycle management can be found in its control over the life-cycle *mix* of its flexible packaging products. Recognizing the maturity of cellophane, Du Pont developed a strong position in polyethylene and in other new packaging materials. While *maintaining* its leadership in flexible packaging by reshaping the life cycle of cellophane, the company also provided for *growth* by adding new products to strengthen its product mix.

- During the mid-1950s, Procter & Gamble's Gleem had attained a strong position in the toothpaste market. But the total market was growing at a slow rate, and P&G wanted to grow faster. Having introduced Crest as the first decay-preventive dentifrice, P&G found the way to explosive growth by obtaining endorsement of the new toothpaste by the American Dental Association—an achievement that had evaded other manufacturers for years. P&G thus reshaped the life cycle of the new dentifrice. Crest's share of the toothpaste market *quadrupled* between 1958 and 1963, while the sales curves of other brands of toothpaste showed strong signs of obsolescence, declining on the average more than 15 percent.

- Decades after the introduction of Jell-O, General Foods succeeded in converting it from a mature to a growth product by a revamping of marketing strategy. GF changed the Jell-O formula, repackaged the product and repriced it, found a host of new uses for Jell-O, and publicized them to the housewife through stepped-up advertising. Today, Jell-O remains one of GF's biggest selling and most profitable products.

- Aggressive life-cycle management was also demonstrated when International Business Machines introduced its "Series 360" computers early 1964. By the early 1960s, competition in this field had rapidly become severe. IBM controlled three-quarters of the computer business, but intensified competition was shortening the life cycles of its computer line. Management foresaw that the rapid growth it had enjoyed in the 1950s would soon slow down unless the company undertook a major shift in product and marketing strategy.

    The solution adopted by IBM was to rapidly obsolete its own equipment—much of which had been on the market for less than four years. At the same time, the company moved to secure its entrenched position in computers by providing an expandable system that would make it uneconomic or inefficient for customers to switch to competing systems as their computer needs grew.

    While there is no substitute for solid marketing judgment, these examples serve to suggest that the odds on making good decisions will be increased if management knows where its products stand—individually and collectively—in their respective life cycles.

Life-cycle Analysis

One proven means of positioning a company's products in their life cycles—a way that has proven effective for some forward-looking companies—is life-cycle analysis. This may be described as a disciplined, periodic review resulting in (a) a formal audit that pinpoints each product's position in its life cycle, and (b) a profile of the life-cycle mix of the product line as a whole.

Although the steps followed by marketing management in carrying out the first part of a life-cycle analysis may vary among companies, the following are typical:

1. Develop historical trend information for a period of three to five years (longer for some products). Data included will be unit and dollar sales, profit margins, total profit contribution, return on invested capital, market share, and prices.
2. Check recent trends in the number and nature of competitors; number and market-share rankings of competing products, and their quality and performance advantages; shifts in distribution channels; and relative advantages enjoyed by competitive products in each channel.
3. Analyze developments in short-term competitive tactics, such as competitors' recent announcements of new products or plans for expanding production capacity.
4. Obtain (or update) historical information on the life cycles of similar or related products.
5. Project sales for the product over the next three to five years, based on all the information gathered, and estimate an incremental profit ratio for the product during each of these years (the ratio of total direct costs—manufacturing, advertising, product development, sales, distribution, etc.—to pretax profits). Expressed as a ratio—e.g., 4.8 to 1 or 6.3 to 1—this measures the number of dollars required to generate each additional dollar of profit. The ratio typically improves (becomes lower) as the product enters its growth period; begins to deteriorate (rise) as the product approaches maturity; and climbs more sharply as it reaches obsolescence.
6. Estimate the number of profitable years remaining in the product's life cycle, and—based on all the information at hand—fix the product's position on its life-cycle curve: (a) introduction, (b) early or late growth, (c) early or late maturity, or (d) early or late obsolescence.

Developing the Life-cycle Profile

Once the life-cycle positions of all the company's major products have been determined, marketing management proceeds to develop a life-cycle profile of the company's entire line. Again, this involves a series of steps:

1. Determine what percentages of the company's sales and profits fall within each phase of the product life cycle. These percentage figures indicate the present life-cycle (sales) profile and the present profit profile of the company's current line.
2. Calculate changes in the life-cycle and profit profiles over the past five years, and project these profiles over the next five years.
3. Develop a target life-cycle profile for the company, and measure the company's present life-cycle profile against it. The target profile, established by marketing management, specifies the desirable share of company sales that should fall within each phase of the product life cycle. It can be determined by industry obsolescence trends, the pace of new product introduction in the field, the average length of product life cycles in the company's line, and top management's objectives for growth and profitability. As a rule, the target profile for growth-minded companies whose life cycles tend to be short will call for a high proportion of sales in the introductory and growth phases.

With these steps completed, management can assign priorities to such functions, as new-product development, acquisition, and product-line pruning, based on the discrepancies between the company's target profile and its present life-cycle profile. Once corporate effort has been broadly allocated in this way among products at various stages of their life cycles, marketing plans can be detailed for individual product lines.

4. The Fear of Innovation

Donald A. Schon

*The modern industrial corporation is required to undertake techno-
logical change, change that is destructive to the corporation's stable state.
Schon examines the risks and uncertainties involved and their implications for management policy.*

THERE IS a "rational view" of innovation. According to this view, innovation is similar to other major functions of an organization—such as sales,
accounting, or production. Therefore, if we accept the rational view, we
say that innovation is a *manageable process* in which risks are controlled
by mechanisms of justification and review.

In this article, I want to show that the rational view of innovation
ignores or violates actual experience. In light of that experience, the notion
of innovation as an orderly, goal-directed, risk-reducing process must
appear as a myth. I shall explore some of the ways in which it is a myth,
then go on to show that when an organization lives by the myth it can
discover that it has made innovation impossible.

Implicit in the rational view is the notion that skilled men can anticipate and control the risks of innovation. Phrases like "the management of
innovation" suggest that we can foresee and quantify the likely dangers and
rewards of a technical project and weigh them against the likely risks and
rewards of alternative efforts. By selecting only those projects whose
benefits justify their anticipated costs, by playing risks off against one another—in short, by a process of justification, decision, and optimization—
we can (it is assumed) keep the risk of innovation within bounds.

Risk has its place in a calculus of probabilities. It lends itself to quantitative expression—as when we say that the chances of finding a defective
part in a batch are 2 out of 100. In the framework of benefit-cost analysis,
the risk of an innovation is how much we stand to lose if we fail, multiplied by the probability of failure.

Reprinted from *International Science and Technology,* 14 (November,
1966), pp. 70–78. Used by permission.

Uncertainty is quite another matter: A situation is uncertain when it requires action but resists analysis of risks. For example, a gambler takes a risk in an honest game of blackjack when, knowing the odds, he calls for another card. But the same gambler, unsure of the odds, or unsure of the honesty of the game, is in a situation of uncertainty.

How does this apply to technical innovation? Men involved in technical innovation in a corporation confront a situation in which the need for action is clear but where it is by no means clear what to do. This situation is painful and full of anxiety for the individuals and, in a sense, for the corporation as a whole. The corporation is not designed for uncertainty—where there are no clear objectives to reach, no measures of accomplishment, and where it is not clear what to try to control. A corporation cannot operate in uncertainty, but it is beautifully equipped to handle risk. It is precisely an organization designed to uncover, analyze, evaluate, and operate on risks. Accordingly, *the innovative work of a corporation consists in converting uncertainty to risk.*

The work begins with more information than can be handled and operates on this information, at lower levels of the corporation, until clear alternatives of action, together with their probable benefits and risks, can be defined. At this point, management can play the investment game—the game of deciding where to put its bets. The game requires analysis of investment alternatives, estimating their markets, costs of technical feasibility, and making investment decisions. The game is played with competitive corporations as opponents. The rewards and punishments of the game can be measured in dollars.

In the process of innovation, everything is done to permit decision on the basis of probable dollar costs and dollar benefits. In the process, the corporation converts the language of invention to the language of investment. Instead of talking about materials, properties, performances, experiences, experiments and phenomena, the corporation talks of costs, shares of market, investment, cash flow, and dollar return.

The conversion of uncertainty to risk takes varying forms, depending on the *kind* of uncertainty to be dealt with. Technical innovation involves many different kinds of uncertainty. Some of these spring directly from the non-rational character of the process of invention; others are only indirectly related to that process. I will be concerned here with the uncertainties springing from determination of technical feasibility, novelty, and market.

One focus of uncertainty is in the question: Can it be done? Is it technically feasible?

In the process of invention, the requirements to be met change continually in response to unexpected findings. At any time, these may turn a good risk into a poor one—or an indifferent idea into an idea of great promise. We can describe these changes in terms of curves of technical difficulty. For example as an investigator works over a period of time, he may first encounter his most difficult problem and later on only minor ones whose solutions he knows he can attain if he works long enough. If we plot his progress over time against "difficulty" or "demands of the solution with respect to the state of the art" the curve may look like this:

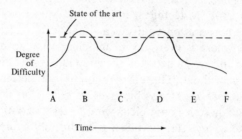

Here, the investigator must surpass the state of the art at *B,* whereas his subsequent tasks are well within the state of the art.

Or there might be a number of separate peaks. For example, in considering the development of new semiconductor materials, we would have to identify separate peaks for the development of high-purity materials and for the development of high-yield production techniques. The curve might look like this:

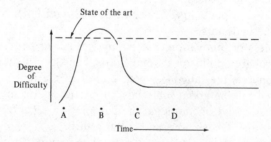

Such curves would not be a source of major uncertainty if it were possible always to identify ahead of time the problems and their degree of difficulty. Small improvements in the properties of materials—for example, raising by a few degrees the melting point of an alloy or increasing slightly the abrasion resistance of a plastic coating—may require no more than the continued application of known methods. On the other hand, achieving these improvements can turn out to be extremely difficult.

It is not always apparent, even to a skilled investigator, whether he is working on a minor problem of adjustment or a major problem of principle. He cannot place himself on the curve of technical difficulty. He may think he is here,

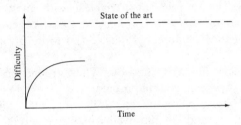

when in fact he is here.

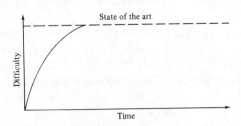

Technical feasibility, therefore, often resists the kind of definition required by the investment game. It may evade definition throughout the entire process of innovation.

Another focus of uncertainty concerns: Who has done it before? Who is doing it now? Even if it knows that others are working in the same field, it cannot be sure how far they have gone. (The development of the automatic light meter for cameras is an example: The company that ultimately achieved commercial success had been spurred on by the belief that a competitor had the product, only to discover, later on, that its competitor did not have the product after all.)

And questions of marketing: Who will buy it? How large will its market be? How much of a share will it get? How long will it last? There are inherent uncertainties about marketing which no amount of information (acquired ahead of time) will resolve—we can see that the process of answering marketing questions occurs over a period of time and that there are bound to be stretches of uncertainty which can only be resolved by the expenditure of time and money, if indeed they can be resolved at all. The uncertainties of marketing are particularly apparent in the case of consumer products. Scotch tape, for example, was originally introduced as a way of mending books. Before its introduction, its makers had no inkling of the huge market potential it offered.

Companies make marketing decisions under pressure of money and time, confronted with more information than they can handle. Although one may be able to predict, in principle, the effects of single-variable changes—price, for example, or color—these variables never act alone.

There are always many relevant variables, with multiple, interacting effects. There is no sure way of learning from past experience, for situations are never identical; differences that appear to be trivial may turn out to be critical.

Moreover, it costs money to find out. The introduction of a consumer product on a national scale is a major enterprise. A single regional market test, with appropriate preparation and follow-up, may cost hundreds of thousands of dollars—and yet the results may not permit formulation of the national picture. *In principle,* uncertainties may be resolvable, but the cost of resolution is high and the very process of resolving may cost more than can be justified.

To this we must add the fact that in the process of development there is interaction between need and technology: The market originally conceived for the product may be ruled out by technical limitations discovered in the process of invention. A different market may suggest itself—in this case, a more limited market. In short, the product for which a market must be anticipated is not an "it" that remains constant throughout the process of development. Rather, the product changes through this process —and its possible market changes with it.

The Cost of Innovation

Throughout the process of technical innovation, decisions about technical feasibility, novelty, and markets—among many other factors—must be made on insufficient evidence, by individuals who have more information than they can handle. The resolution of these uncertainties—the conversion of uncertainty to risk—takes time and money and requires justification in its own right. Its benefits must be balanced against its costs.

The process of innovation has a cost curve, as well as a curve of difficulty, which exhibits characteristic patterns. Let us consider the development of a new metal-to-metal adhesive. It begins in the laboratory when a chemist, working on another problem, notices an adhesive effect and reproduces it. Up to this point, the cost may be in the order of $5000 to $10,000. The chemist shows the effect to the research director, who finds it intriguing and authorizes a search of the report and patent literature, some further experimentation and a first examination of the markets. This may go on for a month or two and bring the total cost to $40,000.

At this point, the research director feels he has something worth presenting to management. Management likes the idea and launches a full-scale development project. The adhesive formulation has certain disadvantages, of course, and the development team makes efforts to improve it, as well as to explore variations of the chemistry involved, so as to "cover all the ground." A detailed analysis of the market—in the automotive, aircraft, and appliance industries—gets under way. It reveals the need for improved handling properties. At the same time, the company undertakes a thorough patent search which suggests that, although the formulation may be novel, the company must try certain other formulations as well, in order to cut off the possibility of later competition from an equally effective product. At the end of six months, the total cost of the effort has risen to $200,000.

Now the company files its patent applications and sets up a pilot production line. The line turns out to have a number of bugs in it; there are many more problems in producing large quantities of adhesive of reliable composition than in making small samples. Because of the scale of effort, modifications in the process become far more expensive than they had been before. Quality control becomes a problem. Shelf life has to be examined. Use tests, which had already been conducted on a small scale, are now undertaken on a large-scale, long-term basis. Meanwhile, word of the development has begun to spread outside the company and management decides to undertake a crash program in order to market the product before fall. A year and $600,000 have gone by.

By the time the first full production line has been set up, the marketing strategy has been settled, the sales force has been educated to the product, the use tests have been completed and evaluated, quality-control techniques have been established, two years have elapsed, and $1.2 million has been spent. Now the company can market the product—even though bugs in production, reliability, and quality still crop up. The product may or may not achieve the volume anticipated for it. The company may or may not make a profit.

The process described here takes no longer and is no more expensive than most product and process developments as they occur in medium-to-large firms. To be sure, there are instances of new products that have been invented, developed, and brought to the point of marketing for as little as $5000. But at the other extreme are examples of products that took 10 years and $20 million. Regardless of scale, however, the shape of the development-cost curve remains relatively constant.

Often, the first invention—the first demonstration of an effect—takes no more than a month or two and a few thousand dollars. As the company takes its first exploratory steps, the rise in the rate of expenditure is slow. As the company passes further checkpoints, the rate of expenditure in-

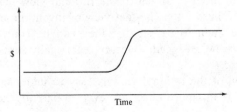

creases. The total commitment grows logarithmically. Each new major commitment requires complementary commitments. Only when the product or process reaches commercialization does the curve begin to level off.

The development-cost curve takes on meaning when it is put in the context of the corporate investment game and the conversion of uncertainty to risk. Despite the careful efforts of many companies to establish checkpoints beyond which they will not go without adequate justification, they find themselves having to make investment decisions on insufficient evidence in a general climate of uncertainty. As they begin to climb the slope of the curve, they rather quickly reach what appears to be a point of no return. At this point, the executive vice president can say to the president: "We have put in so much. We may as well put in a little more and find out whether the investment is worthwhile." To which the president can always reply: "Don't throw good money after bad." But when this point is passed there comes another point: where the mistake—if the development is a mistake—is too big to admit. Large-scale developments of the kind undertaken by supercorporations or the military may proceed for months or years beyond the point where they should have stopped; they continue because of massive commitments to errors too frightening to reveal. They have their own momentum. In these cases, the personal commitment of the people involved in the development, the apparent logic of investment, and the fear of admitting failure, all combine to keep the project in motion until it falls of its own weight.

The problem of innovation within the corporation is, therefore, a problem of decision in the face of continuing uncertainty. A man must take leaps—not once, at the beginning of the process, but many times throughout the process—always in the face of uncertainty and on the basis of inadequate information. The need for such leaps of decision grows out of the uncertainty inherent in the process. A company cannot escape it by careful planning, or by gathering exhaustive data. The uncertainties *resist* resolution—and the process of attempting to resolve them is itself a form of commitment.

Then why the rational view? Why the belief that innovation is manageable? One key to the answer lies in the very non-rationality and uncertainty of the process. A man may state the rational view when he is describing a process in which he has no part, or when he is trying to tell others how to do it, or to exhort others to do it, or, again, when he is reassuring himself about it. In short, the rational view may function as a device. It is an idealized, after-the-fact view of invention and innovation—as we would like them to be, so that they can be controlled, managed, justified. It is a view designed to calm fears, gain support, or give an illusion of wisdom.

The attraction of the rational view is easy to understand. Uncertainty is frightening. It is far more cheering, even apparently necessary, to believe that invention and innovation are rational, deliberate processes in which success is assured by intelligent effort. As a result, uncertainty becomes taboo, unmentionable—especially in the context of important corporate decisions. It is necessary to have a *clear, rational view* of where we have been and where we are going. It is necessary to believe that the future is essentially predictable and controllable, if only we gather the right facts and draw the right inferences from them. We suppress the surprising, uncertain, fuzzy, treacherous aspects of invention and innovation in the interest of this therapeutic view of them as clear, rational, and orderly. Armed with this myth, managers make decisions and mobilize resources. They and their subordinates must then live out the actual uncertainty of this process.

But there is another answer to the question: Why the rational view? This answer focuses on its partial truth and on its utility.

The rational view of invention and innovation is more nearly correct for more nearly marginal inventions. The less significant the invention, the more the process tends to be orderly and predictable. The more radical the invention, the less rational and predictable.

Let us take up the question of degree of novelty—how does this affect the organization within which innovation occurs? We can state a general rule here: The more peripheral the development, the less change required for acceptance, the more the development will tend to conform to the rational view. But the question of degree of novelty is more complex than this simple rule would suggest. For example, a technically insignificant invention—such as one that provides individually packaged food products—may require major changes in marketing. On the other hand a major technological invention, as was true with the invention of nylon, may require surprisingly little change in textile machinery. There is an unusual optical effect: What looks like trivial change from afar may appear, close-up, to be monumental.

For example, consider the replacement of a natural material by a synthetic—a disruption that may threaten several levels of a company at once: The established technology will be rendered obsolete. Men who have built up craft skills over decades will suddenly find their skills irrelevant to the new problems. Production will change from batch processing of materials to a continuous chemical process. New means of controlling product quality, production scheduling, and inventory will have to be devised. The far greater productive capacity of the new machines will require new marketing concepts: The old volumes will no longer be adequate. It may be necessary to double or triple the volume of sales, at lower prices, in order to keep the company's net profit constant. New accounting methods will be required. The very strategy of sales will have to change. In short, the business—and hence the nature of the corporation—will no longer be the same.

Not the least of the effects of technological innovation is on top management itself. For top management, the cumulative effects of all these changes may be overwhelming. If the president came up through the business and draws his confidence from his intimate knowledge of the details of the present operation, technological innovation threatens to throw him onto completely unfamiliar ground. He understood the old business, but he does not understand the new one. How can he manage if he does not understand the business he is in? Where is he to draw the resources of experience he needs in order to trust his own judgments? Is he to become completely dependent on the proponents of the new product or process? He is faced with a crisis of both self-confidence and trust in others.

In brief, technological innovation disrupts the stable state of corporate society. On every level, it affronts the society's vigorous and continuing efforts to stay as it is. To this onslaught, the corporate society responds in a variety of ways. Some of the more evident are these:

- It rejects the effort at innovation. It puts down the idea, fires or demotes the men associated with it, and makes its further discussion taboo. Many corporate pasts are littered with discarded efforts of this sort—begun, then stopped, then relegated to corporate limbo.
- It allows the effort to continue, but isolates it from the rest of the corporation. In this way, research projects—or whole research departments—may function in a vacuum, cut off from the contacts that are essential to their ever coming to reality.
- It contains the threat, allowing it to proceed, but on a level so much reduced that the innovation is always far short of critical mass.
- It seeks to convert the threat to an activity acceptable within the corporate society. Efforts at radical innovation become product improvements or service to production or sales, which can be carried on without disrupting effect.

These are straightforward negative responses. But the corporation cannot respond to innovation in an exclusively negative way. It cannot, because it believes itself to be committed to technological innovation as essential to corporate growth. Innovation is something the corporate society must both espouse and resist.

- It may compartmentalize innovation, permitting it to occur in one part of its business while preventing it from occurring in others.
- It may oscillate between support and resistance, confusing corporate members by an on-again, off-again approach to change.
- It may resist innovation while not appearing to do so, while in fact proclaiming the official doctrine of innovation. For example, it

may encourage the development of new product ideas only to find consistently that none of them meets the stringent criteria laid down in advance (just as a mother may want her son to get married but never approves of the girls he brings home); or it may foster a research effort, only to reject or ignore its results.

These strategies do not usually represent a conscious pose or a management deception. They are responses of a corporate society to two requirements which are equally legitimate—even necessary—but unfortunately in conflict with one another.

The society of a corporation attempts to maintain a stable state. This effort is not inertia, but conservative dynamism. The various forms of corporate resistance to change which reflect themselves as obstacles to technological innovation are processes of *conservation*—processes which are essential to the survival of any social or biological organism. Active conservatism is the natural state of organisms. It is nonsense to say that companies should throw off this old-fashioned habit. But it is the crisis of the modern industrial corporation that it is required to undertake technological change—change that is destructive of its stable state—in order to survive. This is the paradox which makes the corporation so vulnerable. This is the paradox which accounts for its ambivalence to innovation and, yet, forces it to adopt new forms and styles of change.

5. Government and the Innovation Process

J. Herbert Hollomon and Members of the Center for Policy Alternatives, M.I.T.

What can the federal government do to encourage socially desirable innovation? The authors trace the relationships of a wide variety of U.S. government programs to technological innovation, and based on this— and the experience of other countries—they offer some recommendations to Congress.

GOVERNMENTS in all modern industrialized countries work to promote and shape technological development. Each has apparently concluded that the free action of the market is not sufficient to achieve the desired long-term goals of technological strength and independence.

A great variety of U.S. government programs have an important relationship to technological innovation. Many, if not most, were not intended to affect innovation; they embrace, instead, a diversity of societal goals, including increasing the availability of goods and services, protecting society from the adverse consequences of technology, and benefiting specific sectors such as manufacturing, small business, labor, consumers, or the disadvantaged. These goals represent sometimes conflicting purposes, and many of the programs and activities directed toward them are undertaken independently of each other. For these reasons, it is useful for conceptual purposes to organize these government programs and activities into a framework by which their relationship to technology and especially to innovation can be analyzed. (See Figure 1.)

Reprinted in abridged form from *Technology Review* 81 (May, 1979), pp. 30–41. © 1979 by The Alumni Association, M.I.T. The original report was prepared by the Center at the request of the Office of Technology Assessment of the U.S. Congress. It is available from the Center, Room E40-250, M.I.T., Cambridge, Mass. 02139.

J. Herbert Hollomon is Japan Steel Industry Professor of Engineering at M.I.T. and director of the Center for Policy Alternatives. George Heaton was the project manager.

U.S. programs relating to technological innovation can be grouped into 13 areas. The first six respond to perceived deficiencies in resources, externalities, or the distribution of the fruits of technological activity. The first 11 areas focus primarily on the supply side, the intention being to affect what the industrial and labor sectors are able to deliver; the last two areas include policies to stimulate technology by affecting the demands of consumers and workers.

Thirteen Program Areas

Technology assessment	1 The assessment of new and existing specific technologies	Support of infra structure	7 Support for the science base necessary for the new technology
Direct regulation	2 Direct regulation of the research or development of new products and processes	Industry and labor market structure	8 Policies to affect industry structure which may affect the development of technology
	3 Direct regulation of the production, marketing and use of new or existing products		9 Policies affecting supply and demand of man-power resources having an impact on technological change
Enhancement of technology	4 Programs to encourage the development and utilization of technology in and for the private goods and services sector	Domestic economic and foreign trade policy	10 Economic policies with unintended or indirect effect on technological innovation
	5 Government support of technology for public services where consumers are the primary users		11 Policies affecting international trade and investment
	6 Support for the development of technology where the federal government is the primary user	Consumer and worker demand	12 Policies intended to create shifts in consumer demand
			13 Government policies responding to worker demand having impact on technological change

FIGURE 1

Because these reflect independent, and sometimes even conflicting, societal goals, there are difficult choices of emphasis among them; thus policy toward innovation becomes implicit in many political decisions as well as explicit in some.

In the course of the research on which this article is based, we made a detailed study of existing government programs affecting innovation. This resulted in a series of matrices relating policies and innovation effects. Such matrices illustrate what programs have emphasized or neglected. For example, Figure 2, which concerns the encouragement of private-sector technological development, reveals that there is no major, across-the-board support for basic civilian technology. Foreign experience, which is presented later, suggests a new program of this kind which might be effective in the U.S.

To complement this policy-oriented approach, our study also attempted an analysis of the impact of government actions on the innovation process in six major U.S. industries: aircraft and aircraft engines, automobiles, carpets, synthetic materials, iron and steel, and semiconductors.

We found a wide variety of federal impacts on innovation with significant industry-to-industry differences. For example, defense procurement and federal research and development support have shaped both the semiconductor and aircraft engine industries, and research and development performed by the federal government was an important force in the aircraft engine industry. Federal regulation of its products in the areas of emissions, safety, and fuel economy have shaped recent changes in the auto industry. Energy pricing policies have influenced the development of synthetic materials and energy conservation. Demands for safety and environmental quality have been important in determining the course of investments and innovations in the iron and steel industry. Higher minimum wages are held to have speeded the introduction of new equipment in the carpet industry, while restrictions on wool imports hastened the use of synthetic fibers.

These examples suggest that there are strikingly different patterns of government influence on innovation in the U.S. Out of this panoply of causes and effects, we select several categories for special comment.

- We conclude that government purchases and support for research and development have been particularly important in encouraging major innovations. A pattern of rapid technological advance, many new entrants, and economies resulting from production experience is evident in the electronics industry, especially the development of integrated circuits, and in the aircraft engine industry.

   This does *not* mean that encouraging entry through procurement is *always* effective in stimulating innovation. Indeed, our evidence strongly indicates that large projects directly performed by government for the development of products and production process equipment are likely to be quickly made obsolete by the rapid pace of innovation in industry, and their results have not found widespread use.

One reason appears to be industry's superior knowledge of critical details of the production process and its interaction with product design.

- Actions which complement normal competitive pressures for change on an industry often appear to be more effective in promoting innovation than those that do not relate to market forces. In these cases industry is doubly motivated to innovate. For example, while minimum standards for auto emission control were adopted only as mandated, the automobile industry has thus far met fuel economy standards well in advance of legislated deadlines. It is now responding with a major innovation: electronic microprocessors to control engine performance for both fuel economy and lower levels of emissions. In this case, conservation requirements and competitive forces acted together to stimulate change.

  Pollution control regulations, which were not supported by marketplace incentives, appear to have encouraged retrofits on existing technologies instead of innovation in newer and more efficient systems. Indeed, there is a strong suggestion in our experience with pollution control that a system of effluent charges would have encouraged innovation by marshalling competitive forces while specific requirements actually discouraged innovation by working against these forces.

- The timing and quality of a regulatory intervention appears to be critical with respect to its influence on technology and innovation. Unless the needed infrastructure, such as trained people, is in place or created concurrently to meet the regulatory requirement, severe dislocations may result. Moreover, regulation may impose such high costs and stringent constraints that innovation is discouraged or impeded.

  Nevertheless, there are many examples of innovations enabled or enhanced by regulation. Especially when regulation is steady and gradual, we find that effective and innovative technological solutions often appear. On the other hand, intense pressure for rapid change may force industry to patch up an existing technology rather than risk the failure of a radical innovation.

- No one government policy or technology can be recommended as a key to effective stimulation of change. Many factors over which the government has only indirect control work together to enhance the climate for major product innovation and to affect the usefulness of governmental initiatives. These include the availability of

FIGURE 2

Programs to Encourage the Development and Utilization of Technology In and For the Private Goods and Services Sector

Dissecting one of the 13 program areas through which U.S. policy affects technology: encouraging the development and use of technology in private goods and services sectors. At least two score federal programs impact at various levels — market research, technical research, development, and commercialization — on the way technology is used in these sectors, and this chart attempts to organize this plethora of impacts for analysis and evaluation.

Manner of Action	Stages of the Innovation Process			
	Market Research	Technical Research	Development/ Engineering	Production and Commercialization
Transfer of technology to the firm		Anti-trust regulations: joint R & D exemption; compulsory licensing		
		Technology utilization programs (e.g., N.A.S.A., S.B.A.)		
		Diffusion programs for R & D from government laboratories		
		Diffusion of R & D funded by government (e.g., A.S.R.A., N.T.I.S.)		
		Agricultural extension services		
		Government-university-industry cooperation (e.g., Sea Grant)		

Reducing costs of innovation

Direct funding of R & D (e.g., D.O.E.)

Special tax treatment for R & D

Anti-trust regulations: licensing, joint R & D (S.B.A.)

Compulsory licensing under government procurement

Agricultural extension services

Investment tax credits

Modernization assistance

Increasing reward of innovation

Patent and license system

Government procurement

Demonstration projects

Decreasing probability of commercial failure

Government procurement

Market information

Decreasing probability of technical failure

Provision of technical information (e.g., N.T.I.S.)

Invention evaluation   Demonstration projects

private venture capital, the supply and mobility of key personnel, competitive conditions in the industry, and others. Lack of balance or lack of any one critical factor may be a barrier to innovation. Timing, interaction with other programs, and the details of implementation are often crucial.

Learning from Our Competition

Foreign experience can offer several useful lessons about why and how specific government policies succeed or fail in stimulating innovation under certain circumstances.

Japan: Technology Identified with Growth

The distinguishing feature of Japanese technology policy has been its total and complete identification with economic growth policies. The Japanese have made the development and use of technology the backbone of industrial growth. Low-technology and inefficient industries unable to compete with firms in the developed western countries have been allowed to die; protective policies have been used only to aid the development of emerging high-technology industries.

Both large and small business enterprises are recognized as important in the industrial structure, and—though large firms appear to spearhead Japan's export drive—the government nevertheless has a strong policy for support of the technological and business infrastructure of small firms.

Japanese policy has stressed the commercialization of technology in contrast to its creation. Until very recently, little funding for research and development emanated from the government; research and its commercial development have been left to industry, while the government has concentrated heavily on creating an effective environment for its industry. In this respect, the government's role in technology and innovation has been highly indirect.

Government "technology policy" has thus consisted principally of the following elements:

- Heavy emphasis on technical education and training to provide highly skilled manpower resources for industry.
- Emphasis on technologies responding to large-scale demands in the consumer market, in contrast to investments in basic research and development, "big science," and national-prestige projects.
- Strong export orientation for the economy, with Japanese industries competing with the most technologically advanced international firms. This has led to careful manipulation of the industrial structure to prepare sectors and firms to meet international competition with limited protection for infant industries until they are prepared to compete in the international market.

- Elimination of technologically weak companies.
- Mandatory licensing of technologies attaining dominant market positions in order to avoid technology monopolies by Japanese firms.
- Government support for industry through analyses of export markets and available foreign technologies, tax credits and deductions for industrial research and development, and accelerated depreciation for research, development, and pilot plant facilities.

The U.K.: Emphasis on Basic Research

British government policy has focused heavily on supporting research and development in basic fields. This orientation has led the British to make major contributions to science and technology—in particular to areas of "big science" such as defense, nuclear energy, and space. But this emphasis has been heavily on the supply side, with only modest attention given to market demand for the products of research and to the problems of commercializing promising new technologies.

Private-sector initiatives have not been key features in the British experience. Most of the key decisions on technologies to be developed by the country have been made by the British government rather than the private market. Industry-wide research associations have been fostered by the government to respond to the needs of the private sector; they encourage incremental improvements in mature industries. The government has concentrated on its own resources and on the university system to expand the country's base of technical and scientific knowledge. Although the universities have developed strong programs in basic science, there has been less attention to industry-related technology.

Nor have the British followed a strong manpower policy to prepare technical personnel specifically for the needs of industry and technological change. The industrial environment has been marked by poor relations with the labor force, low worker mobility, and strong worker resistance to change.

Several British programs, however, merit close attention as important experiments by the government to bring technologies to the commercial stage:

- The National Research and Development Corporation (N.R.D.C.) has been closely watched as an experiment in government-industry partnership with relatively favorable results. N.R.D.C. supports innovation by paying part or all of the development costs of promising innovations, by licensing public-sector technologies, and by entering into joint ventures with private companies.
- The Launching Aid Program has as its objective the reduction of commercial risk facing manufacturers of new products and processes, using as its principal vehicle interest-free loans to a de-

veloper, which are repayable as a levy on sales or licenses. Unlike N.R.D.C., this program has not been marked by significant success; its investments have flowed primarily into government-designated projects rather than into private market initiatives.

- The Preproduction Order Support Program aims at encouraging industry to utilize advanced manufacturing equipment. The Department of Industry buys equipment from manufacturers and lends it to selected industrial users who have an option to purchase after a trial period. This program has shown some success, particularly in machine tools where it effectively speeded the introduction of numerical control technology.

France: Maintaining Independence

French science and technology policy has been characterized by heavy government support of civilian technology, notably in such high-technology fields as computers, aircraft, and nuclear energy. It is consistent with the highly centralized administrative structure of the government, characterized by strong direction and control and emphasis on long-range planning.

Most technology policy has been dictated by France's political commitment to industrial and technological independence. The objective of maintaining at least one domestic supplier in every important industry—a policy frequently requiring extensive government subsidies to weak industries—has had mixed results in stimulating innovative entrepreneurial behavior.

French policymakers have linked technological and economic growth policies more closely than the British. Great emphasis has been given to strengthening the industrial structure by encouraging mergers of companies into stronger national entities to respond to foreign competition. Strengthening the technological base of such firms has been a key objective. Similarly, the French have emphasized industrial participation in the training of manpower resources.

There are "concerted action programs" in critical areas, with committees created to coordinate research; "thematic action programs" designed to coordinate interdisciplinary applied research among laboratories normally undertaking basic research projects; "pre-development aid" to help research organizations launch work on new technologies; "development aid" in the form of loans to meet the development costs of private firms; and a variety of tax incentives.

All research and development operating expenses are fully deductible for income tax purposes; there is accelerated depreciation of research and development facilities; tax deductions are allowed for capital invested in research and development facilities by new organizations; and a payroll tax supports worker retraining programs. In addition, the government supports the National Agency for the Valorization of Research to help researchers, inventors, and small firms in developing innovations.

West Germany: Support in the Private Sector

In contrast to France, Germany relies more on market forces and industry-government-university cooperation than on government regulation and control to foster innovation. Government assistance is normally granted only if market strength seems to assure ultimate success; hence the German government's direct role in developing such major technologies as electronics and computers, much as in the U.K. and France.

Most German aid, however, seeks to influence the "climate" for innovation through indirect measures. The principal thrust of German policy is to reduce the costs of research and development to private firms and to encourage large, technically-based corporations in advanced areas. The relatively high level of cooperation which exists among industry, universities, and government is a positive factor in the German environment for innovation.

Several programs are of particular interest:

- There is an extensive network of research institutes supported largely by federal and state governments, ranging from basic (for example, the Max Planck Institutes) to applied industry-oriented research.
- "Big science" and "key technology" programs receive high priorities; the latter are focused specifically on industrial innovation and include direct government cost-sharing with industry.
- Under the "first innovations" program, the government meets 50 per cent of the cost of commercial development of a promising new technology with an interest-free, forgivable loan; if the effort fails, the loan is cancelled.
- The availability of venture capital is assured through an independent consortium of banks supported by government guarantees; the consortium purchases equity shares in new companies undertaking innovative projects.

A Congressional Agenda for Innovation

On the basis of what is known about current U.S. programs to encourage technological innovation, industry's response to these programs, and the foreign experience reviewed in the previous section, the authors propose that several policy issues merit consideration in the U.S. The following paragraphs summarize possible Congressional initiatives and the consequences which can be hypothesized to flow from them.

- The Congress should consider providing for the direct support of broadly applicable technology of importance to industry. Currently, the U.S. provides no direct support for such development, unlike other industrialized countries where this support is prominent. The argument for the support of non-mission-oriented research rests on the fact that the social returns on technological innovation are frequently greater than the returns which accrue to any individual inventor or developing company.

  Congressional initiatives might include: authorizing government procurement of innovative products at prices which provide for an indirect subsidy of research costs; advanced research responsive to social goals; and exclusive patent rights for individuals and firms making inventions under federally-supported research.

- The Congress should consider a more appropriate role for the national laboratories in the support of technological innovation. Most of our national laboratories—Brookhaven, Oak Ridge, and Los Alamos, for example—were set up to support specific government missions such as nuclear weapons development or space research. Many have now expanded their roles beyond the original missions, and in some cases changing government policies have led to redefinitions of their activities. The result is that many of the national laboratories now compete directly with private industry in performing research on technology of commercial significance. Options available to the Congress include the definition of explicit missions for the national laboratories, including new research roles which extend instead of duplicate existing research activities; and the development of guidelines to help funding agencies decide which projects to fund in-house, which to assign to the national laboratories, and which to support in the private sector.

- The Congress should consider measures to help new firms and inventors enter the market. New and small firms have been shown to be leading innovators, often because they are formed on the basis of a new idea or product and have great flexibility in introducing radically new products.

  The Congress could ease the process of entering the market for new firms and individual inventors/entrepreneurs by providing for selective use of government procurement policy, stricter enforcement of anti-trust laws, assistance to new firms in meeting regulatory requirements, and greater patent protection for small innovators.

- The Congress should consider programs to promote the diffusion of existing technologies and technical information within the private sector.

  Several instruments could be used to overcome the rigidities which tend to discourage wide application of technologies and thereby to give advantages to large enterprises. These might include creation of local technical centers, support for cooperative activities among small firms, support for technology information/communication systems, compulsory licensing of technologies to competitors when leading firms reach a certain market share, and government purchases of technology for resale to new users.

- The Congress should consider new ways of implementing environmental and safety requirements to encourage innovative technologies and safer products and materials. Regulatory legislation should be designed to encourage innovative compliance technologies; examples would include strict liability for pollution damage, effluent taxes, provision for joint research and development for pollution control, and government support for efforts to achieve regulatory goals through technological change.

- The Congress should consider an integrated manpower policy to strengthen the innovation process and to alleviate the disruptive impacts which rapid technological change can have on employment. There should be training to prepare manpower resources for future technological developments and at the same time training to help workers adjust to existing dislocations. A comprehensive manpower program should include continuing forecasts of future skill requirements in different sectors and strategies for helping scientific and technical education adapt to these future trends.

- The Congress should support continuing analyses of the needs and potential of U.S. industries and of the impact on them of government programs, including regulation and tax policy, and of foreign innovation. The relationship between government actions and technological innovation varies significantly in different industrial sectors, and government policy-making is often severely hampered by the lack of sector-specific analyses of this relationship.

- The Congress should consider supporting a national capability for anticipating hazards arising from existing and new technologies. The benefits and hazards associated with a technological change too often go unrecognized until the hazards reach crisis proportion and threaten the benefits which accompanied them. Several policies deserve consideration, including a centralized agency to strengthen hazard analysis, government support for development of this discipline in universities, worker and consumer education, and a hazard analysis requirement for industrial firms.

- The Congress should focus on the demand for new technologies as well as on the supply. Government support of research and development in the context of innovation represents an effort to affect the supply of new technologies. But policies which work to stimulate demand have often been shown more effective in eliciting innovative products and processes. Government procurement is one notably successful example, and environmental regulation may sometimes work in a similar fashion to change demand. New demand-oriented policies might include mechanisms to create new or expanded markets for new technologies (procurement, user subsidies, and regulations) and to directly influence consumer demand for the products of innovation.

II

STRATEGY
AND PLANNING

A.

Corporate Strategy

CORPORATE STRATEGY is fundamentally a matter of choosing goals and developing time-phased plans of action for their attainment. Cohen and Cyert outline the general procedures involved in formulating, implementing and monitoring strategic plans. Ansoff and Stewart pay special attention to the strategies of technology-based businesses from the standpoint of the desired degree of linkage between ongoing operations and research and development activities.

Corporate strategy, of course, also embraces the identification and evaluation of potential opportunities and the possible means through which these opportunities might be realized. Marcy explores the alternatives available for acquiring new technology with special reference to the steps to be followed and the pitfalls to be avoided in negotiating licensing agreements. Steiner concentrates on mergers and acquisitions as means of achieving strategic ends.

6. Strategy: Formulation, Implementation, and Monitoring

Kalman J. Cohen and Richard M. Cyert

Cohen and Cyert view strategic planning as a nine-step process, beginning with the formulation of corporate goals and ending with the measurement, feedback, and control of results.

THE STUDY of corporate strategy within graduate schools of business has been under way for many years. With the growing complexity of the world and with the increased size of business firms, the need for planning and the development of a corporate strategy has become recognized in the business firm. While many areas of management have been subjected to scientific analysis, the strategy area continues to be characterized by a commonsensical judgmental approach.

This paper is an attempt to impose structure upon the various problems inherent in the process of formulating, implementing, and monitoring corporate strategy in modern business firms. We begin by identifying the relevant considerations in the strategic planning process and then discussing the manner in which formal models can prove useful to executives in dealing with various subproblems. The paucity of valid, normative propositions in the corporate strategy literature indicates the need for a more scientific approach to this important field.

The nine major steps that constitute the strategic planning process are as follows: (1) formulation of goals; (2) analysis of the environment; (3) assigning quantitative values to the goals; (4) the micro-process of

Reprinted from *The Journal of Business*, 46 (July, 1973), pp. 349–367. Used by permission. Note: Many of the footnotes in the original article have been abbreviated or omitted for reasons of space.

Kalman Cohen is Distinguished Bank Research Professor, Graduate School of Business Administration, Duke University. Richard Cyert is President of Carnegie-Mellon University.

strategy formulation; (5) the gap analysis; (6) strategic search; (7) selecting the portfolio of strategic alternatives; (8) implementation of the strategic program; (9) measurement, feedback, and control.[1] This paper will review these nine steps and present selected ideas that demonstrate how the strategic planning process could be improved through use of analytical procedures. The nine steps should not be viewed as a once-and-for-all process of strategic planning, but, rather, as a continuous, ongoing process.[2] The whole procedure is a dynamic feedback process that has neither a beginning nor an end; it is merely for expository convenience that we label the first step as formulating corporate goals.

I. Formulation of Goals

The first step in the strategic planning process can be viewed as the development of the arguments in the corporate utility function. This specification is made by the coalition responsible for the top-level management of the corporation. Corporate goals must stem from participants within the organization. The goals of a small firm under control of a single entrepreneur are determined solely by him. The goals of a large corporation under control of professional managers are determined by a coalition which typically includes the chairman of the board, the president, and a select group of the more important vice presidents. The group is characterized as a coalition because no one dominates it in the way that a single entrepreneur may dominate his organization.

The final set of arguments in the utility function for the corporation must be accepted by the individuals who are responsible for implementing the policy of the corporation. This acceptance can be induced in a variety of ways that have been characterized by organization theorists as "side payments." At this stage, the goals are specified in qualitative rather than in quantitative terms. Some goals relate to measurable entities such as earnings per share, total sales, share of market, return on investment, rate of growth in sales, rate of profit growth, and so forth. Other goals represent management aspirations which are more difficult to measure: for example, a desire to be the most advanced electronics firm in the United States, a desire to be a leader in community improvements, a desire to be ecologically responsible, and so forth.[3]

In the formulation of corporate goals, the relationships between those goals and the goals of the participants in the organization should be con-

---

[1] Some other attempts to present a conceptual framework for the strategic planning process are presented in George A. Steiner, *Top Management Planning* (New York: Macmillan Co., 1969), chap. 2.

[2] This point is aptly illustrated in H. Igor Ansoff, "Toward a Strategic Theory of the Firm," in *Business Strategy,* ed. H. Igor Ansoff (Baltimore: Penguin Books, 1969), esp. fig. 6.

[3] A detailed discussion of the variety of goals pursued by business firms is provided in Steiner (n. 1 above), chaps. 6–7.

sidered by the coalition. . . . It is clear from even casual observation that there is no formal weighting process by which the goals of each participant are incorporated into the goal structure in a systematic fashion. Further, it is also clear that each individual does not have an equal vote in determining the goals of an organization. Nevertheless, if the organization is to function effectively, its goals must in some sense be an amalgam of the goals of the participants.

A frequent phenomenon in organizations is the formation of subunits and of subunit goals. These subunits, which are usually work groups, become the object of the participants' identification. Group norms arise and may exert more influence over the individual than the organizational goals. The norms of the group may at some time be in conflict with the organizational goals and the subgroup actions contrary to the interests of the total organization. Still the individual may, in fact, substitute the goals of this subunit for the organizational goals. Hence, in formulating organizational goals, the coalition should consider the effect that they will have on subunit goals and on the potential formation of subunits.

Clearly the corporate goals must be viewed from the standpoint of the social values that are held by members of the coalition. It is necessary to differentiate between the social goals that are proper for the organization to hold and those that are proper for the individual participant to hold. For example, there may be a conflict for some firms between pollution control and profit. This conflict becomes particularly strong when the society has not passed the appropriate laws which embody its social values and the corporation is left with the problem of voluntarily reducing its profit in order to contribute to some social goal. . . . In the final analysis, however, business firms are profit-seeking organizations, and society depends on them to seek profit as a means of achieving the optimum allocation of resources.

In summary, we have stressed the fact that goal formulation is a process of determining the arguments in the corporate utility function. The particular set of goals that the corporation selects must take into account the personal goals of the members of the organization and the goals of subunits. The coalition must also consider the problem of social goals and the extent to which they are going to be represented in the corporate goal structure. In this first step of the strategic planning process, no attempt is made to assign quantitative values to the set of elements in the goal structure.

II. Environment and the Firm

The organization and the environment are parts of a complex interactive system. The actions taken by the organization can have important effects on the environment, and, conversely, the outcomes of the actions of the organization are partially determined by events in the environment.

These outcomes and the events that contribute to them have a major impact on the organization. Even if the organization does not respond to these events, significant changes in the organizational participants' goals and roles can occur.[4]

Most organizations attempt to learn from interaction with the environment and respond to changes caused by the environment. Both the learning and response are easiest when the environment is disjoint. In such cases, the causal links among the sectors of the environment are relatively short and events in one sector are likely to have only minor effects on events in other sectors. The organization can then usefully partition such a disjoint environment and consider the sectors in isolation. For example, a multinational firm selling products under different brand names in each of several countries can change policy in one market and analyze the effects without considering interactions with other markets. The learning and response are more difficult for the organization when the environment is complex and long chains of causal links and events in one sector have profound effects on other sectors. In such an environment, the organization must consider the whole sequence of possible effects of any action it takes. For example, large steel companies must consider the effects that a price increase will have on various sectors of the environment—on labor unions, competitors, consumers, and government.

The parts of an environment that are relevant differ according to the type of organization. For the business firm, economic conditions are of prime importance. When the economy is in an expansionary period, many possible actions can yield the necessary resources to allow the firm to survive and grow. Conflict with other organizations in the environment will be minimized since all organizations can readily meet their basic resource requirements. Conflict within the organization will also generally be reduced because the preferences of the various coalition members can be more easily satisfied.

*   *   *

In contrast, when economic conditions are unfavorable, goal attainment becomes more difficult and the firm will devote increasing attention toward its goal set. Continued failure to meet its goals without any apparent possibility of increasing resources generally results in a reduction of goal values. In the face of economic adversity, typical firm responses are to tighten operations by postponing expansion plans, engaging in cost-cutting drives, reducing the number of participants, and so on. The extent of these actions depends on the amount of slack in the organization. At the

[4] See Paul Lawrence and Jay W. Lorsch, *Organization and Environment: Managing Differentiation and Integration* (Boston: Division of Research, Graduate School of Business Administration, Harvard University, 1967).

beginning of unfavorable economic conditions, the organization will usually have considerable slack accumulated during more favorable times. If economic conditions continue at a low level for an extensive period of time, it becomes increasingly difficult to remove slack without reducing services that were previously considered essential. Eventually this set of events will lead to changes in the organizational structure. Some roles may be eliminated completely and other roles may be extensively modified. Serious internal conflict among the individual participants will occur and will result in participants leaving the organization both voluntarily and involuntarily.

The impact of changing economic conditions is reduced if the organization is prepared for them. Thus, organizations attempt to plan ahead; as a basis for planning, forecasts must be made of future changes in economic conditions. These forecasts are, of course, more accurate when the economic environment is relatively stable over time. The organization has more difficulty in learning the structure of the environment and accurately predicting its future states when the environment is highly volatile. Unfortunately, these are the circumstances when forecasts are most essential.

For whatever planning horizon the firm uses, it is necessary to make predictions for the entire planning period. In particular, it is necessary to make predictions of various aggregate economic variables which are relevant for the firm. These aggregates include GNP, price indices, unemployment rates, and similar measures of the state of the economy at benchmark dates during the planning period. It is desirable that these predictions be made at the corporate level and transmitted to the operating units of the firm as a basis for their specific planning. In this way, all planning activity of the firm is conducted under a uniform set of predictions. The predictions will not necessarily be single-valued estimates. The firm may find it useful to develop several plausible alternative economic scenarios and to require its operating units to formulate plans for each alternative.[5]

In addition to aggregate economic predictions, it is necessary for the firm to make predictions about future conditions in the industries and markets in which it operates. An industry forecast is usually made in terms of the total dollar sales expected for the industry. From such forecasts, the firm can predict its future sales over the planning period by making assumptions about the market shares that it will obtain. In making these assumptions the firm must make predictions about the behavior of its present and potential competitors.[6] Estimates must be made of the prices

---

[5] For a survey of various approaches to forecasting the future environment, see Steiner (n. 1 above), chap. 8.

[6] The importance of analyzing competitors is stressed in S. Tilles, "Making Strategy Explicit," in Ansoff (n. 2 above), pp. 186–90.

competitors will charge, of their advertising policies, and of the product changes competitors will make. In this regard it is highly useful for firms to maintain an elaborate information system on their competitors. Relevant information on competitors can be obtained from public sources such as financial statements, from information gathered from the firm's salesmen, and from executives who meet rival executives at professional meetings. All of these sources can be utilized to build up a data base on each of the firm's major competitors.

III. Establishment of Quantitative Targets

After goals have been qualitatively formulated and after the environmental analysis has been completed, the firm's coalition is in a position to establish quantitative targets. Quantitative targets essentially impute quantitative values to those previously formulated goals that are capable of being stated in quantitative terms. These quantitative targets are often usefully established for planning purposes in terms of rates of growth. Thus one goal may be that the firm's profit should grow at some specific annual rate over the planning horizon. Part of the process of establishing quantitative targets also involves weighting the importance of the various targets. Thus, the firm conceivably might weight achievement of its sales goal more than achievement of its profit goal. This weighting is important when the firm may be in a position to achieve some but not all of its goal set. Given the weighting it is then possible to specify strategies which are appropriate when it is impossible to attain all the various targets. Goals stated in terms of absolute levels rather than rates of change require target dates to be specified. It is generally necessary for a plan to have values for the relevant goals specified for various benchmark dates. This is frequently done, permitting the firm to project *pro forma* balance sheets and profit and loss statements for the individual years within the planning horizon.

One useful heuristic for planning is the process of "backward induction."[7] This approach requires that a specific set of desired values be established for the various goals for the final period of the planning horizon, for example, 5 years from now. The planners specify, for instance, the values the firm should have for sales, profit, capital investment, and so on during the fifth year. On the basis of these specifications, the planners work backward to see where the firm must be in the fourth year if it is to achieve the goals in the fifth year and so on back to the first year of the plan. This process of backward induction is a useful addition to the planning process. It enables the planner to establish a viable

[7] An explanation of backward induction is presented in Morris H. DeGroot, *Optimal Statistical Decisions* (New York: McGraw-Hill Book Co., 1970), pp. 277–78.

plan for the entire planning horizon. Several iterations may be required, and, in this process, goals may be modified.

*   *   *

IV. The Microprocess of Strategy Formulation

The fourth major step in the planning process can be referred to as "the microaspects of strategy formulation." Each operating unit in the corporation formulates its own strategic plan over the relevant time horizon. The time horizon chosen for strategic planning will vary depending upon the nature of the firm, but 5 years is a typical time horizon for strategic planning in business organizations. It often will be desirable for some qualitative aspects of the strategic plan to be formulated over a 10- or 20-year horizon, even though detailed quantitative projections may be made only for an intermediate-term time horizon such as the next 5 years.

Before each operating unit can develop its own strategic plan, it is necessary for the senior executives of the corporation (or their staff members) to provide the managers of the operating unit with some background information. This centrally provided information should consist of at least the following items:

a. Some guidelines concerning the nature of the strategic planning process should be provided. The emphasis should be put on actively involving relevant executives in the planning process in order to focus their attention on strategic considerations. Especially at the level of the operating units, there is a tendency for managers to worry primarily about immediate problems. A formalized planning process is necessary to induce managers to think seriously about long-term strategy for the operating unit.

b. The relevant goals that top management wants the operating unit to be concerned with should be explicitly stated.

c. All operating units should be provided with the results of the broad analysis of the economic environment undertaken in corporate headquarters. To the extent that relevant technological or product-market forecasts were centrally made, these should also be transmitted to appropriate operating units. There may be economies in having some of the technological and product-market forecasts made centrally even though they are relevant only to particular operating units in the corporation.

On the basis of this corporate information, each operating unit should develop its own strategic plan, in both qualitative and quantitative terms. A major activity which each operating unit must undertake in developing its strategic plan is a critical, thorough analysis of the environment for its own particular mix of products and markets. A reasonably broad definition of the operating unit's product-market mission needs to be adopted for this purpose. Given this broad view of its product-market posture, the operating unit must attempt to analyze its external environment to discover significant economic, market, and technological developments. As part of its environmental analysis, the operating unit must identify its major present and potential competitors. In addition, the operating unit should make an internal analysis to uncover those areas in which it has had problems and successes in the past in order to diagnose hitherto unrecognized strategic obstacles and opportunities. In the light of these external and internal analyses, the operating unit must then determine where its comparative advantage exists.

This analysis should result in a set of recommended strategic programs for each operating unit. Several types of recommendations may be relevant. These might involve pricing strategy, product-line strategy, marketing strategy, programs of cost reduction for existing products and markets, new products to be developed, new markets to be entered, major research and development expenditures, major advertising campaigns, and major physical investments. In proposing the operating unit's diversification into additional products and markets, recommendations should be made as to whether this diversification should be accomplished by means of internal growth or through external acquisition. Enough detailed information should be given in the verbal discussion and the quantitative projections so that executives at higher levels in the corporation can independently determine the impact of undertaking, postponing, or rejecting each element in the recommended strategic plan.

V. The "Gap Analysis"

The fifth major step consists of aggregating upward the strategic plans formulated by each operating unit to obtain aggregate strategic plans for the corporation as a whole and for any relevant subdivisions. This upward aggregation of the specific quantitative projections made by each operating unit for the next 5 years can readily be done by a process of simple summation. Equally important, however, is the upward aggregation of the qualitative, verbal aspects of each operating unit's strategic plan. (The hierarchical pattern utilized in the upward aggregation process should be carefully chosen to make the most logical sense for the particular corporation. It might first involve consolidating the operating units into departments, then consolidating the departments into divisions, then consolidating these divisions into groups, and, finally, consolidating the groups into the corporation. Of course, the number of levels present in this upward aggregation process, and the particular labels attached to each level of consolidation, will differ from firm to firm.)

The immediate aim of the aggregation is to enable a "gap analysis" to be performed at higher organizational levels in the firm.[8] This "gap analysis" might be made only at the corporate-wide level, or, instead, preliminary gap analyses might be made at each of the "collection points" at lower organizational levels (for example, initially at the departmental level, then at the divisional level, and finally at the group level) prior to the corporate-wide gap analysis.

Regardless of the organization level at which the gap analysis is performed, the procedural aspects of it are much the same. In particular, the projected performance for the corporation as a whole (or for whatever organizational subdivision the gap analysis is being performed) is compared to the quantitative targets which have been established for the corporation (or the appropriate subdivision). Since the corporation generally has multiple goals, the gap analysis should be done for each goal. Thus for each goal of importance to the corporation, the projected figures will be subtracted from the targets established for that goal in order to develop a perceived gap. For any particular goal, for example, earnings per share, this perceived gap can be expressed as a function of time (for example, year-by-year over a 5-year horizon). Thus, the gap analysis process can be usefully viewed as developing a "perceived-gap matrix," as illustrated in table 1. The rows in this matrix designate the various corporate goals, for example, total sales, earnings per share, some measure of geographical dispersion, and so forth. The columns of this matrix correspond to various

TABLE 1. An Example of a Perceived-Gap Matrix

Corporate Goals	Time Periods in the Planning Horizon				
	Year 1	*Year 2*	*Year 3*	*Year 4*	*Year 5*
Total sales revenue (million $)	+ 2.5	− 7.3	−10.9	−18.7	−28.3
Earnings per share ($ per share)	+ 0.05	− 0.11	− 0.31	− 0.80	− 1.35
Index of geographical dispersion (percentage)	−15	−13	− 9	− 7	− 6

points of time within the planning horizon, for example, years one, two, three, four and five. The entries in this matrix are the perceived gaps along each goal for each particular point of time. The manner in which this perceived-gap matrix can be used to initiate strategic search will be discussed in connection with step six below.

[8] A different approach to the gap analysis is discussed in H. Igor Ansoff, *Corporate Strategy* (New York: McGraw-Hill Book Co., 1965), chap. 8.

VI. Strategic Search

A gap between the goals specified at the corporate level and the predicted achievement developed through the microanalysis stimulates the firm to search for new strategies in order to achieve its goals.[9] The strategic search process generally first focuses on internal activities. For example, the firm may begin its search by reviewing its price strategy to see whether it can achieve its goals by raising prices. More broadly, the firm may review its entire marketing strategy. Another area for search is the cost structure of the firm with a view toward establishing a strategy for cost reduction. Still another area for internal search is research and development. All of these areas, and others which may be undertaken, fall into the category of internal search.

If the measures discovered by internal search do not entirely close the gap, the firm then turns to external search. In this phase the firm begins to examine the environment with a view toward bringing new resources into the firm to enable it to achieve its goals. Frequently this is accomplished through a strategy of acquisition of other firms. In general, the firm searches for acquisitions which would result in economies of scale or positive externalities. An economy of scale would result from an acquisition that would enable the firm to use some of its resources more intensively, for example, by producing or distributing a new product with already existing facilities or manpower. Positive externalities would result from a new (complementary) product whose sale would increase the sales of the firm's present products, from elimination of overlapping facilities (such as branch or headquarters offices), from the acquisition of new technical talent, and so forth. A frequent source of economies resulting from acquisition is the more intensive utilization of capable managers. It is clear that in any economy, including the U.S. economy, there is a significant shortage of good managers. Thus, firms which have capable managerial talent may be able to benefit from acquisitions that do not appear to be a synergistic fit. However, because of the ability of the acquiring firm to supply good management, these acquisitions may prove highly successful.

There is at present in the United States much evidence that legal power will be invoked to restrict the acquisition policy of firms. This development reduces the efficacy of external search and increases the importance of internal search. This change in turn emphasizes the need to develop organizational policies that will permit managers with entrepreneurial ability to advance within the firm. Thus it is important that planning activity not restrict initiative by developing inflexible policies; instead, the

---

[9] A general discussion of the empirical process of search behavior within an organization is presented in James G. March and Herbert A. Simon, *Organizations* (New York: John Wiley & Sons, 1958), esp. pp. 173–74, 180. A discussion of search behavior which focuses more directly on issues of corporate strategy is contained in Ansoff, ibid.

planning process should induce division managers to feel responsible for developing new business ideas as part of the strategic plans for their own divisions.

VII. Selecting the Portfolio of Strategic Alternatives

In the sixth step of the strategic planning process, the perceived-gap matrix was used to trigger several different types of strategic search. The purpose of this search is to develop a strategy set that consists of possible strategic actions. Each of the members of this set is a strategic action that might be undertaken by the corporation as a whole (or by appropriate subdivisions). For example, a strategy set might include proposals for changes in pricing policy, major cost-reduction campaigns, changes in product design, new market introduction plans, diversification into specific new product-market alternatives, major investments in physical facilities, and the acquisition of particular products or of entire firms.

The fact that a set of possible strategic actions has been developed does not imply that each action will be adopted as part of the strategic plan. From the strategy set, management selects a particular portfolio of strategic actions; this portfolio constitutes the corporation's new strategic plan.[10]

The seventh step of the strategic planning process, as we have described it, focuses on the way in which corporations should develop a strategic plan. Because of the rather casual manner in which strategic planning is approached in most corporations, however, little emphasis is placed on the portfolio aspects of the problem. The usual approach is to judge each proposed action as it is uncovered in the search process strictly on its own merits. If the proposed action proves acceptable at this point, then the action is adopted as part of the new strategic plan. When enough proposed actions are adopted in this manner to close the perceived gap (or if the gap is closed by lowering the goal values), strategic search is terminated and the new strategic plan has been formulated. One deficiency in this typical approach is that management fails to evaluate interactions among possible strategic actions. A more complete analysis from a portfolio viewpoint will often lead to a different evaluation of a particular proposed action because of interaction effects. A second deficiency of the usual approach is that strategic search may be prematurely terminated.

*   *   *

The difficulty of the coalition's making an objective evaluation of proposed actions is complicated by the loss of information as proposals

[10] See E. Eugene Carter and Kalman J. Cohen, "Portfolio Aspects of Strategic Planning," *Journal of Business Policy* 2, no. 4 (Summer 1972), pp. 8–30.

filter upward through the organizational hierarchy. So many details concerning proposals are eliminated in "the selling process" that it becomes
virtually impossible for coalition members to analyze interaction effects
even if they so desired. Thus, each coalition member sponsoring a proposal
becomes an "uncertainty absorber" with respect to the proposed actions
that he advocates. This situation effectively forces the coalition into the
necessity of making personal judgments concerning the competence of its
members in the guise of selecting a strategic plan. In order to minimize
personal conflict among coalition members, the coalition frequently adopts
rules of thumb to allocate strategic resources among organizational subunits in some objective but nonoptimal manner, for example, budgeting
research and development expenditures in proportion to sales and authorizing automatic reinvestment of depreciation charges.

VIII. Implementation of the Strategic Program

Once a portfolio of strategic alternatives has been established for the
corporation (as well as for each group, division, department, and operating unit in the corporation), the next step in the strategic planning process
is implementation of the program. We will focus on the implementation
problem from the standpoint of overall corporate strategy, but analogous
considerations also apply at other levels in the organizational hierarchy.

In order to develop an operational procedure for implementing the
agreed-upon strategic program, it is necessary to decompose the broadly
stated strategy into a time-phased sequence of plans regarding such actions
as new product developments, new market introductions, external acquisitions, capital investment projects, management development, manpower
recruitment, and so forth. The various activities necessary to implement
any particular strategy should be defined in terms of each type of resource
required. It is common practice to reduce this specification of resource
requirements to monetary terms. Unfortunately, in many firms, the underlying detail is then lost and only the dollar budget for the strategic program remains as a permanent control document. With this loss of detail
and transformation into monetary terms, a subtle change in attitudes also
occurs. In place of the inspiration and imagination displayed in the development of the plan, management has merely a set of monetary constraints within which it must operate. This primary emphasis on monetary
considerations has the effect of replacing the manager's entrepreneurial
spirit with a bureaucratic attitude. The long-term goals of the strategic plan
are displaced by the short-term goal of operating within budget.

In arguing that the financial budget should not be the sole form to
which the strategic plan is reduced, we nonetheless acknowledge that
financial budgets are essential. The various forms of short-term plans and
budgets should be consistent with the strategic plan. Such interaction can

be accomplished by initially defining the plans and budgets for the coming year as the first-year components in the quantitative projections developed as part of the 5-year strategic plan. If necessary, of course, these initial figures for the coming year can then be further disaggregated in the short-term planning and budgeting process.

It is obvious that any attempt to forecast the future (especially several years ahead) is bound to be subject to errors. Unfortunately, however, many planning and budgeting systems place undue reliance upon the accuracy of the underlying forecasts. More realistically, strategic plans and their accompanying operating budgets should be formulated on a contingency basis. Some type of decision-tree analysis may be a useful planning aid for this purpose. At a minimum, operating budgets for the next year as well as strategic plans for the next 5 years should be in a variable budget format, rather than the more usual fixed budget format. To the extent possible, however, various major contingencies should be envisioned and probabilities of occurrence assigned to each one. Alternative plans of actions can then be developed for each contingency having a sufficiently high probability of occurrence. Obviously, in this regard, some type of computerized planning and budgeting model would be extremely helpful in developing suitable contingency plans.

In order to implement any specific strategic program successfully, it is necessary to obtain enthusiastic cooperation from executives at various levels of the corporation. One way of achieving acceptance of the strategic plan by lower-level executives is to have these executives actively participate in the planning process. The approach to strategy formulation that we have described requires such participation in the process of developing the plan (especially in the microprocess of strategy formulation and in strategic research).

It is critical as part of the implementation process to examine the formal organizational structure.[11] Although major changes in structure will occur relatively infrequently, it is nevertheless important to determine whether minor modifications will increase the likelihood of achieving the goals specified by the strategic plan. By organizational structure we mean the particular description of the roles of the organization, the allocation of decision-making power, and the placing of responsibility. There must be a matching of the structure with the requirements for decision making, coordination, and control emanating from the plan. Generally changes in organizational structure are made along the centralization-decentralization dimension. The strategic plan should be analyzed to determine whether the organizational structure should be shifted in either direction. For example, if the firm acquires a new product that has little relationship to

---

[11] An appropriate framework for this purpose is presented in Russell L. Ackoff, *A Concept of Corporate Planning* (New York: John Wiley & Sons, 1970), chap. 5.

the current product mix, it may be desirable to decentralize decisions relating to the new product. Such decentralization places decision-making power in the roles where appropriate information and knowledge exist.

Speaking more generally, the main factors affecting the degree of decentralization of an organization are its size, the environment (benign or hostile), subunit interdependency, and technology. As an organization grows larger, the cost of maintaining centralized control increases. If the environment is hostile (in the sense that mistakes will be easily exploited by competitors), there will be an increased tendency toward centralization. Similarly, if there is a high degree of interdependency among subunits, more centralization is often necessary. If the technological changes associated with the firm's activities require large investments in order to exploit them, the tendency to centralize is increased. Technological changes that reduce the costs of communications provide an impetus toward decentralization. In order to relate the strategic plan effectively to the organizational structure, management should determine whether there will be any significant changes in size, environment, subunit interdependency, and technology resulting from the plan. If so, modifications of the organizational structure should then be made as part of the implementation process.

IX. Measurement, Feedback, and Control

An essential component in the strategic planning process is the development of operational measures of the extent to which the corporation and appropriate subunits thereof are in fact adhering to the agreed-upon plan.[12] Additional information should also be developed to help management determine whether the strategic plan may no longer be appropriate. Corporate targets have already been specified in operationally measurable quantitative terms (see Section III above). It is, therefore, relatively simple to obtain periodic measurements of corporate performance (or subunit performance), and to relate these in a time-phased manner to the targets.

It must be recognized, of course, that any attempt to measure performance and to provide feedback on the degree of goal attainment is an evaluation process which introduces possible pitfalls.[13] Once the "rules of the game" have been laid down, the players can be expected to alter their behavior so as to "look good" according to the "scorecard" which

[12] For a discussion of some common approaches to the measurement, feedback, and control aspects of strategic planning, see Kenneth R. Andrews, *The Concept of Corporate Strategy* (Homewood, Ill.: Richard Irwin, Inc., 1971), chap. 7.

[13] For a discussion of some pitfalls that may arise, see E. Kirby Warren, *Long-Range Planning: The Executive Viewpoint* (Englewood Cliffs, N.J.: Prentice-Hall, Inc., 1966), chap. 5.

is kept on them. Therefore, it is essential that the summary evaluative measures conform as closely as possible to the important corporate goals. It also is important that the detailed measures used for ex ante decision analyses are exactly the same as (or at least consistent with) the corresponding measures for ex post performance evaluation. Otherwise, one would expect serious biases to be introduced into strategic decision making and implementation in order to make the performance evaluations look good, often at the expense of the desired corporate objectives.

Dangers inherent in the measurement and feedback process are intensified when attention is focused solely on one type of summary figure, for example, ROI (return on investment), defined as the income after taxes allocated to a profit center divided by the total funds (or investment) utilized by that profit center. Most strategic expenditures are of such a nature that they produce net cash outflows in their early years, accompanied (hopefully) by net cash inflows in later years. If the short-term return on investment measure is in jeopardy at a particular profit center for a given year, it would appear easy for the manager of that profit center to eliminate or reduce strategic expenditures this year, in order to have a better short-run performance evaluation. The emphasis on short-run performance is aggravated in organizations where the profit-center manager can expect to hold that particular organizational role for only a few years.

By having many dimensions of performance on which measurements are made and feedback provided, it is less easy for executives to find ways of arbitrarily "winning the game" at the expense of the long-run corporate objectives. In particular, if the various actions required to implement the profit center's strategic program are clearly spelled out (manpower requirements, research and development projects, physical investments, and so forth), then the profit center manager should be required to explain deviations from the various actions specified in the strategic plan.

X. Summary

In this paper we have outlined the nine major steps which comprise the strategic planning process. Our discussion of strategy formulation, implementation, and monitoring is primarily intended as a normative, rather than as a descriptive, presentation. We would expect that the actual process in a few firms which have concentrated on strategic planning would be generally similar to the framework that we have sketched. We have not, however, made any conscious attempt to describe the manner in which this process is conducted in any particular firm. Unfortunately, we do not believe that most firms approach strategic planning in the serious, logical manner that we have advocated. Thus, this present paper must be regarded as being normative in nature, rather than an empirical description of the strategic planning process in real organizations.

The nine major steps into which we have divided the strategic planning process can be usefully grouped into three phases: formulation, implementation, and monitoring of strategy. Strategic planning should be viewed as being a repetitive, cyclic process. Any firm should repeat this entire process periodically, for example, annually.

The first seven steps together constitute the formulation phase. A prerequisite to any serious attempt to undertake strategic planning is the specification of the overall goals of the organization. This is normally the responsibility of the coalition comprising the top management of the firm. Although initially the goals are stated in qualitative terms, it is ultimately necessary to formulate goals in quantitative terms, for example, as a sequence of target values over several time periods. Before quantitative targets can be meaningfully assigned to the goals, however, it is necessary to analyze relevant portions of the environment in order to determine the type of performance that may generally be feasible. For a business firm, one of the most significant aspects of the environment is the general condition of the economy. Aggregate economic predictions must also be transformed into more specific predictions concerning the various industries and markets in which the firm operates. After specific quantitative goals have been established at the corporate level, it is then critical for the various operating units independently to establish their own strategic plans. A corporate-wide aggregation of the plans produced by each operating unit then provides a prediction of the total corporate performance that would result if no further changes in direction were provided by central management. This implied corporate performance is then compared to the quantitative corporate goals to indicate what gaps there may be in predicted goal achievement. When there are significant positive gaps, that is, when aspirations exceed expected performance, strategic search is initiated both at the corporate level and in various operating units. The objective of strategic search is to discover possible new strategic actions that will improve the performance of the firm beyond that implied by the aggregation of the previously prepared microplans. The senior executives in the firm are then responsible for selecting a particular portfolio of strategic actions from the set of possible strategic actions uncovered in the strategic search process. This portfolio constitutes the new strategic plan for the corporation, thus ending the strategy formulation phase.

Implementation of the strategic plan constitutes the second major phase of the strategy process. The basic problem of implementation is to put the strategic plan into effective action. One of the critical steps in implementing the strategy is to decompose the broadly stated plan into a time-phased sequence of specific action programs. This basically is a specification of the various types of resources that will be required at particular dates in order to achieve the planned strategy. Another critical aspect of the implementation process involves considering possible changes in the organizational structure of the firm if these will increase the likelihood of achieving the plan.

The final phase in the strategy process involves monitoring the extent to which the plan has been effectively implemented and remains appropriate. This requires that various relevant aspects of performance be measured and compared with corresponding aspects of the plan. The behavioral effects of any measurement, feedback, and control system need to be considered to avoid inducing types of motivation that lead to undesirable forms of behavior.

It is our view that the framework we have suggested for the strategic planning process can lead to formulation of serious research efforts that will develop techniques for improving the effectiveness of strategic planning. Such research efforts can be expected to proceed in at least two different directions. On the one hand, some aspects of the strategic planning process can be formulated in rigorous quantitative terms, and the power of management-science techniques and computer systems can be brought to bear to help improve those aspects of the process where the relevant issues can be sharply and definitively stated. On the other hand, some other aspects of strategic planning, which typically have been viewed in qualitative terms and approached solely on the basis of judgment, wisdom, and experience, can be subjected to a more rigorous scientific analysis by the use of the behavioral sciences. We are not maintaining that strategic planning will ever be reduced to a fully automated process in which executive judgment is unnecessary. We do believe, however, that further research efforts will put into clearer focus those areas where executive judgments are essential, thus enabling executives to perform better those tasks in which they have a comparative advantage. This will be possible only when other aspects of the strategic planning process (the ones in which quantitative models, computer-based information systems, and behavioral science concepts possess some comparative advantage) are more rigorously analyzed and understood. The end result will be an improved process of strategic planning, in which the judgment, wisdom, and experience of executives are combined with the judicious use of quantitative and scientific concepts in a manner which effectively exploits the comparative advantages of each component and participant in the process.

Even without waiting for further research efforts to be successfully completed, however, most firms can greatly improve the effectiveness of their strategic planning process by adopting the framework that we have outlined in this paper. Such a framework does not necessarily involve the use of sophisticated quantitative models and computer techniques. Rather, it requires only that the executives in a business firm devote some serious efforts to the strategic planning process and recognize the critical problems inherent in it. Most executives are fully capable of participating effectively in this process if they only take the time to do so. Preoccupation with short-term operating problems unfortunately reduces the attention that most executives pay to strategic planning. It is clear, however, that for the well-being of particular firms as well as our entire economic system, major attention must be paid to produce more effective strategic planning systems in most American corporations. It is only by having effective strategic planning processes that the American economy will have the ability to provide the innovations and adaptations which are necessary to produce an efficient allocation of economic resources in the dynamic society in which we now live.

7. Strategies for a Technology-based Business

H. Igor Ansoff and John M. Stewart

Systematic analysis of a company's technological profile makes it possible to achieve more profitable results. This is the classic article on the relationship between strategy and technology.

WITH THE GROWING impact of technology on business and the growing prominence of research and development in the spectrum of corporate activities, considerable attention has been directed to the special problems of the R&D function: its organization, its planning and control, its budgeting, and especially the stimulation and management of creativity.

In technology-based industries, however, a subtler but no less significant complex of problems has escaped the recognition of many managers who are daily grappling with its symptoms and manifestations. This is the array of new problems and requirements imposed on the technology-based corporation.

In industries such as chemicals, electronics, or aerospace, the implications of technology for corporate business strategy, organization, and planning and control are often decisive. Consider two examples:

- A few years ago a profitable small manufacturer of high-quality electronic components was acquired by one of its major customers, a top-ranking aerospace corporation. Within months it had been "helped to death" by its acquirer, much to the latter's puzzlement. The subcontracts which it had accepted from the parent, apparently at a fair price, presented challenging technical problems.

Reprinted from the *Harvard Business Review*, 45 (November–December, 1967), pp. 71–83. © 1967 by the President and Fellows of Harvard College.

H. Igor Ansoff is associated with the European Institute for Advanced Studies in Management, located in Brussels, and the author of the pathbreaking Corporate Strategy *(New York: McGraw-Hill, 1965). John Stewart is a director of McKinsey & Co., Inc., Management Consultants.*

What had not been apparent was that a small development and manufacturing organization could not turn itself overnight into a research-oriented aerospace hybrid.

- A large international industrial products company was plagued with cost and schedule overruns after stepping up its new product introductions. Introduction costs were continually being underestimated, and the production of other product lines was repeatedly disrupted, because, as it later turned out, management had failed to "shift gears" in its schedule, cost, and inventory controls to fit the advanced rate of product introduction. Cost of the lesson— more than $2 million.

Such problems as these have lately become a source of explicit and increasing top-management concern. This is natural, indeed inevitable, since R&D activities have grown until today in many industries they rank among the two or three heaviest consumers of company funds.

Management Issues

In this article we propose to consider the characteristic parameters of technically intensive businesses, describe their observed impact on major management processes and decisions, and discuss some of their important implications for such issues as these:

- *Business strategy.* Is our R&D investment consistent with our corporate strategy? Should we invest in the same technologies as our competitors, or in different ones? How can we identify the threats and/or profit opportunities from the technology of competitors within our own industry and those in other industries?
- *Organization.* How can we maximize the flexibility of our organization structure in the face of rapid technological change? How should our organization structure and work assignments be changed as products mature through their life cycles? How can technology best be transferred from R&D to manufacturing and marketing?
- *Planning and control.* How should we formulate and specify research objectives? Should we control research differently from development? How can project planning and control be integrated with periodic functional reporting?
- *Marketing.* What kind of product/market strategy should we follow? What technical advantages in our products, at what cost or investment level, will be needed to give us a substantial competitive advantage?

Our object is to suggest a conceptual framework which will help top management in its efforts to define and resolve them. Such a framework, applied to a hypothetical company, is shown in *Exhibit I* (see page 73).

The technological parameters we shall examine are the research versus development mix, the degree of downstream coupling, the shape of the product life cycle, the R&D investment/expense ratio, and the proximity to the "state of the art."

After discussing each of these in turn, we shall consider how they are related to four basic types of marketing strategy—recognizing that most companies will need a mixed strategy and that the different elements of the mix may vary over time.

Research vs. Development

The two concepts of "research" and "development" have become so closely linked in management thinking by the expression *R&D* that important differences between them are often ignored in executive decision making. This becomes particularly apparent when companies attempt to apply the lessons of their research experience to problems in development, or vice versa.

Rather than attempt to formulate a generally acceptable definition of the two concepts, we shall simply use the terms "R-intensive" and "D-intensive" to denote a tendency toward the basic and experimental on the one hand, and a tendency toward commercial product design on the other. Most companies, of course, fall somewhere in between, but they can best be described in terms of the two extremes.

R-intensive

These organizations in general display six characteristics:

1. *They work with indefinite design specifications.* Since management can usually identify the problem but cannot specify the desired solution, the task of the R-intensive organization is to discover and evaluate *alternative* solutions, rather than to implement a single solution.
2. *They tend to "broadcast" objectives and market data among technical people, rather than channel specific kinds of information to individuals.* Being unable to present specific requirements to research, they use broadcast communications to stimulate generation of alternatives that will be consistent with top management's objectives and strategy.
3. *They are nondirective in work assignments.* Since design specifications in R-intensive companies are less definite, and technical insight and potential contribution are individual rather than group attributes, managers must permit freedom for individual initiative and progress rather than assign individuals to specific parts of a well-defined solution.

4. *They maintain a continuing project evaluation and selection process.* Research is constantly turning up alternative solutions of varying worth, and these supersede previous solutions. Moreover, a move by a competitor, or results achieved on another project, may obsolete a piece of research or change its priority.

5. *They stress the perception of significant results.* Where a research problem has not been tightly structured, the solutions—even if found—are not always obvious. An essential skill of the technical manager is his ability to recognize technically or commercially significant results. The history of invention is replete with instances, like Carruther's discovery of nylon, where a flash of insight into the possibilities of wholly unanticipated experimental results led to great discoveries that might otherwise have been missed.

6. *They value innovation over efficiency.* Economy in performing research is less important than achieving a markedly better solution with clear market or profit advantages. Innovation is therefore prized, even when it entails the sacrifice of efficiency in organizational structure, planning, or control.

D-intensive

In contrast, these organizations can usually be recognized by four characteristics:

1. *Well-defined design specifications.* With the research essentially complete, the development objective is reasonably clear, and performance tests can be specified early during design. The technical task is not to create new alternatives but to reduce available alternatives to a single solution for implementation.

2. *Highly directive supervision.* The work to be done is highly interrelated from the beginning of design to successful testing; managers tend to specify objectives, give orders, and carefully measure performance. The relatively large number of people in the D-intensive organization—designers, test engineers, draftsmen, production engineers—also call for a more structured management approach than is required in the R-intensive company.

3. *Sequential arrangement of tasks.* Unlike the R-intensive organization where many people can work in parallel, the D-intensive organization requires a disciplined sequencing of tasks, with sophisticated controls to ensure that technical objectives are achieved within planned time and cost limits. Scheduling tends to be thorough and precise, as in manufacturing. When faced with trade-off decisions between efficiency and innovation, managers will usually opt for efficiency and higher output.

4. *Vulnerability to disruption by change.* Given its relatively high manpower commitment, its sequencing of tasks, and its relative prox-

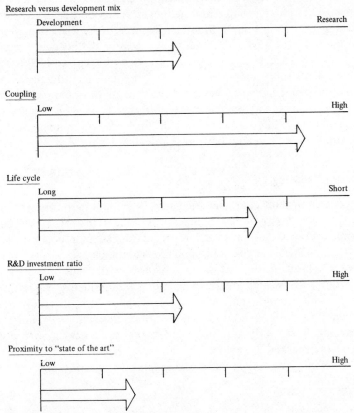

Research versus development mix

Development   Research

Coupling

Low   High

Life cycle

Long   Short

R&D investment ratio

Low   High

Proximity to "state of the art"

Low   High

EXHIBIT I.   Profile of a Technically-based Business

imity to actual production in the new product development process, the D-intensive organization can be severely affected by managerial or administrative changes ordered in specifications or objectives in midstream.

Given these differing characteristics, the hazards of managing a D-intensive organization with management concepts and controls suited to the R-intensive company, or vice versa, should be apparent. Consider this example:

The president of a technically based electronics company was convinced that a strong research department was the key to innovative products and high profits. The department generated plenty of ideas but few marketable products—a situation to which the president reacted by further increasing the research staff. The company's better marketing, manufacturing, and financial managers began resigning in disgust. Profits dropped; so did the company's stock. Not long thereafter, the president was replaced by a new man from the outside.

President No. 2 began by strengthening the functions that had atrophied during the research binge and hangover. Then he began to trim the research staff, which by some estimates was three times what the company could support. In the seven years since the advent of the new president, the company has successfully marketed a series of technically innovative products against strong competition. Its development, manufacturing, marketing, and financial functions are now equal to its most formidable competition. The quality and management of research, despite a substantial staff reduction, has suffered no serious decline, but the management processes to support that research have been drastically altered.

Downstream Coupling

A second important characteristic of high-technology businesses is the degree of *downstream coupling*—that is, the extent to which the success of the company's product introduction process depends on communication and cooperation between the R&D and the manufacturing and marketing functions, which are further "downstream" toward the customer. Clearly, industries differ in their downstream coupling requirements. Some need a great deal of information and interaction, with as little filtering as possible; others need little or none. Being aware of the coupling requirement and managing it properly not only can avert the frictions that are so frequent at the marketing-engineering interface, but also can channel the familiar conflicts between manufacturing and engineering toward more productive ends.

Critical Balance

It is useful to distinguish three degrees of coupling: high, moderate, and low. High coupling requires close interaction among the technical, manufacturing, and marketing functions of the business. Accurate and detailed market information is essential to adequate product line planning. The selection of R&D projects is influenced heavily by manufacturing costs, availability of raw materials, abilities of the marketing organization, and countermoves by competition. Minimizing the disruptive effect of new product introductions on manufacturing is critical. Tight control of product quality is essential to successful customer applications and minimum service engineering effort. Finally, time pressure on all functions is usually acute.

Many technically based industries require exceptionally high coupling. In specialty plastics, for example, the functions of product and process development, production, and field technical service must be closely linked by a tightly knit communication, decision, and control process—an effect that management has often vainly tried to achieve by shifting the technical service group from marketing to development, or to production, or independently to the chief executive. Some companies have completed this organizational cycle more than once.

In a highly coupled organization management is usually concerned about the downstream effect of new product introductions and about the marketing and production impact of R&D actions. The coupling-conscious management of one chemical company, wary of a proposed $3 million investment in a new chemical process developed by a recent acquisition, kept pressing for more information. The facts confirmed their misgivings: more than $20 million of additional investment would be required before the parent company's target rate of return could be achieved. The $3 million "down payment" was not approved.

In such companies, management must maintain a constant balance of influence among development, production, and technical service to the customer. If development becomes too strong, uneconomic products or processes are rammed into manufacturing, and current customer complaints must defer to future development work. If technical service is too powerful, future development is downgraded in the interest of extinguishing the fire-of-the-minute. Occasionally, manufacturing is strong enough to reject desirable product changes in the interest of maintaining high efficiencies, or to schedule output to maximize machine utilization rather than to meet customer commitments. In a highly coupled organization, correct balance among these three technically competent functions is dynamic rather than static. Changes in the company's competitive situation, technical strengths, and capacity utilization, among others, force management to keep readjusting to current conditions.

Interfunctional Control

In a highly coupled organization, moreover, functional dividing lines may create serious problems. Since objectives on either side of the marketing-engineering interface can and often do drift apart, some kind of results-oriented interfunctional control is needed to keep pulling them back together. Sending two men—one from each function—on customer complaint calls is one way. Organizing functionally, with cross-functional responsibilities for project completion is another. Giving senior executives corollary duties that straddle functional lines (a tricky business) can also help to reduce the problem. This can take the form of making the vice president for R&D responsible for training technical service men, or of giving a marketing staffer the job of coordinating all functions to complete an application project.

Although interfunctional responsibility may narrow the gaps between functions, it cannot eliminate interfunctional boundaries or the impacts that occur across them. Care must be taken to assess these impacts in advance. Too often an executive gives the order to release a design to manufacturing without realizing that subsequent engineering changes will produce unanticipated results. This seems to be particularly true in moderately coupled companies, where manufacturing and engineering often become bitter adversaries because neither really identifies and explains what is happening. However, good engineering-change control practices can correct the problem.

Logical Planning

Still another "problem" interface, especially in moderately coupled companies that lack the formal controls characteristic of highly coupled organizations, is joint product planning by marketing and engineering. In one company, technically competent engineers in marketing found themselves hopelessly at odds with R&D engineers doing market research and market development. Each side was working without discipline or clear executive direction; their positions were based on inadequate data, organizational prejudice, and a minimum of analysis. Senior executives can do much to avert such waste of talent and to prevent such malfunctions in product planning by insisting on a logical process for a new product planning.

Since coupling is essentially an interfunctional problem, however, no single functional vice president can manage it successfully. A general manager, whether a president or a division head, must provide the necessary direction and arbitration.

Product Life Cycle

The concept of the product life cycle is too well known to require exposition here. Life cycles may vary in length from a few months to years or even to decades. In technology-intensive businesses, the length of the cycle may have strategic implications.

Short Cycle

Need for speedy management action and response, high concurrency of activities in product introduction, and approximation rather than precision in technical objectives is characteristic of short-cycle companies. Here business success requires competitive intelligence for early appraisal of competitive moves. As a matter of strategy, an alert company should plan to be among the first to bring out a new product or break into a new market, since competition thereafter will generally force prices down fast, depressing profit margins and return on investment.

Organizationally, the short cycle puts a premium on quick response. To observers in slower moving industries, the short-cycle company appears to be in perpetual chaos. It will tend to favor short-circuit devices—such as product managers, project managers, or interfunctional committees—which speed up the interfunctional transfer of information. Faced with the choice of structuring the organization for economy or for rapid response, management will usually pick fast response, even at high cost. Many short-cycle companies, for example, maintain separate engineering-change organizations; these are nonexistent in companies characterized by long product life cycles.

Functional planning in a short-cycle business is usually overlapping or simultaneous. Manufacturing may begin to frame its plan, and marketing may set target dates for product introduction, before R&D planning is complete. Plans are often remade in the short-cycle company; the result is a series of increasingly accurate approximations of introduction dates, product specifications, and detailed plans for market introduction.

Short-cycle companies need close coupling between product marketing specialists and technical staff. Marketing managers tend to be knowledgeable about technology, and they often contribute substantially to product definition and development.

Long Cycle

In this type of business the converse is generally true. With adequate time to learn about competitive market developments and to plan to counter them, there is no need for unusual market sensitivity. In the long-cycle company emphasis is on established procedure and routine. Organization is usually functional. Managerial decisions usually favor economy and efficiency at the expense of rapid response.

Moreover, planning is usually sequential—that is, detailed R&D is completed before the manufacturing and marketing planning is begun. Manufacturing and marketing are seldom deeply involved in technical planning. In fact, the technical staff may include market research specialists to help with the long-range R&D planning.

Again, in long-cycle companies, marketing people are often unfamiliar with the specific technical problems or objectives. The marketing group tends to be volume-oriented rather than response-oriented, since new technical problems are rare and coupling between marketing and technical people is low.

Shift in Characteristics

Occasionally, companies and industries undergo a shift in product life-cycle characteristics. In the 1940's and 1950's, for example, as computers replaced punched-card data processing equipment, the cycle shortened noticeably. One painful consequence of this shift was that many managers who had been highly successful in the era of punched cards were unable to adjust to the planning and control, organizational structure, and strategy implications of the shorter life cycle.

The same adjustment problem may arise when companies diversify. Managers in the oil business, as a case in point, often have trouble adjusting to the shorter cycle and more rapid product obsolescence characteristic of the petrochemical business. The problem is still more acute for petrochemical managers whose companies integrate downstream—say, entering the plastics business.

To take a manager trained in the oil business, move him within a few years to a petrochemical subsidiary, and then to a plastics operation is to subject his personal adaptability and the flexibility of his management methods and outlook to the severest possible test.

Investment Ratios

How much should be spent on research and development? How should the investment be apportioned between basic and applied research projects? The questions are not easy to resolve.

As yet, there is no generally accepted measure of R&D investment. Of late, the familiar practice of expressing R&D investment as a percentage of sales has been falling into disrepute—and rightly so, since the results of R&D are not realized immediately and, in fact, affect sales instead of being affected by them. Measures that begin to do justice to R&D's mission of protecting corporate assets from technical obsolescence treat the R&D investment as a percentage of total investment or of profits or cash flow.

However measured, the ratio of R&D investment/expense is important. High ratios, we may note, are characteristic of technically intensive industries such as pharmaceuticals, chemicals, and electronics; low ratios are characteristic of nonintensive industries such as food, lumber, and cement.

"High" Effects

In our view, high investment ratios have four significant implications for management:

1. *They require a serious and continuous evaluation of technology procurement alternatives:*
   - Whether to buy technology through licensing or through hiring consultants.
   - Whether to buy a company in order to acquire the latest technology in an unfamiliar field.
   - Whether to hire top people with the specific technical competence desired.

- Whether to develop additional technical competence by internal training in order to stay competitive.

Where R&D investment ratio is low, it may be possible to develop technology within the company with relatively low risk of being outpaced by competition. Higher ratios characteristically allow less lead time and make the acquisition of technology a more attractive alternative. In any case, they call for constant review of the alternatives by a corporate-level group which is sensitive to significant competitive moves in the field.

2. *They usually accelerate product and process change.* This, in turn, requires an adaptive organization, which can quickly shift to new levels of efficiency and effectiveness as technology changes the work to be done. The source of the change in a high-ratio company can be either external or internal. Externally, competitors investing in the same technology may obsolete a market, a plant, or an investment—compelling the organization to respond swiftly. Internally, research and development results can produce similar pressures for change. In a company with a high R&D investment ratio, a major criterion of organization is therefore the ability to adapt to new technology without sacrificing market share or efficiency.

3. *They usually mean a dynamic product market.* Such markets, where products readily substitute for one another and where emphasis rapidly shifts from new product development to low unit cost and vice versa, impose three special requirements.

    The first is clear visibility of resources, permitting management to cut off a development project quickly or to switch resources into a new technology.

    The second requirement is explicit strategy formulation. An explicit strategic framework permits clear definition of project alternatives and enables managers to choose more wisely among them.

    The third special need is a well-developed planning system to permit the company to redirect its resources promptly and effectively. The system must be explicit, providing for control of technical resources consistent with strategy by tying R&D closely to annual corporate planning and control.

4. *They require closer supervision of technical efforts.* Since the company is highly dependent on technology for competitive survival, senior managers need to know more about technical problems and performance. They should be aware of the long-term corporate effects of lower level decisions and have a good grasp of the time and cost implications of particular technological developments. This is important because technology in high-ratio companies usually has a substantial effect on other functions. Thus any executive making a substantial investment in technology will need assurance that these effects are consistent with his total objective.

"Low" Implications

In general, the effects of low R&D investment/expense ratios are the converse of those described above. Technology can be developed internally within competitive lead times—or, in some industries, purchased with the capital equipment into which technology has been incorporated by the manufacturer. Organization structure need not be highly adaptive; since technical developments are evolutionary, only occasional changes in functional structure will be needed. Resources need not be specially identified because historical accounting data on expense and investment adequately reflect the impact of product or process replacements. Finally, marketing does not have to be closely coupled with the technological functions, since marketing needs can be communicated via top management or through formal planning and control mechanisms.

Critical Mass

Our evidence indicates that R&D efforts are almost entirely ineffective below a certain critical level.

This level is not easy to pinpoint, but it may be located in a very general way by examining the technical results of competitors. Has a given company developed successful commercial products? How long did it lag the industry leader in developing competitive technology? What is its record of innovation? How old is its current product line?

When it is possible to do so, arraying the competitive results of a series of companies against the amount of technical effort expended by each should suggest the approximate level of resources below which little or no results can be expected.

The question of critical mass is complicated by the factor of quality. Since high-quality research personnel can generate a return out of all proportion to their number, quality as well as quantity affects the critical mass. For want of any real yardsticks of quality, such an analysis must be highly judgmental.

Another complicating factor is the mix of disciplines found in the technical staff. Managers working with interdisciplinary groups have repeatedly noted that even in technical efforts of similar quantity and quality one mix of disciplines will result in higher innovation and output than another.

One company maintained a staff of 16 highly qualified Ph.D.'s in a remote laboratory for several years before the president decided to find out why they had produced no significant results. The problem, as he eventually learned, was threefold: the staff lacked direction, it was too research-oriented, and it was too small. Noting that his chief competitor had a development effort strongly directed at visible, emerging market needs and staffed by no less than 150 development engineers, only a sprinkling of whom were Ph.D.'s the president belatedly remodeled his own company's department to match.

State of the Art

For most managers, the term "state of the art" denotes the frontier of a technology. Inside this boundary, but not beyond it, reliable and tested technical solutions are available.

However, state of the art has different implications in research and in development. For research, it denotes the frontier at which investigators seek to discover new phenomena or to devise a solution to a known problem. For development, it implies the less rarefied zone where the validity of a solution has already been proved, but a successful commercial application remains to be achieved. For development, in other words, the state of the art hinges heavily on economics as well as on technology.

Boundary Distance

How close a company's technology is to the state of the art has important implications for management planning and decision making. These implications may be considered under three headings: (1) stability, (2) predictability, and (3) precedent.

Stability is a function of distance from state of the art. A company working near the state-of-the-art boundary must keep trying for rapid advances like those through which it achieved its current position. At the same time, it must be alert to possible breakthroughs by competitors resulting in either a major advance in product or a major reduction in costs.

Top managers in such firms should be keenly aware of their dependence on a well-developed technological intelligence system. Surveillance of literature, attention to competitive developments, and attendance in scientific societies should all be encouraged.

For companies well back from the boundary, radical breakthroughs are unlikely. Technical progress is evolutionary, with little innovation. Breakthroughs by immediate competitors are no serious threat; the danger is that breakthroughs in other industries and other technologies may obsolete the entire mature technology.

Predictability is low for companies near the state-of-the-art boundary. Since their researchers are working in areas of partial knowledge, the nature and, even more, the timing of results are difficult to foresee.

Conversely, far from the boundary of the state of the art, where breakthroughs are unlikely, predictability is high. Specific small improvements in products or processes can be foretold with confidence and timed with a high degree of accuracy; their achievement depends on the resources invested rather than on technical innovation.

Precedent, which underlies so much management activity, is sparse near the state-of-the-art boundary. In view of the uncertainty and lack of precedent, senior executives cannot afford to demand infallibility in middle managers' decisions. Their task, it must be recognized, differs greatly from that of their counterparts in companies far from the state of the art, who can rely on established management doctrine that prescribes the scope of managerial discretion and assures the manager that he is well within his responsibility—and even may guide many of his individual decisions.

The implications of stability, predictability, and precedent are substantial in the areas of planning and control. Near the state of the art, a company must settle for more approximation and less precision in goals and standards. Thus planning and control systems must be tailored accordingly. In such a company, judgment is critical, and precision is often specious.

Failure to take account of these implications may be exceedingly costly. In one diversified company, an electronics division devoted to the development and marketing of highly sophisticated microwave equipment was expected to plan as far ahead and in as much detail as the industrial products divisions did. When the division manager continued to protest that the requirement was unrealistic, he was replaced by an accountant. Within 15 months, half of the technical people had left, and all momentum was gone from the R&D program.

Rate of Change

Besides the company's distance from the boundary, the rate of advance in the state of the art itself must be considered. Since this is largely a function of the investment, heavier R&D expenditures (and a higher critical mass) are the rule when the boundary is moving rapidly. It is important, however, to remember that in view of the differences between research and development, total resources invested are not an adequate clue to the effectiveness of a particular company's investment. Development budgets normally tend to be much larger than research budgets; but a large development input, unless balanced by an equally strong research component, is of little use when the boundary is fluid.

Rapid change in the state of the art means rapid obsolescence of managerial decisions. Planning assumptions are more quickly superseded by events. Since even the most carefully made capital investment decisions may turn out badly, rapid payback of investment or flexibility in capital facilities, or both, become crucial. In this situation, executives who take their one- and two-year plans very seriously may with some justice treat five-year planning as a paper exercise.

Rapid change in the state of the art creates more opportunities and more blind alleys for technical management. It puts a premium on the ability to cut off projects before their proliferation saps the main effort. Moreover, it requires some degree of management sophistication in all the main aspects of the technology. Technological progress is seldom monolithic. Management should have some knowledge of the directions being pursued by important competitors, including smaller companies with highly competent research teams which sometimes outperform even the large laboratories.

Sensitivity to potentially profitable ventures is a valuable managerial asset, and an executive who possesses it may well be forgiven for otherwise unforgivable administrative weaknesses.

The need for flexible organizational response to new technology is still another requirement imposed by fast-moving technology. This need extends beyond the R&D function to selling, production, and distribution. In a highly coupled technical company, for example, all the sales engineering and application people may have to undergo frequent retraining. Production departments may have to adapt to new processes, new tooling, and even new kinds of operating equipment.

During a rapid development period, manufacturing efficiency is far less important than it is in the case of a maturing product. In the early days of solid-state electronics, transistor yields on the order of 10% of the total material committed to the process were more than adequate for substantial profits. A little later on, crystal manufacturers had to achieve 80% to 90% yields. But when the next technical advance occurred, production management again had to be content with 10% yields until the product line matured. When the cycle of product technology moves as rapidly as this, all management systems are severely strained.

What does all this mean to the manager? At a minimum, it means using great care and judgment in borrowing other companies' techniques. Also, it suggests that the type, accuracy, detail, and quite possibly frequency of planning in a technically intensive division of a conglomerate company ought to be quite different from that of a mature technology division. And for a company whose technology is maturing, it may suggest the desirability of substituting a more formal, precise system of management for the stimulating but inefficient turmoil of infant technology.

Marketing Strategy

We have examined the characteristic parameters of technically intensive businesses and their impact on strategic, administrative, and operating problems of top managers. By way of summary, let us consider the impact of these characteristics on a strategic issue: the timing of the technologically intensive firm's entry into an emerging industry. The alternatives may usefully be grouped into four major marketing strategies, recognizing that most companies will—or should—adopt a blend of these according to the requirements of their different markets or product lines:

- *First to market*—based on a strong R&D program, technical leadership, and risk taking.
- *Follow the leader*—based on strong development resources and an ability to react quickly as the market starts its growth phase.
- *Application engineering*—based on product modifications to fit the needs of particular customers in a mature market.
- *"Me-too"*—based on superior manufacturing efficiency and cost control.

Each of these strategies has different strengths and weaknesses in particular competitive situations. Intelligent selection and execution of the appropriate strategy normally will strengthen the company's competitive posture.

First to Market

This risky but potentially rewarding strategy has a number of important ramifications throughout the business: (a) a research-intensive effort, supported by major development resources, (b) close downstream coupling in product planning, and moderately close coupling thereafter, (c) high proximity to the state of the art, (d) high R&D investment ratio; and (e) a high risk of failure for individual products.

The implications of these have been discussed earlier. Taken together, they outline a clear philosophy of business. The company must recruit and retain outstanding technical personnel who can win leadership in the industry. It must see that these technical people are in close and useful communication with marketing planners to identify potentially profitable markets. It must often risk large investments of time and money in technical and market development without any immediate return. It must be able to absorb mistakes, withdraw, and recoup without losing its position in other product lines. As the nature of the market clarifies, initial plans must quickly be modified and approximation refined into precision.

Perhaps most important, top management must be able to make important judgments of timing, balancing the improved product development stemming from a delayed introduction against the risk of being second into the market. Such a company must have more than its share of long-range thinkers who can confidently assess market and competitive trends in their earliest stages and plan with both confidence and flexibility.

Follow the Leader

This marketing strategy implies: (a) D-intensive technical effort, (b) moderate competence across the spectrum of relevant technologies, (c) exceptionally rapid response time in product development and marketing on the basis of finished research, (d) high downstream coupling of R&D with marketing and manufacturing, and (e) superior competitive intelligence.

The company that follows this strategy is—or should be—an organization that gets things done. It uses many interfunctional techniques, responds rapidly to change, and often seems to be in a perpetual fire drill. It has few scientists on its payroll, but some of the best development engineers available. Its senior executives are constantly concerned with maintaining the right balance of strengths among the technical, marketing, and manufacturing functions so that the company can respond effectively to the leader's moves in any of these three areas.

Application Engineering

This strategy requires: (a) substantial product design and engineering resources but no research and little real development, (b) ready access to product users within customer companies, (c) technically perceptive salesmen and sales engineers who work closely with product designers, (d) good product-line control to prevent costly proliferation, (e) considerable cost consciousness in deciding what applications to develop, (f) an efficiency-oriented manufacturing organization, and (g) a flair for minimizing development and manufacturing cost by using the same parts or elements in many different applications.

The applications-engineering strategy tends to avoid innovative efforts in the interest of economy. Planning is precise, assignments are clear, and new technology is introduced cautiously, well behind the economic state of the art. Return-on-investment and cash-flow calculations are standard practice, and the entire management is profit-oriented.

"Me-too"

This strategy, which has flourished in the past decade as never before, is distinguished by: (a) no research or development, (b) strong manufacturing function, dominating product design, (c) strong price and delivery performance, and (d) ability to copy new designs quickly, modifying them only to reduce production costs.

Competing on price, taking a low margin, but avoiding all development expense, a company that has adopted this strategy can wreak havoc with competitors following the first-to-market or follow-the-leader strategies. This is because the "me-too" strategy, effectively pursued, shortens the profitable period after market introduction when the leaders' margins are most substantial. The "me-too" strategy requires a "low-overhead" approach to manufacturing and administration, and a direct hard sell on price and delivery to the customer. It does not require any technical enthusiasm, nor does it aim to generate any.

8. Acquiring Technology—Licensing Do's and Don'ts

Willard Marcy

Marcy outlines the procedures to be followed and the pitfalls to be avoided in seeking out new technology and negotiating agreements for its use.

BASICALLY there are three general methods for acquiring new technology: develop it internally; purchase it essentially fully developed; or license it from somewhere else in various stages of development. The differences between these methods are primarily matters of degree rather than differences in kind. Licensing from others is in an intermediate position between the other two.

Some advantages and disadvantages of each method are given in Table 1. Let us look first at the major advantages. In-house research and development leads to the acquisition of basic, totally proprietary knowledge and provides an opportunity to train specialists in new technologies. Purchasing technology requires little or no research and development, involves relatively low risk and enables quick entry into the marketplace. Acquiring technology through licensing, though usually involving some further research and development, provides a relatively fast entry into production with relatively low financial needs, and provides time for the training of specialists. Using this approach supply and demand can be adjusted relatively easily in different and/or new markets. It is an effective way to arrive at short or medium-range diversification. Acquiring technology by

Reprinted from *Research Management,* 22 (May, 1979), pp. 18–21. Used by permission.

Dr. Marcy is Vice President in charge of the Patents Program for the Research Corporation, a foundation established to help identify, develop, and license inventions emanating from universities and other similar institutions.

TABLE 1. Methods of Acquiring Intellectual Property

	In-House R&D	Licensing-In	Purchasing Technology
Advantages	Can obtain own basic proprietary knowledge Extensive training of specialists possible before production begins	Can obtain some proprietary knowledge and know-how Risk calculable before investment Relatively low research and development expense Moderately fast to get to production phase Some training of specialists possible before production begins Financing needs relatively low Effective way to arrive at short or medium-range diversification Can adapt supply to demand in different and/or new markets	Little or no research and development needed Quick to get into production Technical and financial risks low
Disadvantages	6–10 years expense required before larger investments possible High risk High cost	Search for suitable projects needed License fees required Moderately high costs	Proprietary knowledge minimal Training specialists possible only after production begins Low competitive technological advantage Previously vested interest endangered Purchase cost high

licensing enables one to invest only in those technologies where the risks are calculable.

In reference to major disadvantages, in-house research and development requires 6 to 10 years of expense before larger investments in plant and market development are possible. In-house R&D also involves high risk and high cost. While purchasing technology involves low risk, the purchase cost is usually high. Vested interests are endangered and low competitive technological advantage is frequently present. Little or no specialist training is possible until after production begins. Acquiring technology by licensing involves costly searches for suitable projects and the payment of license fees.

Procedural Activities

Let me turn now to procedural activities connected with the acquisition of technology through licensing. One way to summarize these is to set forth some do's and don'ts during different phases of activity, (Table 2). While these activities are generally sequential they also overlap and require some attention and study throughout both the initial acquisition and further development phases.

Preacquisition studies should be made to examine in-depth all available external technical information and internal production, marketing and financial capabilities, limitations and requirements. Similar thorough studies of external markets, both domestic and foreign, are essential. Included should be an analysis of the competition and its capabilities. Be careful, however, not to believe in-house market surveys without firm confirmation by objective outside market studies. The preacquisition studies will most often be carried out by a single individual or a small two- or three-man team.

A positive decision based on the preacquisition study conclusions sets off a much broader and costlier study involving several internal departments. These more comprehensive in-house studies should expand on and elaborate the previous studies, using research and development, engineering, production and marketing personnel and facilities. It is well to organize an interdisciplinary team for this effort and to include company management representation in the study. All phases of the technology to be acquired should be studied. If essential information is missing, it should be sought and obtained, either through internal or external means. Particularly important to have is an understanding of the real opinion of the ultimate consumer of the new products, not just the conjecture or opinion of the in-house staff or intermediate marketing organizations. To be avoided at all costs at this juncture is a not-invented-here attitude or negative inputs from production, marketing or financial groups which can overweigh positive factors or even kill an embryonic venture. Beware, however, that the new technology is not too far from existing product lines.

If the results of these intensive in-house studies are positive, and a management decision to proceed is made, an effective well-balanced organization to develop and exploit the acquired technology is essential. At this point legal, financial and managerial inputs are needed as well as continuing efforts from all the groups previously involved. The success or failure of new technology in an existing company is determined by how well this exploitative effort is organized, managed and operated. Some writers strongly recommend that a separate new venture group be set up along lines similar to and using the techniques of small successful entrepreneurially-oriented, high technology companies.

In any event essential elements in a new venture group include a corporate-level product champion with responsibility as manager of the venture, a well-balanced interdisciplinary team working under the product champion, a sponsor at a high management level, technical and marketing gatekeepers to monitor the flow of information to others on the team, and a key research and development scientist or engineer.

Care should be taken, however, to prevent domination of the venture by one or more of the team members, particularly an exceptionally creative scientist or engineer. Care should also be taken to avoid spreading the organization too thinly; each team member should have time to develop and analyze detailed information about the venture and to communicate adequately with other team members.

The law department or outside counsel should make detailed investigations of patent-antitrust implications, legal restrictions on marketing and fund transfer, and governmental regulations, both domestic and foreign. Legal hindrances in these areas may well be critical factors to the ultimate success of the venture. At the minimum, such factors can seriously affect its ultimate cost and capital needs. In view of these pitfalls, the law department must be involved in negotiating licenses for patent rights and know-how, but should be only part of a negotiating team. Other members of this team should have technical and business backgrounds. It should always be remembered that licensing technology is a friendly act between two willing parties, not an adversary proceeding. Legal counsel frequently becomes overly protective in an attempt to avoid future problems.

Corporate management should be interested in and kept aware of the venture team's progress on a frequent basis. Involvement of management during the entire procedure provides an essential top level awareness and balance that will help to keep the venture from taking unrealistic directions. Management should question frequently such matters as capital needs, legal restraints, market estimations and acceptability of the proposed products. Such questioning provides the venture team members with a periodic overview which brings needed perspective to temper judgments based on too intimate familiarity with massive amounts of details.

TABLE 2.   Do's and Don'ts In Acquiring Intellectual Property

Do's	Pre-Acquisition	Initial In-House Studies	Organizing for Exploitation	Managerial Consideration	Financial Consideration	Legal Consideration	Decision Making
Study Internal Technical, Marketing and Financial Needs	X	X		X	X		X
Study External Markets	X	X					
Analyze Competition	X	X					
Determine Ultimate Consumer Opinion		X	X				
Develop Interdisciplinary Team			X				
Adopt Strategic Plan			X	X	X	X	X
Find Product Champion & Put Him in Charge			X	X			X
Set Up A New Venture Group			X				
Provide a Balanced Organization							
Use Techniques of Successful Enterpreneurially-Oriented Companies							
Develop Realistic Capital Needs				X	X		X
Study Patent-Antitrust Implications				X	X	X	
Determine Legal Restrictions on Marketing and Fund Transfer				X		X	
Analyze Government Regulatory Environment				X	X	X	
Acquire Know-How Plus Patents						X	
Enlist Strong Management Support				X			
Require Frequent Management Questioning				X			
Have and Maintain Enthusiasm, Patience and Persistence							X
Face Facts and Have Courage to Terminate							X

Don'ts	Pre-Acquisition	Initial In-House Studies	Organizing for Exploitation	Management Involvement	Financial Considerations	Legal Considerations	Decision Making
Believe In-House Market Surveys Without Objective Outside Market Studies	X	X		X			X
Back New Technology Too Far From Existing Product Lines		X		X			
Spread Organization Too Thinly			X	X			X
Expect Quick Positive Results			X	X			X
Allow Existing Production and Marketing to Kill Project With Negative In-Puts		X					X
Allow Not-Invented-Here Attitude to Prevail		X					
Allow In-House Research to Suffer From Licensing In or Purchase of Technology				X			X
Allow Legal Counsel to be Exclusive Negotiators			X	X		X	
Use Licensing-In for Defensive or Market Control Purposes Only			X	X		X	X
Allow Creative Scientist or Engineer to Dominate				X			
Allow Negative Financial Department In-Put to Overweigh Other Positive Factors		X		X	X		X

103

Summing Up

Acquiring technology through licensing and subsequently exploiting it successfully is not easy. Quick positive results are not to be expected. If they occur, good judgment, fortuitous circumstances and luck are responsible, with emphasis on luck. Management and the entire venture team must develop and maintain unflagging enthusiasm, patience and perspective must also be maintained, leading to realistic evaluations during the course of the venture. All involved must determine to face facts and have the courage to terminate the venture should overwhelming hard evidence, not opinions or suppositions, so indicate.

In this short paper I have tried to summarize some basic principles the use of which will increase the chances of developing successful new ventures based on intellectual property acquired primarily through licensing. The principles discussed seem to recur over and over again in the literature on the subject, but are, by no means, all there are. These principles appear almost axiomatic in well managed and well run industrial organizations, but are all too often overlooked, minimized or forgotten in the welter of minutiae and press of time to which we are all subjected today. However, if they are kept in mind and used during all stages of development in acquired intellectual property, a more profitable and less costly final result will eventuate.

9. Diversification Planning

George A. Steiner

Diversification means entry into new product lines, processes, services or markets. Steiner discusses mergers and acquisitions as a means to this end.

ENTERPRISES must specialize to exploit a given environment. But all environments change, and they must, therefore, diversify to permit adaptation to new environments. If they do not diversify they will become extinct. Hence, the injunction: diversify or die.

Chance has and will continue to play an important role in successful diversification. In the long run, however, the "luckiest" will be those whose diversification is rooted in thoughtful and soundly conceived planning. This is not news to most managers, but precisely what to do about it is not always clear. The literature purporting to tell a manager what to do is rather voluminous, but the pieces are scattered and not always consistent. Nevertheless, there is a growing body of knowledge and experience from which are discernible a number of major guides for better planning of diversification. This chapter seeks to identify those outstanding policies, strategies, and actions which have brought successful diversification.

Meaning of Diversification by Acquisition and Merger

Diversification means entry into new product lines, processes, services, or markets. A beginning can be made at identifying diversified firms by using the broad U.S. business groupings in the *Standard Industrial Classi-*

Reprinted with permission of Macmillan Publishing Co., Inc. from *Top Management Planning* by George A. Steiner. Copyright © 1969 by The Trustees of Columbia University in the City of New York.

George Steiner is Professor Emeritus of Management and Public Policy in the Graduate School of Business Administration at the University of California, Los Angeles.

fication Manual. All business and services are classified in the SIC into 89 major groups (called 2-digit categories). At a minimum, diversification may be said to exist when a company does business in two or more of these broad categories. But they are, perhaps, too broad. For instance, the category "electrical machinery, equipment, and supplies" includes such diverse products as highpower transformers, household stoves, refrigerators for homes, telephones, spark plugs, and x-ray equipment. A better classification to determine degree of diversification probably is the next level of classification. For transportation equipment, for instance, the next level of classification includes these groups: motor vehicles and motor vehicle equipment; aircraft and parts; ship and boat building and repairing; railroad equipment; motorcycles, bicycles, and parts; and miscellaneous.

More generally, diversification may be defined as producing a new product or service, or entering new markets, which involves importantly different skills, processes, and knowledge from those associated with present products, services, or markets. The simple diagram in Chart 1 illustrates the spectrum.

Diversification defined in this way can proceed upon the basis of research on and development and production of new products within a company, or mergers and acquisitions. The first, of course, is designed to produce internal growth and the second is called external growth.

Major Reasons for Diversification

A business, being a dynamic organization run by individuals with diverse and multiple motivations, finds many reasons for diversification. While most of what is said in this section is applicable to internal diversification, the focus is on acquisitions and mergers. There are many very important things an acquisition can do for a company which explain its popularity, as follows:

Growth

Charles Thornton, Chairman of the Board of Litton Industries, one of the most spectacular growth companies through acquisitions, said: "We grow not just to stay in business but to have a virile, stimulating atmo-

CHART 1. Expansion vs. Diversification

Products \ Markets	Present	New
Present		Diversification
New	Diversification	Diversification

sphere. The strength of the U.S. is in an industrial base that is ever-growing. Growth is associated with progress, the means to accomplish more things. Profit is only one of the motives. A stronger motive is a deep, pioneering spirit." By all odds, growth is the most outstanding reason for diversification through mergers.

Avoid Dependence on One Product Line

If a company feels that it cannot achieve its objectives by sticking to its traditional line of business, it may offset this uncertainty by acquisition. W. R. Grace, an old shipping company, decided its traditional business was not good enough and today is an important producer of chemicals, operates an airline, is engaged in outdoor advertising, makes paper, and produces oil.

Stability

Like growth, although not as much a fetish, American businessmen are strongly motivated to seek continuous sales and profit growth with a minimum of fluctuations about the trend line. Instability can result from many events. Cyclical, seasonal, and secular shifts in demand are important causes, but changes in models, in the life cycles of different products of the line, the impact of variations of raw material prices on finished goods prices and demand, or delays in getting component parts, can bring instability.

Furnish Needed Technical Know-How

This is a motivation of growing significance which has many aspects. A company may wish to get into a new line of business, for example, for which it does not have the technical know-how, and does so by acquisition.

Reduce Costs by Using Company Distribution Systems

It is quite possible, of course, for a company with an effective distribution system to reduce cost per unit distributed by adding new lines. A number of the food distributors have sought this objective in recent years. Campbell Soup, for example, added Pepperidge Farm products to its system for this reason.

Breaking into International Markets

U.S. expansion abroad raises problems not found when tried at home, and many businessmen have found the most expedient method to make foreign entry is to acquire an interest in or merge with a foreign-based firm. General Electric's acquisition of Machines Bull in France is an illustration of this company's efforts to break into the computer market in Europe. Campbell Soup has acquired a biscuit maker in Belgium, and Heinz has acquired food processors in Holland. A number of large European companies have reversed this process in the U.S.

Acquisition of Tax Write-Offs

Many acquisitions have been made simply because the acquirer wants the benefit of the operating tax loss carry-forward of the acquired. When Textron acquired American Woolen and Robbins Mills, this apparently was in mind and did reduce substantially the company's effective federal income tax.

Solve Competitive Problems

Competitive threats create the occasion for business marriages. If you make shortening and find that ready-made mixes are cutting into your market, you do as Procter & Gamble did and acquire Duncan-Hines and make cake mixes yourself.

Other Reasons for Acquisitions

This by no means exhausts the list of reasons for acquisitions. A few others may be given without illustration or comment, as follows: to use surplus cash, to offset unfavorable geographic locations, to utilize waste or by-products, to use basic raw materials, to use excess productive capacity, to capitalize on distinctive knowledge, to capitalize on a company's basic research, to limit competition, to control patents, to complete a product line with a sufficient spread of models and prices, to take advantage of tax laws, to acquire new and needed management, and to increase borrowing capacity.

Why Diversify Rather Than Build from Within?

Many of the above objectives can be met by internally-managed diversification. There are a number of compelling reasons, however, why many companies wish to meet their objectives by acquisition or a combination of external and internal growth, rather than relying on internal diversification.

Acquisition saves a company time. It takes time to develop a research organization, particularly in an advanced technology industry; and it takes time to build a new productive facility and operate it. Where time is important, companies can save themselves years by acquiring these resources in another company.

One element of business risk may be eliminated. If a company is not familiar with the management or substance of a new research effort, a new engineering problem, or a new productive operation, there may be less risk in finding these activities in a suitable state of performance in another company and acquiring it.

The cost may actually be less to a company by acquiring another rather than duplicating its capabilities by building from within. Following World War II, for instance, many companies found they could gain productive facilities through acquisition much more cheaply than through their own construction programs. This also was obviously much faster and permitted companies to take advantage of a great surge in consumer demands. Sometimes, too, it is possible for a company to find another whose book value is below replacement costs.

Sometimes it is possible for a company to finance an acquisition more easily than to finance internal expansion. This can happen, for example, when a large flotation of securities by a company at a particular time might not be well received. In such a case, the company might acquire another company by an exchange of stock and require no public acceptance of securities.

This does not exhaust the reasons why a company may wish to acquire another rather than build from within, or to solve other problems through internal means, but it does specify the more important ones.

Planning Steps and Principles

There are two different approaches to diversification, namely, the *ad hoc* and the planned. There can be little question about the fact that the planned acquisition program is more likely to be the more successful. Very well, what is sound planning for a particular company or problem? Every company differs from every other and diversification problems of a particular company may differ over time.

There do exist, however, fundamental procedural steps and principles which, when understood and wisely adapted and applied to particular situations, can assure successful diversification. A number of suitable how-to-do-it diversification planning steps exist in the literature.* They naturally vary depending upon the company and writer. A brief series of steps is shown in table 1.

* See, for example, Theodore A. Andersen, H. Igor Ansoff, Frank Norton, and J. Fred Weston, "Planning for Diversification Through Merger," *California Management Review,* Summer 1959; Sidney Cottle, "Four Steps to Diversification Planning," *Business Quarterly,* Summer 1963.

TABLE 1.   One List of Diversification Steps

1. Establish comprehensive and integrated over-all corporate objectives, goals, strategies, and policies.
2. Develop specific objectives, goals, and policies for new-product internal growth or diversification by acquisition and merger.
3. Develop and explore new ideas for (a) new products and their internal development or (b) acquisition or mergers, or (c) both.
4. Screen new ideas through appropriate criteria to sort out those deserving further analysis and development.
5. Gather facts and analyze them to determine the economic and technical feasibility of further development or acquisition proposals.

The above sequence of steps is suitable both to internal product development and acquisition. Beyond this point, requirements are sufficiently different to justify a separate sequence for each type of diversification.

INTERNAL PRODUCT DEVELOPMENT:

6. Complete research and development.
7. Test the prototype for production and sale.
8. Produce and sell.
9. Control to insure that actions take place in conformance with plans to achieve basic objectives and goals.

ACQUISITION AND MERGER:

6. Discuss with prospective marriage partner the proposed acquisition or merger and explore problems and opportunities.
7. Negotiate the terms of acquisition or merger.
8. Integrate the two companies to the extent desirable.
9. Periodically review the results to determine whether actions are in conformance with plans.

Source: George A. Steiner, "Why and How to Diversify," *California Management Review,* Vol. VI, No. 4 (Summer 1964), p. 17.

Role of Corporate Planning

Effective comprehensive corporate planning is indispensable to top-quality diversification planning. This, together with actual experience in acquisitions, is a fundamental principle for successful acquisitions. It is difficult to see how a diversification program can be successful without a clear definition of objectives. Acquisitions are means to ends and in making them it obviously is important to know what the ends are.

In determining objectives, and in devising means to achieve them, the strengths and weaknesses of the diversifying company must be honestly and penetratingly set forth. There is no substitute for a company identifying its own particular capabilities and limitations. These, in conjunction with objectives, provide invaluable clues to the most appropriate diversification moves. A company with a weak research department may see clearly its need to acquire a company with a strong technological team. A company that knows it has a poor distribution capability may more easily see the need for merging with one having a strong marketing arm than if it does not recognize the magnitude of its weakness.

The evaluation should cover thoroughly the traditional elements of a company, such as marketing programs, technical talent, managerial capabilities, financial strength, and so on. It should also probe deeply into unique strengths and weaknesses. These may suggest opportunities which would otherwise be undiscovered.

Broad strategic approaches may be of four types: vertical, horizontal, concentric, and conglomerate. Vertical mergers are those in the same product line (or line of business) and involve integration from basic raw materials to the ultimate sale to consumers. A steel ingot producer acquiring an iron ore mine as well as a steel fabricating company would be engaging in vertical merger.

Vertical integration, of course, has many advantages. It may benefit from specialization and the continuous control over the flow of materials. In this way, sales and profits may be improved through reduced costs, and may be more stable. But there are also dangers. Diseconomies of scale of parts of the integration may adversely affect profits, and a company may find itself in competition at too many points in the flow of materials. Vertical integration may also encourage federal antitrust action.

Horizontal mergers are those which join producers of similar products at the same stage of manufacture and distribution. A chemical company acquiring other chemical companies, or an electronic company acquiring other electronic companies, is involved in horizontal integration through merger.

Acquisition of a company producing the same or very closely related products also, of course, permits specialization with consequent efficiencies. Such a merger may help a company to produce at closer to capacity, thereby improving profitability. If an acquisition is too close to the product line of the acquiring company, however, it may be guilty of reducing competition by acquiring competitors and run afoul of the antitrust laws.

Concentric mergers are those in which the merged parties have a common thread of interest. This common thread may be in product areas, as when a shortening manufacturer acquires a cake mix producer; it can be in the manufacture of comparable products, which is close to horizontal merger; or it can be in terms of a common marketing arrangement as has been the case with mergers in the food industry. It may result from technical complementarity as when Litton Industries acquired Monroe to provide cross-fertilization between its computer scientists and office machinery know-how to make and market a desk computer.

Conglomerate mergers bring unrelated product lines of business into a company. The growth of Textron, for example, has been in diverse unrelated lines of business. Thorough planning and imaginative management are required to select those acquisition strategies fitting each company. It is this fact, rather than the specific strategies, that I wish to emphasize here.

Screening Criteria

Once the basic objectives and strategies have been established it is important to develop more detailed screening criteria. These may be considered tactics, but actually they represent a combination of strategy and tactics. The basic purpose of this further elaboration obviously is to provide a better basis for searching for and evaluating prospective acquisitions. Screening criteria not only save much time but also should make more certain that objectives are met.

The Borden Company's basic objective in its acquisition drive, in the words of Chairman of the Board Francis Elliott, is "not only to strengthen our organization immediately but, more importantly, to broaden the foundation on which we can build for the future." Some of the screening requirements are as follows: The company must be well-established in its own business, be able to upgrade Borden earnings, and be guided by astute, experienced management. It must also have growth potential through expansion by adding new products or by a deeper penetration of markets—a tactic described by Elliott in one of his favorite phrases as "geographic roll-out."

Screening criteria vary, of course, among companies. Generally, however, it would seem important that the following categories (not in any particular order of importance) be considered in developing the standards against which new ventures must be judged. Where appropriate, standards should take into account past trends and, more importantly, future prospects. These criteria should include:

a. Size of company
b. Market share
c. Growth potential
d. Type of business
e. Profitability
f. Pricing and financing
g. Management compatibility

Other criteria can also be considered, to name a few: research and development strength and fit, timing of entry into a new field, timing of acquisition, marketing methods, type of manufacturing process, antitrust considerations, potential for joint product development, joint marketing potential, and location.

Each firm must consider factors such as these and determine for itself which are important in an acquisition. Once done, it also may be desirable to place weights on the more significant factors.

Locating Companies to Acquire

With a carefully developed statement of objectives, strategies, and tactical screening standards as described above, a company is in a strong position to find the "right" company.

Staff work in the search stage may involve an analysis of industry sales projections to find those with growth potential of interest to a company, and identification of particular concerns which might fit the acquirer's needs. In many other ways, staff can narrow the focus so that approaches can be made on a "rifle-shot" and not a "buck-shot" basis.

Good staff work builds up an enormous amount of information over time that is indispensable to a company with an active continuous acquisition program. Although expensive, the probable payoff of effective staff work is very high relative to cost.

A source of information about companies to be acquired, which may and should parallel acquisition staff activities, are members of the board of directors. Other important sources are investment bankers, commercial bankers, consultants, and business brokers who concentrate on acquisitions.

Evaluating Prospective Candidates for Merger

If companies are acquired according to specification, as they would be with the type of screening standards discussed above, it will be possible often to tell at a quick glance whether a company deserves fuller evaluation. For a major acquisition the evaluation should, of course, be thorough and rigorous. Among other things this would include the following:

1. *General History and Background of the Company.* Included here would be the identification of and brief biographical statements on the officers; stock ownership distribution; important recent changes in organization, management, products, etc.; reputation in the industry, and similar matters. This background information should, of course, be prepared and evaluated in terms of the interests of the acquiring company.
2. *Financial Evaluation.* Included should be collection and evaluation of balance sheet and profit and loss statements over an appropriate period of time. This evaluation should penetrate deeply into the current financial condition of the company, its liquidity, its financial problems, the extent to which it corresponds to standard financial

ratios of the industry and the acquiring company, the extent to which it will strengthen or weaken the financial position of the acquirer, the possible ways to finance acquisition, whether the acquisition will or will not dilute the acquirer's stockholders' equity, and the price which seems appropriate to pay for the acquisition.

To make such evaluations the financial data should be reviewed to assure that financial statements are comparable and can be evaluated properly with those of the acquiring company. For example, it will be important to know whether assets are valued at original cost less depreciation, or on some other basis.

3. *Operations.* Under operations would be included the collection and evaluation of information about products manufactured. Included would be the type of products, volume, costs in relation to sales price, quality, stage in life cycle, and other considerations of importance to the acquiring company. Markets served also must be examined in terms of share held, nature of consumers, consumer loyalty, geographic distribution, etc. The location of the plants of the company might be included, together with an examination of the productivity of facilities, replacement needs, operating capacity, and actual capacity being used. It may be important to have a complete analysis of research and development capability, capability in managing production lines, and competence in distributing products.

Analysis of future prospective demand for the products usually is important. This should be related to prospective costs of production to determine potential profit. The analysis may include methods by which the acquiring company may increase output per dollar of capital outlay, reduce product cost by engineering improvements, raise quality without raising cost, and in other ways enhance profit prospects. By eliminating some plants, or by expanding capacity of some plants, the profit picture may be much improved. At any rate, the real emphasis must be on the future and not the past.

4. *Management Capabilities.* If the acquiring firm wishes to retain present management in the acquired firm, there ought to be an analysis of the quality of management and its compatibility with management in the acquiring firm. The quality of management is not as easy to evaluate as financial and operating data, but in a real sense the marks given the company on these evaluations are a direct reflection of managerial capability. But other matters must be considered, such as motivations, loyalty, reputation, competence in specific functions, innovative capabilities, and age distribution.

5. *Resume of Fit.* If there is a prescribed set of standards for acquiring firms, the net conclusion should specify the kind of a fit the acquired company has with the screening criteria. Should it be

acquired? If so, what is the price that ought to be paid? How should the acquisition be financed? What does the acquiring company have to do to assure that the prospects for the future as projected in the evaluation actually are achieved?

Negotiating the Acquisition

When all the above has been accomplished, the acquiring firm must then determine its strategy for approaching the prospective partner. In setting this strategy the acquiring company should be in a position to answer a number of questions. For example, if the to-be-acquired company is healthy and successful there must be an answer to such questions as: Why should we merge with you? What is our advantage? If we do sell, how will our company fit into yours? What, precisely, will be the relationship of our top management with yours? What are your plans for our managers and employees?

These are natural questions and if the answers to them are not thought through, or are unsatisfactory to the receiver, the acquisition is not likely to take place. If they are answered to the satisfaction of the prospective acquirer, the conversation quickly may get into more detailed areas suggested by the interests of each party.

In whatever approach is used, secrecy should be a guiding consideration. Rumors of impending negotiations bring with them too many problems for both companies. Changes in stock price may jeopardize financing plans, employees of either company may get upset, other firms may become interested in the prospective merger and try to stop it, and so on.

The list of causes for a breakdown of negotiations is long, but probably the one most frequently of highest importance is price and financing. Coming to a conclusion about what is a sound purchase price is difficult and inevitably a matter of controversy between buyer and seller. It will depend not alone on financial considerations but on prospects in an uncertain world and the bargaining power of both sides. A first approach to the question is to ask what is being purchased. What is being purchased, of course, are assets used in a going operation. One measure of the value of the business will be the current market price of all shares outstanding. There are obvious difficulties in accepting completely this answer. Another approach is to capitalize earnings. The future earnings of the company can be projected and capitalized at a rate which presumably a prudent investor would pay.

Integrating the Companies

Planning for the integration of the companies once the acquisition is agreed to will depend much upon the motive for the acquisition and the plans for its relationship to the acquired. For example, if the acquired company is in effect allowed to be a decentralized, virtually autonomous profit center under its old management, the problems of integration will be considerably less than if the new company is to be completely managed by the acquiring firm. In either event, however, there will be very important "people problems" as well as operational problems.

This is not the place to lay out in any detail guidelines which should govern integration planning and operating. A few points may be made, however, as illustrations.

First, the acquiring company should have a set of policies governing many matters relating to the relationships of people, such as promotion, filling managerial vacancies, compensation and benefits, and replacement.

Second, there should be explicitly stated policies about managerial planning and control.

Third, an effort should be made to create good communications between the two companies in order to build up an atmosphere of mutual trust and understanding. There should be a forthright facing of problems and issues.

Fourth, if operations and organizations are to be integrated, the sooner the task begins the better. Preplanning should avoid delays and procrastination which can only bring headaches.

Fifth, unprofitable assets should be disposed of as quickly as possible. These should have been discovered before negotiations get under way and probably should have been discussed in negotiations.

Sixth, managers of the acquired company should be architects of change and properly motivated. Obviously to do this successfully requires careful planning of the integration in which management tasks are evaluated, managers to fill them are identified, and the means to motivate managers are determined.

Seventh, when managers in the acquired company fail to measure up to what is expected of them, they should be removed promptly. Whatever has happened, however, prompt changes should be made among personnel who are not performing properly.

Postaudit

The final step in merger should be a postaudit of results. This should, of course, be tailored to each situation, but the principle of review is sound since it requires an examination of past mistakes and successes from which future experiences can benefit. A postaudit should provide a sober evaluation of the profitability of the venture. If it turns out that all or part of the venture is a loser, that which is not working out should be sold. It is easy to become wedded to a past decision, and it is human to find it hard to admit error. If a company has a policy to disinvest unprofitable parts of a business, and if it matches that policy with a rigorous postaudit, it will be easier to get rid of failing acquisitions.

Major Considerations in Successful Acquisitions

Six fundamental factors for successful acquisition stand above all others.

Involvement of the Chief Executive

There is no substitute for the personal involvement of the chief executive. The president must provide the driving force, the initiative, in acquisition. No acquisition program will move without his consent and interest. Even though his interest is expressed, it is still necessary for him to get involved personally if the program is to succeed. Another reason he should get involved is that acquisition is his job, and if he does not get personally involved he clearly will not be doing his job. Company presidents like to talk to other company presidents, not to their junior officers, when serious business is discussed. Furthermore, the president often must get approval from his board of directors for his acquisition program, which, of course, makes this a matter demanding his personal attention. Finally, the chief executive has experience in the industry, knows people, knows how they think, and has information about candidates for acquisition that staff may not possess. This point is more pertinent for acquisitions of companies in the same or a similar line of business as that of the acquirer. In general, however, the experience of the chief executive gives him an insight, an intuitive feel for important considerations, that is of great value in making successful acquisitions.

Importance of Planning

Companies that have been most successful have learned the value of formalizing their approach to acquisitions and have made full-time staff assignments to do this. The formalization of acquisition procedures encompasses thorough planning throughout the entire process as well as clear and detailed methods for evaluations through the decision-making stages. To paraphrase a current product's slogan, things go better with planning.

Importance of the Expert

Acquiring other companies is a complex activity that brings together the expertise of many disciplines—investment banking, tax analysis, accounting, law, economics, and management, to name a few—details of any one of which may, if ignored, turn success into disaster. A management entering this field for the first time, therefore, should have at its disposal the services of reputable experts on acquisitions.

Value of High Stock Price-Earnings Ratios

Price-earnings ratios are of great significance in the growth of many companies. The reason is that if a company with a high stock price-earnings ratio acquires one with a low price-earnings ratio, and after the merger the price-earnings ratio continues to be high, there is a net gain to stockholders of both companies.

Avoidance of Companies in Distress

Some companies look for others in distress with the hope of adding something to the combination that will correct a deficiency and revitalize an ailing enterprise. With few exceptions these integrations do not work out much better than the situation of the girl who marries a man to reform him.

The Quality of Management is a Major Consideration

While some companies have sought others with weak managers and, by replacing them with strong managers, have made handsome profits, this is not a game with odds in its favor. Generally, rapidly growing companies have not enough top managers to put into failing enterprises.

B.

Product-Market Planning

MARKETING STRATEGY begins where corporate strategy leaves off. Its key components are products and markets. Ames shows how a product plan should be prepared and executed if the company is to attain its market goals efficiently and effectively. Conley, Day, and Robinson, Hichens, and Wade all address the subject of product portfolio analysis—but from different vantage points. Conley links the concept of experience curves to the Boston Consulting Group's version of the portfolio. Day concentrates on the diagnosis of inappropriate and misleading applications when the basic assumptions of this approach are violated, the measurements are wrong, or the resultant strategies are not feasible. Robinson *et al.* show how the use of portfolios can be extended to include new dimensions of evaluation and new uses such as the appraisal of major competitor strategies.

10. Keys to Successful Product Planning

B. Charles Ames

Ames discusses the need for product planning and shows how this planning can be carried out.

NEW PRODUCTS fail because marketing executives, already overloaded with existing product responsibilities, lack time to plan the market entry of the new ones. Minor products never realize their full potential because marketing managers are too busy trying to meet their major goals.

This is why more and more businesses have turned to the product manager concept.[1] The results, in many cases impressive, have included:

- Better definition of each product's market, future direction, and needs, and a clearer conception of the company's relative competitive position and opportunities
- Clearer understanding of the economic consequences and market impact of alternative decisions and strategies for each product
- More explicit and better-integrated product goals (for example, volume, profit, market share, and so forth) and sounder specific programs in all areas of the business for their achievement

Reprinted from *Business Horizons*, 9 (Summer, 1966), pp. 49–58. © 1966 by the Foundation for the School of Business at Indiana University. Used by permission.

B. Charles Ames was a principal of McKinsey & Co., Inc., at the time of writing. He is now President and Chief Executive Officer of Reliance Electric Inc.

[1] For a company selling several products to the same general market, the product manager form of organization is a logical way to make certain that each product gets its fair share of time and attention from the various functional groups that affect its flow into the marketplace. On the other hand, a company selling the same product or products to a number of different market or industry segments often finds a *market* or *industry manager* setup the best way to make sure that the particular requirements of each market or industry are met. In either case, planning is the core responsibility of the job—and the same concepts apply.

- For key line executives, better understanding of these goals and strategies and of the efforts they will require
- More effective implementation and follow-up of agreed-upon plans, and more timely adjustments when needed to strengthen product positions and profits.

Consider the recent experience of a leading electronics manufacturer. For years, this company had dabbled in the nuclear instrumentation field with little success. Its sales growth had lagged behind competition, and profits were too slim to support the development efforts needed to keep pace with the field. Understandably, management had its doubts about this business, but problems in other product areas were always more important. For some time, the instrumentation business was allowed to drift.

Eventually, under pressure of these mounting problems, a product manager was assigned full-time to the company's nuclear instrumentation line. His charter: to develop a plan for getting some market momentum behind the line—or a plan for withdrawing from the business.

Within three months, the product manager was convinced that the potential of the nuclear instrumentation line alone was too limited to justify the company's continued interest. But he had also identified a real opportunity to expand into the much broader and more attractive controls field. Accordingly, the plan he submitted called for adding technical staff and acquiring a small, foreign manufacturer to obtain the broader base of products the company would need to compete in the controls area. His plan was adopted, and today his product line is the fastest-growing and most promising segment of the company's entire business.

Such successes, however, are far from universal. In fact, a great many companies that adopted the product management concept in hopes of improving profitability through better product planning have been sorely disappointed. Here is a recent example:

A marketing vice-president in the basic metals field complained,

> We moved to a product management setup because we thought we could improve our profits if we had product managers with full-time responsibility for planning to improve the mix of products moving through our plants. But it's beginning to look like we were kidding ourselves. Our product management group costs us $150,000 a year, but I can't honestly say our product mix is any better today than it was in the beginning. Our product managers have put all kinds of plans together, but not one of them has really done the job we wanted.

How is it that product managers have importantly improved product planning in some companies—and failed so abysmally in others? The blame for bad product planning, usually pinned on the hapless product manager, should more often he laid at top management's door. Too often, companies adopt the product management concept and then proceed to make it impossible for the product managers to do their jobs. Too often, management fails to define the product manager's planning responsibilities or to provide him with the direction and support he needs to plan effectively.

The purpose of this article, then, is two-fold: to define the planning job that should be expected of a product manager, and to outline what top management needs to do to enable the product manager to plan effectively.

What Should the Manager Plan?

From its early start in consumer goods companies, the product management concept has rapidly spread into other industries. Today, product manager assignments are as common for electronic gear and heavy machinery as for toothpaste or baby food.

Within such a broad spectrum of products and marketing requirements, product-manager assignments understandably show important differences in focus and structure. A product manager for toothpaste is primarily concerned with advertising, promotion, and packaging, the keys to his product's success. In contrast, a product manager in the heavy equipment field is likely to spend most of his time on individual account analysis, production costs, and product specifications.

Despite such differences, however, all product manager jobs have an identical core. Whatever his product assignment, the product manager's basic responsibility—in fact, his very reason for being—is *effective planning and coordination of the activities that are vital to his product's success.*

In my experience, successful product management groups are distinguished by four basic approaches to planning.

First, the product managers develop written plans for their product lines, incorporating in some form the five basic elements illustrated in figure 1. Despite many variations in content and format, its function is always to define explicitly product and market needs and opportunities and indicate what can be done to meet and exploit them. There is nothing magical about a written product plan but it does reduce the chances of planning gaps or outright errors. It also provides a far better basis for top management evaluation.

Second, the planning emphasis is focused on relatively few areas— those that can make or break the product. These vary from product to product. Often, even for the same product, they will vary over the course of time. For example, one product manager for a consumer package item, who had limited his detailed planning to advertising and promotion, was obliged to shift much of his effort to product and package improvement when his two major competitors began gaining market share through advances in these areas.

Third, product managers range across organization lines in their planning, focusing on the activities crucial to product success wherever these activities may be located functionally. Often, they work their ways into areas that would normally be considered remote from their sphere of influence, such as production or design engineering. To do so without running into organization conflicts, of course, they must have both personal stature and the necessary top management support.

For example, a product manager for small electric motors found his product costs nearly 25 per cent out of line and his market position slipping rapidly. Although positioned in the marketing department, he took the lead in planning a cost reduction project that significantly changed both the engineering and the manufacturing of his product, enabling it to again meet market and competitive requirements. Without actually doing the planning himself, he initiated and coordinated the entire project. There were no organizational repercussions, for everyone recognized that the changes were essential to regaining a strong market position—and that the product manager was most knowledgeable about what needed to be done.

Fourth, product planning is a continuous process, not a one-shot effort. Of course, the product manager's planning efforts may peak at certain times—for example, when he is required to draw up a formal over-all plan for his business. But he is constantly following up on actual results, initiating new plans, and modifying old plans to make certain that his product's volume and profit goals are achieved. In effect, he serves as a nerve center for his product area. He keeps in touch with developments inside and outside the company, communicates and defines the need for program changes to all functional departments, and sees to it that everything necessary is done to ensure his product's success in the marketplace.

Of course, these ground rules are much easier to define than to follow. But unless they are followed, the chances are that management will not be pleased with the product manager's planning.

What Top Management Can Do

In my observation, companies that have profited most from product management consistently follow certain common ground rules to optimize the planning of their product managers:

1. Start with the right raw material
2. Spell out the product manager's planning responsibilities in detail, and communicate them clearly throughout the organization
3. Structure the product manager's job so that he has time to plan
4. Provide guidance and direction so that he doesn't have to plan in a vacuum.

These rules are so elementary it is hard to see how or why they would ever be overlooked. Yet it is surprising how often, simply because management has neglected these fundamentals, the product manager fails to do the planning job expected of him. Several examples from my own experience will serve to illustrate.

The Right Raw Material

To chart the course his company should follow, the product manager must analyze the economics of his product's business, what the market opportunities are, what his company must do to capitalize on them, and what the payoff will be if successful. This is his plan. If it is soundly conceived,

FIGURE 1. Five Components of the Product Plan

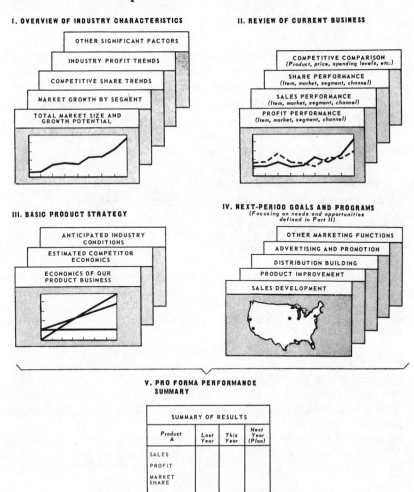

I. OVERVIEW OF INDUSTRY CHARACTERISTICS

- OTHER SIGNIFICANT FACTORS
- INDUSTRY PROFIT TRENDS
- COMPETITIVE SHARE TRENDS
- MARKET GROWTH BY SEGMENT
- TOTAL MARKET SIZE AND GROWTH POTENTIAL

II. REVIEW OF CURRENT BUSINESS

- COMPETITIVE COMPARISON (Product, price, spending levels, etc.)
- SHARE PERFORMANCE (Item, market, segment, channel)
- SALES PERFORMANCE (Item, market, segment, channel)
- PROFIT PERFORMANCE (Item, market, segment, channel)

III. BASIC PRODUCT STRATEGY

- ANTICIPATED INDUSTRY CONDITIONS
- ESTIMATED COMPETITOR ECONOMICS
- ECONOMICS OF OUR PRODUCT BUSINESS

IV. NEXT-PERIOD GOALS AND PROGRAMS
(Focusing on needs and opportunities defined in Part II)

- OTHER MARKETING FUNCTIONS
- ADVERTISING AND PROMOTION
- DISTRIBUTION BUILDING
- PRODUCT IMPROVEMENT
- SALES DEVELOPMENT

V. PRO FORMA PERFORMANCE SUMMARY

SUMMARY OF RESULTS			
Product A	Last Year	This Year	Next Year (Plan)
SALES			
PROFIT			
MARKET SHARE			

his product business should get the management decisions and commitments that are needed. If it is not, his chances for management support are limited. Thus it is he, more than anyone else, who determines the success or failure of the company's business in his product area.

When the consequences of his planning assignment are reduced to this equation, it is clear that outstanding abilities are essential in his position. And, in fact, the companies that get good planning from their product managers do not settle for less.

Well-Defined Responsibilities

Many well-qualified product managers never really do the planning job they should because they (or others in the company) do not fully understand what it involves. "Planning" is such a vague term, and the product manager's charter is frequently so broad, that such confusion is almost inevitable unless the scope of the assignment and the expected results are clearly and carefully defined.

Within the marketing area, these planning responsibilities are fairly easy to specify: the product manager recommends goals and programs for advertising, promotion, distribution development, and so forth, as they relate to his product area. He seldom has trouble getting these plans approved, since the men responsible for executing them are typically in his own functional area. But, as we have seen, his planning responsibilities extend beyond the marketing area, and outside its boundaries the possibilities of misunderstanding and conflict are much greater. Special care should be taken, therefore, to ensure that the product manager and other functional groups understand the precise scope and content of his planning charter.

Consider the predicament of one company where the product managers' planning assignments were not carefully defined:

> Product Manager A became so involved in trying to plan everything that he never left his office. Soon he was out of contact with line managers as well as with the market. Consequently, his plans—though impressively detailed and comprehensive—were simply not responsive to his product's needs.
>
> By pushing his planning too far in areas outside the marketing group, Product Manager B got into serious conflict with certain line managers who believed he was trespassing on their responsibilities. Their refusal to cooperate made it impossible for him to do an effective planning job.
>
> Precisely to avoid such conflicts, Product Manager C confined his planning to the sales forecasting area and spent most of his time in expediting orders, fielding customer inquiries, and other sales support activities. In effect, he abdicated the planning role that management had expected him to fill.

Since these three product managers were among the most capable men in the entire organization, management tended to blame the product manager concept itself for the planning fiasco. Actually, of course, these men never had a chance to plan effectively, since neither they nor those with whom they had to work had ever been told what management expected them to do.

The implications of this example are clear. Just as it is the product manager's primary responsibility to plan, it is management's responsibility to provide him with a clear charter and a definite sense of direction in his planning. It is management's responsibility, too, to see to it that the product manager and the rest of the organization have a clear common understanding of how his planning responsibilities will be carried out.

Time to Plan

If planning is the core of the product manager's job, it should clearly receive top priority. Yet I know many product managers who are so bogged down with other responsibilities that they have no time to do the planning expected of them.

In one company, inadequate planning had made the entire product management group the target of top-management dissatisfaction. The product managers found they were averaging more than fifty hours a week on the job. An analysis of how they were using their time (Table 1) showed that they had good reason to feel discouraged and frustrated.

TABLE 1. Product Manager Time Usage (hours spent in a typical week)

	Product Manager		
	A	*B*	*C*
Sales administration	17.5	24.0	24.5
Sales support	10.5	11.5	11.0
International sales	11.0	12.0	8.5
Planning	3.5	5.5	5.5
Trade meetings, special projects, and so forth	7.5	7.0	5.5
Total	50.0	60.0	55.0

Obviously, their activities represented more than a full platter. In fact, their jobs had been overloaded with sales administrative activities from the start, and—as management belatedly agreed—something had to give before they could spend more time on planning.

Compare this with the situation of a packaged goods company, where a major effort had been made to structure the product managers' jobs around their planning responsibilities. As figure 2 shows, this company's product managers are expected to prepare, during the third quarter of each

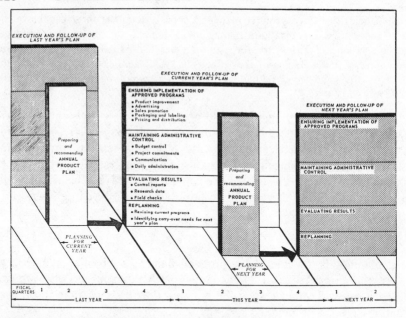

FIGURE 2. The Product Manager's Planning Cycle

year, a written plan for their product for the year ahead. Beyond this peak planning period they have various implementation, administration, and control responsibilities. But all these activities are defined in relation to the job of preparing the annual product plan.

For example, the stated purpose of the product managers' field checks is to "evaluate the results of existing programs for your products and size up the need for new ones." This put them in a position to strengthen their product plans as well as to avoid slipping into the role of supersalesmen, to the detriment of their planning effectiveness.

The marketing vice-president of this company actually used the chart shown in figure 2 to show new product managers how their job responsibilities are all keyed to planning. In addition, he regularly checked the time usage pattern of each of his product managers and counseled with them to correct any imbalance that threatened to interfere with the planning job. Clearly, the success of this product group was no accident.

Guidance and Direction

Unless product plans are tied both to over-all company objectives and to other functional planning, they can get so far out of line with management's intent or with the capabilities of other departments as to be unworkable. The disappointing experience of a large plastics converter shows what can happen when product planning is done in a vacuum.

The president of this company was convinced that it could be made more profitable by targeting the marketing effort at the right market segments and gearing all functional activities (sales, product development, and production, for example) to support it. Accordingly, three product managers were added to the sales manager's staff to spearhead the planning job. However, no further effort was made to get the company operating on a planned basis. The product managers were on their own with virtually no counseling from top management and no planning system to tie into.

Understandably, their efforts to develop useful plans for their product areas were futile. In some cases, product plans were never even developed; in others, they were unrealistic or totally unrelated to over-all company goals. After two years, with the company no closer to operating by plan than it had been at the start, the product management concept was abandoned. It was impossible, the president concluded, to plan in such a complex and volatile business.

Admittedly, any plastics converter operates in a fast-moving, highly competitive environment. But the fact that he must contend with a host of variables is an argument for good planning, not against it. Proof of this point can be seen in the experience of a competing company in exactly the same field.

Top management had decided they could improve their planning substantially by appointing product managers, each of whom would be responsible for drawing together all the plans for a given product area. These assignments, it was recognized, would have to be fitted into the company's total marketing process, and the new product managers would need extensive coaching. Accordingly, the marketing vice-president worked closely with the product managers, making sure that his personal inputs and knowledge of over-all company objectives were factored into their plans. Figure 3, which shows how the new planning system was worked out, is a modified version of the diagram management used to secure understanding and acceptance throughout the organization of the product manager's planning role.

In this company, in contrast to its competitor, the importance and effectiveness of the planning effort has never been doubted. Nor has the product managers' contribution to the over-all planning process ever been questioned. The difference stems from the plain fact that one company gave their product managers guidance and direction in their planning assignment, while the other company did not.

Whether a product manager successfully carries out his planning assignment depends largely on whether top management creates the proper

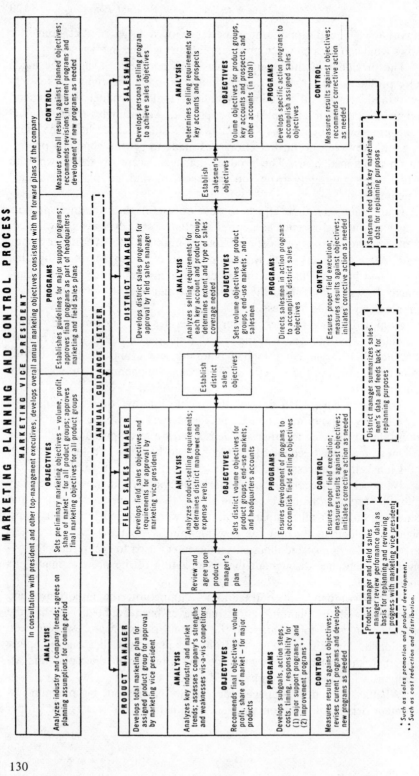

MARKETING PLANNING AND CONTROL PROCESS

MARKETING VICE PRESIDENT

In consultation with president and other top-management executives, develops overall annual marketing objectives consistent with the forward plans of the company

ANALYSIS
Analyzes industry and company trends; agrees on planning assumptions for coming period

OBJECTIVES
Sets preliminary marketing objectives — volume, profit, share of market — for all product groups; approves final marketing objectives for all product groups

PROGRAMS
Establishes guidelines for major support programs; approves final programs as part of headquarters marketing and field sales plans

CONTROL
Measures overall results against planned objectives; recommends revisions in current programs and development of new programs as needed

---

ANNUAL GUIDANCE LETTER

PRODUCT MANAGER

Develops total marketing plan for assigned product group for approval by marketing vice president

ANALYSIS
Analyzes key industry and market trends; assesses company's strengths and weaknesses vis-a-vis competitors

OBJECTIVES
Recommends final objectives — volume profit, share of market — for major products

PROGRAMS
Develops subgoals, action steps, costs, timing, responsibility for (1) major support programs* and (2) improvement programs**

CONTROL
Measures results against objectives; revises current programs and develops new programs as needed

Review and agree upon product manager's plan

FIELD SALES MANAGER

Develops field sales objectives and requirements for approval by marketing vice president

ANALYSIS
Analyzes product-selling requirements; determines district manpower and expense levels

OBJECTIVES
Sets district volume objectives for product groups, end-use markets, and headquarters accounts

PROGRAMS
Ensures development of programs to accomplish field selling objectives

CONTROL
Ensures proper field execution; measures results against objectives; initiates corrective action as needed

Establish district sales objectives

DISTRICT MANAGER

Develops district sales programs for approval by field sales manager

ANALYSIS
Analyzes selling requirements for each key account and product group; determines extent and type of sales coverage needed

OBJECTIVES
Sets volume objectives for product groups, end-use markets, and salesmen

PROGRAMS
Directs salesmen in action programs to accomplish district sales objectives

CONTROL
Ensures proper field execution; measures results against objectives; initiates corrective action as needed

Establish salesmen's objectives

SALESMAN

Develops personal selling program to achieve sales objectives

ANALYSIS
Determines selling requirements for key accounts and prospects

OBJECTIVES
Volume objectives for product groups, key accounts and prospects, and other accounts (in total)

PROGRAMS
Develops specific action programs to accomplish assigned sales objectives

CONTROL
Measures results against objectives; recommends corrective action as needed

Salesmen feed back key marketing data for replanning purposes

District manager summarizes salesmen's data and feeds back for replanning purposes

Product manager and field sales manager review performance data as basis for replanning and reviewing progress with marketing vice president

* Such as sales promotion and product development.

** Such as cost reduction and distribution.

FIGURE 3.   Marketing Planning and Control Process

environment. In the last analysis, all this requires is attention to funda-mentals: starting with the right men, carefully defining their planning responsibilities, structuring their jobs properly, and providing the necessary guidance and direction. Far too many companies, because they neglect these steps, have needlessly cut themselves off from the important benefits they might have received from effective product management.

11. Experience Curves as a Planning Tool

Patrick Conley

The total cost of many products declines by a fixed percentage each time the cumulative number of units produced is doubled. This implies that market share is vital in determining profitability, and that new products are doomed to lackluster financial performance unless they capture a dominant market position.

THE WELL-KNOWN learning curve relates the direct-labor hours required to perform a task to the number of times the task has been performed. For a wide variety of activities, this relation has been found to be of the form shown in exhibit 1, in which time to perform decreases by a constant percentage whenever the number of trials is doubled. Plotted on log-log scales, this relation becomes a straight line with a slope characteristic of the rate of "learning," such as that shown in exhibit 2.

A 20 percent reduction in hours for each doubling of performances—or what is called an 80 percent curve—is typical of a very wide variety of tasks. The concept of continuing improvement "forever," which is apparent in exhibit 2, is often disturbing. However, one must recall that the base of the curve is *not* time but trials and that the number of trials required to make a given percentage improvement grows enormously as

Reprinted from *Experience Curves As A Planning Tool: A Special Commentary.* (Boston: The Boston Consulting Group, Inc., 1970). This paper first appeared in the *IEEE Spectrum* (June, 1970), published by the Institute of Electrical and Electronic Engineers. The article is based on extensive research conducted by the Boston Consulting Group which resulted in the book, *Perspectives on Experience* (Boston, 1968, 1970 and 1972), a detailed examination of the implications of the experience effect.

Patrick Conley was a vice president of The Boston Consulting Group, Inc. at the time of writing.

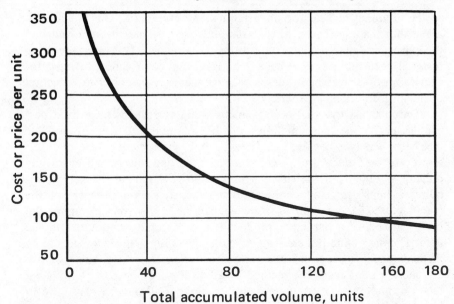

EXHIBIT 1.   Representation of Experience Relationships Graphically on a Linear Scale

learning occurs. Thus, for all practical purposes, learning in most instances eventually becomes so slow that it appears static.

The experience effect, quantitatively similar to the learning curve phenomenon, includes all costs, not just direct-labor costs. It is quite general and seemingly applies to most of the activities undertaken within a corporation. In particular, it applies to the start-up of new plants and even to "automated" operations.

Cost as a Function of Learning

Since experience increases the efficiency of an operation, it naturally reduces the cost of that operation. This fact has frequently been used for estimation and prediction.[1] In fact, observers have noted that costs go down *by a fixed percentage* each time the number of units produced doubles. Recent studies by The Boston Consulting Group serve to augment these observations. There is every reason to believe that each element of cost declines in such a way that total cost follows a composite "experience" curve.

If costs are measured in dollars, it is necessary to eliminate inflation when observations are made over a substantial period of time. Deflation of cost figures thus becomes more important when growth rates are slow,

[1] Cole, R. R., "Increasing utilization of the cost-quantity relationship in manufacturing," *J. Ind. Eng.,* pp. 173–177, May–June 1958.

so the doubling of trials or units requires several years. One might also argue that material costs, when large and fixed, should be removed and the experience effect applied only to the value added. However, removing material costs turns out to be a relatively minor correction in most instances; in other instances, these costs are themselves subject to reduction through substitutions ("experience?").

The fact that the total cost of many products declines by a fixed percentage each time the cumulative number of units produced is doubled has been widely recognized and used for cost prediction and control.[2] However, cost data are usually proprietary and always mechanically difficult to obtain for individual products, so research on the subject requires a high degree of cooperation and assistance on the part of the manufacturer. A common problem encountered when one examines the historical cost of a particular product is a series of discontinuities in the data. The discontinuities are usually associated with changes in accounting methods and are expensive and tedious to rationalize. Also, since we are considering *total* costs, the method of allocating indirect costs becomes a factor in multiproduct companies, and traditional allocations may have to be adjusted to achieve the desired precision.

EXHIBIT 2.   Representation of Experience Relationships Graphically on a Log-Log Scale

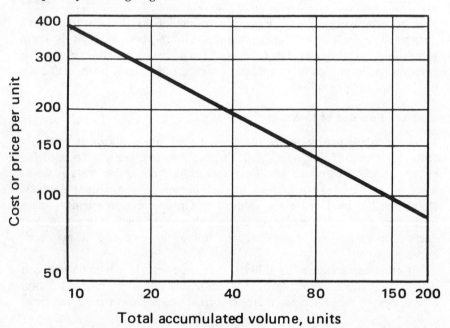

Total accumulated volume, units

[2] Hirschmann, W. B., "Profit from the learning curve," *Harvard Business Rev.*, vol. 42, pp. 125–139, Jan.–Feb. 1964; and Andress, F. J., "The learning curve as a production tool," *Harvard Business Rev.*, pp. 87–97, Jan.–Feb. 1954.

Costs and Market Share

In spite of long-standing awareness of the learning-curve phenomenon and its effect on costs, the broader experience effect and its obvious strategic implication seem until now to have been overlooked. If cost declines predictably with units produced, the competitor who has produced the most units will probably have the lowest cost. Since the products of all competitors have sensibly the same market price, the competitor with the most unit experience should enjoy the greatest profit. Furthermore, it should be clear that very substantial differences in cost and profit can exist between competitors having widely different unit experiences. Of course, this assumes that all competitors have equal access to resources and patents and that the competitors are all reasonably efficient.

Price and Experience

Assuming that costs can be made to decline at a predictable rate such as that shown in exhibit 2, we can examine the related price curves for possible correlation. In general, we find most price curves to have either the form shown in exhibit 3 or that shown in exhibit 4, with a strong predominance of the former type. In these idealized examples, as well as in the actual ones to be discussed later, we are plotting industry unit price (or weighted average unit price if several sizes or grades are involved) against total historical industry units on logarithmic scales. The costs shown are average industry costs, weighted by the unit production of each competitor. (If these prices are plotted with appropriate costs for the individual competitors' experience, the slope of the price line will *appear* to vary if the competitor is gaining or losing market share substantially.)

In exhibit 3, the constant-dollar price shows little or no decline during phase A, a steep slope of around 60 percent in phase B, and a moderate 70 to 80 percent slope in phase C. The relatively level price exhibited in phase A is associated with the introductory period in which price is set somewhat below initial cost and not changed as volume grows. If this price is held too long, competitors enter, and all add capacity until a "shakeout" price decline occurs in phase B. When prices reach a "reasonable" level above costs, they continue to decline with cost, as shown in phase C.

Characteristically, the dominant producer is losing his share of the market during phase A. During phase B, market shares may shift considerably as the more aggressive competitors struggle for dominance, using price as a major weapon. In phase C a stable competitive situation is again established with possibly a different dominant competitor than the one in phase A.

In exhibit 4, the price is brought down more nearly in parallel with cost—usually in an attempt to discourage the entry of competition. Although initial margins are less, final margins are usually greater.

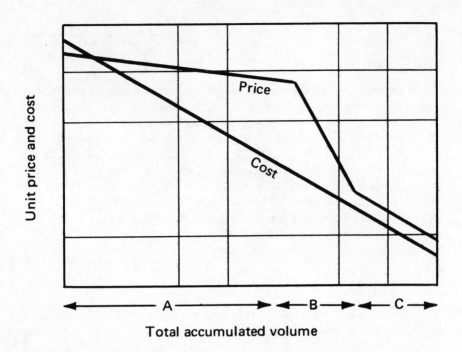

EXHIBIT 3. A Characteristic Pattern of Costs and Prices

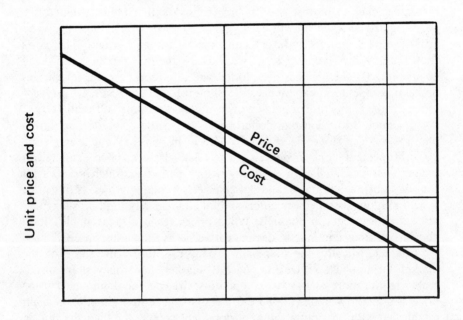

EXHIBIT 4. An Alternative Pattern of Costs and Prices

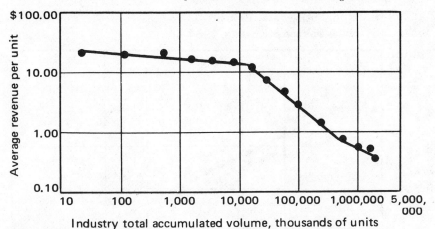

EXHIBIT 5.   Revenue Curve for Silicon Transistors during the Period from 1954 to 1968

There is nothing inherent in the price characteristics shown in exhibits 3 and 4 that reveals one to be "better" than the other. One might expect a wide variety of patterns between the two types shown; however, such variation does not appear to occur in practical instances.

It must be remembered that these idealized curves are typical of those obtaining in uninhibited competition and are exclusive of the influence of inflation. One must also be certain to avoid thinking of them as plots against *time*. Although time increases with experience, the curves are plotted against *units produced* and may be quite irregular with respect to time.

Observations of Price Behavior

Price data are relatively easy to acquire and, when adjusted by means of a GNP deflator,* they can be plotted as shown in exhibits 5 through 8. These exhibits are typical of many, many similar ones for a very wide variety of products. Exhibits 5 and 6 show the two classical forms of price behavior in semiconductors. Exhibit 7 is considered typical of the chemical industry. Exhibit 8, for facial tissues, has an unusual break in the price pattern. This break shows what happened when an element in the distribution chain was omitted and the factory picked up the eliminated unit's markup.

The 1965–1966 data for integrated circuits in exhibit 6 are particularly remarkable, since each point represents an average *monthly* price. The

---

* The GNP deflator is a factor used to correct prices for any given year to what they would have been in the base year by removing the average inflation in the gross national product.

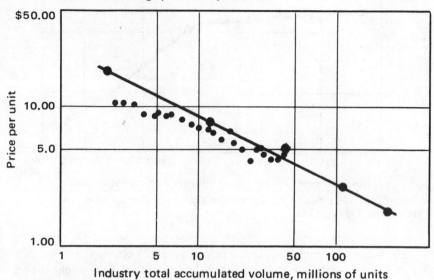

● Monthly price data, 1965-66
● Annual average price data, 1964–68

EXHIBIT 6. Price Curve for Integrated Circuits

clustering of points, shown strongly in the progressive data at the high-volume end of exhibit 8, is indicative of declining growth rate in the product. Such a decline (with its resulting cluster) is often the precursor of a price break when it occurs in the location of phase A of exhibit 3.

From the data shown, as well as from the long-acknowledged behavior of costs, one can conclude that prices behave in a remarkably predictable and regular manner and that, in constant dollars, prices tend to decline.

EXHIBIT 7. Polyvinyl Chloride Price Curve (1946–1968)

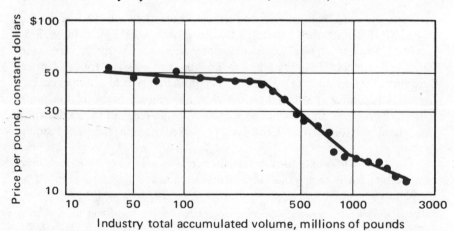

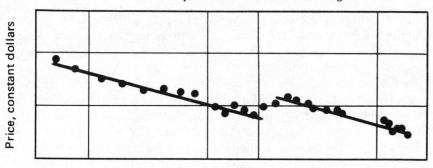

Total accumulated volume

EXHIBIT 8.   Price Curve for Facial Tissues (for the Years 1933–1955 and 1961–1966)

Break points are perhaps difficult to foresee, but they are associated with declining growth rates in the presence of a price "umbrella." Once again, the plots are in terms of total units produced and not in terms of time.

Product Strategy Implications

Since prices and costs tend to decline with units produced and since the producer with the largest stable market share eventually has the lowest costs and greatest profits, then it becomes vital to have a dominant market share in as many products as possible. However, market share in slowly growing products can be gained only by reducing the share of competitors who are likely to fight back. It may not be worth the cost to wrest shares away from competent competitors in low-growth products. The value—in terms of improved cost and increased volume—of an increase in market share can be calculated with the aid of the experience curve. The investment required to increase one's share in the market can be compared with the calculated value, and, after suitable allowances for risk factors, the decision can be made. The company should remember, however, that most competitors will price at out-of-pocket cost rather than close a facility.

But all products at some time enjoy a period of rapid growth. During rapid growth, a company can gain share by securing most of the *growth*. Thus, while competitors grow, the company can grow even faster and emerge with a dominant share when growth eventually slows. The competitors, pleased with their own growth, may not stage much of a contest even when the company is compounding its market share at their eventual expense. At high growth rates—say 20 to 30 percent in units—it is possible to overtake a competitor in a remarkably few years.

The strategic implication is that a company should strive to dominate the market, either by introducing the product, by segmenting the market, or by discouraging competitors' growth in rapidly growing areas by preemptive pricing or value. Developing and introducing new products, though a good road to dominance, involve considerable cost and uncertainty. Similarly, it is difficult to identify a market segment that can be isolated from those segments in which competitors have more experience and lower costs. However, the history of business abounds with examples of successful segmentation. The key is to find a segment the company can protect over a long period of time. In contrast, the idea of preempting market by price or value concessions is intuitive in most business organizations. Although price competition is usually resisted, it is often cheaper than the more intangible weapon of added value.

The Product Portfolio

The products of a firm can be categorized into four groups in terms of market share and growth rate. Exhibit 9 depicts such a matrix.

Category 1: Products with a High Market Share but with Low Growth

Products in category 1—those whose growth is equivalent to the growth rate of the GNP—are *not* attractive areas for investment, but they are the main source of reported earnings and cash. They are usually products for which a dominant market share is held. Their good earnings are sometimes used inappropriately to justify continued investment in the hope that growth can be increased, whereas the proper objective is to maximize cash flow consistent with maintaining market share.

Category 2: Products with a High Market Share and Rapid Growth

Products in category 2 are those that, if dominant share can be maintained until growth slows, will become the high dollar earners of category 1. These products are heavy consumers of cash and earnings, and those for which leading market position must be maintained. To attempt to extract high earnings from these products during their growth phase will usually blight the growth and sacrifice the dominant position. If continued until growth slows, such "bleeding" will move the product into category 4 instead of into category 1.

EXHIBIT 9.   Product Growth and Market Share

	High Market Share	Low Market Share
High growth rate	category 2	category 3
Low growth rate	category 1	category 4

Category 3: Products with a Low Market Share but Rapid Growth

Category 3 includes products in which a dominant market share must be achieved before growth slows or a marginal position will be "frozen in." These products demand a heavy commitment of financial and management resources. Since such resources are limited, the number of such products in the portfolio must be limited. If resources are not available to move a product in this category into a dominant market position, then it is usually wise to withdraw from the market.

Category 4: Products with Low Market Shares and Slow Growth

The final category comprises the "dogs"—products that consume far more than a just amount of management attention. They can never become satisfactorily profitable and should be liquidated in as clever and graceful a manner as possible. Outright sale to a buyer with different perceptions can sometimes be accomplished. Often pricing in a manner to upset competitors is a useful adjunct to liquidation. In any event, investment in such areas should be discontinued.

It is useful to examine a corporation's products and try to classify them into the foregoing categories. Lack of balance becomes rapidly evident and plans can be laid to add and drop products to achieve a more nearly satisfactory portfolio. It must be remembered that we are talking of products, not industries, although some industries are sufficiently simple in product diversity that they behave as single products. An unbalanced product portfolio produces some typical cash-flow symptoms. If the company has too many dominant, slow-growth products, it will usually have a low growth rate coupled with excess cash and inadequate investment opportunity. Having too many high-growth products will produce cash deficiencies as well as rapid growth. Too many low-share, low-growth products will result in inadequate cash *and* inadequate growth. With time, the balance of a product portfolio will automatically change if no deletions or additions are made.

Control Implications

Market dominance by product is the key to profitability and it can be achieved by expenditures and investments during the rapid-growth phase for a given product. The source of the funds should be mature or slowly growing products in which dominance has already been achieved and in which expense and investment are no longer intense. It is important to avoid control procedures that stifle the rapid-growth phase; yet when growth slows, it is vital to secure maximum cash flow and avoid investment overshoot.

Budgeting and control systems should be quite different for the two categories, and different objectives should be set for the product managers. Clearly, the main objective in managing the rapidly growing product should be market penetration, whereas the goal for the dominant mature product should be to maximize cash flow. In both cases the total costs should be managed to follow the experience-curve slope appropriate to the industry. A control system that sets appropriately designed goals for market share, cash flow, and cost progress is more likely to produce continuing growth in reported earnings than a system that merely stresses product-line profitability.

To use the experience-curve effect in the control system and the management decision process, the company must have comprehensive data on costs and market share. If such data can be obtained, the company will have a powerful tool. Needless to say, the successful implementation of a competitive strategy also depends upon the reaction of competitors. The route to a dominant share of a growing market lies in discouraging competitors from adding capacity or increasing their capability to produce the product. An estimate of the key competitors' decision processes is thus invaluable in planning competitive interaction.

Forecasting

The use of the experience curve to forecast prices—both for products and for purchases—is obvious. Again, one must use care to deflate the raw data and reinflate the forecast. Use of the GNP deflator has been most satisfactory and, in particular, better than the sector deflator.* (If the sector deflator is used, one is likely to erase evidence of the effect sought.) Obviously, the resulting forecast carries a forecast of inflation rate that is included in the deflator projection. The forecast of price-break points is much more difficult than projecting an existing trend—even in the presence of strong inflation, if capacity in the industry seems high and if prices appear soft, it may be wise to initiate the break, since the leader in a severe price decline usually is the gainer in market share.

Conclusions

The fact that manufacturing costs tend to follow an experience curve not only is useful for cost control and forecasting but also has a profound implication for prices and profits. In particular, it is strongly suggested that the producer of a particular product who has made the most units should have the lowest costs and highest profits. The potential profita-

---

* The sector deflator is a correction factor to be applied to prices in a particular sector of the economy—for example, chemicals—to adjust for the inflation that has occurred in that particular economic sector.

bility of a mature product should be closely related to the market share it enjoys in its particular segment.

The products of a company can be grouped by market share and growth rate in order to prescribe appropriate management of products in each group. Substantially different management objectives should be pursued in each of the four categories described. The important strategic issues of product selection, price policy, investment criteria, and divestment decisions can be more effectively addressed in the context of the experience curve than in other ways—*even if no actual data are ever collected or actual curves plotted.*

12. Diagnosing the Product Portfolio

George S. Day

This article examines the critical assumptions, measurement problems and application issues that may distort the strategic insights and conclusions to be drawn from product portfolio analysis.

THE PRODUCT portfolio approach to marketing strategy formulation has gained wide acceptance among managers of diversified companies. They are first attracted by the intuitively appealing concept that long-run corporate performance is more than the sum of the contributions of individual profit centers or product strategies. Secondly a product portfolio analysis suggests specific marketing strategies to achieve a balanced mix of products that will produce the maximum long-run effects from scarce cash and managerial resources. Lastly the concept employs a simple matrix representation which is easy to communicate and comprehend.

With the growing acceptance of the basic approach has come an increasing sensitivity to the limitations of the present methods of portraying the product portfolio, and a recognition that the approach is not equally useful in all corporate circumstances. Indeed, the implications can sometimes be grossly misleading. Inappropriate and misleading applications will result when:

- The basic assumptions (especially those concerned with the value of market share dominance and the product life cycle) are violated.
- The measurements are wrong, or
- The strategies are not feasible.

Reprinted from the *Journal of Marketing,* 41 (April, 1977), pp. 29–38. Used by permission.

George S. Day is Professor of Marketing in the Faculty of Management Studies, University of Toronto. He won the 1977 Alpha Kappa Psi Foundation Award for this article "for its significant contribution to the furtherance of the practice of marketing."

144

This article identifies the critical assumptions and the measurement and application issues that may distort the strategic insights. A series of questions are posed that will aid planners and decision-makers to better understand this aid to strategic thinking, and thereby make better decisions.

What Is the Product Portfolio?

Common to all portrayals of the product portfolio is the recognition that the competitive value of market share depends on the structure of competition and the stage of the product life cycle. The earliest, and most widely implemented example is the cash quadrant or share/growth matrix developed by the Boston Consulting Group.[1] Each product is classified jointly by rate of present or forecast market growth (a proxy for stage in the product life cycle) and a measure of market share dominance.

The arguments for the use of market share are familiar and well documented.[2] Their basis is the cumulation of evidence that market share is strongly and positively correlated with product profitability. This theme is varied somewhat in the BCG approach by the emphasis on relative share—measured by the ratio of the company's share of the market to the share of the largest competitor. This is reasonable since the strategic implications of a 20% share are quite different if the largest competitor's is 40% or if it is 5%. Profitability will also vary, since according to the experience curve concept the largest competitor will be the most profitable at the prevailing price level.[3]

The product life cycle is employed because it highlights the desirability of a variety of products or services with different present and prospective growth rates. More important, the concept has some direct implications for the cost of gaining and/or holding market share:

- During the rapid growth stage, purchase patterns and distribution channels are fluid. Market shares can be increased at "relatively" low cost by capturing a disproportionate share of incremental sales.
- By contrast, the key-note during the maturity stage swings to stability and inertia in distribution and purchasing relationships. A substantial growth in share by one competitor will come at the ex-

---

[1] Described in a number of pamphlets in the Boston Consulting Group's *Perspectives* series, authored by Bruce D. Henderson. For adoptions, see "Mead's Technique to Sort Out the Losers," *Business Week,* March 11, 1972, pp. 124–30.

[2] Sidney Schoeffler *et al.,* "Impact of Strategic Planning on Profit Performance," *Harvard Business Review* 52 (March–April, 1974): 137–45; and Robert D. Buzzell *et al.,* "Market Share—A Key to Profitability," *Harvard Business Review* 53 (January–February, 1975): 97–106.

[3] Boston Consulting Group, *Perspectives on Experience* (Boston: 1968 and 1970), and "Selling Business a Theory of Economics," *Business Week,* September 8, 1974, pp. 43–44.

pense of another competitor's capacity utilization, and will be resisted vigorously. As a result, gains in share are normally both time-consuming and costly.

Product Portfolio Strategies

When the share and growth rate of each of the products sold by a firm are jointly considered, a new basis for strategy evaluation emerges. While there are many possible combinations, an arbitrary classification of products into four share/growth categories (as shown in Exhibit 1) is sufficient to illustrate the strategy implications.

Low Growth/Dominant Share (Cash Cows)

These profitable products usually generate more cash than is required to maintain share. All strategies should be directed toward maintaining market dominance—including investments in technological leadership. Pricing decisions should be made cautiously with an eye to maintaining price leadership. Pressure to over-invest through product proliferation and

EXHIBIT 1. The Cash Quadrant Approach to Describing the Product Portfolio [a]

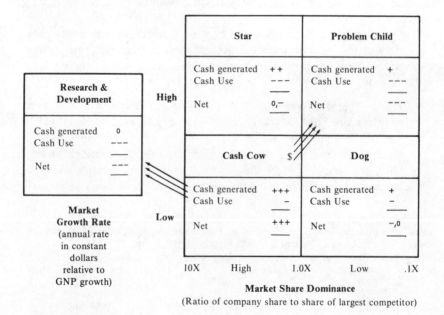

a Arrows indicate principal cash flows.

market expansion should be resisted unless prospects for expanding primary demand are unusually attractive. Instead, excess cash should be used to support research activities and growth areas elsewhere in the company.

High Growth/Dominant Share (Stars)

Products that are market leaders, but also growing fast, will have substantial reported profits but need a lot of cash to finance the rate of growth. The appropriate strategies are designed primarily to protect the existing share level by reinvesting earnings in the form of price reductions, product improvement, better market coverage, production efficiency increases, etc. Particular attention must be given to obtaining a large share of the new users or new applications that are the source of growth in the market.

Low Growth/Subordinate Share (Dogs)

Since there usually can be only one market leader and because most markets are mature, the greatest number of products fall in this category. Such products are usually at a cost disadvantage and have few opportunities for growth at a reasonable cost. Their markets are not growing, so there is little new business to compete for, and market share gains will be resisted strenuously by the dominant competition.

The slower the growth (present or prospective) and the smaller the relative share, the greater the need for positive action. The possibilities include:

1. Focusing on a specialized segment of the market that can be dominated, and protected from competitive inroads.
2. Harvesting, which is a conscious cutback of all support costs to some minimum level which will maximize the cash flow over a foreseeable lifetime—which is usually short.
3. Divestment, usually involving a sale as a going concern.
4. Abandonment or deletion from the product line.

High Growth/Subordinate Share (Problem Children)

The combination of rapid growth and poor profit margins creates an enormous demand for cash. If the cash is not forthcoming, the product will become a "Dog" as growth inevitably slows. The basic strategy options are fairly clear-cut; either invest heavily to get a disproportionate share of the new sales or buy existing shares by acquiring competitors and thus move the product toward the "Star" category or get out of the business using some of the methods just described.

Consideration also should be given to a market segmentation strategy,

but only if a defensible niche can be identified and resources are available
to gain dominance.

Overall Strategy

The long-run health of the corporation depends on having some products that *generate* cash (and provide acceptable reported profits), and
others that *use* cash to support growth. Among the indicators of overall
health are the size and vulnerability of the "Cash Cows" (and the prospects for the "Stars," if any), and the number of "Problem Children"
and "Dogs." Particular attention must be paid to those products with large

EXHIBIT 2. Balancing the Product Portfolio

(Diameter of circle is proportional to product's contribution to total company sales volume)

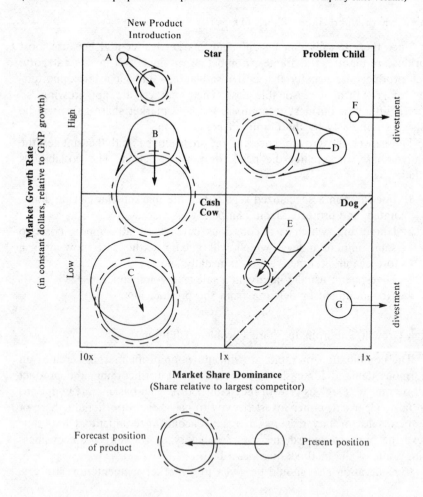

cash appetites. Unless the company has abundant cash flow, it cannot afford to sponsor many such products at one time.

The share/growth matrix displayed in Exhibit 2 shows how one company (actually a composite of a number of situations) might follow the strategic implications of the product portfolio to achieve a better balance of sources and uses of cash. The *present* position of each product is defined by the relative share and market growth rate during a representative time *period*.

The *future* position may be either (a) a momentum forecast of the results of continuing the present strategy, or (b) a forecast of the consequences of a change in strategy. It is desirable to do both, and compare the results. The specific display of Exhibit 2 is a summary of the following strategic decisions.

- Aggressively support the newly introduced product A, to ensure dominance (but anticipate share declines due to new competitive entries).
- Continue present strategies of products B and C to ensure maintenance of market share.
- Gain share of market for product D by investing in acquisitions.
- Narrow and modify the range of models of product E to focus on one segment.
- Divest products F and G.

Pitfalls in the Assumptions

The starting point in the decision to follow the implications of a product portfolio analysis is to ask whether the underlying assumptions make sense. The most fundamental assumptions relate to the role of market share in the businesses being portrayed in the portfolio.

What Is the Role of Market Share?

All the competitors are assumed to have the same overhead structures and experience curves, with their position on the experience curve corresponding to their market share position. Hence market share dominance is a proxy for the *relative* profit performance. Other factors beyond market share may be influential in dictating absolute, profit performance (e.g., calculators versus cosmetics).

The influence of market share is most apparent with high value-added products, where there are significant barriers to entry and the competition consists of a few, large, diversified corporations with the attendant large overheads (e.g., plastics, major appliances, automobiles, and semi-conductors). But even in these industrial environments there are distortions under conditions such as:

- One competitor has a significant technological advantage which can be protected and used to establish a steeper cost reduction/experience curve.
- The principal component of the product is produced by a supplier who has an inherent cost advantage because of an integrated process.
- Competitors can economically gain large amounts of experience through acquisitions or licensing, or shift to a lower (but parallel) cost curve by resorting to off-shore production or component sourcing.
- Profitability is highly sensitive to the rate of capacity utilization, regardless of size of plant.

There are many situations where the positive profitability and share relationship becomes very tenuous, and perhaps unattainable. A recent illustration is the building industry where large corporations have suffered because of their inability to adequately offset their high overhead charges with a corresponding reduction in total costs. Similar problems are also encountered in the service sector, and contribute to the many reasons why services which are highly labor-intensive and involve personal relationships must be approached with extreme caution in a product portfolio analysis.

There is specific evidence from the Profit Impact of Market Strategies (PIMS) study[4] that the value of market share is not as significant for consumer goods as for industrial products. The reasons are not well understood, but probably reflect differences in buying behavior, the importance of product differentiation and the tendency for proliferation of marginally different brands in these categories. The strategy of protecting a market position by introducing line extensions, flankers, and spin-offs from a successful core brand means that product class boundaries are very unclear. Hence shares are harder to estimate.

Similarly, joint costing problems may be difficult to untangle. For example, Unilever in the U.K. has 20 detergent brands all sharing production facilities and marketing resources to some degree.

When Do Market Shares Stabilize?

The operating assumption is that shares tend toward stability during the maturity stage, as the dominant competitors concentrate on defending their existing position. An important corollary is that gains in share are easier and cheaper to achieve during the growth stage.

There is scattered empirical evidence, including the results of the PIMS project, which supports these assumptions. Several qualifications must be made before the implications can be pursued in depth:

[4] Schoeffler et al. and Buzzell et al. (note 2 above).

- While market share *gains* may be costly, it is possible to mismanage a dominant position. The examples of A&P in food retailing, and British Leyland in the U.K. automobile market provide cases in point.
- When the two largest competitors are of roughly equal size, the share positions may continue to be fluid until one is finally dominant.
- There are certain product categories, frequently high technology oriented, where a dominant full line/full service competitor is vulnerable if there are customer segments which do not require all the services, technical assistance, etc., that are provided. As markets mature this "sophisticated" segment usually grows.

What Is the Objective of a Product Portfolio Strategy?

The strategies emerging from a product portfolio analysis emphasize the balance of cash flows, by ensuring that there are products that use cash to sustain growth and others that supply cash.

Yet corporate objectives have many more dimensions that require consideration. This point was recognized by Seymour Tilles in one of the earliest discussions of the portfolio approach.[5] It is worth repeating to avoid a possible myopic focus on cash flow considerations. Tilles' point was that an investor pursues a balanced combination of risk, income, and growth when acquiring a portfolio of securities. He further argued that "the same basic concepts apply equally well to product planning." The problem with concentrating on cash flow to maximize income and growth is that strategies to balance risks are not explicitly considered.

What must be avoided is excessive exposure to a specific threat from one of the following areas of vulnerability:

- The economy (e.g., business downturns).
- Social, political, environmental pressures.
- Supply continuity.
- Technological change.
- Unions and related human factors.

It also follows that a firm should direct its new product search activities into several different opportunity areas, to avoid intensifying the degree of vulnerability.

The desire to reduce vulnerability is a possible reason for keeping, or even acquiring, a "Dog." Thus, firms may integrate backward to assure supply of highly leveraged materials. If a "Dog" has a high percentage

[5] Seymour Tilles, "Strategies for Allocating Funds," *Harvard Business Review* 44 (January–February, 1966): 72–80.

of captive business, it may not even belong as a separate entity in a portfolio analysis.

A similar argument could be used for products which have been acquired for intelligence reasons. For example, because of the complex nature of the distribution of lumber products, some suppliers have acquired lumber retailers to help learn about patterns of demand and changing end-user requirements. In this case, the business was acquired for reasons outside the logic of the product portfolio, and should properly be excluded from the analysis.

Can the Strategies Be Implemented?

Not only does a product portfolio analysis provide insights into the long-run health of a company; it also implies the basic strategies that will strengthen the portfolio. Unfortunately, there are many situations where the risks of failure of these strategies are unacceptably high. Several of these risks were identified in a recent analysis of the dangers in the pursuit of market share.[6]

One danger is that the company's financial resources will not be adequate. The resulting problems are enormously compounded should the company find itself in a vulnerable financial position if the fight were stopped short for some reason. The fundamental question underlying such dangers is the likelihood that competitors will pursue the same strategy, because they follow the same logic in identifying and pursuing opportunities. As a result, there is a growing premium on the understanding of competitive responses, and especially the degree to which they will be discouraged by aggressive action.

An increasingly important question is whether government regulations will permit the corporation to follow the strategy it has chosen. Antitrust regulations—especially in the U.S.—now virtually preclude acquisitions undertaken by large companies in related areas.

There is less recognition as yet that government involvement can cut both ways; making it difficult to get in *or out of* a business. Thus, because of national security considerations large defense contractors would have a difficult time exiting from the aerospace or defense businesses. The problems are most acute in countries like Britain and Italy where intervention policies include price controls, regional development directives and employment maintenance which may prevent the replacement of outmoded plants.

The last implementation question concerns the viability of a niche strategy, which appears at the outset to be an attractive way of coping

---

[6] William E. Fruhan, "Pyrrhic Victories in Fights for Market Share," *Harvard Business Review* 50 (September–October, 1972): 100–107.

with both "Dogs" and "Problem Children." The fundamental problem, of course, is whether a product or market niche can be isolated and protected against competitive inroads. But even if this can be achieved in the long-run, the strategy may not be attractive. The difficulties are most often encountered when a full or extensive product line is needed to support sales, service and distribution facilities. One specialized product may simply not generate sufficient volume and gross margin to cover the minimum costs of participation in the market. This is very clearly an issue in the construction equipment business because of the importance of assured service.

Pitfalls in the Measures

The "Achilles' Heel" of a product portfolio analysis is the units of measure; for if the share of market and growth estimates are dubious, so are the interpretations. Skeptics recognize this quickly, and can rapidly confuse the analysis by attacking the meaningfulness and accuracy of these measures and offering alternative definitions. With the present state of the measurements there is often no adequate defense.

What Share of What Market?

This is not one, but several questions. Each is controversial because they influence the bases for resource allocation and evaluation within the firm:

- Should the definition of the product-market be broad (reflecting the generic need) or narrow?
- How much market segmentation?
- Should the focus be on the total product-market or a portion served by the company?
- Which level of geography: local versus national versus regio-centric markets?

The answers to these questions are complicated by the lack of defensible procedures for identifying product-market boundaries. For example, four-digit SIC categories are convenient and geographically available but may have little relevance to consumer perceptions of substitutability. Furthermore, there is the pace of product development activity which is dedicated to combining, extending, or otherwise obscuring the boundaries.

Breadth of Product-Market Definition?   This is a pivotal question. Consider the contrast between time information display devices *or* medium-priced digital-display alarm clocks.

Narrow definitions satisfy the short-run, tactical concerns of sales and product managers. Broader views, reflecting longer-run, strategic planning concerns, invariably reveal a larger market to account for (a) sales to untapped but potential markets, (b) changes in technology, price relationships, and supply which broaden the array of potential substitute products, and (c) the time required by present and prospective buyers to react to these changes.

Extent of Segmentation?   In other words, when does it become meaningful to divide the total market into sub-groups for the purpose of estimating shares? In the tire industry it is evident that the OEM and replacement markets are so dissimilar in behavior as to dictate totally different marketing mixes. But how much further should segmentation be pushed? The fact that a company has a large share of the high-income buyers of replacement tires is probably not strategically relevant.

In general the degree of segmentation for a portfolio analysis should be limited to grouping those buyers that share situational or behavioral characteristics that are strategically relevant. This means that different marketing mixes must be used to serve the segments that have been identified, which will be reflected in different cost and price structures. Other manifestations of a strategically important segment boundary would be a discontinuity in growth rates, share patterns, distribution patterns and so forth when going from one segment to another.

These judgments are particularly hard to make for geographic boundaries. For example, what is meaningful for a manufacturer of industrial equipment facing dominant local competition in each of the national markets in the European Economy Community? Because the company is in each market, it has a 5% share of the total EEC market, while the largest regional competitor has 9%. In this case the choice of a regional rather than national market definition was dictated by the *trend* to similarity of product requirements throughout the EEC and the consequent feasibility of a single manufacturing facility to serve several countries.

The tendency for trade barriers to decline for countries within significant economic groupings will increasingly dictate regio-centric rather than nationally oriented boundaries. This, of course, will not happen where transportation costs or government efforts to protect sensitive industry categories creates other kinds of barriers.

Market Served Versus Total Market?

Firms may elect to serve only just a part of the available market, such as retailers with central buying offices or utilities of a certain size. The share of the market served is an appropriate basis for tactical decisions. This share estimate may also be relevant for strategic decisions, especially if the market served corresponds to a distinct segment boundary. There is a risk that focusing only on the market served may mean overlooking a significant opportunity or competitive threat emerging from the unserved portion of the market.

Another facet of the served market issue is the treatment of customers who have integrated backward and now satisfy their own needs from their own resources. Whether or not the captive volume is included in the estimate of total market size depends on how readily this captive volume can be displaced by outside suppliers.

What Can Be Done?

The value of a strategically relevant product-market definition lies in "stretching" the company's perceptions appropriately—far enough so that significant threats and opportunities are not missed, but not so far as to dissipate information, gathering and analysis efforts on "long shots." This is a difficult balance to achieve, given the myriads of possibilities. The best procedure for coping is to employ several alternative definitions, varying specificity of product and market segments. There will inevitably be both points of contradiction and consistency in the insights gained from portfolios constructed at one level versus another. The process of resolution can be very revealing, both in terms of understanding the competitive position and suggesting strategy alternatives.[7]

Market Growth Rate

The product life cycle is justifiably regarded as one of the most difficult marketing concepts to measure—or forecast.

There is a strong tendency in a portfolio analysis to judge that a product is maturing when there is a forecast of a decline in growth rate below some specified cut-off. One difficulty is that the same cut-off level does not apply equally to all products or economic climates. As slow growth or level GNP becomes the reality, high absolute growth rates become harder to achieve for all products, mature or otherwise. Products with lengthy introductory periods, facing substantial barriers to adoption, may never exhibit high growth rates, but may have an extended maturity stage. Other products may exhibit precisely the opposite life cycle pattern.

The focus in the product portfolio analysis should be on the long-run growth rate forecast. This becomes especially important with products which are sensitive to the business cycle, such as machine tools, or have potential substitutes with fluctuating prices. Thus the future growth of engineered plastics is entwined with the price of zinc, aluminum, copper

---

[7] George S. Day and Allan D. Shocker, *Identifying Competitive Product-Market Boundaries: Strategic and Analytical Issues* (Boston: Marketing Science Institute, 1976).

and steel; the sales of powdered breakfast beverages depends on the relative price of frozen orange juice concentrate.

These two examples also illustrate the problem of the self-fulfilling prophecy. A premature classification as a mature product may lead to the reduction of marketing resources to the level necessary to defend the share in order to maximize net cash flow. But if the product class sales are sensitive to market development activity (as in the case of engineered plastics) or advertising expenditures (as is the case with powdered breakfast drinks) and these budgets are reduced by the dominant firms then, indeed, the product growth rate will slow down.

The growth rate is strongly influenced by the choice of product-market boundaries. A broad product type (cigarettes) will usually have a longer maturity stage than a more specific product form (plain filter cigarettes). In theory, the growth of the individual brand is irrelevant. Yet, it cannot be ignored that the attractiveness of a growth market, however defined, will be diminished by the entry of new competitors with the typical depressing effect on the sales, prices and profits of the established firms. The extent of the reappraisal of the market will depend on the number, resources, and commitment of the new entrants.

Pitfalls from Unanticipated Consequences

Managers are very effective at tailoring their behavior to the evaluation system, *as they perceive it*. Whenever market share is used to evaluate performance, there is a tendency for managers to manipulate the product-market boundaries to show a static or increasing share. The greater the degree of ambiguity or compromise in the definition of the boundaries the more tempting these adjustments become. The risk is that the resulting narrow view of the market may mean overlooking threats from substitutes or the opportunities within emerging marget segments.

These problems are compounded when share dominance is also perceived to be an important determinant of the allocation of resources and top management interest. The manager who doesn't like the implications of being associated with a "Dog," may try to redefine the market so he can point to a larger market share or a higher than average growth rate. Regardless of his success with the attempted redefinition, his awareness of how the business is regarded in the overall portfolio will ultimately affect his morale. Then his energies may turn to seeking a transfer or looking for another job, and perhaps another prophecy has been fulfilled.

The forecast of market growth rate is also likely to be manipulated, especially if the preferred route to advancement and needed additional resources is perceived to depend on association with a product that is classified as "Star." This may lead to wishful thinking about the future growth prospects of the product. Unfortunately the quality of the review procedures in most planning processes is not robust enough to challenge such distortions. Further dysfunctional consequences will result if ambitious managers of "Cash Cows" actually attempt to expand their products through unnecessary product proliferation and market segmentation without regard to the impact on profits.

What will surely create problems is to have an inappropriate reward system. A formula-based system, relying on achievement of a target for return on investment or an index of profit measures, that does not recognize the differences in potential among business, will lead to short-run actions that conflict with the basic strategies that should be pursued.

Alternative Views of the Portfolio

This analysis of the share/growth matrix portrayal of the product portfolio supports Bowman's contention that much of what now exists in the field of corporate or marketing strategy can be thought of as contingency theories. "The ideas, recommendations, or generalizations are rather dependent (contingent) for their truth and their relevance on the specific situational factors." [8] This means that in any specific analysis of the product portfolio there may be a number of factors beyond share and market growth with a much greater bearing on the attractiveness of a product-market or business; including:

- The contribution rate.
- Barriers to entry.
- Cyclicality of sales.
- The rate of capacity utilization.
- Sensitivity of sales to change in prices, promotional activities, service levels, etc.
- The extent of "captive" business.
- The nature of technology (maturity, volatility, and complexity).
- Availability of production and process opportunities.
- Social, legal, governmental, and union pressures and opportunities.

Since these factors are situational, each company (or division) must develop its own ranking of their importance in determining attractiveness. In practice these factors tend to be qualitatively combined into overall judgments of the attractiveness of the industry or market, and the company's position in that market. The resulting matrix for displaying the positions of each product is called a "nine-block" diagram or decision matrix. [9]

[8] Edward H. Bowman, "Epistemology, Corporate Strategy, and Academe," *Sloan Management Review*, Winter, 1974, pp. 35–50.

[9] William E. Rothschild, *Putting It All Together: A Guide to Strategic Thinking* (New York: AMACOM, 1976).

Although the implications of this version of the product portfolio are not as clear-cut, it does overcome many of the shortcomings of the share/growth matrix approach. Indeed the two approaches will likely yield different insights. But as the main purpose of the product portfolio analysis is to help guide—but not substitute for—strategic thinking, the process of reconciliation is useful in itself. Thus it is desirable to employ both approaches and compare results.

Summary

The product portfolio concept provides a useful synthesis of the analyses and judgments during the preliminary steps of the planning process, and is a provocative source of strategy alternatives. If nothing else, it demonstrates the fallacy of treating all businesses or profit centers as alike, and all capital investment decisions as independent and additive events.

Despite the potential pitfalls it is important to not lose sight of the concept; that is, to base strategies on the perception of a company as an interdependent group of products and services, each playing a distinctive and supportive role.

13. The Directional Policy Matrix— Tool for Strategic Planning

S. J. Q. Robinson, R. E. Hichens, and D. P. Wade

The authors introduce a nine-cell product evaluation matrix, incorporating new evaluative dimensions, and apply it in novel ways.

IN DIVERSIFIED BUSINESS ORGANIZATIONS one of the main functions of the management is to decide how money, materials and skilled manpower should be allocated. Good management allocates resources to sectors where business prospects appear favourable and where the organization has a position of advantage. In a reasonably stable economic environment the normal method of comparing the prospects of one business sector with another, and for measuring a company's strengths and weaknesses in different sectors, is to use historical and forecast rates of return on capital employed in each sector to provide a measure of the sector's prospects or the company's strength. But records and forecasts of profitability are not sufficient yardsticks for guidance of management in corporate planning and allocation of resources, because

a. They do not provide a systematic explanation
   1. Why one business sector has more favourable prospects than another.
   2. Why the company's position in a particular sector is strong or weak.
b. They do not provide enough insight into the underlying dynamics and balance of the company's individual business sectors and the balance between them.

Reprinted with permission from *Long Range Planning* Journal, 11, no. 3 (June, 1978), pp. 8–15.

S. J. Q. Robinson is in the Corporate Planning Division of Shell Chemicals U.K. Ltd. Messrs. Hichens and Wade are with Shell International Chemical Co. Ltd.

c. When new areas of business are being considered, actual experience, by definition, cannot be consulted.

d. World-wide inflation has severely weakened the validity and credibility of financial forecasts, particularly in the case of businesses which are in any way affected by oil prices.

Corporate managements which recognize these shortcomings bring a variety of other qualitative and quantitative considerations to bear on the decision-making process in addition to the financial yardsticks. These are described in the following sections.

Outline of Technique

The basic technique of the Directional Policy Matrix is to identify:

a. the main criteria by which the prospects for a business sector may be judged to be favourable or unfavourable; and

b. those by which a company's position in a sector may be judged to be strong or weak.

Favourable in this context means with high profit and growth potential for the industry generally.

These criteria are then used to construct separate ratings of "sector prospects" and of "company's competitive capabilities" and the ratings are plotted on a matrix. The ratings can be plotted in various ways. Figure 1 displays the position of a number of different sectors in a hypothetical company's portfolio. Alternatively, the matrix can be used to display all the competitors in one particular business sector, since the method lends itself to evaluating competitors' ratings as well as those of one's own company.

Details of Technique

Scope of the Analysis

The detailed techniques have been developed by reference to the petroleum-based sector of the chemical industry, but the general technique is applicable to almost any diversified business with separately identifiable sectors. In the chemical industry business sectors can generally be identified with product sectors, since these form distinct businesses with well defined boundaries and substantial competition within the boundaries.

Any particular geographical area may be defined for study. For the majority of petroleum-based chemicals it has been found most convenient to consider economic blocs (e.g., Western Europe) since there is generally greater movement of chemicals within these blocs than between them.

The time scale of assessment is the effective forecasting horizon. This

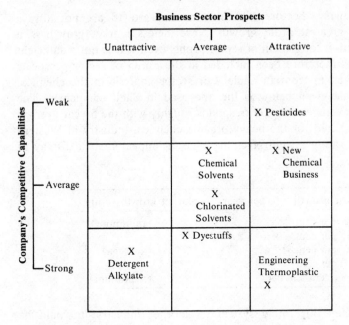

FIGURE 1.   Positions of business sectors in a hypothetical company's portfolio

will vary according to the business growth rate and the lead time needed to install new capacity or develop new uses. For most petroleum-based chemicals a time scale of 10 years has been found appropriate.

Analysis of Business Sector Prospects

There are four main criteria by which the profitability prospects for different sectors of the petroleum-based chemical business may be judged. These are:

    a. Market growth rate;
    b. Market quality;
    c. Industry feedstock situation; and
    d. Environmental aspects.

Some of these criteria are not applicable to other industries and other criteria have to be introduced. Industry feedstock situation, for example, would not be of significance in evaluating sectors of the engineering industry. Market growth and market quality, however, are fundamental to any analysis of business sector prospects.

The significance of these four criteria and the way in which they are rated is as follows:

Market Growth. Sectors with high market growth are not always those with the greatest profit growth. Nevertheless market growth is a necessary condition for growth of sector profits even if it is not a sufficient condition. It has therefore been included in the rating of sector prospects on the basis of an appropriate scale. For sector analysis in the chemical industry the scale given below is the one used in Shell companies. The centre point or average rating, corresponds roughly with the 5 year average growth rate predicted for the heavy organic chemical industry in Western Europe. A star rating system gives more visual impact than a display of numerals.

sector growth rate per year	market growth rating	
0–3 per cent	*	(minimum)
3–5 per cent	**	
5–7 per cent	***	(average)
7–10 per cent	****	
10 per cent and over	*****	(maximum)

When applying this rating system to another industry it would be necessary to construct a different scale with a centre point appropriate to the average growth rate for that industry.

The other criteria are used to qualify the basic forecast of growth of demand so far as their effect on growth of profits is concerned.

Market Quality. Certain sectors of the chemical industry show a consistent record of higher and/or more stable profitability than others.

Market quality is difficult to quantify; in order to arrive at a sector rating it is necessary to consider a number of criteria in relation to the sector and try to assess their impact. The following are some of the more important questions:

a. Has the sector a record of high, stable profitability?
b. Can margins be maintained when manufacturing capacity exceeds demand?
c. Is the product resistant to commodity pricing behaviour?
d. Is the technology of production freely available or is it restricted to those who developed it?
e. Is the market supplied by relatively few producers?
f. Is the market free from domination by a small group of powerful customers?
g. Has the product high added value when converted by the customer?
h. In the case of a new product, is the market destined to remain small enough not to attract too many producers?
i. Is the product one where the customer has to change his formulation or even his machinery if he changes supplier?

j. Is the product free from the risk of substitution by an alternative synthetic or natural product?

A sector for which the answers to all or most of these questions are yes would attract a four or five star market quality rating.

Industry Feedstock Situation. Normally in the chemical industry, expansion of productive capacity is often constrained by uncertainty of feedstock supply. If this is the case, or if the feedstocks for the sector in question have a strong pull towards an alternative use, or are difficult to assemble in large quantities, this is treated as a plus for sector prospects and attracts a better than average rating.

Conversely if the feedstock is a by-product of another process, and consumption of the main product is growing faster than the by-product, pressure may arise, either from low prices or direct investment by the by-product producer, to increase its consumption. This would attract a lower than average rating.

Environmental (Regulatory) Aspects. Sector prospects can be influenced by the extent of restrictions on the manufacture, transportation or marketing of the product. In some cases the impact of such restrictions is already quantifiable and has been built into the forecasts of market growth. If it has not, it must be assessed if there is a strongly positive or negative environmental or regulatory influence to be taken into account for the product.

Analysis of a Company's Competitive Capabilities

Three main criteria have been identified by which a company's position in a particular sector of the chemical business may be judged strong, average or weak. With suitable adaption they can probably be applied to the analysis of companies' positions in almost any business sector. The three criteria are:

a. Market position;
b. Production capability; and
c. Product research and development.

The significance of these criteria and the ways in which they are rated is shown below. In general it is convenient to review the position of one's own company in relation to that of all the significant competitors in the sector concerned as this helps to establish the correct relativities.

Normally the position being established is that of the companies *today*. Other points can be plotted for one's own company to indicate possible future positions which might result from implementing alternative investment proposals and product strategies.

Market Position. The primary factor to consider here is percentage share of the total market. Supplementary to this is the degree to which this share is secured. Star ratings are awarded against the following guidelines:

***** Leader. A company which, from the mere fact of its pre-eminent market position is likely to be followed normally accompanied by acknowledged technical leadership. The market share associated with this position varies from case to case. A company with 25 per cent of West European consumption in a field of ten competitors may be so placed. A company with 50 per cent in a field of two competitors will not be.

**** Major Producer. The position where, as in many businesses, no one company is a leader, but two to four competitors may be so placed.

*** A company with a strong viable stake in the market but below the top league. Usually when one producer is a leader the next level of competition will be three star producers.

** Minor market share. Less than adequate to support R & D and other services in the long run.

* Current position negligible.

Production Capability. This criterion is a combination of process economics, capacity of hardware, location and number of plants, and access to feedstock. The answers to all the following questions need to be considered before awarding a one to five star production capability rating:

PROCESS ECONOMICS. Does the producer employ a modern economic production process? Is it his own process or licensed? Has he the research and development capability or licensing relationships that will allow him to keep up with advances in process technology in the future?

HARDWARE. Is current capacity, plus any new capacity announced or building, commensurate with maintaining present market share? Does the producer have several plant locations to provide security to his customers against breakdown or strike action? Are his delivery arrangements to principal markets competitive?

FEEDSTOCK. Has the producer secure access to enough feedstocks to sustain his present market share? Does he have a favourable cost position on feedstock?

Product Research and Development. In the case of performance products this criterion is intended to be a compound of product range, product quality, a record of successful development in application, and competence in technical service. In other words, the complete technical package upon which the customer will pass judgment. In awarding a one to five star rating, judgment should be passed on whether a company's product R & D is better than, commensurate with, or worse than its position in the market.

In the case of commodity products, this criterion is not relevant and is not rated.

Assignment of Ratings—Plotting the Matrix

The most straightforward method of assigning ratings for each of the criteria is discussion by functional specialists. They should be drawn from the particular sector of the company's business which is being studied and assisted by one or two non-specialists to provide the necessary detached viewpoint and comparability with other sector assessments.

Although members of the group may differ in the initial ratings which they assign, it is usually possible to arrive at a set of consensus ratings. Where there are still unresolved differences, a representative rating can generally be obtained by averaging. More sophisticated methods of sampling opinion have been designed, using computer techniques, but experience shows that the group discussion method was to be preferred as the end result is reached by a more transparent series of steps which make it more credible both to those participating and to management.

Simplified System

In the simplified form of the technique each of the main criteria is given an equal weighting in arriving at an overall rating for business sector prospects and for company's competitive capabilities. This system of equal weighting may be open to question in comparing certain business sectors but has been found to give good results when applied to a typical chemical product portfolio.

In converting star ratings into matrix positions it is necessary (in order to avoid distortion) to count one, two, three, four and five stars as zero, one, two, three, four points respectively. One star is thus equivalent to a nil rating and a three star rating scores two points out of four and occupies a midway position where three points out of five would not. The working of the system is illustrated by the hypothetical example in Table 1. In this, the technique is being used to assess the competitors in a particular business sector.

Weighting System

In certain businesses it is unrealistic to suppose that each factor is equally important, in which case an alternative method of analysing company's competitive capabilities can be used, introducing objectively determined weightings.

An example of such weightings is given in Table 2. This is taken from a particular study on speciality chemicals, in which the four functions

    a. Selling and distribution;
    b. Problem solving;
    c. Innovative research and development; and
    d. Manufacturing.

were considered to be the most important.

TABLE 1. Examples of Simplified Weighting System

Product sector: Product X is a semi-mature thermoplastic suitable for engineering industry applications. There are two existing producers in Western Europe and a third producer is currently building plant.

Sector prospects analysis (Western Europe, 1975–1980)

		Stars	Points
Market growth	15–20% per year forecast	*****	4
Market quality			
Sector profitability record?	Above average.		
Margins maintained in over-capacity?	Some price-cutting has taken place but product has not reached commodity status.		
Customer to producer ratio?	Favourable. Numerous customers; only two producers so far.		
High added value to customer?	Yes. The product is used in small scale, high value, engineering applications.		
Ultimate market limited in size?	Yes. Unlikely to be large enough to support more than three or four producers.		
Substitutability by other products?	Very limited. Product has unique properties.		
Technology of production restricted?	Moderately. Process is available under licence from Eastern Europe.		
Overall market quality rating:	Above average.	****	3
Industry feedstock	Product is manufactured from an intermediate which no other outlets. itself requires sophisticated technology and has	****	3
Environmental aspects	Not rated separately.	—	—
Overall sector prospects rating			10

166

Companies competitive capabilities analysis (Competitors A, B and C)

	A	B	C	A	B	C
Market position Market share	65%	25%	10%	****	***	***
Production capability Feedstock	Manufactures feedstock by slightly outdated process from bought-in precursors	Has own precursors. Feedstock manufactured by third party under process deal	Basic position in precursors. Has own second process for feedstock			
Process economics	Both A and B have own 'first generation' process supported by moderate process R&D capacity		C is licensing second generation process from Eastern Europe			
Hardware	A and B each have one plant sufficient to sustain their respective market shares		None as yet. Market product imported from Eastern Europe			
Overall production capability ratings				****	***	**(*)
Product R&D (in relation to market position)	Marginally weaker	Comparable	Stronger	****	***	**(*)
Overall competitors' ratings				10/12	6/12	4/12

TABLE 2. Example of Weightings on Company's Competitive Capabilities Axis

	Businesses			
	W	X	Y	Z
Selling and distribution	2	3	6	3
Problem solving	2	4	3	1
Innovative R&D	4	1	0	1
Manufacturing	2	2	1	5
	10	10	10	10

Interpretation of Matrix Positions

The results of the hypothetical example in Table 1 can be plotted on the matrix as shown in Figure 2.

Since the various zones of the matrix are associated with different combinations of sector prospects and company strength or weakness, different product strategies are appropriate to them. These are indicated by the various key words which suggest the type of strategy or resource allocation to be followed for products falling in these zones.

The zones covered by the various policy key words are not precisely defined by the rectangular subdivision arbitrarily adopted for the matrix. Experience suggests that:

a. The zones are of irregular shape;
b. They do not have hard and fast boundaries but shade into one another; and
c. In some cases they are overlapping.

The most appropriate boundaries can only be determined after further practical experience of comparing business characteristics with positions plotted in the matrix.

Matrix Positions in the Right Hand Column

Leader. Competitor A, the largest producer with the lowest unit costs and a commanding technical situation, is in the highly desirable position of leader in a business sector with attractive prospects. His indicated strategy is to give absolute priority to the product with all the resources necessary to hold his market position. This being a fast growing sector he will, before long, need to install extra capacity. Although in all probability he is already earning satisfactory profits from Product X his current cash flow from this source may not be sufficient to finance a high rate of new investment. In that case the cash must be found from another sector of his

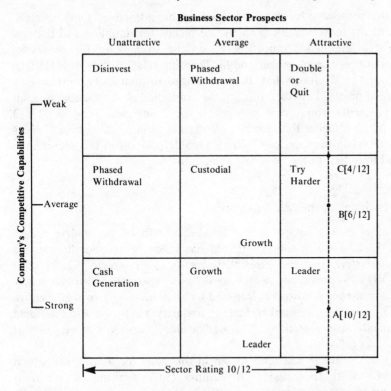

FIGURE 2. Comparison of competitive capabilities—Product X.

business. Later, as the growth rate slows down Product X should be able to finance its own growth and eventually to become a net generator of cash.

However, in this hypothetical example, competitor A's position on process and feedstock economics is threatened by second generation processes. This suggests that he may need to strengthen his process R & D. A production capability of one star below market position reflects A's slight weakness in this area.

Try Harder. Competitor B is in this position. It implies that products located in this zone can be moved down towards at least an equality position by the right allocation of resources. However competitor B does not appear to have any very special advantages in this sector and unless he can strengthen his position by, for example, licensing one of the new processes, he may be condemned to remain No. 2. This is not necessarily an unacceptable position in the short term but is likely to become increasingly vulnerable with the passage of time.

Double or Quit. This is the zone of the matrix from which products that are destined to become the future high fliers should be selected. A company should not normally seek to diversify into any new sector unless the prospects for it are judged to be attractive. Only a small number of the most promising should be picked for doubling and the rest should be abandoned. Competitor C, on the strength of his successful feedstock process development and his licensing relationships with Eastern Europe for the X process has already decided to double, i.e., invest in a commercial plant. He is therefore on the borderline of the Double or Quit and Try Harder zones: his production capability and product R & D ratings are both higher than his present market rating. Competitor C faces a more uncertain prospect of reaching a viable position in this sector than if he had been first in the field like competitor A.

Matrix Positions in the Middle Column

Business sectors falling in the middle column of the matrix are in general those in which market growth has fallen to around the average for the industry. In many cases they are the high growth sectors of a decade or two previously which have now reached maturity. Sector prospects can range, however, from 0.33 (below average) to 0.66 (above average) according to market quality, industry feedstock situation and environmental considerations. The significance of the key words in this column is as follows:

Growth. Products will tend to fall in this zone for a company which is one of two to four major competitors (four star market position) backed up by commensurate production capability and product R & D. In this situation no one company is in a position to be a leader and the indicated strategy for the companies concerned is to allocate sufficient resources to grow with the market in anticipation of a reasonable rate of return.

Products in this zone will in general be earning sufficient cash to finance their own (medium) rate of expansion.

Custodial. A product will fall in the custodial zone of the matrix when the company concerned has a position of distinct weakness either in respect of market position (below three star), process economics, hardware, feedstock or two or more of these in combination. Typically, custodial situations apply to the weaker brethren in sectors where there are too many competitors. The indicated strategy in these situations is to maximize cash generation without further commitment of resources.

Matrix Positions in the Left Hand Column

Business sectors falling in this column are those in which a growth rate below the average for the industry as a whole is combined with poor market quality and/or weaknesses in the industry feedstock situation and environmental outlook. A typical case would be a sector in which the product itself is obsolescent and is being replaced by a quite different product of improved performance and environmental acceptability or one in which the product is serving a customer-dominated industry which has fallen into a low rate of growth.

Cash Generation. A company with a strong position in such a sector can still earn satisfactory profits and for that company the sector can be regarded as a cash generator. Needing little further finance for expansion it can be a source of cash for other faster growing sectors.

Phased Withdrawal. A company with an average-to-weak position in a low-growth sector is unlikely to be earning any significant amount of cash and the key word in this sector is phased withdrawal. This implies that efforts should be made to realize the value of the assets and put the money to more profitable use. The same policy would apply to a company with a very weak position in a sector of average prospects.

Disinvest. Products falling within this zone are likely to be losing money already. Even if they generate some positive cash when business is good, they will lose money when business is bad. It is best to dispose of the assets as rapidly as possible and redeploy more profitably the resources of cash, feedstock and skilled manpower so released.

In general, unless the prospects for the sector have been completely transformed as the result of some rapid technological or environmental change, it will be rare for a well managed company to find that any of its business sectors lie within the disinvest area; it will be more usual for a company to be able to foresee the decline in sector prospects in the phased withdrawal stage.

The Second Order Matrix

The second order matrix enables one to combine two parameters of an *investment* decision. This is distinct from examining the parameters of product strategy, the object of the first order matrix. In this instance we are relating the product strategy parameters with our priorities in non-product strategy notably location and feedstock security aspects.

Table 3 shows a classification of the business sectors in Figure 1, in order of priority for resources. It will be noted that new ventures and double or quit businesses only receive attention after those with proven profitability or cash generation have been allocated sufficient resources to get the best advantage from existing commitments.

Table 4 shows a list of non-product strategic options. These will usually have been developed at the corporate level and the company management will have a clear idea of relative preferences.

These two desiderata can then be combined in the second order matrix shown as Figure 3. It will be noted that three of the businesses appear twice, as their future development can be used to satisfy alternative non-product priorities, whereas three of them do not appear at all.

TABLE 3.   Classification of Business Sectors in Order of Priority

Criteria	—Matrix position —Profit record —Other product related criteria —Judgement
Category I	Hard core of good quality business consistently generating good profits. Example: Engineering thermoplastic
Category II	Strong company position. Reasonable to good sector prospects. Variable profit record. Examples: Dyestuffs. Chlorinated Solvents
Category III	Promising product sectors new to company. Example: New Chemical Business
Category IV	Reasonable to modest sector prospects in which the company is a minor factor. Variable profit record. Example: Chemical Solvents
Category V	Businesses with unfavourable prospects in which the company has a significant stake. Example: Detergent Alkylate

TABLE 4.   Non-Product Strategic Options

Category	
1	—Joint venture to make olefins with petroleum company having secure oil feedstocks.
2	—Make maximum use of land and infrastructure at existing sites.
3	—Develop new major coastal manufacturing site in the EEC.
4	—Develop a foothold in the US market.
5	—Reduce dependence upon investment in Europe in order to spread risk. Develop manufacturing presence in, *inter alia,* Ruritania.

This matrix gives a very convenient method of presentation of priorities and feasible alternatives, from which the most appropriate decisions can be more easily resolved.

Other Uses of the DPM

In addition to the applications described, the Directional Policy Matrix can be used in several other ways.

Analysing the Dynamics and Financial Balance of the Portfolio

The general shape of the product matrix plot for a diversified business will give an insight into its financial position. Thus a company in which the majority of products plotted fall in the mature phase (cash generator or custodial) may be expected to generate more cash than it needs to

Product Rating by Category

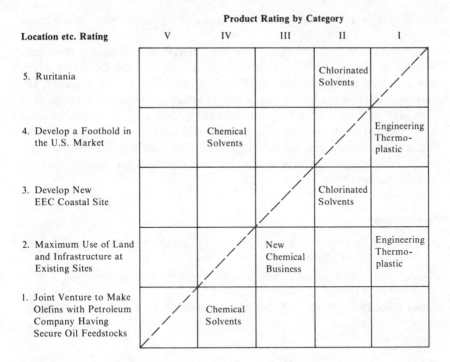

Location etc. Rating	V	IV	III	II	I
5. Ruritania				Chlorinated Solvents	
4. Develop a Foothold in the U.S. Market		Chemical Solvents			Engineering Thermo-plastic
3. Develop New EEC Coastal Site				Chlorinated Solvents	
2. Maximum Use of Land and Infrastructure at Existing Sites			New Chemical Business		Engineering Thermo-plastic
1. Joint Venture to Make Olefins with Petroleum Company Having Secure Oil Feedstocks		Chemical Solvents			

FIGURE 3.   Second order matrix.

pursue its total strategy. If so it must either seek new areas of business in the double or quit or try harder areas, or else act in effect as a banker to other businesses.

Conversely a company that has the majority of its individual product sectors in the double or quit, try harder or leadership areas will need more cash if it is to pursue the opportunities open to it.

Ideally the overall strategy should aim at keeping cash surplus and cash deficit sectors in balance, with a regular input or promising new business coming forward from research or to take up the surplus cash generated by the business already in or moving into the mature phase.

Building up a Picture of Competitors

The DPM can also be used to build up a qualitative picture of the product portfolios of other companies. Some insight into competitors' market positions, production capability and product R & D is in any case a prerequisite to arriving at one's own company's ranking in a particular sector. The matrix analysis will perform a useful function in codifying this information and highlighting areas where more needs to be obtained.

Once competitors' matrices have been plotted, and assuming that competitors will base their investment decisions on broadly the same logic, one can gain an insight into their likely future moves. For example, the matrix analysis will identify the points at which a competitor's production capability is weaker than his market position and hence will indicate that he is likely to lose market share unless he strengthens his position by further investment in manufacturing plant. Conversely it will also identify where production capability is stronger and a competitor is likely to seek to gain market share.

Bibliography

Planning a Chemical Company's Prospects, published by the Royal Dutch/ Shell Group of companies.

Perspectives: The Product Portfolio. The Growth Share Matrix. The Boston Consulting Group.

BARRY HEDLEY, "Strategy and the 'Business Portfolio,' " *Long Range Planning,* Vol. 10, February, 1973.

C.

Organizing for New Products

MOST COMPANIES find it virtually impossible to develop significant new products internally within organizational frameworks designed primarily to support current product-market operations. New organizational procedures and structures seem to be required.

The basic new product problem is defined in broad terms in extracts drawn from the classic Booz, Allen & Hamilton monograph on the subject. Johnson and Jones, in an equally classic piece, describe how a new product department should be organized. Wilemon and Hulett point out, however, that this type of arrangement functions well only when the new offerings in question bear a relatively close relationship to current product-market activities. For the identification and evaluation of new business opportunities which might lie somewhat further afield they recommend the venture group approach. Roberts takes a somewhat different tack, looking at the organizational challenge from the standpoint of the key staffing roles to be fulfilled in the innovation process. The Vanderwicken article from *Fortune* magazine concludes this section. An unusual piece, it is included because it offers a rare glimpse into the new product development efforts of Procter & Gamble, one of the nation's best-managed and most successful consumer goods companies.

14. A Program for New Product Evolution

Booz, Allen & Hamilton, Inc.

If the concept is accepted that products are the medium of business conduct, then business strategy is fundamentally product planning.

1. Products Defined in Business Terms

WHEN A COMPANY selects and develops a product, it is determining its customers, competitors, suppliers, facilities, skill needs, and the socio-economic environment that will form the perimeter of its opportunity for success.

Before proceeding with this premise, it is necessary to establish a common understanding of a new product. Here, it refers to a product that is new to the company, even though it may have been made in some form by others. Whenever the product is new to the company, the problems inherent will not have previously been faced by management and must be handled as a new product.

A product has two key dimensions. *Technology*—the fund of knowledge, technical and otherwise—enabling the product to be economically produced and *markets*—to whom and how the product is to be sold—enabling profitable distribution. These two characteristics are inseparable. An invention is not a new product until it is produced and distributed in a form that people can and will buy.

As shown in chart 1 there are varying degrees of product newness in each of the two dimensions. In the technological dimension, the requirements may range from no new technical knowledge, machinery or plant, to an entirely new spectrum of technical and production knowledge. The marketing requirements also range from no change in customers, selling, or channels of distribution to a need for developing new customers, a new

Reprinted from *Management of New Products*, pp. 7–12. © 1968 Booz, Allen & Hamilton Inc. Used by permission.

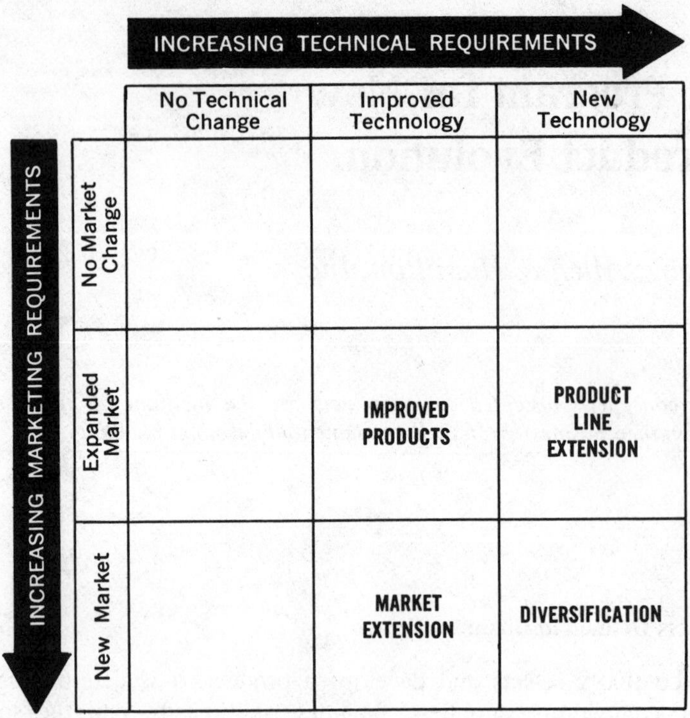

INCREASING TECHNICAL REQUIREMENTS

	No Technical Change	Improved Technology	New Technology
No Market Change			
Expanded Market		IMPROVED PRODUCTS	PRODUCT LINE EXTENSION
New Market		MARKET EXTENSION	DIVERSIFICATION

INCREASING MARKETING REQUIREMENTS

CHART 1.   Two-dimensional Characteristics of Products

sales force, and new distribution channels. Numerous variations in the degree of newness lie along both dimensions of this grid.

So far, two major dimensions of new products have been identified—technology and markets. Now a third is added—product evolution—or the time it takes to bring a product into existence. Chart 2 illustrates this dimension. As indicated by the arrow, a new products program begins with company objectives, which include product fields of interest, profit aims, and growth plans. The more specifically these objectives can be drawn, the greater guidance will be provided the new products program. For example, the company with the objective to grow ("no matter what field, so long as it is profitable") provides little, if any, guidance. On the other hand, if an objective is set—for example—to operate only in the field of high quality electronic measuring instruments, a starting point for guidance has been established.

Finally, it seems clear that the new products activity is a complex and often sizeable activity embracing the whole company. To manage such a complex activity, it is necessary to break it into functions and stages that can be managed.

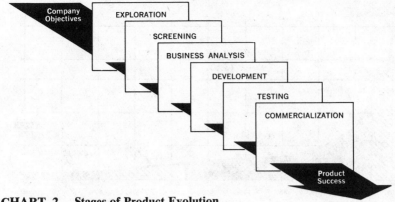

CHART 2. Stages of Product Evolution

2. The Stages of New Product Evolution

The new product process can be broken down into manageable stages for planning and control. Study of case histories reveals that there are six fairly clear stages, although the labels for such stages vary from company to company. These six stages also shown on chart 2 are:

- EXPLORATION—the search for product ideas to meet company objectives.
- SCREENING—a quick analysis to determine which ideas are pertinent and merit more detailed study.
- BUSINESS ANALYSIS—the expansion of the idea, through creative analysis, into a concrete business recommendation including product features and a program for the product.
- DEVELOPMENT—turning the idea-on-paper into a product-in-hand, demonstrable and producible.
- TESTING—the commercial experiments necessary to verify earlier business judgments.
- COMMERCIALIZATION—launching the product in full-scale production and sale, committing the company's reputation and resources.

Steps in these stages are further described in the Appendix.

3. Basic Characteristics of the New Product Process

The *decay curve for ideas* is characteristic of the process. As shown in chart 3 this is represented by the progressive rejection of ideas or projects by stage in the new product process. Although the rate of rejection varies some between industries and more markedly among companies,

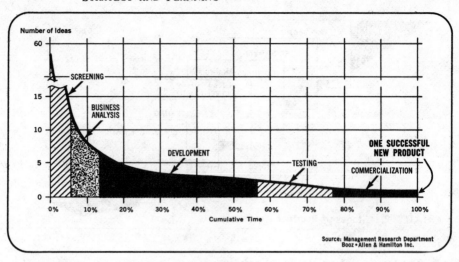

CHART 3.   Mortality of New Product Ideas
(By Stage of Evolution · 51 Companies)

the general shape of the decay curve is typical. As will be noted, it takes some 58 ideas to yield one successful new product.

Viewed from top management perspective, the process of new product evolution involves a series of management decisions. Each stage is progressively more expensive as measured in expenditures of both time and money.

Chart 4 shows the rate at which expense dollars are spent as time accumulates for the average project in a sample of leading companies. This illustrative chart is an industry average; the dotted line shows an all-industry average of capital expenditures concentrated in the last three stages of evolution.

4. The Objective of New Product Selection

Effectiveness in product selection can be measured in part by examining the degree to which projects in the company combine low risk and high payout. Most companies make a profit without approaching this degree of selectivity. However, profits tend to improve markedly in companies when management consciously seeks combinations of low risk and high payout, however rare.

5. The Opportunity for Improvement

Most companies do make a profit just like most men do make a living. But men and companies vary greatly in their level of earnings. The rate of

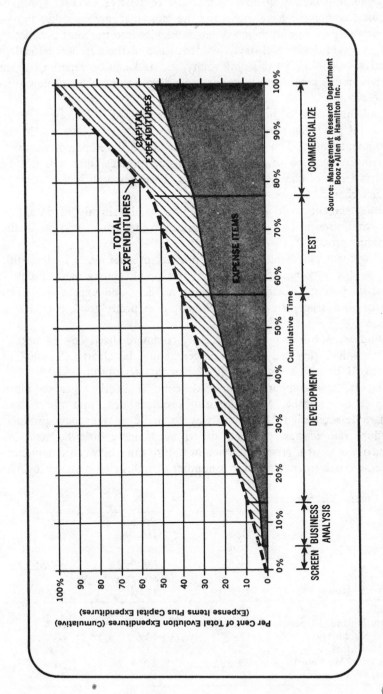

CHART 4.   Cumulative Expenditures and Time
(By Stage of Evolution • All-Industry Average)

181

growth can be generally taken as a measure of relative success. Throughout history, companies have prospered the most that, among other things, have purposely channeled their available energies into the most productive tasks they could devise and have avoided waste of their resources on less productive tasks. Against this philosophy, the data can be examined again to see how much companies today are spending on unsuccessful new product projects.

Of all the dollars of new product expense, almost three-fourths go to unsuccessful products; about two-thirds of these waste dollars are in the "development stage." Thus, about eight out of ten development scientists and engineers may be said to be working on projects that will not be justified in terms of commercial usefulness (basic research is not included here). See chart 5.

If management could decrease this waste only slightly, it would in theory—and often in fact—greatly enhance its effective manpower in the new product process.

Management judgment in the new product process meets its final test at the last stage—commercialization. At this point, management has pronounced its product worthy and says so publicly and expensively. The record for an average of prominent companies is pretty good, considering the hazards.

A study of 366 new products recently commercialized (by 54 prominent companies) revealed that 67 percent could be clearly classified as successful, 10 percent as failures, and 23 percent as doubtful.

However, few companies can take comfort in the success-failure average of two to one. Most doubtful products drift into the failure column, unless redesigned in some way to make another new product. The failure rate of new products differs surprisingly little between industries, but there is a great difference in failure rates between companies. The average performance rate for a number of industries is shown below.

Rate of Commercial Success

	New Product Ideas	Product Development Projects	New Products Introduced
		Success Percentages	
All Industry Groups	1.7%	14.5%	62.5%
Chemical	2%	18%	59%
Consumer Packaged Goods	2%	11%	63%
Electrical Machinery	1%	13%	63%
Metal Fabricators	3%	11%	71%
Non-Electrical Machinery	2%	21%	59%
Raw Material Processors	5%	14%	59%

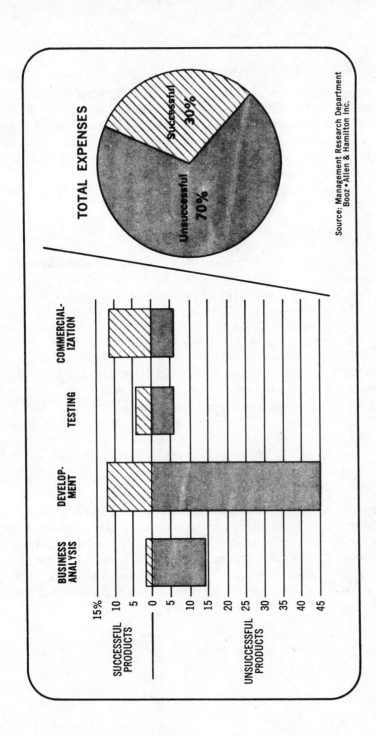

CHART 5. Effectiveness of New Product Expenditures

6. Conclusions on New Product Evolution

In examining the management process of new product evolution, the conclusion is reached that heavy attention should be focused on the first three stages. As will be remembered, these are the idea or concept stages. Experience of major companies indicates that most products fail because the idea or its timing was wrong and not because the company lacked the knowledge to develop and commercialize the product.

The following points emphasize the importance of the earlier stages of product evolution:

- In the commercialization stage, failures should occur rarely in well managed and adequately financed companies because successful companies know pretty well how to produce and sell. Such companies feel that their failures can usually be traced to an earlier stage and reflect weakness in the product concept itself.
- Failures that occur in the testing stage, while not as expensive as commercialization failures, are significant in the manpower and dollar losses incurred. Too many products fail in testing for non-technical reasons. Many of these problems could have been anticipated before development if the product concept had been evaluated more fully at the earlier stages of evolution.
- As for the development stage, experienced companies in R&D say, in effect, "Our men can develop anything. Show me enough sales and enough profit, and we'll spend the necessary time and money to develop it." Most *development* work, after all, should and does take place within technology largely understood at the outset of the project.

Therefore, well-managed companies can concentrate with advantage on the early stages of determining "what should be developed." It takes just as long and just as much money to develop a new product failure as it does to create a spectacular winner in the market place. There are plenty of problems to solve in the world. The secret of success is to be working on the problems which have solutions for which there is a marketable demand.

APPENDIX
Program Improvement Guidelines

The following list of points, made without comment, has helped increase success in many companies seeking to analyze, change, and improve their new product programs.

EXPLORATION

1. *Determine the product fields of primary interest to the company.*
   - Analyze major company problems.
   - Evaluate the company's principal resources.
   - Identify external growth opportunities ready for exploitation—expanding markets, technological breakthroughs, or rising profit margins.
2. *Establish a program for planned idea generation.*
   - Identify idea-generating groups.
   - Give them a clear concept of the company's interest fields.
   - Expose creative personnel to idea-generating facts.
   - Conduct exploratory technical research.
   - Utilize team approach.
   - Minimize distractions from current problems.
3. *Collect ideas through an organized network.*
   - Designate an idea collection point.
   - Establish comprehensive idea collection procedures.
   - Cover selected outside sources of ideas.
   - Solicit ideas actively and directly.
   - Consider each idea first on a "can-do" basis.
   - Treat the idea man with care.

SCREENING

1. *Expand each idea into a full product concept.*
   - Translate the idea into business terms.
   - Identify the key business implications of the product concept and its development.
   - Prepare a written proposal of the product idea.
2. *Collect facts and opinions, which are quickly available, bearing on the product idea as a business proposition.*
   - Select evaluation techniques to fit the specific idea.
   - Identify the best sources of facts and qualified opinions.
   - Use quick and inexpensive fact-gathering methods.
   - Apply strictly the principle of "diminishing returns" to fact-gathering.
3. *Appraise each idea for its potential values to the company.*
   - Estimate the magnitude of the profit opportunity.
   - Assess the investment, time, and risk requirements.

185

- Check the idea against other selection criteria.
- Provide for subsequent review of ideas discarded or shelved.

BUSINESS ANALYSIS

1. *Appoint persons responsible for further study of each idea.*
   - Select a small product team, representing major departments that would be affected by the product.
   - Tailor team size and composition to the nature of the product.
   - Select team members on the basis of their self-interest.
2. *Determine the desirable market features for the product and its feasibility.*
   - Determine characteristics of the market and its trends.
   - Appraise both competitors and their products—existing and potential.
   - Conduct experimental market and technical research, within budget limits established for preliminary investigation.
   - Identify "appeal" characteristics that would differentiate and sell the product.
   - Establish feasibilty of developing and manufacturing a product with these features.
3. *Develop specifications and establish a definite program for the product.*
   - Evaluate various business alternatives to determine desired product specifications.
   - Establish a timetable and estimate expenditures to evolve this product through succeeding stages.
   - Reduce the proposed idea to a specific business proposition in terms of time, costs, manpower, profits, and benefits.

- Get top management approval or revision of the product idea in terms of its specifications and program before authorizing the development stage.

DEVELOPMENT

1. *Establish development projects for each product.*
   - Explode the product proposal into as many projects as are required for administrative control.
   - Schedule these projects within the approved budget and timetable for the product.
   - Maintain the product team for company-wide coordination.
   - Pinpoint responsibility of all team members and identify them in all reports and records.
   - Establish yardsticks for measuring performance and progress.
2. *Build product to designated or revised specifications.*
   - Exhaust available information.
   - Maintain security against outside information leaks.
   - Continue market studies as a basis for enhancing product salability.
   - Hold to agreed specifications or make formal revisions by repeating the specification stage.
   - Keep top management informed; report promptly anticipated changes in objectives, schedule, or budget.
3. *Complete laboratory evaluation and release for testing.*
   - Complete laboratory tests to determine basic performance against specifications.
   - Provide checks and balances through organization and procedure to assure objectivity of product appraisal.

- Apply commercial rather than scientific standards to determine product release point.
- Prepare management report summarizing product description and characteristics; report project completion.

TESTING

1. *Plan commercial experiments necessary to test and verify earlier judgments of the product.*
   - Expand product team, if required.
   - Outline the nature and scope of commercialization phase.
   - Identify the major factors that must prove out to support successful commercialization.
   - Establish the standards by which product performance and market acceptance will be judged.
   - Plan test methods, responsibility, schedule, and cost.
   - Construct a testing program and recommend it to top management for their support and approval.
2. *Conduct in-use, production, and market testing.*
   - Continue laboratory testing.
   - Design and test production facilities.
   - Submit products to customer use for "abuse" testing.
   - Conduct test marketing programs in line with plans for commercialization.
   - Survey company, trade, and user reactions to the product and its commercialization program.
3. *Make final product decision; freeze design.*
   - Interpret test findings objectively; drop or modify products which fail tests.
   - Incorporate test findings in pro-

duct design and commercialization plans.
   - Detail the program for full-scale production and sales with a schedule, budgets, and manpower.
   - Recommend the product and its commercialization program, with full supporting data, to top management for final product decision.

COMMERCIALIZATION

1. *Complete final plans for production and marketing.*
   - Establish patterns for over-all direction and coordination of the product.
   - Expand product team to encompass all departments involved.
   - Designate individuals responsible for each part of the commercialization program.
   - Assure that these individuals work out all program details to fit coordinated plan.
2. *Initiate coordinated production and selling programs.*
   - Brief all participating personnel.
   - Maintain established program sequence and schedule.
   - Provide feedback mechanisms for program corrections.
3. *Check results. Make necessary improvements in product, manufacturing, or sales.*
   - Make design changes promptly to correct "bugs."
   - Work continuously for cost reduction and quality control.
   - Shape the product and its program to meet competitive reaction and changing internal pressures.
   - Maintain necessary team members until the product is a going commercial success, absorbed by established organization.

15. How to Organize for New Products

Samuel C. Johnson and Conrad Jones

If a steady stream of new products is the key to continued success, then specialized organization is the answer to the question of how to make the most of them. This is the classic article on this subject.

Location and Responsibility

THE SELECTION and development of new products must, in the final analysis, be the responsibility of top management. Not only does this determine the fundamental nature of a business, but the product line establishes the limit of opportunity for maintaining and expanding a company. Also, product plans are at the heart of competitive strategy; they are the starting point for over-all corporate planning, since they determine capital, personnel, and facility requirements.

Of course, top management cannot carry out such a responsibility by itself. The question is how to go about organizing for it.

Need For Control

A typical company shows many symptoms of the need for systematic control of this complex activity, such as:

- The executives who want new products, but do not know or cannot agree on what kinds of products to be interested in.
- The laboratory crowded with development products, but with few new products coming out, and too many of these not paying off.

Reprinted from the *Harvard Business Review*, 35 (May–June, 1957), pp. 49–62. © 1957 by the President and Fellows of Harvard College.

Samuel Johnson is Chairman of S. C. Johnson & Son, Inc. Conrad Jones is a Group Vice President of Booz, Allen & Hamilton, Inc., Management Consultants.

- The "orphan" project that goes on and on because nobody has given it the thought or had the heart to kill it.
- The "bottomless hole" product that took three times as long and cost five times as much as expected, and finally got to market behind all other competitors.
- The product with "bugs" that were hidden until 10,000 came back from consumers.
- The "me too" product that has no competitive reason for existence.
- The scientific triumph that turned out to have no market when someone thought to investigate it.

No single existing department can be held responsible for these problems in the new product process; all are involved in it. If the rate of activity is more than a handful of projects—and large companies count their development projects in the hundreds—top management simply does not have the time to assume direct supervision and coordination of all the tasks involved. Thus, more and more companies are reaching the conclusion that somebody must be put specifically in charge of the new product effort and held accountable for it.

Special Department

Executives considering the establishment or operation of such a department have three fundamental questions to answer.

- How can I define the new product function clearly enough to delegate responsibility?
- How should I structure this department in my company organization?
- How should this department be staffed, and how will these people operate?

Each company must find the answers, of course, in terms of its own unique characteristics and requirements. However, there are fundamental concepts that can be drawn from the experience of others to provide a useful frame of reference. In the interests of brevity and consistency, we shall confine ourselves to illustrations from a single case study of S. C. Johnson & Son, Inc., makers of Johnson Wax products.

Case Study

The idea for the organization of a new products department at S. C. Johnson & Son, Inc., grew out of examination of the management problems inherent in new product activity.

An active and growth-minded company, especially in an industry characterized by products of relatively short life cycles, has many items in varying degrees of creation and exploitation. Every department of the company is involved in some degree and some way. At any given moment a cross section of the workday of the company would show a bewildering tangle of interrelated activities and decisions on new products.

This diverse activity, multiplied by 100 or more projects, forms a maze in which it is all too easy to lose the thread of continuity. Problems breed rapidly in such an environment. However, the administrative problems that arise can be traced to these basic needs:

- *Classification*—to determine what handling each kind of new product proposal ought to receive.
- *Coordination*—to assure continuity and cooperation in evolution of each new product from idea to market introduction.
- *New knowledge*—to provide information for decisions on products with which the company has had no direct prior experience.

Analysis of these needs leads to the concepts underlying new product organization.

Classification

A large part of the problem of assigning responsibilities has proved to be a simple lack of definition. Identification of the new product function began to emerge at S. C. Johnson & Son, Inc., when the different kinds and degrees of product "newness" were related and defined so that responsibility for each kind could be sorted out and assigned. Definition rests on these concepts:

- A "product" is conceived by the matching of a technology and a market and therefore has two principal "dimensions."
- A product can be "new" in either one or both of these two dimensions.
- "New"—for the purposes of company organization—means only that the product is new to this company.

The simplest classification of new products can now be drawn by arraying the broad technological and market objectives of the company against each other, by degrees of newness in two dimensions, as shown in exhibit I. This chart unlocks the complex departmental relationships involved in the evolution of new products; different products are handled differently, in accordance with the kind of newness involved in each case.

This, then, is the first function of a new products department—to identify, isolate, and classify each new product idea. And this implies an objective, company-wide viewpoint.

			INCREASING TECHNOLOGICAL NEWNESS ⟶	
	PRODUCT OBJECTIVES	**NO TECHNOLOGICAL CHANGE**	**IMPROVED TECHNOLOGY** To utilize more fully the company's present scientific knowledge and production skills.	**NEW TECHNOLOGY** To acquire scientific knowledge and production skills new to the company.
	NO MARKET CHANGE		**Reformulation** To maintain an optimum balance of cost, quality, and availability in the formulas of present company products. Example: use of oxidized microcrystaline waxes in Glo-Coat (1946).	**Replacement** To seek new and better ingredients or formulation for present company products in technology not now employed by the company. Example: development of synthetic resin as a replacement for shellac in Glo-Coat (1950).
INCREASING MARKET NEWNESS	**STRENGTHENED MARKET** To exploit more fully the existing markets for the present company products.	**Remerchandising** To increase sales to consumers of types now served by the company. Example: use of dripless spout can for emulsion waxes (1955).	**Improved Product** To improve present products for greater utility and merchandisability to consumers. Example: combination of auto paste wax and cleaner into one-step "J-Wax" (1956).	**Product Line Extension** To broaden the line of products offered to present consumers through new technology. Example: development of a general purpose floor cleaner "Emerel" in maintenance product line (1953).
	NEW MARKET To increase the number of types of consumers served by the company.	**New Use** To find new classes of consumers that can utilize present company products. Example: sale of paste wax to furniture manufacturers for Caul Board wax (1946).	**Market Extension** To reach new classes of consumers by modifying present products. Example: wax-based coolants and drawing compounds for industrial machining operations (1951).	**Diversification** To add to the classes of consumers served by developing new technical knowledge. Example: development of "Raid" – dual purpose insecticide (1955).

EXHIBIT I.   Classification of New Products by Product Objective

Coordination

When the responsibilities of the marketing department and the R&D department are overlaid on the product classification chart, a large area of joint responsibilities shows up, as indicated by exhibit II. Where there are joint responsibilities, there is a need for coordination of the people and activities involved—and it is exactly here, and here only, that the authority of the new products department is required.

Coordination means providing continuity for a new product through its full process of evolution, including:

- *Exploration*—searching for ideas to meet company product objectives.
- *Screening*—weighing technological, market, and other considerations which determine whether or not the idea is of interest to the company.

PRODUCT EFFECT	NO TECHNOLOGICAL CHANGE Does not require additional laboratory effort.	IMPROVED TECHNOLOGY Requires laboratory effort utilizing technology presently employed, known, or related to that used in existing company products.	NEW TECHNOLOGY Requires laboratory effort utilizing technology not presently employed in company products.
NO MARKET CHANGE Does not affect marketing programs.		Reformulation	Replacement
STRENGTHENED MARKET Affects marketing programs to present classes of consumers.	Remerchandising	Improved Product	Product Line Extension
NEW MARKET Requires marketing programs for classes of consumers not now served.	New Use	Market Extension	Diversification

KEY: Research and Development Department   Marketing Department

Joint Responsibility of R & D and Marketing Departments

EXHIBIT II. Relationship of New Product Responsibilities by Department

- *Proposal*—analyzing and converting an idea into a concrete recommendation, and deciding to undertake a development project.
- *Development*—turning an approved idea into a demonstrable and producible item.
- *Testing*—conducting the product and market tests required to confirm earlier judgments and to finalize plans for production and marketing.
- *Commercialization*—launching the new product full-scale in both production and distribution.

Coordination also means maintaining communication and directing the relationships of personnel in all company departments, as required in each phase of this complex evolution process; for every company department is involved in some way and to some extent in every one of these six phases. For example:

> The development of "J-Wax," a combination cleaner and paste wax for automobiles, introduced successfully last spring, required decisions by the *marketing department* on the sales opportunity and the effect on automobile products already in the line; by the *R&D department* on the per-

EXHIBIT III.   Requirements for Information Outside the Scope of Present Business

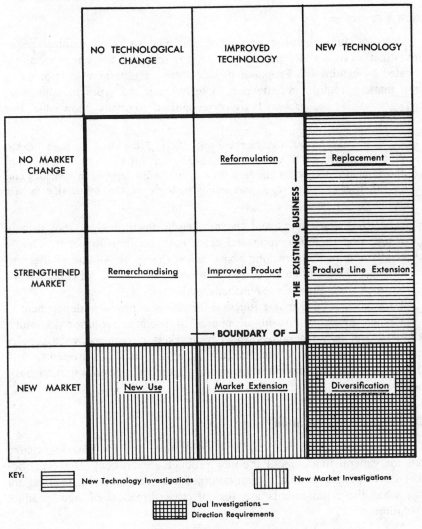

	NO TECHNOLOGICAL CHANGE	IMPROVED TECHNOLOGY	NEW TECHNOLOGY
NO MARKET CHANGE		Reformulation	Replacement
STRENGTHENED MARKET	Remerchandising	Improved Product	Product Line Extension
NEW MARKET	New Use	Market Extension	Diversification

THE EXISTING BUSINESS — BOUNDARY OF

KEY:

New Technology Investigations

New Market Investigations

Dual Investigations — Direction Requirements

formance characteristics that could be achieved; by the *production department* on the adaptability of present machinery; and by the *administrative
departments* on the availability of necessary working capital and personnel.

Only a few weeks of lost motion in the coordination of this product
would have cost heavily in the competitive advantages resulting from the
early introduction date actually achieved.

Thus a second and more fundamental function of the new products
department is to guide the continuity of evolution for proposed new products from exploration to commercial products, and promote interdepartmental cooperation during each step of this process. And this implies
independent status for the department, reporting to the chief executive
officer.

New Knowledge

New product planning, operation, and analysis often require special
investigation or activity beyond the present scope of the business, as indicated by exhibit III. Proposed products that involve new technology or
new markets require investigation of techniques and types of consumers
that are outside the present body of recognized company knowledge. For
example:

> The development and marketing of "Raid," the dual purpose insecti-
> cide introduced by S. C. Johnson & Son, Inc., this past summer, involved
> the company deeply for the first time in the technology of insecticides and
> in the needs, habits, and purchasing patterns of the housewife in her
> battle against insects.

The R&D department and the marketing department do not usually
have this kind of information and often have no time to get it. This is
especially true in the screening phase, when the sheer volume of ideas to
be considered would mean constant interruption of the scheduled work
upon which the company's revenues depend.

So there is a third major function for the new products department—
to conduct investigations in all phases of product evolution in which
knowledge of new technology and new markets is required, as a supplement to the activities of the marketing and the R&D departments. And
this implies a staff of specialists trained in technical, marketing, and business research.

Departmental Organization

The need for classification, for coordination, and for new knowledge
sets the general functions of the new products department. However, before developing a plan of organization, agreement must be reached on
just what the requirements are for effective direction of new product
evolution.

A minimum listing calls for a breakdown of requirements of each phase of evolution in terms of three basic steps for each phase—what is to be done, doing it, and evaluating what has been done. This breakdown yields only a sparse outline, but does provide a skeleton for the organizational provisions needed to meet these requirements. The executives of S. C. Johnson & Son, Inc., have agreed on the outline in exhibit IV.

In addition to these basic provisions for each phase, all of the phases in new product evolution should be linked together by added provisions for continuity, control, and completeness:

1. The originator or chief advocate of a proposed product idea should participate formally in all phases until the product is in full production and sale as an established product in the line.
2. The person who will be responsible for marketing the product should participate formally in development of the product, as well as its test marketing.
3. The person who is responsible for development work in the laboratory should participate in formulating design objectives and follow the production on through the testing phase.
4. One organizational unit should guide the complete process of product evolution on every new product.
5. All programs for each phase of product evolution should be spelled out concretely.
6. Check lists should be provided for the programs to be completed in each phase of evolution.
7. Responsibility for each phase, each step, and each task in each product's evolution should be pinpointed on one individual.
8. This responsible individual should have a reporting relationship through which interdepartmental coordination can be promoted fully.
9. Information on all product proposals under development should be consolidated, summarized, and re-evaluated in business terms at frequent intervals.
10. A full case history should be assembled continuously on each new product as it evolves.
11. Criteria for judgment at all points of decision should be pre-established.
12. Development of proposed products should be either actively in work or formally shelved.

Place in Company Structure

Concepts and requirements, when merged, sketch a picture of a department which:

Requirements for effective direction and coordination of product evolution	Organizational provisions needed to meet these requirements
Exploration Phase	
1. Areas of company interest (in terms of potential products) clearly stated and widely understood.	1. A single executive charged with the specific responsibility to focus and coordinate searches for new opportunities in technology and markets.
2. Full and programed coverage of all productive sources of ideas.	2. Specialized personnel, free of responsibilities for present products, to conduct supplementary exploration of unrelated markets and technology in a neutral environment.
3. Complete capture of all ideas for proposed products to assure that each is considered.	3. A central collection station to record and process all ideas and the data supporting them.
Screening Phase	
1. Standards for the measurement of proposed product ideas against company product policy.	1. Authority to determine the criteria and method by which each idea will be judged.
2. Complete and careful consideration of each idea by the persons best qualified to judge each screening factor.	2. Authority to select screening participants and to secure formal replies to specific questions.
3. Evaluation of ideas for their commercial value prior to committing development funds and manpower.	3. Skilled personnel to secure the data necessary for early commercial evaluation and to summarize all facts and opinions as a basis for deciding the disposition of each idea.

Proposal and Development Phases

1. A management commitment of willingness to accept and utilize a product before development is begun.

2. Continuing liaison and agreement between marketing, R & D, other departments, and top management during the development phase.

3. Complete and realistic evaluation of the performance characteristics and market acceptance of the product developed.

1. Formal construction and authorization of a concrete development proposal, in business terms: a product of stated characteristics by a specific date, at an approved development cost.

2. Direction of the interdepartmental relationships required during development; preparation of regular summary status reports to top management.

3. Impartial review and audit of all new product data developed prior to top-management decisions based on these data.

Test Marketing Phase

1. Opportunity to exploit all products developed, even if judged unsatisfactory for further commitment of company resources.

2. Complete and careful programing and control for test marketing, product testing, and early production.

3. Complete and realistic appraisal of product, production, and market testing results.

1. Perspective and personnel to acquire or dispose of products outside established company channels.

2. Coordination and guidance of committee work and the preparation of progress reports to top management.

3. Perspective to help establish evaluation criteria and review results impartially.

EXHIBIT IV. Requirements and Organization of New Products Department

197

- Reports to the executive vice president, in order to provide the stature and independence that are necessary for coordinating interdepartmental programs.
- Participates in actual work in proportion to the degree to which a proposed idea or a product is new to the company.
- Makes no decisions where responsibilities are clearly assigned to other departments.
- Has authority to make required decisions and the budget to implement these decisions in areas where the responsibility is assigned to the department.
- Draws on established departments as much as possible for their services in order to minimize duplications and conflicts.
- Houses its own specialists as required, in order to discharge its specific duties without interfering with other divisions.
- Provides its director with enough staff and freedom to participate in the broad affairs of the top planning committees of the company.

These characteristics call for a small department of specialists with a minimum of routine responsibilities. The operating departments of the company, particularly the marketing and R&D departments, should continue to carry the major work load in all product activities.

The new products department at S. C. Johnson & Son, Inc., reports directly to top management, rather than to R&D or marketing.

Operating Staff

The actual work on each project should be carried out by specific individuals drawn from as many departments as necessary. Each new proposal is unique in its requirements for development from idea to product, and therefore deserves a unique interdepartmental organization to nurture it. It would be impractical to staff the new products department with enough permanent employees to handle the full evolution of every proposed product.

At S. C. Johnson & Son, Inc., two kinds of "task forces" report to the new products director (see exhibit V). These are the principal vehicles for carrying forward new product activities in all departments:

1. *Sponsor groups* formulate a proposal and guide its development. Each group is formally charged, after the screening phase, with responsibility for successful development into a realistic product. The composition of the group is tailored to fit the specific product and its characteristics. Marketing, R&D, and the new products department are always represented; in addition, there may be one or two individuals drawn from other departments.

The sponsor group is a key provision in the organization of this new products department. It is the device through which the department discharges its responsibilities in the proposal and development phases. It provides minimum interference with the established departments and maximum reliance on their existing personnel and services. It represents, in effect, formal recognition of relationships among people who either do or should work together in any successful product development.

2. *Product committees* are formally organized with regular meetings and agenda, and have a large membership drawn from many departments —but the nucleus of each committee is the sponsor group that developed the product. The product committee is responsible for carrying a product, once developed, through to full-scale commercialization. At S. C. Johnson & Son, Inc., where test marketing is of major importance, the committee chairman is usually a product or sales manager.

The minutes of one week's conferences show that the product committee made these decisions:

- Ordered production molds.
- Recommended advertising copy and strategy (for top-management approval).
- Established delivery schedule with suppliers.
- Programmed additional product-in-use tests.

The committee also coordinates all activities of product introduction to the point where line responsibility for the new product has been permanently established and is operating smoothly.

The importance of these task forces is attested by the fact that the phases of new product evolution have come in practice to be called the "sponsor group phase" and the "product committee phase."

Functional Specialization

The over-all responsibilities of the new products department are broken down into four basic areas for purposes of internal organization:

1. *Administrative (internal)*—includes monitoring schedules, processing forms, maintaining records, and preparing reports.
2. *Marketing*—includes marketing research, analysis, and liaison with sales personnel.
3. *Technical*—includes technical research, analysis of technological factors, and liaison with R&D personnel.
4. *Negotiating (external)*—includes contacting outsiders for acquisitions, negotiations, patents, and product exploitation outside company facilities.

Of course, each member of the department participates in many sponsor groups and product committees and shares in a variety of cooperative tasks.

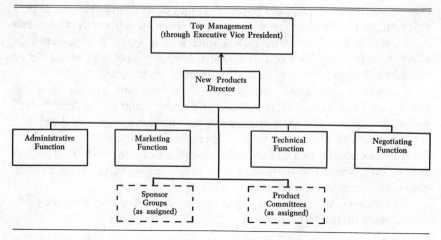

EXHIBIT V.   Plan of Organization, New Products Department,
S. C. Johnson & Son, Inc.

The responsibilities of each position are established in detail and the working relationships in each step of the total process defined. Similarly, the working relationships of the total department with each major department of the company are specified. Such detailing is important to effective operations, and must be tailored to each company. However, the broad division of responsibilities which is shown here is typical of other new products departments that have achieved a comparable level of specialization.

Operating Procedures

Effective communication channels are essential to new products evolution. Organization of the new products department at S. C. Johnson & Son, Inc., has been planned to assure that these communication channels could be easily maintained within the formal lines of organizational authority required for control (see exhibit VI).

The organizational responsibilities and working relationships have been given more specific expression by translating communications into procedures, with forms and records, for the conduct and control of new products activities.

The established procedures—carefully built and integrated—retain considerable flexibility to meet changing circumstances. There is a constant recycling of phases and steps as events unfold, but the recycling is formal, and control is maintained by phase even in the ebb and flow of this creative process.

The most important single form is probably the "product proposal" (exhibit VII) which is the basis of management control. It is this document

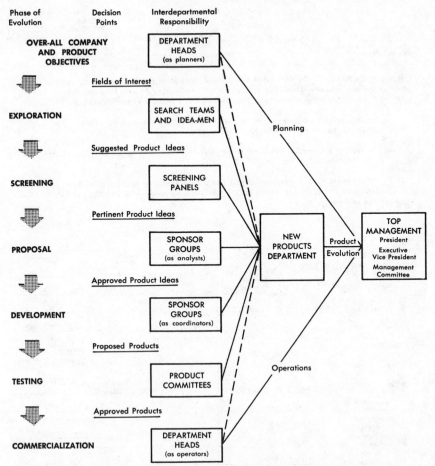

EXHIBIT VI. **Communications for Effective New Product Evolution**

which is prepared by the sponsor group for top management authorization of each new product before development and through which subsequent progress is followed. This form, with its summary data, has the merit of being on one page, and the total company new product effort can be assembled in a loose-leaf book of a size conducive to frequent executive review.

Budget Allocation

Organization and control are most clearly illustrated in the acid test of allocating the product development budget. The budget is allocated and controlled so that the marketing department, R&D department, and the new products department each has its own budget for development work—though, of course, all laboratory projects are actually carried out under

PRODUCT PROPOSAL

S. C. JOHNSON & SON, INC.
PRODUCT
PROPOSAL NO. 27

TYPE	PRIORITY	TITLE	DATE
Diversification	1	Space Deodorant	October 19, 1955

1. PROPOSAL OBJECTIVES: To develop a room deodorant in a pressurized container which performs in a manner which the housewife will recognize as being demonstrably better than competitive products. This is to be accomplished as follows:

    a. by neutralizing offensive odors rather than acting through olfactory desensitization and masking.

    b. by having a clean, fresh, low level odor (such as "the smell of the outdoors after a rain").

The product shall have a cost which will permit competitive pricing to yield a profit consistent with the company profit policy and shall be made with readily available materials and equipment.

2. ESTIMATED RETURN

A. PRESENT TOTAL MARKET FACTORY ANNUAL SALES	$ XX, 000, 000
B. ESTIMATED TOTAL MARKET IN FIVE (5) YEARS	$ XX, 000, 000
C. JOHNSON TARGET ANNUAL SALES (YR.)	$ X, 000, 000
D. ESTIMATED ANNUAL GROSS PROFIT _____%	$ X, 000, 000

3. ESTIMATED INVESTMENT

A. Est. SPONSOR GROUP PHASE COSTS	$ XX, 000
B. PRODUCT COMMITTEE PHASE COSTS	$ XX, 000
C. INTRODUCTION COSTS	$ XXX, 000
D. CAPITAL EXPENDITURES	$ XX, 000
E. TOTAL	$ XXX, 000

4. SCHEDULE

	PROPOSED	ACTUAL
A. APPROVAL OF PRODUCT PROPOSAL		Oct 31, 55
B. DEVELOPMENT START DATE	Nov 7, 55	Nov 7, 55
C. PRESENTATION OF DEVELOPMENT REPORT	Feb 17, 56	
D. PRESENTATION OF TEST MARKET PLANS	Mar 9, 56	
E. PRESENTATION OF FINAL SALES PLANS	Aug 24, 56	
F. FULL SALE BEGINS	Oct 1, 56	

5.

		BUDGET CURRENT SIX MONTHS TO 7 19 56	NEXT SIX MONTHS TO ____ 19 ___
A. R & D	(INSIDE)	$ X, 000	$ X, 000 $
	(OUTSIDE)	$ 000	$ 000 $
B. MRKTG.	(INSIDE)	000	000 $
	(OUTSIDE)	$ X, 000	$ X, 000 $
C. OTHER	(INSIDE)	$	$ $
	(OUTSIDE)	$	$ $
D. TOTAL		XX, 000	$ XX, 000 $

6.

		DIVISION
A. CHAIRMAN	W. M. Schmick	Mktg.
B.	C. T. Rood	R & D
C.	R. A. Graef	Adm. Mgt.
D.		
E.		
F.		
G.		

7. APPROVAL OF ITEMS INDICATED

ALL	Samuel C. Johnson NEW PRODUCTS DIRECTOR	10-20-55 DATE
1, 4F, 5B	R. W. Carlson MARKETING VICE PRESIDENT	10-25-55 DATE
1, 4C, 5A	J. V. Steinle R & D VICE PRESIDENT	10-28-55 DATE
1, 4, 5	H. M. Packard EXECUTIVE VICE PRESIDENT OR MANAGEMENT COMMITTEE	10-31-55 DATE

A-4   REV. 2

EXHIBIT VII.   Sample Product Proposal Form

the administration of the R&D department, and all market testing under the marketing department.

The product development budget components, with requisitioning authority and accounting procedure, are charted in exhibit VIII along with the budget components for basic research and the service functions of R&D.

It should also be noted that S. C. Johnson & Son, Inc., has product managers in its marketing department, who retain primary responsibility for their own product improvements. However, over-all control and co-ordination are exercised by the new products director, and the product manager is, in effect, a predetermined sponsor group chairman.

Only when the new products department function is conceived clearly enough to establish budget and accounting procedure for its area of responsibility is it practicable to consider that the organization has been defined.

EXHIBIT VIII. Basic Components of the Research and Development Budget (**Showing requisitioning authority and accounting procedure for expenditures**)

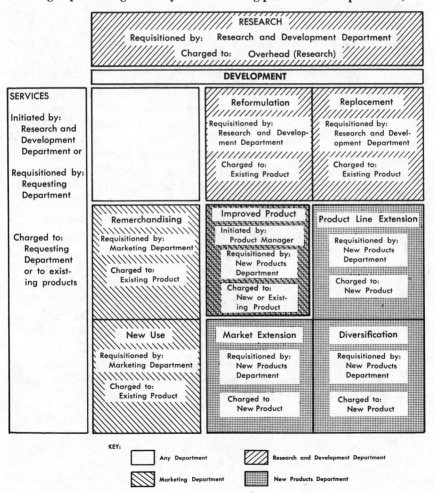

Conclusion

Every management that is convinced of the importance of new products is faced with this question of how to organize the new product function. At S. C. Johnson & Son, Inc., the program has been placed under a new products department, which reports to top management. Company executives see such noticeable benefits as these:

- The total product strategy of the company has been clarified and is scheduled toward specific products, which is the only possible approach to realistic long-range company plans.
- Enthusiasm of persons on product development teams is often lifted by the knowledge that management has already agreed to utilize the developed product and that management knows which individuals are working on it.
- Sponsor group and product committee activities are developing broader management skills for individuals at all levels, and their group efforts are clearly stimulating more creative ideas.
- The profit potential of projects is higher, because product selection standards have been upgraded and controlled toward the goal of maximum return on available resources and manpower.
- Lost effort has been reduced, with a lower mortality of products after development, thereby relieving staffing pressures in technical manpower and minimizing personal disappointments.
- Top management has a more complete picture of the current new product status in factual, condensed business terms; decisions are more prompt and based on fuller information.
- Management has been relieved of many part-time coordinating and supervisory requirements and has more time for analysis and judgment at critical decision points.
- In addition to the ideas generated, development on a number of long-considered new products is finally crystallized, and so more new products than ever before are on the way to market.
- The time required for a new product to go from idea to market place is noticeably faster because group work anticipates problems and devises solutions well in advance.
- Products created are more successful because the sales features are designed into the product proposal by team thinking before a full-scale development project is ever begun.

16. A Systems Approach to Corporate Development

David L. Wilemon and Porter L. Hulett

Most corporations are designed to "maintain" established businesses rather than to create new ones. This article discusses a systematic approach to developing new products and businesses for the large organization.

ONE OF THE MOST SIGNIFICANT challenges facing corporate executives is adaptability, i.e. changing their organizations to fit tomorrow's dynamic market environment. Ten plus years for product life cycles, for example, have often been telescoped to 3–5 years and sometimes less. Changing market demands, rapid growth in science and technology, foreign competition, and increased activity in research and development are but a few of the forces that are contributing to the evolutionary changes firms are now witnessing. No longer do corporations have the privilege of playing the game of 'catch up', rather, they must now detect, initiate, and most importantly, they must manage change to remain viable.

Barriers to Corporate Adaptability

In auditing corporate capabilities, executives frequently conclude that their organizations are designed primarily to 'maintain' established corporate functions rather than meet the challenges demanded by rapidly

Reprinted from *Long Range Planning*, 5 (March, 1972), pp. 46–51. Used by permission.

David Wilemon is a professor in the School of Management at Syracuse University. Mr. Hulett is an executive with a broadcasting company in Roanoke, Virginia. This article is based on their research on venture management in several high technology companies.

changing environmental demands.[1] In addition, managers frequently lament over the inability of their organizations to cope in an innovative vein with their external environment.

In recognizing the need for flexible environmental response capabilities, more and more companies are seeking various new organizational approaches which encourage individual initiative and creativity in finding and developing new business opportunities. As a consequence, a few progressive firms have begun to utilize such activities as new business development departments, venture groups, new product task teams, and new business research and development teams. Their missions are similar—finding new markets and business for their 'host' organization.

The objective of this paper is to view these emerging approaches to new business development in a larger context as critical components of a corporate 'refounding process'.[2] As entrepreneurs founded businesses, so must managers of large organizations devise methods to 'refound' new businesses, if they are to profitably adapt to the requirements of environmental change and its demands.

A Corporate "Refounding Process"—A Systems Approach

The purpose of the corporate refounding model described here is to depict one approach by which the 'refounding' process can be achieved. Such an approach provides a framework whereby a company may more adequately maintain itself in a state of adjustment with its operating environment. The approach discussed starts with the corporate long-range planning function and if successful, ends with the commercialization of new products and businesses (see figure 1). The basic responsibility of the Long-Range Planning Group in the total process is assisting in establishing corporate objectives and growth policies, and assisting in planning and the necessary corporate resources to achieve the company's desired growth objectives.

To assist in formulating and developing growth policies, however, the Long-Range Planning Group needs to know the status of the corporation in terms of its current businesses, especially as they are reflected at the

---

[1] Mack Hanan, Corporate Growth Through Venture Management, *Harvard Business Review*, p. 43 (Jan.–Feb. 1969). Also see R. W. Peterson, New Venture Management in a Large Company, *Harvard Business Review* (May–June 1967). He states (p. 68): "The chief deterrent to the success of a new venture in many cases is that the company is organized to run *today's* business. As a result, the structure for giving birth to tomorrow's business is often attached to, and dominated by, an organization fully occupied with the present."

[2] The term "Refounding Process" comes from R. W. Galvin's article "The Refounding Process in Business", appearing in the *Journal of Marketing*, Vol. 30, pp. 1–2 (Oct. 1966). The term is used in a more comprehensive vein in this paper.

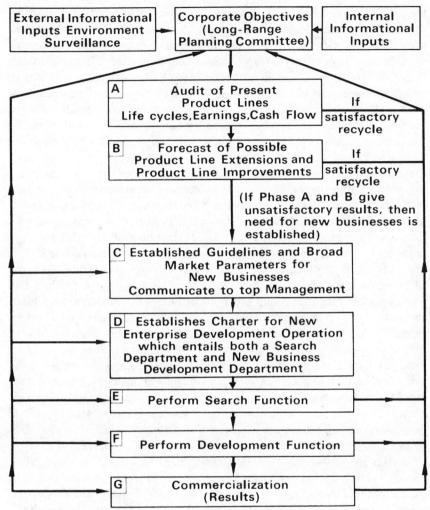

FIGURE 1.   Systems View of New Enterprise Development Activities

level of the individual product lines. This requires an intensive, multidimensional audit of the corporation's product lines to determine their significance to the company's long-term plans and growth prospects. In addition, it requires constant surveillance of the external environment and the internal variables and conditions which may affect the potential future directions which the corporation can take. The audit of the external variables, for example, entails auditing those changes in the market, society and the economy, for example, which affect the company while the internal data surveillance entails continuous analysis of information generated internally by the company's operations. Both kinds of informational inputs may signal needed corporate changes. As depicted in figure 1 (Phase A) the auditing process includes an in-depth analysis of both present and the project future of the company's existing product lines in terms of profits, cash flows, competitive pressures, costs, and forecasted life cycles. Once the audit for Phase A is completed, the Long-Range Planning Group then compares the results of the product line audit to the objectives which have been established for them. If the results of the audit are considered satisfactory, then the long-range planning system is recycled and planning for a new period commences. If, however, the audit is considered unsatisfactory to achieve desired objectives, further audits and analyses of the product lines are required. Those managers involved with managing the product are encouraged to seek product line improvements and to seek methods by which the product lines can be extended for additional profitability and customer satisfaction (Phase B). Projections for proposed product line improvements and extensions in terms of profits, cash flow data, costs, and so forth, are then sought. If projected earnings and other factors are considered satisfactory for the product line improvements, then the planning system recycles. If, however, the project results of product line improvements and extensions are not considered satisfactory to achieve the desired corporate objectives, then a 'need' for new businesses is established. Once the need for new products and businesses has been established by the long-range planning group it then becomes their function to *communicate* their findings to top management. In some cases the report of the Long-Range Planning Group to top management includes broad recommendations outlining some broad potential avenues for corporate development. (Phase C) If management agrees that new business development is essential to the long term objectives of the company, a decision may then be made to either establish or activate (if one is in existence) and develop a 'charter' for a New Enterprise Development Operation as depicted in Phase D which contains both a *New Business Search Department* and a *New Business Development Department*. The New Business Search Department is responsible for performing "searches" for new product and business ideas while the New Business Development Department is responsible for developing viable new business ideas produced by the Search Department (Phases F and G). An in-depth analysis of Phases D, E, F and G are examined in the following sections.

Establishing the New Enterprise Development Operation

The spectrum of alternatives which can be considered in developing new businesses is broad and can range from the external acquisition of a new business to developing new businesses and products via an internal new product/new business development program. To generate new businesses via external acquisition often entails the formation of an 'external acquisition group'.

This paper concentrates primarily on internal new product development activities as a means of establishing new products and businesses for a company. An internal New Enterprise Development operation may take many forms. As previously alluded, the approach described here entails both a *New Business Search Department* and a *New Business Development Department*.

The responsibility for establishing the 'charter' delineating the mission of the New Enterprise Development group largely should fall to the manager directly charged with the mission for generating new businesses. In developing his charter he is often assisted by a committee composed of key corporate officers, the Long-Range Planning Group, and various line and staff personnel.

A basic necessity of those charged with creating the charter is to examine the objectives (i.e., scope as set forth by long-range planning operations) and refine them into more meaningful and concrete guidelines which can then be used by all the personnel in the New Enterprise Development Group. A rather typical charter for a New Enterprise Operation, containing both a *Search Department* and a *New Business Development* operation might resemble the following.[3]

Charter for Search Operations—Conduct searches and make evaluations of new product ideas within the parameters outlined by long-range planning and outside the short term interests of the corporate operating divisions for new and expanding markets. Such new business ideas should allow the firm to gain some proprietary position (hopefully through patent protection) and show considerable promise in developing corporate revenues.

Charter for Development Operations—Prepare a full and in-depth analysis of business ideas proposed by the new business search operations and recommend and implement a complete market entry plan. The business development plan should include production facility requirements, production and marketing manpower needs, product concepts, advertising and promotion strategy, channels of distribution to be used plus a complete financial analysis relating new cash inflows to original and anticipated capital investment over the expected lifetime of the business culminating in an anticipated after tax cash inflow sufficient to provide X per cent R.O.I. over T_n years. In making the analysis and recommendation, use should be made of various analytical techniques as they are needed.

After delineating the scope of his charter and eliciting top management approval, the New Enterprise Development manager needs to coordinate it with Long Range Planning.

Organizationally, it is not unusual for the manager of the New Enter-

[3] For a rather detailed description of the criteria one company employs in selecting and evaluating new businesses, see: R. C. Springborn, New Ventures Division at W. R. Grace & Company. *Research Management*, XII (No. 4), pp. 276–277 (July 1969).

prise Operation to report to the Chief Executive Officer or at least at the company's vice-presidential level. The New Enterprise Development Manager usually draws his personnel from the various line and staff functions of the company. Frequently managers charged with New Enterprise Development Operations attest that it is most desirable if the group members are assigned to them on a full-time basis—if their services can be spared from their normal work units.

Moreover, while not always feasible, managers responsible for New Enterprise Development operations almost always recommend separating their operations from the mainstream of the company's normal activities. One advocate of this approach put it this way:

> As a simple illustration, let's look at a corporation having three operating divisions, each with its own sales, production, and technical departments. These established operations are concentrating daily on producing goods, distributing them, selling them, and improving them, all within the framework of sales forecasts and profit objectives. This leads to a multitude of short-term programs and pressures which greatly limit the division's freedom to explore wholly new developments, especially in business fields not related to existing business. New business development is a long-term proposition; if it is too closely associated with operating functions, it tends to be neglected, restricted, or even cannibalized when operating problems occur.[4]

In addition to separating the New Enterprise Development Operations from the 'mainstream' operating groups, management also needs awareness that the personnel associated with New Enterprise Development Operations cannot normally be evaluated by the same yardsticks as a line manager or staff person. As one manager related, "you just don't know when you're going to have a breakthrough on a new idea—it may be tomorrow and again you may fail completely."

New Business Search Department

The Search operation is both an entrepreneurial and a market oriented function whose responsibility is to find either existing or potentially profitable markets located within the broad market parameters originally set forth by long range planning and further refined by the New Enterprise Development charter. Although the search function may involve reviews of present corporate capabilities and technologies in terms of *new* markets, it also may involve investigating entirely new technologies and new markets for the company. In other words, its primary orientation may be towards finding new market opportunities, utilizing existing corporate capabilities in a different vein or in exploring markets and new tech-

---

[4] R. M. Adams, An Approach to New Business Ventures, *Research Management,* XII (No. 4), pp. 257–258 (July 1969).

nologies entirely. In two high technology firms, for example, the activities of their Search Departments were devoted almost exclusively to seeking applications in new markets of their company's technology. The search activities in these cases required intensive interfacing with the technical laboratories of their companies.

A Search group may consist of three or four relatively young, imaginative men from various backgrounds, i.e., marketing, production, engineering, etc. In one company, their function was to assess ideas which could be obtained from a number of sources, such as market research data, trade literature, salesmen, outside inventors, consulting firms, licensing organizations, consumer studies, etc. Their output in terms of a report for those ideas which appeared to have commercial potentials included a preliminary investigation of the product idea to determine both its financial and its market feasibility. The output of a search group of a large packaging firm, for example, consisted of the following: A technical and marketing feasibility report on the use of paperboard cans for packaging a high volume convenience food. The report included a study of market trends and projections for packaging these products and as assessment of the feasibility of entering the market with a substitute package concept. The technical modifications necessary to use paperboard cans for the new application were also detailed. Preliminary estimates of the potential sales and profits for the proposed product line were also developed in the report.

If a Search group's output appears favorable, the normal course of events is to present the idea to the New Business Development Department for further analysis of its commercial potentialities and development.

In some cases, if the new product idea is accepted by the New Business Development Dapartment, the 'searcher' for the idea may then join the development group as a regular team member; he may serve as a consultant; or he may recycle back and begin his search activities again on a new product idea.

It should be noted that while some companies use many of the same personnel for both the new business search and development functions, others have employed separate teams of personnel. One manager responsible for a new business development operation in a large technical company explained his rationale for separating the personnel in the two functions this way:

> There's a big difference in the activities that are performed in the New Business Search and Development areas. In our Search operations, for example, I need creative people—people who have lots of imagination, who will constantly ask, "Will this idea work? Where? What is the size of the market? Who can assist me in developing it?" and so forth. Now, the skills required of the people in our Development Department are a little different. They need to know about distribution, advertising, contract agreements, and how to develop, launch, and maintain a product. I'm not saying

a man can't do both, some can, but we've been most successful in separating the Search and Development functions.

At the present time there are no clear indicators regarding whether having a distinct Search group and a distinct Development group is more effective than combining the two functions into an 'integrated team approach.'

New Business Development Department

The New Business Development group has the responsibility, often by the use of 'venture teams' to further evaluate the new business ideas presented by the search group through a series of analytical steps. The use of venture teams in new business development operations is a relatively new organizational approach for actualizing innovation. Its emergence has been fostered as a result of the need to give direct responsibility to a specific group for the development of new business potentials. Their primary objective is to make an in-depth analysis of the commercial feasibility of new business ideas. The scope of their responsibility varies from company to company. Some companies, for example, require their new business development groups to continue with the idea until it is ready for market launch while others recommend that the development group actually launch the product. One of the major advantages in using a venture management approach in the business development operations is that it potentially can foster an entrepreneurial spirit.[5] Entrepreneurship and risk-taking by the venture team is a key ingredient to the effective development of new businesses. As one manager stated: "A venture group has to be entrepreneurial—they can't be regimented since each product idea is different—you can't build a mold for this kind of team." Key managers and staff personnel with broad experience, often composed of marketing, finance, manufacturing, and from the technical areas, are chosen for V-team assignments. Although venture team members usually are drawn from the existing functions of the company, it is not a necessary condition for venturing. One company, for example, had a venture team completely composed of experts recruited from outside the company.

Through the use of various forms of venture teams, large corporations are not only able to capitalize on the strength of their functional expertise but they also are able to approach the flexibility and adaptability typically

---

[5] Venture team management differs from traditional product management concepts in that venture managers most often have full line authority over their immediate team members whereas product managers do not possess line authority and must, therefore, rely more on interpersonal skills in performing their role. As defined here, the venture team approach also differs from the task force and special project team approach in that the latter are normally confined to working on very specific, isolated problems as contrasted to venture teams who have the broad spectrum of responsibility in developing entire new business programs.

associated with smaller firms and so necessary when coping with rapidly changing market environments.

The responsibilities of the venture team begin once the team members have been chosen and they have accepted the new business or product idea from the Search team. The function of the V-team during the initial phases of its operation is to further examine the market potentials for the proposed ideas under consideration and to further delineate the potential market and its characteristics. As one New Business Development Manager stated: "Our objective is to put a lot of meat on the ideas that the guys in the Search Department give us."

Most importantly, the financial implications of the proposed product for the company must be further delineated. The V-team, for example, needs to further examine the new business proposal to determine if it can gain a proprietary position for a product in a particular market; to refine the volume forecasts potentially available; and to estimate the probable life cycle of business; the raw material resources required; manufacturing cost data, manpower requirements, etc. In addition, efforts are made to delineate the market into likely segments to assess preliminary marketing strategies. If the New Business Development Department does not anticipate that the proposed new product is ready for further development, they may ask the Search Department to additionally refine the idea or a decision may be made by the development group to drop the idea.

An analysis is also conducted of any competitive products (if any) that are currently serving the market. Three products are analyzed to determine particular characteristics which may affect salability. This process helps calculate the survival propensity for the new product. In addition, this step helps guide the firm in developing their own product concepts and in providing the necessary user-benefit characteristics to satisfy projected market requirements. Once this has been completed, the development group should further redefine and estimate as accurately as possible, changes in costs, revenues, and sales volumes over the life of the proposed new business. Information of this nature further clarifies the financial implications of the project. If the results of this research, after being related back to the guidelines set up in the charter, are unfavourable, the project may be recycled back for additional basic research, it may be dropped, or it may be modified by the development group. If, however, the proposed project continues to have a promising potential, the V-team normally will be concerned with generating alternative product prototypes. One approach is to generate a reasonably broad spectrum of prototypes and then analyze each alternative to determine which one will best fit the particular needs of the proposed market. In discussing the importance of prototype development, a development manager for a large consumer goods manufacturer stated:

This is the crucial stage in the development of a product. We need to know:
How does it look? How does it feel? What are the important physical
properties? Does it do what we want it to do in terms of customer communication? What does the price/value relationship look like for potential
customers? This is how you learn about a new product.

By taking a fairly broad approach at prototype generation, alternative
concepts will evolve that can be implemented into the final product plan.
This procedure also aids in formulating and projecting future extensions
and modifications for the product. After alternative prototypes have been
developed, the next step involves screening the most likely ones and conducting additional tests on them. The venture team in other words attempts
to make realistic market acceptance projections for the surviving product
candidates. As one manager explained:

> In anticipating market reaction you have to proceed experimentally. We'll
> put new products in the market on an experimental basis and set up pilot
> operations in a plant. We can then gain maximum feedback on the utility
> of the product and an understanding of how to modify the products. Then
> we continually assess the utility and the cost to see what we're going
> to get back from the product . . . You learn a lot about your product with
> this sort of dialogue with the market.

After additional analysis and testing, if the proposed product still looks
acceptable in terms of the market, raw material requirements, processing
capabilities, and the established objectives, the venture team continues to
move toward commercialization. However, if the product concept proved
unsatisfactory or unacceptable, new product concepts or further evaluation
will be necessary. In the more drastic cases, however, the product may still
be terminated as unfeasible.

One of the most important phases in the development operations is
developing a specific marketing mix plan which included price, product,
promotion, distribution, advertising, and sales strategies. The marketing
expert on the venture team has primary marketing strategy formulation
responsibilities for the marketing mix. In addition, the facilities and resource requirements are further refined which encompasses estimating manpower and equipment needs to produce the proposed product at output
levels consistent with the proposed volume objectives. Simultaneously, the
team continually monitors the projected market potential, the expected
R.O.I., sales volume, and the projected growth rate of the proposed
product. This information is estimated over the expected lifetime of the
potential business. Usually included at this point are the alternative future-
oriented marketing mix strategies. These are concerned not only with the
benefits derived from short-term commercialization, but also with the long-
run implications of product strategy formulation.

The final phase in the new business development operation involves commercializing the product which involves the assignment of specific responsibilities for market entry according to the market commercialization plan developed by the venture team. The assignment for administering the new product can be assigned to an existing division within the company or it may be spun-off as a new division.

There is no set pattern in terms of the venture team assignments at the time of commercialization. As one venture manager stated:

> We've used all kinds of approaches . . . No two ventures call for the same treatment. People and circumstances differ and require individual attention and treatment.

The flexibility indicated here is another indication of adaptability of venture management.

The results of the commercialization process are monitored by both the operating group responsible for the new product and the Long-Range Planning Group. Operating changes and requirements are then evaluated and acted upon.

Conclusions

The refounding process eliminates many of the problems inherent in organizations designed primarily to maintain existing businesses and yet it capitalizes on the inherent strengths of those organizations, i.e., its managerial expertise. By establishing the New Enterprise Development Operations as a separate entity from the more routine corporate undertakings, the group can function more effectively since it will be somewhat isolated from the everyday problems of the company. The new business development operations also can be protected somewhat from the myopic and parochial viewpoints which so often seem to flourish in large organizations.

As managers continually wrestle with the problem of keeping their companies dynamic and in a 'state of adjustment' with changing market requirements, we shall undoubtedly see additional approaches to corporate development. Such systems as discussed here are proving too important not to be used.

17. Generating Effective Corporate Innovation

Edward B. Roberts

Roberts suggests some guidelines for staffing, structuring, and strategy-setting when pursuing technological innovation.

EFFECTIVE CORPORATE INNOVATION requires the planned integration of staffing, structure, and strategy.

The four critical areas are these:

- The *staffing* of technical organizations must provide for the several key functions necessary to achieve successful innovation.
- The organization must be *structured* to enhance the flow of technical and market information into research and development.
- The organization's structure must also assure strong links with *marketing,* to assure that innovations effectively move forward into commercial success.
- The company must adopt *strategic planning* methods that improve integration of top management's technical plans with other dimensions of overall corporate strategy.

Five different key staff roles must be fulfilled if innovative ideas are to be generated, developed, enhanced, commercialized, and moved forward in the organization.

- The *creative scientist or engineer,* the source of creativity within the organization about whom so much—perhaps too much—has been written.
- The *entrepreneur* who pushes the technical idea (it may be his or someone else's) forward in the organization toward the point of commercialization.

Reprinted from *Technology Review,* 80 (October–November, 1977), pp. 26–33. © 1977 by The Alumni Association, M.I.T. Used by permission.

Edward B. Roberts is David Sarnoff Professor of Management at the Sloan School of Management, M.I.T.

- The *project manager,* who can focus upon the specifics of the new development and indicate which aspects will go forward, which can be economically supported, and which must be deferred and who can coordinate the needed efforts.
- The *sponsor,* the in-house senior individual who provides coaching, back-up, and large skirts behind which entrepreneurs and creative scientists can hide. His role is that of protector and advocate—and sometimes bootlegger of funds—so that innovative technical ideas survive past the birth stage to gain the confidence of the technical organization.
- The *gate-keeper,* who brings essential information into the technical organization. Gate-keepers come in two varieties: the technical gate-keeper and the market gate-keeper; both of them account disproportionately for the information that is used in developing innovative ideas and moving the resulting processes and products forward into manufacturing and the marketplace.

In studies of many research and development organizations over the last 15 years, we have observed deficiencies primarily in all but one of these key roles needed for organizational effectiveness. The role of creative scientist seems to be over-emphasized; organizations tend to assume that having creative people on the payroll guarantees effective development of new products, new processes, and product improvements. This assumption is far from correct, and it has tended to cause systematic neglect of the other functions necessary for effective innovation.

This observation is important in the light of our conclusion that each of the several roles required for effective technical innovation presents unique challenges and must be filled with very different types of people, each type to be recruited, managed, and supported differently, offered different sets of incentives, and supervised with different types of measures and controls. Most technical organizations seem not to have grasped this concept, with the result that all technical people tend to be recruited, hired, supervised, monitored, evaluated, and encouraged as if their principal roles were those of creative scientists. But only a few of these people in fact have the personal and technical qualifications for scientific inventiveness; a creative scientist or engineer is a special bird who needs to be singled out and cultivated and managed in a special way. He is probably a strong, innovative, technically well-educated individual who enjoys working on advanced problems, often as a "loner."

The entrepreneur is a special person, too—creative in his own way, but his is an aggressive form of creativity appropriate for selling an idea or a product. The entrepreneur's drives may be less rational, more emotional than those of the creative scientist; he is committed to achieve, and less concerned about how to do so. He is as likely to pick up and successfully champion someone else's original idea as to push something of his own creation. Such an entrepreneur may well have a broad range of interests and activities; and he must be recruited, hired, managed, and stimulated very differently from the way a creative scientist is treated in the organization.

The project manager is a still different kind of person—an organized individual, sensitive to the needs of the several different people he's trying to coordinate, and an effective planner; the latter is especially important if long lead time, expensive materials, and major support are involved in developing the ideas that he's moving forward in the organization.

The sponsor may in fact be a more experienced, older project manager or former entrepreneur who now has matured to have a softer touch than when he was first in the organization; as a senior person he can coach and help subordinates in the organization and speak on their behalf to top management, allowing things to move forward in an effective, organized fashion. Many organizations totally ignore the sponsor role, yet our studies of industrial research and development suggest that many projects would not have been successful were it not for the subtle and often unrecognized assistance of such senior people acting in the role of sponsors.

Finally, there is the information gate-keeper, the communicative individual who, in fact, is the exception to the truism that engineers do not read—especially that they do not read technical journals. If you're looking for a flow of technical information in a research and development organization to enhance new product development or process improvement, you have to look to these gatekeepers.

But those who do research and development need market information as well as technical information. What do customers seem to want? What are competitors providing? How might regulatory shifts impact the firm's present or contemplated products or processes? For answers to questions such as these research and development people need people I call the "market gate-keepers," engineers or scientists, or possibly marketing people with technical backgrounds who focus on market-related information and communicate effectively to their technical colleagues. Such a person reads trade journals, talks to vendors, goes to trade shows, and is sensitive to competitive information. Without him, many research and development projects and laboratories become misdirected with respect to market trends and needs.

The significant point here is that the staffing needed to cause effective innovation in a technical organization is far broader than the typical research and development director has usually assumed; our studies indicate that many ineffective technical organizations have failed to be innovative solely because one or more of these five quite different critical functions has been absent.

The Social Aspects of Technology

The structure of an organization also affects the success of its creative efforts. The need, of course, is for an interrelationship which enhances the flow of the right kind of information into and through the technical organization, assures its appropriate use there, and encourages the flow of results of technical programs from the research and development group to the other parts of the organization where they can be made to count.

No research and development organization produces a profit. At best such organizations can produce the technical bases that will permit the firm's marketing and manufacturing activities to produce the profit. Thus the search for effective, profitable innovation must embrace the interface relationships that bring information into research and development and move its results forward to other parts of the firm.

My colleague Professor Thomas J. Allen is responsible for some of the best studies in the country on the factors that affect technical information flow in an organization. He has found, for example, that if you separate two technical people by 60 or 70 feet, you've suppressed the likelihood of technical communication by two-thirds; separate them by another 70 feet and you've essentially eliminated 90 per cent of the possibility of technical communication between them; furthermore, he finds no difference in the impediment to communication between 3,000 miles and 3,000 feet.

He has also found that the social relationships between technical people are critically related to the technical relationships between the same people. The person with whom you go to lunch or dinner is also the person with whom you'll talk about new technical ideas; the sources of technical problem-solving ideas within the firm correlate strongly with the sources of information about the Sunday afternoon football game.

Professor Allen's approach emphasizes the social aspects of managing a technical organization, an area that technical managers have seldom considered. If technology is to be useful in product improvement, new products, and new business, we must take a broader, more cultural view of what in fact takes place in the creation and enhancement of technical information flows.

Choosing Among a Spectrum of Venture Strategies

Thus far I have emphasized issues related to information flow in innovation—where the ideas really come from and how they reach that critical point within the firm in which they will be thoughtfully considered. Now we come to a still more crucial issue: if the information comes into the firm and if the firm has the technical know-how and other resources for using that information, then what has to be done to cause those innovative technical products to be developed and to move forward into the marketplace? Organization structures to link research and development outputs to the market vary greatly, and I shall limit my discussion here to the so-called venture strategies.

Firms have moved in many very different directions in their efforts to respond to venture opportunities—new products and new business areas—presented by technological innovation. The spectrum of the firm's possible involvements is wide, ranging from the low commitment of undertaking venture capital activities to invest in someone else's development of a new business idea all the way to the other extreme of intensive internal venture management typical of companies like 3M.

For any given opportunity, each firm must select from within this spectrum the appropriate approach, depending on the available staff, the firm's general strategy, the resources available to move products forward into the market, and the characteristics of the markets into which the new products are to be moved.

To make clear the nature of these alternatives and the process of choosing among them, let me trace one company's experiences over the past 15 years trying to develop broad new business bases.

This multi-billion-dollar corporation began its venture strategy organization in 1960. For the first four years it followed a venture capital approach of investing in the start-up phases of high-technology firms—a policy the management called "window on technology," designed to provide varied perspectives on the sources of new technology and on new market opportunities. After four years in which the firm invested in 11 companies, the management concluded that "window on technology" was not providing adequate information and insights on the launching of broad, ambitious new businesses. So the venture capital approach was replaced by an internal venture research and development organization—a special laboratory group to develop new technical ideas. The firm's principal business was in the field of materials, and the new group's goal was to develop new product systems heavily dependent on special materials properties and know-how which would be forward-integrated in the market relative to the company's other businesses. Over a five-year period the firm spent $40 million of corporate funds in this activity; the result was two new products, both of which failed.

So at the end of five years management concluded that it was time to close out on this internal venture research and development approach. But the firm was still committed to creating new products and new businesses, and so management conceived of an opportunities analysis group to study broad ranges of market opportunities and pinpoint global business areas into which the firm should move. During the next two years, this opportunities analysis group presented eight major new business proposals to the executive committee of the company, and they scored a perfect record: the executive committee rejected every one. At the end of that period, the company was ready to scrap this approach for getting into new businesses.

But management remained committed to the need for venturing forth into new markets, so the company adopted its present internal venture strategy of trying to develop small business based on off-the-shelf commercial exploitations to test on a pilot basis the company's ideas for different markets. And in fact, during the past several years this firm has been somewhat successful in entering a few new market areas.

My point is not to emphasize this last apparent success, which may, in fact, soon turn into a failure. My point is rather to emphasize how much work and time are necessary to create a basis for meaningful diversification, and how many different approaches are available from which to choose.

Looking back at all of our studies of venturing, I think we have learned a few—not many—things:

- First, long-term persistence is required for any success in venturing into major new business endeavors. New-venture development of new products and new businesses is not something to go into for a year or two or three or four; it's something to which you had better have a long-term commitment supported by the belief that it matters that you succeed.
- Second, almost every successful new venture strategy is somehow dependent upon either copying or coupling to the strengths of small-company technical entrepreneurship. This is true whether you're engaged in venture-capital investments in new, high-technology companies, or in joint ventures trying to combine the technical ideas of a small new firm with the capital base and distribution capability of a large firm, or trying to create an environment in your own large firm that mimics in important dimensions the creative, aggressive, entrepreneurial milieu of the small, high-technology-based enterprise. Our studies demonstrate that the kinds of people who leave large, high-technology firms to form successful new companies are the same kinds of people who, when they stay in the large firm, are the key entrepreneurs behind new venture development there.
- Third, no generalizations are possible on the subject of which strategy for new-venture development really works. For example, Minnesota Mining and Manufacturing Co. has for 30 years followed a strategy of depending upon internal venture stimulation with a beautiful organizational approach for creating and exploiting new ideas. In recent years Dow Chemical Co. has taken a very different

approach, utilizing venture capital investment and outside technology acquisition as a strategy for building profitable new businesses. Through the medium of Exxon Enterpises—a still different strategy which appears to have strong merit and high possibility of success—Exxon is piecing together venture capital, joint ventures, and in-house research and development results into the base for significant new business entities.

These strategies are examples of success to be looked at carefully, but no individual or company can expect to be successful merely by mimicking any one of these strategies. The approach that works for one firm may not work for another, even if both firms do the right kinds of things about staffing and structure, because there remains the need to develop a formal technical strategy within the firm.

How to Win Profits by Planning Technology

Our studies reveal that most corporations have ignored technological strategy as an element of overall corporate strategy. For some reason, most firms limit their attention to financial and marketing strategies and planning, ignoring technology as a major area for assessment, planning, and strategic development.

No firm can divorce product from the technology embodied in that product. When we talk about the competitive positions of product lines two to five years hence, we are almost of necessity talking about the underlying technological basis of these product lines. An executive who wants to look at his firm's direction in the next half decade must start by profiling the competitive product positions of his company and studying the product and technology strategy options available to him.

What dimensions and approaches are relevant to monitoring technical performance? Which key projects need to be monitored by top management, and in what ways? For every product subcategory of the firm, where does the firm stand? Is the product's leadership clear? Are you in a product/technology parity position, or are you in a catch-up position with respect to your competition? Where were you with respect to those measures three to five years ago? Where will you be three to five years hence?

As you try to answer these questions for each major product or subproduct, you may be surprised and dismayed at what is revealed about the technological strengths and weaknesses built into your technical posture. You ought to have a deliberate strategy for technological development in each product category, and you especially need strategies for those products where you find yourself somewhat frightened as you analyze your future position.

Research and development should not be done on good faith. You should do research and development for strategically justified reasons, according to a clear strategy that says what you are trying to achieve and that gives you some measuring points at which you will be forced to evaluate and further justify what is being done. Can you find a way to take the offensive, launching forward with new technology in a bold way? Or are you going to be adaptive and exploitative, countering whatever the competition does and trying to make the best of a weak technical position?

What about related product areas—not the ones you're presently in but those that are close to these familiar areas? Is your present posture well defined? Do you have a strategy for the future? Are you going to be aggressive? If your chief competitor branches into a related area where he hasn't previously been, how will you respond? What about new products and new technologies? Do you have a technical program that will support your posture and strategy? Do you have research and development resources that match these intentions?

What about major manufacturing processes? Do you change them because manufacturing people tell you they have problems, or do you have a strategy? Do you want to change your firm's present manufacturing process, or do you want merely to respond to whatever the competition does by keeping even on the cost per unit item?

How do senior technical and general corporate managers invest their time with respect to the major new products and new innovative activities of the firm? Do you, in fact, involve the time of top management at the points of leverage that can affect the future of the firm?

At the very beginning of a new technology-based product development activity, a senior manager is able to influence the direction of the project in almost any way he chooses; he can stop it, enlarge it, accelerate it, redirect it, make it go for one piece of the market or another. The top manager's opportunity to be the bold innovator or the aggressive obsoleter of technology is greatest at that earliest stage. As the product moves forward into development, production, and finally marketing, the ability of the executive to influence the outcome goes down—eventually very close to zero.

But if you look at how managers typically spend their time, you find a very different pattern. Studies of this subject seem to indicate that chief executive officers spend trivial amounts of their time on the study and design stages of major new projects, the redirection projects of the firm. Instead the typical chief executive is primarily involved during the production and marketing stages of a project, when it's too late to do anything that can influence the outcome. The lesson from this is simple: if you want to affect the future of your firm, you need not only the right kind of staffing in your technical organizations and the right kinds of structures to enhance information flow in and transfer out. You need a strategic posture which displays critical points for paying attention to certain dimensions of product and technology, and you need to have an allocation of managerial time that brings the best talents of the company to bear on these focal points at the critical time.

References

ALLEN, THOMAS J., *Managing the Flow of Technology*, Cambridge: M.I.T. Press, 1977.

ROBERTS, EDWARD B., "Entrepreneurship and Technology," *Research Management*, Vol. 11, No. 4 (July, 1968), pp. 249–266.

ROBERTS, EDWARD B., and ALAN L. FROHMAN, "Internal Entrepreneurship: Strategy for Growth," *Business Quarterly*, Spring, 1972, pp. 71–78.

18. P&G's Secret Ingredient

Peter Vanderwicken

This article offers a rare glimpse into the new product development efforts of one of the nation's best-managed and most highly regarded consumer goods companies.

ASK ALMOST ANYBODY in the world of business to characterize Procter & Gamble, and chances are you'll get a familiar answer—it's "a marketing company." The cliché implies that only by puffing them up with great gales of advertising can P&G sell its products in such huge quantities. Now, it certainly is true that P&G is very big in marketing—the nation's No. 1 advertiser, in fact. The $200 million that the company spent on TV in its last fiscal year provided one-tenth of the networks' total revenues. And P&G is certainly very *good* at marketing. A company that ranks No. 1 in the U.S. in laundry detergent (Tide), shampoo (Head and Shoulders), toothpaste (Crest), shortening (Crisco), disposable diapers (Pampers), toilet paper (Charmin), and several other consumer products as well has to be doing some very effective marketing. But to repeat that "marketing company" stereotype is to miss the true secret of Procter & Gamble's success.

That secret, in a word, is thoroughness. Procter & Gamble manages every element of its business with a painstaking precision that most organizations fail to approach. Thoroughness extends to the careful and tenacious recruitment of employees, the development of a much-admired executive corps, the design of manufacturing facilities, and the creation and testing of products. By the time a product gets to the marketing stage, the thorough preparation through all the prior stages has already endowed it with an edge on competitors.

Peter Vanderwicken was a staff writer for Fortune *at the time of writing.*

Before Chairman Edward Harness will allow a new product to be put on the market, he insists that its superiority (meaning consumer preference for it) be demonstrated by actual tests. "Some people suggest that product differences in our field are minimal or infinitesimal," he says. "I can't agree. When you find a significant body of women who believe the characteristics of what they want are found in a product—this is the essence of consumerism, giving them what they want."

One of the less obvious benefits of the P&G approach is that it helps employee morale. People who work for P&G believe the products they make and market *are* better. As they see it, they're engaged in something fundamentally worthwhile. The high morale accounts in part for the legendary competitive enthusiasm of the company's salesmen. "They eat, sleep, and dream P&G," says a vice president of a supermarket chain who sees a lot of them. A campus radical of the Sixties who went to work for P&G and then quit to run an arts foundation says of the company as he recalls it: "Their integrity and fairness permeate every dimension of what they do."

Now They're Eating Hyperbolic Paraboloids

The top managers of Procter & Gamble are wise enough to know that preservation of this spiritual vitality is more important than any temporary fluctuations in the operating results. Their ability to take this farsighted view, rather than jerking the company from one course to another in response to breezes in the market, derives in part from the leaders' own longevity. The men who reach the top have usually spent most of their careers at the company. Howard Morgens, who stepped aside for Harness in April, was chief executive for seventeen years. Now chairman of the executive committee, Morgens has thought a lot about what has made P&G successful. "We take the long-term view and work for the long-term future," he says. "Anyone can improve his earnings over two or three years."

Procter & Gamble's thoroughness is most apparent in the development of new products, the lifeblood of any consumer-goods company. P&G spends well over $100 million a year on research. Contrary to the general impression that consumer-goods companies belch forth new products in rapid succession, P&G has introduced only two since 1970. One was Sure, an antiperspirant, and the other was Pringle's, a new kind of potato chip. Not infrequently, the company spends a decade or more perfecting a product before bringing it to market. Work on Pringle's began back in the mid-Fifties.

The development of Pringle's is a classic case of recognizing a need in a consumer market and then painstakingly working away to meet it. Americans gobble up roughly $1 billion worth of potato chips a year, but for the manufacturers, potato chips have always had their problems. They are so fragile that they are rarely shipped more than 200 miles, and even at that distance, a quarter of the chips get broken. They also spoil quickly—they can't remain on the shelf for more than two months. These characteristics have kept potato-chip making a fragmented industry and nobody had applied much technology to the product since it was invented in 1853.

Aware of these problems because they sold edible oils to the potato-chip industry, P&G executives set out to solve them. Rather than slicing potatoes and frying them in the traditional way, engineers developed a process somewhat akin to papermaking. They dehydrated the potatoes, reconstituted them as a mash, then pressed them for frying into a precise shape that a mathematician would call hyperbolic paraboloid.

That geometrical form looks like a potato chip, is easy to manufacture, and permits the chips to be stacked neatly on top of one another in a hermetically sealed container that resembles a tennis-ball can. Pringle's stay whole and have a shelf life of at least a year. They are selling regionally in the U.S. at a rate that, if they were distributed nationwide, would make them a $200-million-a-year product.

Shampooing Half a Head

After the lab work has been done on a new product, the division that will manufacture it takes over and finances all further development and testing. In some companies, division managers are reluctant to take on new products because the costs of introduction are heavy and hold down short-term profits. P&G avoids this impediment to innovation in several ways. Its executives reiterate in each annual report that they attach no significance to such matters as quarter-to-quarter wobbles in earnings. They also budget by brand, rather than by division, so that a division manager's record is not marred by the cost of a new introduction.

There is, however, a formidable obstacle to the introduction of a new product: the ironclad requirement that any proposed product has to have a demonstrable margin of superiority over its prospective competitors. P&G reaches a verdict on its own innovations by rigorously testing them against the competition. A development team begins refining the product by trying variations of the basic formula, testing its performance under almost any conceivable condition, and altering its appearance. Eventually, the team gets the product into a few alternative versions that differ only slightly— say in odor or color. Then they start testing variants on hundreds of P&G's own employees.

In the company's Hair Care Evaluation Center, women have half their hair washed with a new shampoo, and half with their regular brand as a control. To analyze detergent performance, technicians in a P&G laboratory wash the laundry of five hundred employees every week. Some tests become a little bizarre. Employees sampling a new toothpaste or mouthwash, for example, enter a laboratory where they breathe through a hole in the wall. A researcher on the other side sniffs their breath to judge the product's effectiveness. A new deodorant is tested similarly, by a professional armpit-sniffer.

If the product passes its tests by employees (who tend to be overly critical, the testers say), P&G presents it to panels of consumers picked at random. In all, P&G queries 250,000 consumers a year (church groups are a favorite target), asking whether this or that product fills their needs and whether they would buy it. To be considered for introduction, the product must win the votes of a majority of consumers in tests against each major competing brand.

The required margin of preference varies from one type of product to another. The company has found, for example, that taste preferences vary greatly, so it is difficult to develop a toothpaste or mouthwash that a panel will favor over competitors by a margin of more than 60 to 40. Accordingly, P&G is satisfied if its entrant is chosen by fifty-five out of a hundred consumers tested.

People's sensitivities to differences in paper products are much less acute. Since the capital investment required to produce paper products is much greater than with many other products, the risks in marketing a newcomer are higher. "If the product is perceived to be superior here," Harness says, "it has to be preferred by a huge amount." For a new toilet paper, the required margin is about 80 to 20. It wasn't just marketing, in other words, that made Charmin No. 1.

A Creative Tension

P&G is no less thorough when it comes to manufacturing. The company's own engineers design or extensively modify most of the production machinery P&G uses. All employees are encouraged to propose ways to reduce costs, but each proposal is carefully tested before it is adopted. The procedure, Harness explains, is that "you get the plan blessed by the engineering division and get an experimental order to jury-rig the machine to see what the new process does. We run EO's all the time on everything."

The critical process in making detergents, for example, is drying and mixing the chemical ingredients to form granules. That takes place in a stacklike "detergent tower." By successively modifying its oldest tower, built in 1946, P&G has been able to increase the output sixfold. If the company had not modified any of the thirteen towers it now has, it would need a total of 108 towers to achieve current production levels. Similar modifications help improve productivity throughout P&G. Its toilet-tissue winders originally turned at 900 feet a minute; now they wind at twice that speed.

Plant managers are judged in part on their ability to devise new ways to cut costs. The resulting not-so-informal competition among plants serves to create both a competitive spirit within the company and an internal tension that keeps operations lean. When the new paper mill at Mehoopany, Pennsylvania, got into full production in 1969, the costs were well below those at the much older mill in Green Bay, Wisconsin. Since then, the Green Bay managers have modified their machines enough to become competitive in cost with Mehoopany. Because methods have been revised in many ways throughout the company, Harness says, "our costs this year are $100 million lower than a year ago."

The Difference 4 Cents Made

And then, of course, there's that famous marketing. Here, too, thoroughness reigns. P&G tests its marketing methods as painstakingly as its products. In some cities with cable TV, one sample commercial goes to homes on one side of a block and another to homes across the street. Researchers will then ask residents whether, and how well, they remember what they saw.

Before a new product is introduced nationwide, P&G tests it in one or more cities that are demographically representative of the nation. The company sets up an initial production line, backs the product with a massive barrage of advertising, and puts it on sale in supermarkets. If a product fails this test, it is normally dropped. But occasionally one gets a second chance.

One product that was not discarded after initial failure went on to become a huge success: Pampers, which now rivals Tide as P&G's best-selling brand. On its first market test, Pampers bombed. The product was priced too high—about 10 cents each, which was more than the cost of buying a cloth diaper and washing it. By simplifying the package, speeding up the assembly lines, and using less costly components, the company gradually got the price down to 6 cents.

As the price dropped, each of three subsequent tests over four years indicated a bigger potential market. So management progressively reduced the profit-margin target and raised the volume target. By the fourth test, the price was right and Pampers took off.

Prior research is supposed to prevent P&G from flopping in its test markets. "My boss said years ago," Harness recalls, "that when you go to test market you should be 90 percent sure. That's our approach." According to one survey, 112 of 204 brands put into test markets in the

U.S. in 1971 failed to make it to nationwide distribution. P&G's success ratio has been better, but nowhere near 90 percent. Of sixteen brands test marketed in the last decade, seven failed to win general distribution.

The Missing Magic

The expansion of a new brand nationwide is reminiscent of a military campaign in its complexity and intensity. Generally, distribution is extended outward from the test markets as production capacity becomes available, until, after six months or a year, the brand is sold throughout the country. P&G may spend $25 million or more promoting a brand in its first year on the market and the company continues to run tests to discover the least expensive combination of ways to reach potential consumers. Surprisingly, giving out samples door-to-door can be the cheapest method of introducing a new brand especially if it is delivered with samples of another brand that shares the cost.

In the last ten years, P&G failed in an attempt to extend a brand beyond its test market on three occasions. Hidden Magic, a hair spray, turned out to have no magic at all. Stardust, a dry bleach, failed to convert housewives from the customary liquid. Cinch, a spray household cleaner just never caught on, and the men at Procter & Gamble still haven't figured out why.

On any brand that flies, P&G expects to recover development and marketing costs and begin earning a profit within three years. Getting into the black, though, is only the beginning of an endless process of trying to hold and expand market share. A typical brand budget provides for a promotion of some kind—a "3 cents off" offer, a coupon, or a premium—about every three months.

Contrary to what might be expected, P&G runs its most attractive promotions not to lure customers when a brand's sales are falling off, but when the demand is highest. Cake mixes sell best before Thanksgiving and Christmas, for example, while soaps and detergents move fastest in the late spring and summer. Promotions are aimed at building market share, and it is easier to increase penetration when the total market is growing. If the product can expand its share then, it may be able to hold some or most of the gain as sales fall off seasonally during the rest of the year.

Similarly, P&G and other manufacturers increase advertising expenditures on their fast-selling brands and reduce them on brands that are doing less well. They figure that a dollar spent advertising a high-volume item will return a greater profit than a dollar spent on a brand with lower volume or a smaller market share.

Daytime television is still the most efficient means of selling soap (and Pampers, too), and Procter owns, produces, and sponsors six long-running

TV soap operas, which get the attention of housewives as their predecessors on radio did for almost half a century. Products such as deodorants and hair sprays, which also appeal to working women and to men, are more efficiently advertised on evening TV.

Once a brand is established, P&G changes it in some major or minor way twice a year. The company recently changed the formulation of its dishwasher detergent, Cascade, to prevent the granules from caking. It added a new ingredient to Downy fabric softener to help minimize the buildup of lint-catching static on clothes in a dryer.

There is a lot of show biz in the soap biz, to be sure, and a good many of the changes seem trivial. A supermarket executive laments: "One year they'll add blue dots to a detergent and say, 'new blue improved,' and the next year they'll take them out." Ed Harness, though, claims there's a good deal less straining for superficial novelty than there was a couple of decades ago, when the industry was more flamboyant.

Up Against the Life Cycle

All the attention P&G gives its existing products represents an effort to cope with an inescapable challenge facing consumer-goods manufacturers. Left unchanged, a packaged product will tend to increase its market share for a few years after it is introduced, hit a peak, and then sink into decline. Though no one knows for sure, many marketing men believe these product life cycles are becoming shorter. A study by the A.C. Nielsen Co. concludes that 85 percent of all new brands can expect less than three years of success before their market shares start declining rapidly. While manufacturers can try to lengthen the life cycle by launching a new advertising campaign or redesigning a package, they don't always succeed. And when they do succeed, the study says, they revive the brand for only an average of fifteen months before it sinks once again.

Procter & Gamble's strategy of frequent, regular improvements, accompanied by an unceasing barrage of advertising, has in most cases virtually overridden the life cycle. Several P&G products introduced long ago are still very much around. Crisco was first sold back in 1912. Ivory soap made its debut in 1879 and is now the most venerable brand sold in American grocery stores. No established P&G product has died in the last ten years.

This stability pays valuable dividends. P&G sells only forty-nine branded consumer products (plus some industrial bulk chemicals and variations of its domestic brands abroad), and that is a rather small number for a $5-billion company. It means that the average P&G brand sold in the U.S. is in itself a sizable business, permitting many economies of scale. And since the company's established products aren't dying off, the sales and profits contributed by newly introduced brands are net gains for the company's growth.

Poised for a Leap Forward

For the last 125 years, Procter & Gamble has been growing at an average rate of 8 percent a year, compounded—one of the most splendid long-run performances in the annals of business. For the last two decades, the company has increased sales, profits, *and dividends* every year without a miss.

Its prospects, moreover, seem pretty bright. After a relatively quiet period of introducing few new products, P&G has seven in test markets, including a fabric softener, a paper towel in a counter-top dispenser, a liquid laundry detergent, and a tampon that the company began developing thirteen years ago. Hopes run high in Cincinnati that the tampon, named Rely, will take a major share of the market from Tampax and Kotex. Demonstrating the new product, P&G executives plunk Rely and Tampax into separate beakers of water to demonstrate their own product's superiority. They are confident enough about the outcome to make an explicit claim on the package: "Rely absorbs twice as much as the tampon you're probably using now."

But Will Thoroughness Work Any More?

To all appearances, the company has great potential for growth abroad. Right now, foreign business accounts for a quarter of its sales and . . . a somewhat larger portion of earnings. Recently sales have been growing faster abroad than in the U.S.—about 35 percent a year—but the president of the international division, William Gurganus, says that he expects foreign sales "to remain one-quarter of our total business."

This statement suggests that Gurganus, at least, believes domestic business is poised for a leap forward. The burst of new brands could well keep sales rising briskly for several years. P&G took 119 years to reach its first billion dollars in sales, nine years for its second, five years for its third, three years for its fourth, and little more than a year for its fifth. At the recent rate of growth, sales could more than double by 1980. If history is a guide, profits would keep pace.

Some analysts on Wall Street, however, express serious doubts whether Procter & Gamble can sustain its remarkable pace. One big question concerns the time-consuming process of testing that is a crucial element in the P&G system. As the life cycles of packaged goods grow shorter, manufacturers are compressing the time they spend in developing new products. A new shampoo is introduced about every three months now, for instance, and each new one threatens the market shares of all those on the shelves. Under such conditions, can P&G continue to spend years developing and testing its products? Can P&G still count on thoroughness?

Morgens and Harness, at least, seem unworried about predictions that their company will have to change its ways. Morgens, indeed, maintains that some trends at work in the society favor the Procter & Gamble style. "The development cycle may be longer in the future," he says, "because of the consumer and environmental movements and the red tape of government. It can take the FDA a year and a half to clear a product, and this is after it's ready to go to market. All this benefits a company like ours which does its research well."

EDITOR'S NOTE: Rely tampons were introduced regionally, starting in August, 1978, achieving full national distribution by February, 1980. P&G had strong evidence to indicate that Rely would also become sales leader in its product category, and based on this it readied plans to introduce a series of related offerings under the umbrella of the Rely brand identity.

In September of 1980, however, P&G voluntarily withdrew Rely tampons from the marketplace in the face of widespread adverse publicity concerning a possible connection between the incidence of toxic shock syndrome (TSS) and the use of tampons in general and the Rely brand in particular. The Food and Drug Administration, charged with the responsibility of acting in this sector, deliberately chose to use adverse publicity as part of a larger regulatory offensive to force P&G to recall this brand as quickly as possible. P&G complied, despite the fact that the evidence linking TSS to Rely was highly fragmentary and that it had not had an opportunity to defend itself in formal proceedings.

The after-tax cost of this recall has been estimated to be a minimum of $75 million. The cost of *not* making this recall—to the general public as well as to P&G—has not been estimated.

III

CONCEPT GENERATION AND EVALUATION

A.

Idea Generation

CONCEPT GENERATION and evaluation refers to those activities that take place before a decision is made to develop a proposed product into a physical entity.

New products, of course, can be no better than the ideas upon which they are based. Von Hippel points out that in many instances the customer not only suggests the need for the new product but actually goes on to develop the offering itself for its manufacturer-supplier. Leaf recommends the systematic evaluation of one's own product performance, sales, and service relative to those of the competition as a source of inspiration.

McGuire describes how concept testing can be used on an equally systematic basis to identify and evaluate new product ideas. Green and Wind concentrate on more sophisticated methodology; they show how complex consumer choices involving multiattribute alternatives can be decomposed through conjoint measurement to yield valuable information for the design and positioning of new product offerings.

Wheelwright and Makridakis look at concept generation and evaluation from a technical perspective. They describe how various technological forecasting methods might be used to help set R&D priorities. Gary Steiner's paper on creativity concludes this section. He looks at idea generation from the standpoint of the individuals engaged in the process and explains how creativity in an organizational context can be stimulated through the appropriate selection of personnel and the proper structuring of the creative environment.

19. Users as Innovators

Eric A. von Hippel

Most successful new products in some industries are developed com-
pletely by the product-user and not by the manufacturer-supplier. The
author discusses his research in this sector and the implications of his
findings for new product development in general.

CONVENTIONAL WISDOM holds that customers articulate needs and manufacturers develop products responsive to those needs. But recent research
on the histories of many innovative and successful new products has resulted in a different view: in some industries, most commercially successful
products are developed by product users, not product manufacturers.

When the User Becomes the Designer

As a preview of what is to follow in this article, an example from our
research data may be helpful.

The methods used in the mid-1950s by semiconductor manufacturers
to bond wires to semiconductor chips were quite unreliable. Three scientists at Bell Telephone Laboratories addressed the problem and developed
thermocompression bonding—a greatly improved method which involved
heating the semiconductor material and pressing the wire against it. When
tests demonstrated the effectiveness of the method, the Bell System developed equipment to implement thermocompression bonding in production—no easy task given the precise control of position, pressure, and
temperature required. The method was adopted by Western Electric start-

Reprinted in abridged form from *Technology Review,* 80 (January, 1978),
pp. 3–11. © 1978 by The Alumni Association M.I.T. Used by permission.

Eric von Hippel is a professor in the Sloan School of Management, Massa-
chusetts Institute of Technology. The artwork in this chapter is by Nancy C.
Pokross, art editor of Technology Review.

ing in 1956–57. Other semiconductor manufacturers soon followed, all building the required production equipment in-house.

Two years later, engineers from Kulike and Soffa, a firm specializing in the design and building of production equipment, began working for Western Electric on various production-machine problems. They concluded that machinery implementing several process innovations—including thermocompression bonding—could be sold commercially, so in late 1959 Kulike and Soffa became the first of several firms to manufacture thermocompression bonders for commercial sale. Kulike and Soffa retains a major share of that market today.

Does the pattern in the example seem familiar? It should be to readers whose business is in manufacturing process equipment or scientific instruments. In studies of the sources of innovation—we have been working on this topic at M.I.T. for the last half-decade—we have found that 60 to 80 per cent of the products sampled in those industries were invented, prototyped, and utilized in the field by innovative users before they were offered commercially by equipment or instrument manufacturing firms.

Scientific Instruments: Users Make What They Need

In the case of scientific instruments, we have studied three samples totaling over 100 commercially successful product innovations. The first sample consisted of the first-commercialized versions of four types of scientific instruments: the first gas chromatograph, the first nuclear magnetic resonance spectrometer, the first ultraviolet spectrophotometer (absorption photo-electric type), and the first transmission electron microscope; these are commercially important instruments widely used in the scientific and industrial communities worldwide. Next, we made a survey of expert users and manufacturers to determine a sample of 44 major improvement innovations—judged on the basis of incremental utility offered to the instrument user—to these four basic instruments. And finally, we selected a sample of 63 minor improvement innovations for transmission electron microscopy—the sampling consisting of all commercially successful innovations which offered any incremental functional utility to any subset of users.

The histories of each of these three samples of scientific instrument innovations (identified in Table 1 as "basic," "major improvement," and "minor improvement" innovations, respectively) were then carefully acquired. We started by identifying the firm which *first* manufactured the product for commercial sale, thus avoiding instances of "me-too" innovation. We then identified and interviewed personnel of manufacturing companies who were involved in the innovation work, and we also interviewed early users of the device. Related products and publications generated prior to the date of first-to-market commercialization were also collected and studied.

TABLE 1

Field of innovations and sample selection criteria *	First device used in the field developed and built:	
	By product user	By product manufacturer
Instrumentation *Scientific instrument innovations:*		
First of type (4)	100%	0%
Major functional improvements (44)	82	18
Minor functional improvements (63)	70	30
Process equipment *Innovations in semiconductor and electronic subassembly manufacturing equipment:*		
First of type used in commercial production (7)	100	0
Major functional improvements (22)	63	21
Minor functional improvements (20)	20	29
Polymers *All engineering polymer innovations developed in the U.S. after 1955 whose production in 1975 exceeded 10 million pounds (6)*	0	100
Additives *All commercialized plasticizers and ultraviolet stabilizers developed after 1945 for use with four major polymers (16)*	0	100

* Numbers in parentheses indicate the number of cases in each sample

After studying the sources of over 160 major and minor innovations in four fields, the author concludes that users of products, rather than their manufacturers, are often the developers of commercially viable new products. A predictive model is not yet available, but the author suggests how managers can determine whether product development by users is common in their industries and how they may capitalize on this source of innovations by establishing special sales and technical service activities.

The result of all this work: in 81 per cent of all the innovation cases studied, we found that it was the user who perceived that an advance in instrumentation was required; invented the instrument; built a prototype;

improved the prototype's value by applying it; and diffused detailed information on the value of the invention and how the prototype device might be replicated. Only when all of these steps were completed did the manufacturer of the first commercially available instrument enter the innovation process. Typically, the manufacturer's contribution was to perform product engineering work which, while leaving the basic design and operating principles intact, improved reliability, convenience of operation, etc.; and then to manufacture, market, and sell the improved product.

The frequency with which this user-dominant innovation pattern appeared in our sample of scientific instrument innovations was, as is indicated in Table 1, strikingly high for basic innovations and for major and minor improvement innovations as well. User-dominant innovation showed no statistically significant relationship to the size—and thus, presumably, to the research and development potential—of the manufacturing company. Furthermore, the pattern of user-dominated innovation appeared to hold for companies which were established manufacturers of a given product line—manufacturers who "ought" to know about improvements needed in their present product line and to be working on them—as well as for manufacturers for whom a given innovation represented their initial entry into a product line.

Our data also showed extensive precommercial diffusion of significant user inventions through "home-built" replications by other users. Indeed, such "home-built" replications were made and used to produce publishable results in every case where more than a year elapsed between the initial published description of a significant new instrument innovation by a user and the introduction of the first commercial model by an instrument firm.

User Innovations in Process Machinery

Having thus discovered a user-dominated innovation pattern in scientific instruments, we next sought to determine whether this was an isolated instance, or whether the pattern held also for other types of innovation in other industries. Because innovation in process equipment is related to such pressing national concerns as the rate of increase of industrial productivity and the international competitiveness of U.S. manufacturers, we decided to focus our next studies on process equipment innovations.

After discussions with people in a range of industries, we decided to work with two samples:

- Process equipment innovations related to the manufacture of silicon-based semiconductors; and
- Process equipment innovations related to the manufacture of electronic subassemblies on printed circuit cards.

These were chosen because we speculated that the amount of innovation by users might vary according to the novelty of the innovations they needed compared with the prior experience of equipment manufacturers traditionally serving those users. If such a relationship existed, we reasoned, a higher proportion of innovations in semiconductor process equipment than in electronic subassembly process equipment should come from users. The former industry was new; it had no established suppliers; the needed new equipment involved near-unique problems of controlling chemical contamination and providing precise, microscopic manipulation on a mass-production scale. Makers of electronics products, on the other hand, enjoyed established relationships with suppliers of subassembly process equipment in the period examined, and the problems to be solved in developing equipment for inserting components into printed circuit boards—for example—did not seem to us extraordinary.

The samples of process equipment innovations studied in each industry were analogous to those used in the scientific instrument study. We focused on a subset of the major process "steps" commercially used in each industry, and for each one of these (such as the insertion of component leads into printed circuit cards) we identified:

- Machinery (if any) used in the initial commercial practice of the process step;
- Major functional improvements made in the process machinery over time; and
- All minor functional improvements in the process machinery used in two process steps, one step taken from each industry examined.

Then, as before, we carefully reconstructed the histories of each innovation which was ultimately adopted in commercially manufactured process machinery. We searched the appropriate technical literature prior to first commercial innovation seeking references to experimental apparatus functionally similar to the commercialized innovation as well as other relevant work, and we interviewed authors of relevant articles. When we identified user-innovator firms we sought out and interviewed personnel in them; and if we had no information on the presence of user-innovators, we canvassed logical potential user-innovator firms to assure ourselves insofar as we could that such user-innovators indeed did not exist.

We found user-dominated innovation patterns very strongly present in the segments of the process machinery industry we sampled. As Table 1 shows, all of the novel machinery used in the initial commercial practice of a process step and more than 60 per cent of the improvements to that machinery were invented, prototyped, and used in commercial production by innovative users before they were manufactured and marketed by process machinery manufacturing companies. Interestingly, we found no significant difference in the proportion of user-dominated innovation present in the two process areas studied, so our initial speculation as to a reason for the occurrence of product development by users in some industries was not supported.

Note that our findings of a high level of user-dominated innovation considerably understate the total level of user involvement in the innovation process. This is because:

- Users can and do sometimes make a considerable contribution to the innovation process without carrying their work far enough to meet our criteria for user-dominated innovation. For example, in four process machinery innovations studied—attributed to the product manufacturer in our results—the users provided machinery manufacturers with the central technical concept used in the innovation; and

- Many process innovations are not embodied in innovative hardware. An example is the preparation of dislocation-free crystal for semiconductor substrate. Although "dislocation-free crystal growers" were eventually produced, initial commercial practice was a matter of modifying the technique used to operate conventional crystal growers. It is logical that users would have a very high involvement in innovations of this type, manufacturers having a role occasionally if the innovation promised additional sales of non-innovation hardware of their manufacture.

But User-dominated Innovation Is Not Universal

Not-yet-published research shows that user-dominated innovation is also characteristic of some process machine categories in addition to the two discussed above and of some types of medical product innovation.

But user-dominated innovation clearly is *not* common in all industries; in some, the conventional relationship of manufacturer responding to user needs by acting as innovator and product developer is strongly applicable. Studies by two of my students, Alan J. Berger and Julian W. Boyden, for example, show that all innovations in a sample of new engineering polymers and new additives for commodity plastics were developed by manufacturers of these products, not by users *(see table 1)*.

In what industries is the user-dominated pattern common, and in what industries is it rare? A model which would quickly and economically answer this question for particular industries would be useful both to policymakers and to innovators. We are working hard to develop such a model, but it is not ready for presentation yet.

The Realm of User-dominated Management

The fact that user-dominated innovation characterizes so many new developments need not be a cause for dismay on the part of those concerned about effective and efficient industrial innovation. Accurate understanding of user need is widely regarded as the most important single factor assuring the success of an industrial innovation. Clearly, users who innovate are in an advantageous position to perceive user needs accurately. User-dominated innovation should therefore have unusual potential for success.

But there remains the question of effective strategies for managing user-dominated innovation processes. If your manufacturing firm is in an industry which turns out to be characterized by user-dominated innovation, how should this finding affect your new-product-development effort?

Figure 1 indicates the position of the first-to-market firm in a user-dominated innovation process. In the following discussion we focus on the appropriate interface of the manufacturer to that process, in contrast to the interface which the manufacturer conventionally has with the user community.

First, consider the conventional interface as shown in Figure 2. In this interface, no distinction is made between innovative and non-innovative (routine) product users, with the result that personnel from market research, sales, and technical service (the three typical interface units) come into contact with innovative users only a small proportion of the time. And when they *do* make such contacts, these units are inappropriately staffed and motivated to make much use of the information which may be available about user-developed products.

The dominant workload of technical services is typically field set-up, debugging, and servicing of existing products. Although minor product modifications are sometimes made by such groups for high-volume customers, the goal in general is to keep the customers happy with the existing products. If, in the course of their work—often performed on customer sites—technical service personnel should be offered information on user home-builts ("Why don't you people start building this? We're sick of making them in our shops."), they are not in a good position to take advantage of it because:

- Technical services is typically not staffed with people able to understand and make a good case for the commercial potential of a user-developed product; and
- Technical services typically has no incentive to gather such information or make such a case.

The typical sales force is set up to *output* information on existing pro-

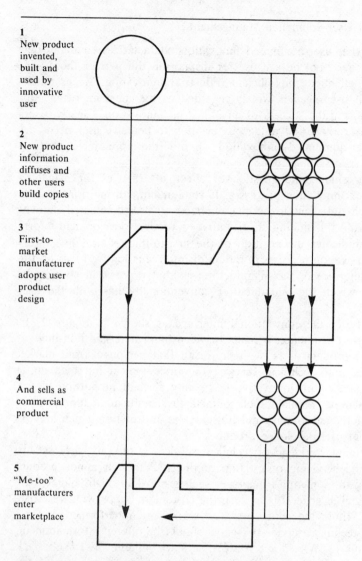

1
New product
invented,
built and
used by
innovative
user

2
New product
information
diffuses and
other users
build copies

3
First-to-
market
manufacturer
adopts user
product
design

4
And sells as
commercial
product

5
"Me-too"
manufacturers
enter
marketplace

**FIGURE 1.   Steps Leading to the Commercialization
of a User-Developed Product**

ducts. It is true that sales people spend much of their time at customer
sites, and so they ought to be in good positions to return information to
their employers on promising user-developed products; but sales departments are typically not staffed with people able to do this job, and the
typical commission and incentive schemes operating on them reward
only sales of existing products. As a result, sales people have not only no
incentive to accurately report on conversations regarding user develop-

ments which might have potential as commercial products; they have an incentive to deflect any such conversations towards the question, "What can I sell you of my present products?"

Finally, consider how the conventionally structured marketing research group would deal with data on user-developed products. Marketing research typically collects and analyzes data on user needs and then attempts to *generate* responsive new product concepts. "Have you any interesting new home-builts we should study?" is an alien question in such a setting. Indeed, any information on such home-builts which users, sales or technical service happens to bring to a conventionally oriented marketing research group's attention would probably be considered only as data on a user need, not as data on both a need *and* a potentially responsive solu-

FIGURE 2

(Below) Product manufacturer's conventional interface to product users. Market research, technical service, and sales departments are typically oriented to communications with users on their needs and the manufacturer's response to those needs. There are multiple barriers, shown by the zig-zagged lines, to flows of information into manufacturers on user-developed products—"solution data," in the author's terminology.

(Right) Proposed manufacturer's interface to innovative users. The reorientation of market research encourages the acquisition by manufacturers of data on user's needs and solutions, and there are special technical service and sales forces to assure that solution as well as need data are embraced and even sought from innovative users.

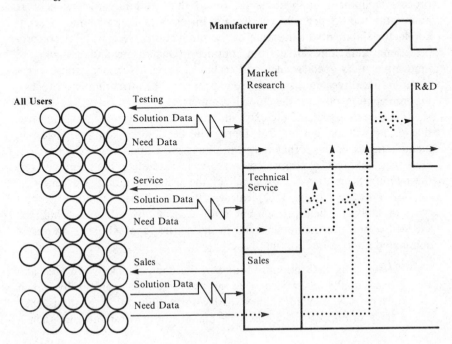

tion. For example, if information comes to marketing research regarding a user prototype which functions better on some dimension than the product manufacturer's existing offering, need analysis methodologies such as multidimensional scaling would probably be invoked; these would ignore how the precision was obtained—the solution data in the user design—noting only that it was needed.

And even if the conventional market research group included the user-solution data in its specification of a new product need, the conventionally organized research and development group receiving such a specification would tend to look at the data on a user's solution with a "not invented here" prejudice.

For these many reasons, the conventional interface which product manufacturers present to their customers offers multiple barriers to the perception and use of information on user-developed products.

Interface Groups for Innovative Users

How should the market interface be modified in an environment in which user-developed home-builts are an important source of new products for the first-to-market manufacturer? The structure in Figure 3 suggests an answer to this question, based on our evidence that product users with a history of product innovation can be identified and separated from the mass of routine product users. For example, in our study of semiconductor process equipment innovations we found that all innovative users were among the top 25 per cent of all users in terms of their volume of semi-conductor shipments at the time of the innovations. Accordingly, we propose separating innovative from routine product users and assigning to innovative users special sales and technical service sections whose organization, incentives, and staffing are appropriate for attracting and processing information on user-developed products.

It is true that some of the extra attention we propose paying to innovative users will be costly. But there will be compensating payback to manufacturers in the form of new products built upon research, development, and field testing performed by a user instead of by the manufacturer, the manufacturer thus saving much of the usual cost of these activities.

For innovative users, technical services should be expanded. Several types of activity—field-proven but not yet generally adopted—could be added by product manufacturers in industries characterized by user-dominated innovation. Among these:

- *User groups*. Commonly found in the computer software area and occasionally elsewhere, user groups are a mechanism by which users may exchange ideas and information on innovations they have developed. The cost to a manufacturer of sponsoring such a

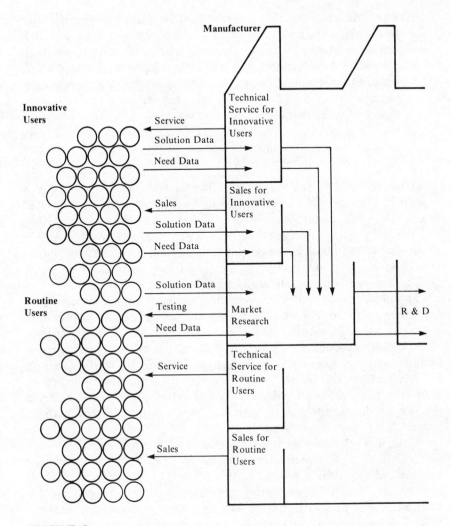

FIGURE 3

group is low, usually taking the form of providing a collection point for such information and disseminating it to members through newsletters and occasional meetings. The benefits in terms of access to the user-generated information is sometimes significant.

- *Applications laboratories.* In many industries, users are commonly invited to propose to manufacturers' applications laboratories their concepts for new applications for existing products. The manufacturer through the applications laboratory provides free or low-cost research and development help in working out the application.

The user gains an effective new process while the manufacturer learns about the need and—often—is shown a user solution which can be developed into a salable new variation on existing products.

- *Custom product groups.* In industries where standard products prove to have usually started as custom products, it is often advantageous for a first-to-market manufacturer to offer good, fast, flexible help to that subset of users whose special needs have previously proved to foreshadow general demand. A good custom products group will induce such users to bring their developments to the sponsoring manufacturer.

A special sales force experienced in the technologies and problems of innovative users should be established to serve those users. As the staff of this sales force gradually prove their competence to the user firms, they will gradually obtain access to user-developed products which the user might wish to have built by an outside supplier, and they will have opportunities to bid on custom products with interesting commercial potential. Such a strategy is well established in some fields today.

Technical service and sales personnel assigned to a manufacturer's innovative users must work under compensation schemes which reward the sale of existing products, the sale of custom products, and information-gathering on user-developed products. Clearly, not all user prototypes or ideas for custom products have enough potential to be worth pursuing, but this problem can be dealt with in a screening process conducted by marketing research; it should not be dealt with by the all-too-common practice of discouraging all information inputs with a policy such as "we don't do custom products."

Marketing research should be encouraged to accept proposals for custom products and user-developed products from sales and technical services and should be organized so that information transfers of this sort are easy and routine. In industries dominated by user-developed innovations, marketing personnel may be able to proceed directly to an exploration of the market potential of the user-developed product itself, just as if the design had come from the manufacturer's own research and development group.

Channels and incentives should be set up to encourage the transfer of information on users' product designs as well as needs from marketing research to research and development. And the latter should be encouraged not to design all new products "from scratch" but to use user designs—often available free—when appropriate.

Management has a role in creating these new arrangements and in keeping an open mind as to the outcome. Many companies start what turn into profitable product lines by making custom products or building to customer designs, then decide that these lines have grown so big that further involvement with custom products could be an unprofitable distraction from the companies' main goals; later such companies wonder why they are having difficulty finding the bases for new product lines.

A Warning: Adopt Thoughtfully

Promising concepts for the management of innovations—and we believe that the management of user-developed products is one—are often prescribed too enthusiastically by researchers at a too-early stage—and then embraced too uncritically by practitioners. To avoid this, we wish to emphasize that strategies for the management of user-dominated innovation are not yet standardized. If you wish to apply the concept before it is routine, we urge you to approach the task flexibly and experimentally.

20. How to Pick Up Tips from Your Competitors

Robin Leaf

Corporate performance in the marketplace can be improved by studying how competitors make, test, distribute, and promote their products.

THE PAST THREE DECADES of international trade have been marked by ever more intense competition among well-managed industrial companies. At the same time, a noticeable shift has taken place in the preoccupations of top managers in the more successful companies. Absorption with products and production processes has given way to an overriding concern with customer needs as the determinant of company strategy.

More recently still, this market focus has taken on an explicitly competitive dimension. Increasingly, the patterns of corporate action are being determined by evaluating, from the customer's point of view, the merits of one's own product performance, sales and service against those offered by one's competitors.

Paradoxically, the better a company becomes at this kind of competitive surveillance, the more difficult it is to do. Success brings growth. Growth enlarges the competitive arena, and at the same time makes it harder to integrate the functional activities that must mesh together for an effective competitive response. Most large companies today, moreover, are in many businesses, so that these functional linkages are needed not only within each business but also between the businesses that make up the total company.

Despite these problems, many large multibusiness companies around the world are rightly respected, not to say feared, as adroit and aggressive competitors. These companies, almost without exception, enjoy a reputa-

Reprinted from *Director*, 30 (February, 1978), pp. 60–62. Used by permission.

Robin Leaf, at the time of writing, was a principal in the Cleveland office of McKinsey & Company, management consultants.

tion for the bold move, the ability to catch their competitors off balance. More often than not, however, their real talent is not for striking out in new directions but for observing and learning from their competitors and applying what they learn with exceptional consistency, imagination and skill. As one senior executive said to me recently, "I tell my managers: 'Never assume that you've got nothing more to learn just because you're well ahead of your competitors at the moment. Even the worst of the lot probably has something to teach you.' "

No self-respecting manager, of course, will admit to not knowing his competition. What sets the outstanding companies apart is not only that they watch their competition but that they do so in such depth and with such dedication. Some actual examples may serve to illustrate the level of effort required, the kind of insights gained and the competitive advantages that can be realised by moving beyond general qualitative assessment to specific quantitative analysis of competitors' performance.

Knowing the Competition

Consider first how three successful UK-based companies studied three aspects of their competitors' performance and used the information to develop their business strategies and set their internal objectives.

Product Performance

A consumer products company, which among many other things makes margarine, uses a consumer panel to make regular evaluations of its own product's relative performance in terms of convenience, quality, colour and texture against competitive margarines made not just in the United Kingdom but around the world.

Many companies, having ranked their own products in relation to their competitors, would leave it at that. But this company went further. Over the years its marketing and technical people have developed a series of technical measures that have proved to be reliable quantitative guides to subjective consumer reactions.

For example, one component of product convenience in the case of margarine is spreadability. To measure it, technical staff drop a small cone from a known height into a pat of margarine and measure the penetration. These quantitative measurements are then correlated with the results of subjective tests carried out with a knife, a pat of margarine and a piece of bread.

Again, one component of product quality in the case of margarine is coolness on the tongue, which happens to be a function of melting speed. Here again the company is not content with subjective impressions—it has actually created an artificial tongue to measure the melting rates of different margarines. And these are only two of a battery of such tests the company has developed to secure accurate quantitative comparisons of the performance of their own products and those of their competitors.

One payoff came a few years ago. A large US producer began test-marketing a new brand of margarine in the United Kingdom, with the evident intention of taking a 10 per cent market share—potentially a major disaster for the UK manufacturer. This company, however, soon established that the invader's product was no better than one of the US brands it had already tested—and found to be barely at parity with its own margarine. Since it offered no clear advantage on quality or convenience, its success would necessarily depend on promotion and price.

The UK company developed its competitive strategy accordingly. It used a fighting brand to attack the American product in the one low-price market where it had some possibility of gaining a foothold. The US margarine, which had attained around two-thirds of its target just after introduction, was soon beaten back to a small fraction of that. It has since been withdrawn from the mainstream of the market.

Knowing the competitor's product was the key to this strategy. Had the UK company not been certain that the new brand had no special appeal to customers, it might have considered repositioning one of its major brands. This would have disrupted other important plans, to say nothing of costing far more money. It was the years of experience with quantitative test results that gave the company the confidence to adopt a low-cost, yet effective defensive strategy.

Cost and Delivery

Product tear-down offers another way for a business to sharpen its own strategies by learning about its competitors' products. The Ford Motor Company, for example, regularly takes its competitors' products to bits to find out exactly how they are made and what their cost structure is likely to be. It has even publicly reported the results.

The process follows a five-step sequence:

1. *Purchase the product.* The high cost of product tear-down, particularly for a carmaker, gives some indication of the value successful competitors place on the knowledge they gain.
2. *Tear the product down—literally.* First, every removable component is unscrewed or unbolted; then rivets are undone; finally, individual spot welds are broken.
3. *Reverse-engineer the product.* While the competitor's car is being dismantled, detailed drawings of parts are made and parts lists are assembled, together with analyses of the production processes that were evidently involved.

4. *Build up costs.* Parts are costed out in terms of make-or-buy, the variety of parts used in a single product and the extent of common assemblies across model ranges. Among the most important facts to be established in a product tear-down, obviously, are the number and variety of components and the number of assembly operations. The costs of the processes are then built up from both direct labour requirements and overheads (often vital to an understanding of competitor cost structures).

5. *Establish economies of scale.* Once the individual cost elements are known, they can be put together with the volume of cars produced by the competitor, and with the total numbers of people he employs, to develop some fairly reliable guides to his economies of scale. Having done this, Ford can calculate model-run lengths and volumes needed to achieve, first, break-even and then profit.

From regularly tearing down the Leyland Mini over the years, Ford's technical and production people had reached two related conclusions: (1) Leyland was not making money on the Mini at its current price; and (2) Ford should therefore not enter that sector of the market as long as current price levels prevailed. Having established these two important points through detailed, factual analyses, Ford was able to make firm strategic decisions.

Sales and Service

My third example is a successful British company that sells most of its products by telephone. To keep its competitive edge, it monitors its competitors' telephone selling activities, using a small panel of marketing and production people. Once each month, posing as potential customers, members of the panel ring up each main competitor and evaluate the responses in quantitative terms: How long the telephone rang, how long it took to reach the right sales person; quality of the reply (assessed with a checklist); product knowledge (another checklist); and sales effectiveness. Panel members also note whether the product in question was in stock and available, or if not, what alternatives were offered. The panel then completes the competitive analysis by ringing its own sales force and asking similar questions.

From all the information gathered by the panel, the company has developed standards of sales and service that give it a sound basis for setting sales force numbers, altering sales training programmes when weaknesses are identified, changing the mix to counter competitive threats when there is evidence of relative product shortages, and separating the perennial issue of sales-force effectiveness from other product problems.

Each of these three companies gained significantly from measuring their competitors' performance. In each case, it is worth noting, the aspect of performance measured lies at the interface between two basic functions of the business. Product performance, as measured by the battery of quantitative measures and the consumer panel, involves both marketing and technology; costs, as measured by product tear-down, are governed both by technology and by production; and sales and service, as measured by competitors' selling activities, are a function of both production and marketing. They are the same three aspects of performance that determine the customer's decision.

Combining Competitive Insights

To see how a company can achieve notable competitive success by combining all three of these measures, compare the two different approaches to new product development taken by two companies which a few years ago, at almost the same time, were each alerted by their marketing departments to an important new market opportunity for an automatic dishwasher.

When the chief executive of the first company learnt from his marketing department about the market growth potential and current competitors' shares, he lost no time setting up an R&D project to develop a suitable machine.

Finding little useful information available on dishwasher design, the R&D director decided to begin by investigating the basic mechanics of the dishwashing process. Accordingly, he set up a series of pilot projects to evaluate the cleaning performance of different jet configurations, the merits of alternative washing-arm designs, and the varying results obtained with different types and quantities of detergent on different washing loads. At the end of a year he had amassed a great deal of useful knowledge. He also had a pilot machine running that cleansed dishes well, and a design concept for a production version. But considerable development work was still needed before the prototype could be declared a satisfactory basis for manufacture.

To complicate matters, management had neglected to establish effective linkages among the company's three main functions—marketing, technology and production. So it was not until the technologists had produced the prototype and design concepts that marketing and production began asking for revisions and suggesting new ideas—further delaying the development of a marketable product.

So much for the first company, with its fairly typical traditional response to market opportunities. The second company, which happened to be Japanese, started with the same marketing intelligence but responded in very different fashion.

First, it bought three units of every available competitive dishwasher. Next, management formed four special teams: (1) a product test group of marketing and technical staff; (2) design team of technologists and production people; (3) a distribution team of marketing and production staff; and (4) a field team of production staff.

The *product test group* was given one of each competitive model and asked to evaluate their performance: dishwashing effectiveness, ease of use, and reliability (frequency and cause of breakdown).

The remaining two units of each competitive model were given to the *design team* of technologists and production people, who stripped down one of each pair to determine the number and variety of parts, the cost of each part and the ease of assembly. The remaining units were stripped down to 'life-test' each component, to identify design improvements and potential sources of supply; and to develop a comprehensive picture of the competitors' technology. Meanwhile, the *distribution team* was evaluating each competitor's sales and distribution system (numbers of outlets, product availability and service offered), and the *field team* was investigating the competitors' factories and evaluating their production facilities in terms of cost of labour, cost of supplies and plant productivity.

All this took a little less than a year. At the end of that time, the Japanese still knew a lot less than their UK rivals about the physics and chemistry of dishwashing, but the knowledge developed by their business teams had put them far ahead. In two more months they had designed a product that out-performed the best of the competition, yet would cost 30 per cent less to build, based on a preproduction prototype and production process design. They also had a marketing plan for introducing the new dishwasher on the Japanese domestic market before taking it overseas. This plan positioned the product relative to competition and defined the distribution system requirements in terms of stocking and service levels needed to meet the expected production rate. Finally, the Japanese had prepared detailed plans for building a new factory, establishing supply contracts and training the labour force.

The denouement of this story is what one might expect: the competitive Japanese manufacturer brought its new product to market two years ahead of the more traditionally-minded British manufacturer, and achieved its planned market share ten weeks later. The traditional company steadily lost money and eventually dropped out of the market.

Linking the Functions

The Japanese company's success, however, was not solely due to its outward-looking, competitive orientation. Just as important within the organisation was management's recognition of the need for interfunctional linkages within the company itself. Only by pooling and sharing the knowledge they had acquired could the technical, marketing and production functions turn it to advantage and outperform their competition.

This recognition is, in my experience, typical of the most successful competitors. By forging strong links between functions, they are better able to keep a close watch on competition, develop competitive strategic responses and, finally, maintain better communications between functions in the day-to-day running of the business.

When a company is small, the man in charge can typically handle the task of competitive surveillance himself. He can keep an eye on his competitors' product performance; he can go to trade fairs or exhibitions to try the products out, and visit customers to find out how well they perform. He can get to know his competitors' costs and delivery performance, monitoring delivery on lost orders, and working out costs from sales literature and maintenance manuals. He can know his competitors' sales and service orgnisations.

Such a man can mobilise the separate functions to meet the competitive challenge and provide the link that coordinates and directs the different parts of the business. He can, for example, challenge his technologists in marketing terms—"That concept will never go down with the customers. Make it more functional; get rid of those sharp edges"— and in production terms—"That design can't be made for the quoted price. Redesign it to take advantage of these low-cost techniques." He can do the same for the marketing staff and for the production department. He knows his factory and how it works.

But small companies that compete effectively tend to grow, and growth brings increasing complexity and specialisation in each function. The result is to push the functions further and further apart. As the company grows it tends increasingly to fragment into separate functional islands, each trying to solve its own problems, each using its own special language and having its own priorities. Marketing people talk about marketing segmentation, market growth, GNP, Nielsens, promotions and product image, and worry about changes in share. Technologists talk about processes, new materials, computer chips, and space-age ideas, and worry about prototype results and technical problems; as regards language and interests, they have little in common with marketing. Production people talk and worry about industrial relations, people arriving on time, suppliers who let them down, and plant and equipment breakdowns and delays; they in their turn have little in common with either marketing or the technologists who, they consider, live in ivory towers.

Should the man responsible for the business concentrate on the individual functions, he will find himself forced to play the role of the small businessman with total responsibility for the competitive success of the business. There are some notable examples of large businesses where one individual does just this; but in general, as a business grows in complexity, this task becomes impossible at some point.

If, however, the man in charge turns his attention to the links between functions, he can insist on external competitive measures and focus on competitive results, while, at the same time, building communications and team work between functions. He can forge a link between *marketing and technology* to look at competitors' product performance. This link may be a project team; it may be *ad hoc,* created in response to a particular problem. (This is frequently better than setting up yet another disconnected staff function with no means of maintaining its own links with the functions from which it came.)

Again, the chief executive can forge links between *technology and production* in the form of joint design teams charged with evaluating competitors' costs and delivery. (Product tear-down has been cited as an example, but much can be learned from a systematic study of literature and visual study of products.) And he can forge links between *marketing and production,* an area where permanent links are particularly needed but are apt to get bogged down in procedures. Occasional projects to review competitors' sales and service can, however, be an effective shot in the arm.

Through such measures, the chief executive of a giant company can manage the linkages among the functions of his business that are vital to effective competitive response—while at the same time freeing himself to concentrate on his single most important mission, that of maximising the competitive vitality of the enterprise.

21. Concept Testing for Consumer and Industrial Products

E. Patrick McGuire

McGuire discusses the various approaches management can take to evaluate the relative merits of proposed new products at early stages in their development.

I. Concept Testing of Consumer Products

THE SPONSOR of a concept test hopes to get advance consumer reaction to a new-product offering by exposing the concept to a consumer jury and analyzing its response. The concept may be presented to the test participants in several different ways—by written description; by picture; by mock-up or prototype versions of the package or the product itself; and by promotional literature or simulated advertising.

Just which combination of these is employed depends in part on how far the company has proceeded in concept planning and development. It depends also on what kind of guidance the company's planners seek from the test.

More than anything else, the underlying rationale for concept testing is that, for a relatively modest investment, it can prevent a company from making costly mistakes. Nevertheless, there are several reasons that keep companies from putting blind faith in the results of their concept tests.

Probably the most serious difficulty is that there is some question of what is really being measured in a concept test. As one observer has noted,[1] researchers variously refer to the testing of advertising execution

---

[1] Edward M. Tauber, "What Is Measured by Concept Testing?" *Journal of Advertising Research,* December, 1972, pp. 35–37.

Reprinted from *Evaluating New Product Proposals* (New York: The Conference Board, CBR 604, 1973), pp. 33–75. Used by permission.

E. Patrick McGuire is Senior Research Specialist at The Conference Board.

or copy; of product positioning; and, most often, of new-product ideas. In each instance one must distinguish between the form of the presentation and the particular execution or design of what is to be conveyed.

The limitations of concept tests, however, do not deter many companies from conducting them. Generally, their planners do follow various guidelines which they believe can help them to avoid misleading test results. Among those mentioned:

- If possible, the primary means of presenting concepts during tests should replicate that of the intended vehicle for promotion (e.g., television, print).[2]
- For concept tests to be reasonably predictive of how consumers will react to the product, the product itself will have to fulfill the promises enunciated in the concept statement.
- It is better to confine consumers' test evaluations to a very few, clearly demonstrable product benefits; including too many may confuse the issue.
- Estimates of market size extrapolated from concept test findings are apt to be highly misleading.

The most common methods[3] of exposing product concepts or prototypes in advance to consumer juries are through:

- Focus-group testing
- Employee panels
- Central location testing
- Use testing

Focus Groups

Freewheeling discussions, along with panel interviewing, are hallmarks of focus groups. Such groups are frequently made up of six to ten individuals who meet—sometimes, on a regular basis—to give their opinions on a company's new-product concepts, package designs, advertisements, and the like.

A focus-group test may take one to two hours to complete. The session is most often conducted as an informal discussion, with the research personnel acting as discussion leaders or perhaps merely as observers. The proceedings of the session are usually tape-recorded for later review and transcription.

[2] This was also one of the principal conclusions of Edward M. Tauber, *op. cit.*

[3] There is some possible overlap and blurring among these methods. For example, persons taking part in central location tests may be enlisted for focus-group interviews or for later participation in product or home-use tests.

Depending partly on their purposes, focus-group discussions may follow an ordered agenda or move along on a relatively unstructured basis. Ordinarily, a company or agency representative at the meeting begins by presenting the participants with a concept statement and then helps to get the discussion started by asking evocative questions about it.

Marketers are thus able to develop clues regarding not only the relative appeal of a particular concept, but also some of the rationale behind the members' preferences. For many researchers, this is seen as one of the principal advantages of using focus-group evaluations.

Employee Panels

A number of the consumer goods producers (and even some manufacturers of industrial products), make regular use of employee panels to appraise new-product concepts or prototypes.[4] Several food firms, for example, report having used employee screening panels for several decades.

It is acknowledged that there may be some problems of bias in using employee panels. In comparisons involving the company's current product offerings, for example, employees may be familiar with these items. However, researchers usually make certain to conceal the actual company or brand identity of products during paired-comparison, triangular or monadic product tests.

It is the practice of some manufacturers of food products to maintain a test kitchen, along with a consumer test facility, and to invite selected employees to visit the test area at regular intervals.

Other companies, including manufacturers of detergents, personal care products, hand tools, etc., report providing selected employees with take-home samples for use and evaluation by them and their families. The employee is also supplied with a product-use and evaluation questionnaire. After several weeks of using the product, the employee completes the questionnaire form, which is then keypunched and processed for EDP analysis.

The companies surveyed that rely on employee test panels are generally enthusiastic about their use. The advantages they mention most frequently are the convenience of such testing, its low cost, the speed with which it can be done, and the ease of retesting. But these companies are not blind to the dangers and limitations. Such panels, some say, probably work best in companies with large, fairly heterogeneous work forces whose

[4] Of course, marketing researchers often use various sample groups for other testing purposes: among the possibilities available from research suppliers; continuous consumer-purchase panels whose purchase diaries indicate brand preferences and switching; store-audit panels by which can be computed measure of market share; territorial sales volume; and other panels used to monitor the size and composition of media audiences.

habits and tastes are unlikely to be much different from those of persons in the target market. Employee panels are a poor bet in any case where the members have an obvious personal interest in the success of a product being tested.

Central Location Testing

Researchers take advantage of the fact that groups of consumers can be interviewed at shopping centers, transportation terminals, and similar locations, for what is known as "central location" testing. Many consumer goods marketers make frequent use of such testing possibilities to evaluate their new-product concepts or prototypes.

The term "central location testing" is sometimes applied also to the controlled exposure of products or concepts to groups of socially related consumers. For example, a women's club which meets monthly may be invited to help in evaluating cosmetic product concepts at its next get-together. (The same organizations are also sometimes the source of focus groups.) In return for members' evaluations, the cooperating organization is usually given a fee and then test participants may be further rewarded with free samples of the sponsoring company's products.

While central location testing may offer many advantages, companies cite some limitations, including:

- *It may be difficult to assemble respondents who are representative of the client's target market.*
- *Interference and distractions at some public testing sites may hinder thoughtful response.*
- *Retesting individual respondents may be difficult if they include a large percentage of transients.*
- *Many respondents may not have the sophistication necessary for certain types of concept testing.*

Use Tests

A company's new product planners may get useful preliminary guidance in developing concepts from consumer juries enlisted for focus-group, central-location, or employee testing. But at some juncture most planners would like to know the reactions of individual consumers who have actually used the product. (And, in the home-testing of some items, there is the advantage that responses may reflect the views of the whole family.) A related question may be how well the product works, and how it is used or misused, under normal use conditions. Product-use tests are standard features in the development programs of many manufacturers of such products as food, beauty and other personal care items, appliances, and the like.

Participants in a use test may be persons selected solely for this purpose. Or they may be persons who took part in earlier testing and whose reactions would again be of interest.

Thus, a soap company, seeking to introduce a new type of soap, will sometimes manufacture several thousand bars in advance and distribute them by mail to households within a selected area. Then a sample of the households is interviewed to get reactions to the product.

Corning Glass Works is one of several firms having its own testing panel. The members—over 1,500 housewives—help in evaluating the company's new cooking utensils. Demographic data about the housewives and their families, including the number of persons in the family, the ages of children, the type of cooking energy used, ownership of other kitchen appliances, etc., are cross-indexed on catalog cards.

Normally, the company asks at least 200 housewives to take part in a particular product test. By rotating those chosen, the company makes certain that no individual panelist is called on too frequently. Of course, the panel members are permitted to retain the cookware they are asked to evaluate. The Corning interviewers later contact the panelists, either in person or by phone. They complete detailed questionnaires covering the respondents' opinions regarding the utensil's durability, ease of use, aesthetic appeals, etc.

Planners who make extensive use of in-home product testing stress that marketers must be wary of potential problems in such testing. These reportedly include:

- Despite precise instructions on product use, a respondent still may misuse the product and then report adversely on its features and properties.
- It is occasionally difficult to determine whether the product was in fact used at all.
- If the product is received as a free sample, this may result in some degree of built-in favorable bias towards the product.
- Some products require long-term testing, and a panelist's commitment to continued use of the product may wane after a while.

"Mini-Market" Testing

Several consumer goods marketers that formerly subjected all their new products to full-scale test marketing now rely, as often as possible, on some form of controlled test marketing (otherwise known as "mini-market" testing).

Like traditional market tests, the mini-market evaluation provides a thorough dress rehearsal for the actual marketing of a new consumer item. Among those who find it desirable to use this test method—for either mid- to final-stage testing of new entries—several advantages are cited. Compared to regular market tests, they say, mini-market checks are quicker, less expensive, and, in their experience, nearly as effective in predicting market acceptance.

The mini-market test is usually carried out in one or more small areas where the marketer is able to control most of the variables affecting the new-product introduction. The controlled test market, from product introduction to store audit of sales results, can usually be completed within six weeks.

The execution of the controlled test market may be by company personnel; but more often, an outside research agency is used. Some agencies will take over the complete distribution of the new product during the control test market. Shipments of the product may be received by the agency's warehouse, and then taken to stores within the test area, priced, and, if desired, billed to the stores by the agency.

Under an arrangement of this kind, agency service personnel will make periodic calls on the stores to ensure that the new product is in stock, that the designated retail price is on each package, and that the agreed upon number of shelf facings have been secured.

During larger-scale market tests, by contrast, it is often difficult to avoid out-of-stock situations or unsatisfactory shelf facings in some retail outlets. In this respect, the controlled test market could turn out to be an idealized situation which is unlikely to be duplicated either in a full test market or in national distribution. For these and related reasons, researchers say the mini-market test nearly always indicates higher levels of sales than can realistically be obtained in national distribution.[5] So, the results are seldom used for direct projection of expected sales on a national basis.[6]

"Fine Screening" of New-Product Proposals—Ralston Purina Company

The Consumer Products Group of the Ralston Purina Company has worked to develop a disciplined approach to new-idea evaluation. It consists of passing new-product ideas through a series of increasingly finer evaluation screens. The screening steps are as follows:

Step A—Judgmental Screening. The first step in the screening process is the responsibility of the new-products department. The department's

---

[5] See E. Sherak, "Controlled Test Marketing and the Projection of Test Marketing Results," *Marketing Review,* February, 1973, p. 17.

[6] However, Market Facts, Incorporated, a marketing research firm, reportedly conducted a series of regression analyses on eight separate controlled test markets. The firm found that when adjustments were made for levels of distribution and out-of-stock situations, the regression model did provide reasonably good projections of national sales.

staff makes an initial rough screening of the several hundred new-products ideas proposed each year. From these it selects the 25 or 30 that seem most promising and worthy of further consideration.

Step B—Preliminary Consumer Reaction Tests. These superior ideas are then subjected to a consumer reaction check. Usually, this consists of exposing selected consumers to a short statement, consisting of a paragraph of no more than 30 or 40 words, which describes a product idea. The consumers are asked to rank the various concepts in the order of interest to them. The consumers participating in these checks are usually procured through central location testing services.

Step C—Preliminary Marketing Criteria Evaluation. Each worthwhile idea identified in the preliminary consumer reaction tests is now evaluated on the basis of the following criteria: probable sales volume, concept uniqueness, incremental value, life cycle, competition, and the purchase situation and consumer appeal within the relevant market.

Step D—Preliminary Feasibility Evaluation. The best surviving prospects from Step C are then submitted to a research and development team which examines the feasibility of their manufacture. The team checks possible conflicts with competitive patents, potential technical difficulties in developing a product, and the amount of money that may be required to produce it. At this stage, manufacturing executives may also be consulted more closely regarding capital investment and production equipment requirements, including the possible use of present facilities for the new product.

Step E—Preliminary Concept Test. An outside marketing research agency is now engaged to find out how well several alternative concept statements for Step B communicate the concept to various consumer groups. The agency attempts to discover, for example, whether consumers will translate a concept statement accurately and thus recognize the advantages the product has to offer. The agency works with a focus group, consisting of six to eight individuals who have some demonstrated familiarity with the type of product in question.

Step F—Final Concept Test. It now becomes necessary to identify those classes of consumers—i.e., the target groups in the market—who will have the greatest interest in the product. A broad sample of consumers is approached and a determination made of the interest level within each of various subsections of the over-all market.

Step G—Final Marketing Potential and Feasibility Evaluation. There is one last step, as a spokesman explains, "before turning the R&D people loose on the project." Once a proposal gets this far and is approved, it becomes an active laboratory project.

The main consideration at this late point is whether the proposed project appears in all respects to be a valid business proposition, in terms of Ralston's standards. The decision to go ahead with final development now requires more highly refined estimates as to probable sales volume, pricing, costs, profits, capital investment, market timing, and competitive factors. If all of these look favorable, the research and development department is authorized to proceed with a product's development, including preparation of test formulas and prototypes for use during the field-test marketing stage still to come.

II. Industrial Product Concept Testing

Companies that undertake the pretesting of industrial product concepts try to obtain information regarding:

- The range or variety of applications and situations for which the new product might be used.
- Identification of various types of users for the proposed product, and the specific needs of each.
- Preferred product attributes.
- Relative importance of proposed features and intended functions of the product on the part of different classes of users.
- Design parameters for the product.
- Cost-benefits of the product to potential users, and general evidence as to pricing possibilities.
- How the product could best be marketed, e.g., advance clues to suitable channels of distribution, promotional requirements, etc.

The usual practice is to have product proposals under consideration first scrutinized by the company's own marketing and sales personnel. Production and purchasing personnel can also help—e.g., a producer of machine tools is a large user of its own products and is therefore able to test and evaluate new-product concepts in its own shops. Companies also solicit the views of distributors and dealers through which the product might be sold.

For some firms, the pretesting of a product idea does not go beyond its own employees or distributors. One reason may be the reluctance of a company to tip its hand to competitors by discussing the product with outsiders. Or a company may settle for the informed opinion of its own staff because it is convinced that customer opinion in this instance—or perhaps in most—would be of little help.

In some instances, the industrial products manufacturer enjoys a close working relationship with the relatively small number of customers that constitute its market. Under such conditions, the manufacturer will often find that its ties and contacts make the job much easier.

Even when the new entry is planned for large or unfamiliar markets, and more effort is required to sound out prospective users, the fact that the latter often stand to benefit by the supplier's product innovation gives them incentive to cooperate.

Many planners consider it desirable to get views from several different points within those firms believed to be logical users of the product. In this way, an attempt is made to obtain the judgments of all individuals who might be influential in their company's purchasing decisions, or who are knowledgeable of their firm's product-plans or needs.

Companies sometimes find it necessary to go beyond the immediate user to pretest the product's marketability. In certain kinds of market situations, for example, it is helpful to test the product concept with the user's customers. There are other instances in which some companies deem it worthwhile—or even mandatory—to check the requirements or interest of a variety of other specifying influences. In the building products field, for example, contacts for this purpose are often made with architects and various agencies of government.

Guides for Concept Testing of Industrial Products

Practitioners recommend that concept tests:

- Make clear the function or functions the new product would perform, possible situations in which it could be used, and how it would be used.
- Portray the product's characteristics in terms that will be readily understood by the respondent.
- Provide a comparison of the product's likely physical and performance characteristics with those of any existing competitive products used to perform a similar function.
- Cite the product's principal advantages and disadvantages.
- Indicate an expected price or price range.

Pretesting Methods

Industrial marketing researchers rely heavily on personal interviews for gathering field information needed for their new-product programs, both in concept and prototype testing. The technique is reported to be especially well suited for probing discussions dealing with complex product concepts, since, in an interview situation, the interviewer can usually sense both the extent of the respondent's comprehension of the product idea under discussion and his reception to the proposal.

When manufacturers need to obtain information from respondents concerning well-defined basic product concepts or specific product features —or when they wish to supplement the data developed earlier through personal interviews—they may be able to do so by means of telephone interviews. (The telephone is usually less helpful for carrying out first-stage interviews dealing with product concepts requiring some kind of demonstration aid.)

Many industrial product companies have at one time or another made use of mail surveys in their new-product research involving either concepts or prototypes. Usually, the purpose is to broaden the base of the investigation and/or to supplement first-hand findings obtained by personal interview.

Not all polling of this kind is done with ad hoc samples of prospective customers. Sometimes the participants are the customers of prospective customers, technical experts in the field or persons in a position to influence or specify purchase of the product, such as architects.

A steel manufacturer, for example, maintains a panel of machine designers who are contacted by mail on a regular basis, and asked for their opinions on new alloys, extrusions, etc. Samples of a proposed new product, along with descriptive literature, are sent to the designers months before the product is to be introduced. Often, company executives say, commentary from the panelists is valuable in suggesting worthwhile modifications of a product before its introduction.

There is general agreement that the mail survey technique is most effective in industrial marketing research when well-defined concepts are involved, and when specific, limited answers are called for.

In circumstances where it can be used effectively, the principal advantage of the mail survey is reported to be its low cost—and speed. Some industrial products firms have been able to obtain a very high rate of return for their mail questionnaires. Others, however, have been left in doubt as to the accuracy of survey findings in instances when the return was small, or when they had no effective way of judging the representativeness of their sample.

Communicating Industrial Product Concepts

One of the major problems in concept testing for industrial product marketers and respondents alike is the presentation, communication, and comprehension of ideas during early project stages. Since the product's sponsor is often attempting to present an abstract concept—at a time when design features, price, and other specifications are probably still tentative—it is hard for the respondent to visualize the new-product idea being presented.

The actual testing of an industrial product concept often requires the use of some sort of demonstration aid. Devices used to convey product ideas to prospective users include detailed specifications, drawings, blueprints, photographs, movies, mock-up scale models, working models, and prototypes.

The means of exposure and method of presentation depend generally on the stage of the product development and on the type of customer to whom it will appeal. Most planners say that, in general, the closer the demonstration aids resemble the actual product, the more accurate and meaningful the results of the tests are likely to be.

Test Problems

The testing of new-product concepts, as well as of prototypes, oftentimes is more of an art than a science, and its practitioners must accept the fact that they will almost invariably have to contend with a number of difficulties.

Certainly, one of the things that any company has to consider when pretesting new-product ideas with prospective users is the risk it runs in disclosing evidence of its activities and interests. Many companies try to minimize this risk by anonymously having their testing carried out by independent research agencies.

Moreover, it takes no small amount of time to develop methods of presenting the concept, to design the test, to locate suitable respondents, to arrange for contacts, to visit respondents or provide them with questionnaires, and to evaluate the results. While this means that concept testing can be costly, the question in a given case, of course, is whether such expense looms large or small in relation to the possible consequences of proceeding without the test information.

There is yet another factor that can render the results of industrial concept pretesting inconclusive: after initial probes, findings may become dated as markets and technology change. Still another possibility is that, even if prototypes are used, it may be difficult to tell what the test results really show. The marketing research manager of a glass producer sums up this problem as follows:

> The biggest limitation is in being unable to forecast what the end product will look like. Broad concepts can be described in general terms and can be understood by the potential user. However, as the study narrows to a more specific product, the product must be described by words, picture, sketch, or prototype. At this time, we must describe the product as we understand it. Obviously, we don't understand it well enough or we wouldn't be testing further. Sometimes it is difficult to be sure if we are testing the product concept, the particular color, or some other part of the prototype shown.

Concept testing cannot be expected, of course, to answer once and for all the many questions that the industrial manufacturer would like to have answered before the final stage of development and market launching. Rather, those experienced with such testing regard it simply as an initial probe for supporting early-stage decisions and guiding future planning. And most continue to employ such testing, when suitable, in the belief that—despite attendant problems and limitations—they are likely to make fewer costly mistakes in their product programs as a result.

Testing Industrial Prototypes

It generally becomes possible at some point—and according to most companies, highly desirable—to pretest the new industrial product's field performance. Prior research will have dealt with the product concept and leaned heavily perhaps on a set of suppositions more or less speculative in nature. Therefore, the conclusions based on investigations thus far—of a product which has hypothetical attributes and which should be able to perform certain hypothetical functions—will in most cases have been conditional.

As a last-stage check prior to some type of limited test marketing or full-scale national introduction, a good many companies will now undertake to evaluate the product and its marketability under selected field conditions. Some of the major objectives of testing at this point are technical, e.g., to test the product in actual use with respect to performance, reliability, design, operating costs, and the like, and also to develop plant experience and facility in manufacturing the product. But marketing planning considerations are also served by such tests which may involve:

- Testing user reaction to the product and its features.
- Testing price possibilities.
- Determining probable order patterns.
- Identifying key purchasing influences.
- Testing the effectiveness of promotional materials and plans.
- Determining the most effective sales approach.

The product-use test is the most common method of advance testing of industrial product performance. Generally, the primary purpose is to verify, prior to its formal introduction, the product's ability to perform as it is supposed to; if it cannot meet certain performance standards, then, of course, the product cannot be successfully sold. As one producer explains, "The marketability of the products we manufacture is highly correlated with performance results, operating costs, and reliability. These factors can be measured through extensive, objective tests within company-operated facilities and by customer use in a testing program."

Test Considerations

When subjecting a new industrial product to actual operating conditions, planners say that it is desirable to have someone from the company on hand when the test is run to see that the product is used properly, to handle unforeseen complications, and to observe the results. Otherwise, the customer might somehow misuse the product, in which case it may be difficult to schedule another trial and the disappointed customer may announce his dissatisfaction to others.

In the case of expendable items having relatively low unit value, selected prospective users are sometimes supplied with trial lots of the product. When it is feasible, the most common practice in testing a durable product is to turn over to prospects a limited amount of the product for on-the-job testing. But some manufacturers are able to install and test such a product first on their own premises. Many manufacturers maintain pilot plant facilities that replicate customer uses and purposes, and prospective customers may be brought in to see new products in operation.

Although it is the practice of some manufacturers to give the new product to the user at no charge, others arrange to sell it to him, perhaps at a reduced price. In either case, the user often agrees to provide, in effect, a limited consulting service; and the manufacturer is permitted to observe the product in operation, to compile performance data, to make necessary adjustments or alterations in the product, and, in some instances, to show the product to any other interested prospects.

Some product testing is prolonged and expensive, especially when costly capital equipment is involved. In the testing done by a textile machinery manufacturer, for example,

> Several prototypes will be thoroughly evaluated by a number of mills prior to the actual go-ahead signal for full manufacturing. Such mill evaluation can take from a couple of weeks to as long as one or two years, depending upon the nature of the product improvement.

By contrast, some products require relatively simple testing. One company was able to place working prototypes of a proposed new product in three separate marketing areas for use under actual operating conditions. At the end of 30 days, it called on the users, conducted long interviews, and picked up the product.

Some Limitations

There are often limits to the thoroughness with which product tests can be profitably observed and evaluated. For one thing, users are sometimes said to be biased in their reports—and in ways not always evident to the sponsor. Some may tend to be overly critical under test conditions, while others may be inclined to report more favorable results than the tests would appear to justify. Also, there is the danger that users may lose interest in the cooperative venture if the testing period must be extended for some reason, or if the product requires excessive attention.

Because of the expense involved in producing prototypes, the placement of a sufficient number of products in representative test situations sometimes poses a problem. Moreover, the company's inability to locate willing cooperators may also limit the possibilities of testing.

22. New Way to Measure Consumers' Judgments

Paul E. Green and Yoram Wind

Conjoint measurement can be used to sort out the relative importance of various product dimensions in complex choice situations. The results can be applied to the design and positioning of new product offerings.

TAKING A JET PLANE for a business appointment in Paris? Which of the two flights described below would you choose?

- A B-707 flown by British Airways that will depart within two hours of the time you would like to leave and that is often late in arriving in Paris. The plane will make two intermediate stops, and it is anticipated that it will be 50% full. Flight attendants are "warm and friendly" and you would have a choice of two movies for entertainment.
- A B-747 flown by TWA that will depart within four hours of the time you would like to leave and that is almost never late in arriving in Paris. The flight is nonstop, and it is anticipated that the plane will be 90% full. Flight attendants are "cold and curt" and only magazines are provided for entertainment.

Are you looking for replacement tires for your two-year-old car? Suppose you want radial tires and have the following three options to choose from:

- Goodyear's, with a tread life of 30,000 miles at a price of $40 per tire; the store is a 10-minute drive from your home.

Reprinted by permission of the *Harvard Business Review*, 53 (July–August, 1975), pp. 107–17. Copyright © 1975 by the President and Fellows of Harvard College; all rights reserved.

Paul E. Green is S. S. Kresge Professor of Marketing at the Wharton School of the University of Pennsylvania. Yoram Wind is also a Professor of Marketing at Wharton.

- Firestone's, with a tread life of 50,000 miles at a price of $85 per tire; the store is a 20-minute drive from your home.
- Or Sears's, with a tread life of 40,000 miles at a price of $55 per tire; the store is located about 10 minutes from your home.

How would you rank these alternatives in order of preference?

Both of these problems have a common structure that companies and their marketing managers frequently encounter in trying to figure out what a consumer really wants in a product or service. First, the characteristics of the alternatives that the consumer must choose from fall along more than a single dimension—they are multiattribute. Second, the consumer must make an overall judgment about the relative value of those characteristics, or attributes; in short, he must order them according to some criterion. But doing this requires complex trade-offs, since it is likely that no alternative is clearly better than another on every dimension of interest.

In recent years, researchers have developed a new measurement technique from the fields of mathematical psychology and psychometrics that can aid the marketing manager in sorting out the relative importance of a product's multidimensional attributes.[1] This technique, called conjoint measurement, starts with the consumer's overall or global judgments about a set of complex alternatives. It then performs the rather remarkable job of decomposing his or her original evaluations into separate and compatible utility scales by which the original global judgments (or others involving new combinations of attributes) can be reconstituted.[2]

Being able to separate overall judgments into psychological components in this manner can provide a manager with valuable information about the relative importance of various attributes of a product. It can also provide information about the value of various levels of a single attribute. (For example, if price is the attribute under consideration, conjoint measurement can give the manager a good idea of how sensitive consumers would be to a price change from a level of, say, 85¢ to one of 75¢ or one of 95¢.) Indeed, some models can even estimate the psychological trade-offs consumers make when they evaluate several attributes together.

The advantages of this type of knowledge to the planning of marketing strategy are significant. The knowledge can be useful in modifying current products or services and in designing new ones for selected buying publics.

In this article, we first show how conjoint measurement works from

[1] R. Duncan Luce and John W. Tukey, "Simultaneous Conjoint Measurement: A New Type of Fundamental Measurement," *Journal of Mathematical Psychology,* February 1964, p. 1.

[2] The first marketing-oriented paper on conjoint measurement was by Paul E. Green and Vithala R. Rao, "Conjoint Measurement for Quantifying Judgmental Data," *Journal of Marketing Research,* August 1971, p. 355.

a numerical standpoint. We then discuss its application to a variety of marketing problems, and we demonstrate its use in strategic marketing simulations. The Appendix provides a brief description of how other research tools for measuring consumer judgments work, and how they relate to conjoint measurement.

How Conjoint Measurement Works

In order to see how to apply conjoint measurement, suppose a company were interested in marketing a new spot remover for carpets and upholstery. The technical staff has developed a new product that is designed to handle tough, stubborn spots. Management interest centers on five attributes or factors that it expects will influence consumer preference: an applicator-type package design, brand name, price, a *Good Housekeeping* seal of endorsement, and a money-back guarantee.

Three package designs are under consideration and appear in the upper portion of Exhibit 1. There are three brand names under consideration: *K2R, Glory,* and *Bissell.* Of the three brand names used in the study, two are competitors' brand names already on the market, whereas one is the company's present brand name choice for its new product. Three alternative prices being considered are $1.19, $1.39, and $1.59. Since there are three alternatives for each of these factors, they are called three-level factors. The *Good Housekeeping* seal and money-back guarantee are two-level factors, since each is either present or not. Consequently, a total of $3 \times 3 \times 3 \times 2 \times 2 = 108$ alternatives would have to be tested if the researcher were to array all possible combinations of the five attributes.

Clearly, the cost of administering a consumer evaluation study of this magnitude—not to mention the respondents' confusion and fatigue—would be prohibitive. As an alternative, however, the researcher can take advantage of a special experimental design, called an *orthogonal array,* in which the test combinations are selected so that the independent contributions of all five factors are balanced. In this way each factor's weight is kept separate and is not confused with those of the other factors.

The lower portion of Exhibit 1 shows an orthogonal array that involves only 18 of the 108 possible combinations that the company wishes to test in this case. For the test the researcher makes up 18 cards. On each card appears an artist's sketch of the package design, A, B, or C, and verbal details regarding each of the other four factors: brand name, price, *Good Housekeeping* seal (or not), and money-back guarantee (or not). After describing the new product's functions and special features, he shows the respondents each of the 18 cards (see Exhibit 1 for the master design), and asks them to rank the cards in order of their likelihood of purchase.

The last column of Exhibit 1 shows one respondent's actual ranking of the 18 cards; rank number 1 denotes her highest evaluated concept. Note particularly that only *ranked* data need be obtained and, furthermore, that only 18 (out of 108) combinations are evaluated.

Computing the Utilities

Computation of the utility scales of each attribute, which determine how influential each is in the consumers' evaluations, is carried out by various computer programs.[3] The ranked data of a single respondent (or the composite ranks of a group of respondents) are entered in the program. The computer then searches for a set of scale values for each factor in the experimental design. The scale values for each level of each factor are chosen so that when they are added together the *total* utility of each combination will correspond to the original ranks as closely as possible.

Notice that two problems are involved here. First, as mentioned previously, the experimental design of Exhibit 1 shows only 18 of 108 combinations. Second, only rank-order data are supplied to the algorithms. This means that the data themselves do not determine how much more influential one attribute is than another in the consumers' choices. However, despite these limitations, the algorithms are able to find a *numerical* representation of the utilities, thus providing an indication of each factor's relative importance.

In general, more accurate solutions are obtained as the number of combinations being evaluated increases. Still, in the present case, with only 18 ranking-type judgments, the technique works well. Exhibit 2 shows the computer results.

As can be observed in Exhibit 2, the technique obtains a utility function for each level of each factor. For example, to find the utility for the first combination in Exhibit 1, we can read off the utilities of each factor level in the five charts of Exhibit 2: U (A) = 0.1; U (K2R) = 0.3; U ($1.19) = 1.0; U (No) = 0.2; U (No) = 0.2. Therefore the total utility is 1.8, the sum of the five separate utilities, for the first combination. Note that this combination was ranked only thirteenth by the respondent in Exhibit 1.

On the other hand, the utility of combination 18 is 3.1 (0.6 + 0.5 + 1.0 + 0.3 + 0.7), which is the respondent's highest evaluation of all 18 combinations listed.

However, as can be easily seen from Exhibit 2, if combination 18 is modified to include package Design B (in place of C), its utility is even higher. As a matter of fact, it then represents the highest possible utility,

---

[3] As an illustration, see Joseph B. Kruskal, "Analysis of Factorial Experiments by Estimating Monotone Transformations of the Data," *Journal of the Royal Statistical Society,* Series B, March 1965, p. 251.

Package Designs

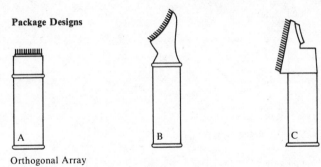

Orthogonal Array

	Package design	Brand name	Price	*Good Housekeeping* seal?	Money-back guarantee?	Respondent's evaluation (rank number)
1	A	K2R	$1.19	No	No	13
2	A	Glory	1.39	No	Yes	11
3	A	Bissell	1.59	Yes	No	17
4	B	K2R	1.39	Yes	Yes	2
5	B	Glory	1.59	No	No	14
6	B	Bissell	1.19	No	No	3
7	C	K2R	1.59	No	Yes	12
8	C	Glory	1.19	Yes	No	7
9	C	Bissell	1.39	No	No	9
10	A	K2R	1.59	Yes	No	18
11	A	Glory	1.19	No	Yes	8
12	A	Bissell	1.39	No	No	15
13	B	K2R	1.19	No	No	4
14	B	Glory	1.39	Yes	No	6
15	B	Bissell	1.59	No	Yes	5
16	C	K2R	1.39	No	No	10
17	C	Glory	1.59	No	No	16
18	C	Bissell	1.19	Yes	Yes	1*

*Highest ranked

EXHIBIT 1. Experimental Design for Evaluation of a Carpet Cleaner

even though this specific combination did not appear among the original 18.

Importance of Attributes

By focusing attention on only the package design, the company's marketing researchers can see from Exhibit 2 that Design B displays highest utility. Moreover, all utility scales are expressed in a common unit (although their zero points are arbitrary). This means that we can compare utility ranges from factor to factor so as to get some idea of their relative importance.

In the case of the spot remover, as shown in Exhibit 2, the utility ranges are:

- Package design $(1.0 - 0.1 = 0.9)$

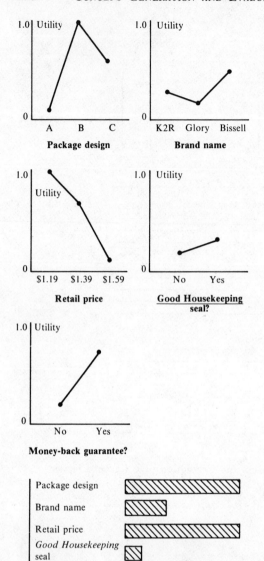

EXHIBIT 2.   Results of Computer Analysis of Experimental Data of Exhibit 1

- Brand name $(0.5 - 0.2 = 0.3)$
- Price $(1.0 - 0.1 = 0.9)$
- *Good Housekeeping* seal $(0.3 - 0.2 = 0.1)$
- Money-back guarantee $(0.7 - 0.2 = 0.5)$

How important is each attribute in relation to the others? The lower portion of Exhibit 2 shows the relative size of the utility ranges expressed in histogram form. As noted, package design and price are the most important factors, and together they account for about two-thirds of the total range in utility.

It should be mentioned that the relative importance of a factor depends on the levels that are included in the design. For example, had price ranged from $1.19 to a high of $1.89, its relative importance could easily exceed that for package design. Still, as a crude indication of what factors to concentrate on, factor importance calculations provide a useful by-product of the main analysis regardless of such limitations.

Managerial Implications

From a marketing management point of view the critical question is how these results can be used in the design of a product/marketing strategy for the spot remover. Examination of Exhibit 2 suggests a number of points for discussion:

- Excluding brand name, the most desirable offering would be the one based on package Design B with a money-back guarantee, a *Good-Housekeeping* seal, and a retail price of $1.19.
- The utility of a product with a price of $1.39 would be 0.3 less than one with a price of $1.19. A money-back guarantee which involves an increment of 0.5 in utility would more than offset the effect of the higher price.
- The use of a *Good Housekeeping* seal of approval is associated with a minor increase in utility. Hence including it in the company's product will add little to the attractiveness of the spot remover's overall offering.
- The utility of the three brand names provides the company with a quantitative measure of the value of its own brand name as well as the brand names of its competitors.

Other questions can be answered as well by comparing various composites made up from the utilities shown in Exhibit 2.

The Air Carrier Study

What about the two Paris flights you had to choose between? In that study, the sponsor was primarily interested in how air travelers evaluated the B-707 versus the B-747 in transatlantic travel, and whether relative value differed by length of flight and type of traveler-business versus vacation travelers. In this study all the respondents had flown across the Atlantic at least once during the preceding 12 months.

Exhibit 3 shows one of the findings of the study for air travelers (business and vacation) flying to Paris. Without delving into details it is quite apparent that the utility difference between the B-707 and the B-747 is very small. Rather, the main factors are departure time, punctuality of arrival, number of stops, and the attitudes of flight attendants.

The importance of type of aircraft did increase slightly with length of flight and for business-oriented travelers versus vacationers. Still, its importance to overall utility was never greater than 10%. It became abundantly clear that extensive replacement of older aircraft like the B-707 would not result in major shifts in consumer demand. On the contrary, money might better be spent on improving the scheduling aspects of flights and the attitudes and demeanor of flight personnel.

The air carrier study involved the preparation of some 27 different flight profiles (only two of which appear at the beginning of the article). Respondents simply rated each flight description in terms of its desirability on a seven-point scale. Only the order properties of the ratings were used in the computer run that resulted in the utility scales appearing in Exhibit 3.

The Replacement Tire Study

The conjoint measurement exercise in the replacement tire study was part of a larger study designed to pretest several television commercials for the sponsor's brand of steel-belted radial tires. The sponsor was particularly interested in the utility functions of respondents who expressed interest in each of the test commercials.

The respondents considered tread mileage and price as quite important to their choice of tires. On the other hand, brand name did not play an important role (at least for the five brands included in the study). Not surprisingly, the most popular test commercial stressed tread mileage and good value for the money, characteristics of high appeal to this group. What was surprising was that this group represented 70% of the total sample.

This particular study involved the preparation of 25 profiles. Again, the researchers sorted cards into seven ordered categories. The 25 profiles, also constructed according to an orthogonal array, represented only one twenty-fifth of the 625 possible combinations.

Potential Uses of Conjoint Measurement

The three preceding studies only scratch the surface of marketing problems in which conjoint measurement procedures can be used. For example, consumer evaluations can be obtained on:

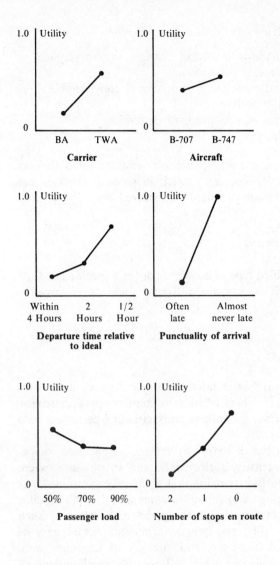

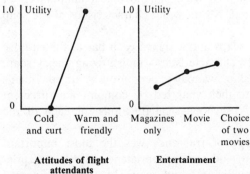

EXHIBIT 3. Utility Functions for Air Travelers to Paris

- New product formulations involving changes in the physical or chemical characteristics of the product
- Package design, brand name, and promotional copy combinations
- Pricing and brand alternatives
- Verbalized descriptions of new products or services
- Alternative service designs

Moreover, while the three preceding examples emphasized preference or likelihood-of-purchase orderings, any explicit judgmental criterion can be used. For example, alternatives might be ordered by any of these criteria:

- Best value for the money
- Convenience of use
- Suitability for a specified type of consumer or for a specified end use
- Ruggedness, distinctiveness, conservativeness, and other "psychological images"

Designing Bar Soaps

In one recent study researchers related the psychological imagery of physical characteristics of actual bars of soap to end-use appropriateness; this study was conducted for the laboratory and marketing personnel of a diversified soap manufacturer.

While the designing of a bar of soap—by varying weight, size, shape, color, fragrance type and intensity, surface feel, and so on—may seem like a mundane exercise, the fact remains that a cleverly positioned bar soap (for example, Irish Spring) can rapidly become a multimillion-dollar enterprise. Still, the extent of knowledge about the importance of such imagery is woefully meager. The researchers formulated actual bars of soap in which color, type of fragrance, and intensity of fragrance were constructed according to a design in which all possible combinations of the experimental factors appeared. All the other characteristics of the soap were held constant.

Respondents examined the soaps and assigned each bar to the end use that they felt best matched its characteristics—moisturizing facial soap, deep-cleaning soap for oily skin, woman's deodorant soap, or man's deodorant soap. The data were then analyzed by conjoint measurement techniques, leading to a set of psychophysical functions for each of the characteristics.

The study showed that type of fragrance was the most important physical variable contributing to end-use appropriateness. Rather surprisingly, the type of fragrance (medicinal) and color (blue) that appeared best suited for a man's deodorant soap were also found to be best for the deep-cleaning soap, even though deep-cleaning soap had been previously classed for marketing purposes as a facial soap. On the other hand, fragrance intensity played a relatively minor role as a consumer cue for distinguishing among different end uses.

In brief, this study illustrated the feasibility of translating changes in various physical variables into changes in psychological variables. Eventually, more detailed knowledge of these psychological transformations could enable a laboratory technician to synthesize color, fragrance, shape, and so forth to obtain soaps that conjure up almost any desired imagery. Moreover, in other product classes—beers, coffees, soft drinks—it appears possible to develop a psychophysics of taste in which such elusive verbal descriptions as "full-bodied" and "robust" are given operational meaning in terms of variations in physical or chemical characteristics.

Verbalized Descriptions of New Concepts

In many product classes, such as automobiles, houses, office machines, and computers, the possible design factors are myriad and expensive to vary physically for evaluation by the buying public. In cases such as these, the researcher usually resorts to verbalized descriptions of the principal factors of interest.

To illustrate, one study conducted among car owners by Rogers National Research, Inc., employed the format shown in Exhibit 4. In this case the researchers were interested in the effects of gas mileage, price, country of manufacture, maximum speed, roominess, and length on consumer preferences for new automobiles. Consumers evaluated factor levels on a two-at-a-time basis, as illustrated in Exhibit 4. Market Facts, Inc., employs a similar data collection procedure.

In the Rogers study it was found that consumer evaluations of attributes were highly associated with the type of car currently owned and the type of car desired in the future. Not surprisingly, gas mileage and country of manufacture were highly important factors in respondent evaluations of car profiles. Somewhat surprising, however, was the fact that even large-car owners (and those contemplating the purchase of a large car) were more concerned with gas economy than owners of that type of car had been historically. Thus, while they fully expected to get fewer miles per gallon than they would in compact cars, they felt quite strongly that the car should be economical compared to others in its size class.

---

[4] Paul E. Green and Yoram Wind, *Multiattribute Decisions in Marketing: A Measurement Approach* (Hinsdale, Ill.: Dryden Press, 1973).

What is more important to you?

There are times when we have to give up one thing to get something else. And, since different people have different desires and priorities, the automotive industry wants to know what things are most important to you.

We have a scale that will make it possible for you to tell us your preference in certain circumstances—for example, gas mileage vs. speed. Please read the example below which explains how the scale works—and then tell us the order of your preference by writing in the numbers from 1 to 9 for each of the x questions that follow the example.

Example: Warranty vs. price of car

Procedure: Simply write the number 1 in the combination that represents your first choice. In one of the remaining blank squares, write the number 2 for your second choice, and so on, from 1 to 9.

Years of warranty

Price of car	3	2	1
$3,000	1		
$3,200			
$3,400			

Years of warranty

Price of car	3	2	1
$3,000	1		
$3,200	2		
$3,400			

Years of warranty

Price of car	3	2	1
$3,000	1	3	
$3,200	2		
$3,400			

Years of warranty

Price of car	3	2	1
$3,000	1	3	6
$3,200	2	5	8
$3,400	4	7	9

Step 1 (Explanation)
You would rather pay the least ($3,000) and get the most (3 years). Your first choice (1) is in the box as shown.

Step 2
Your second choice is that you would rather pay $3,200 and have a 3-year warranty than pay $3,000 and get a 2-year warranty.

Step 3
Your third choice is that you would rather pay $3,000 and have a 2-year warranty than pay $3,400 and get a 3-year warranty.

Sample:
This shows a sample order of preference for all possible combinations. Of course, your preferences could be different.

For each of the six questions below, please write in the numbers from 1 to 9 to show your order of preference for your next new car.

Miles per gallon

Price of car	22	18	14
$3,000			
$3,200			
$3,400			

Miles per gallon

Maximum speed	22	18	14
80 mph			
70 mph			
60 mph			

Miles per gallon

Length	22	18	14
12 feet			
14 feet			
16 feet			

Miles per gallon

Roominess	22	18	14
6 passenger			
5 passenger			
4 passenger			

Miles per gallon

Made in	22	18	14
Germany			
U.S.			
Japan			

Price of car

Made in	$3,000	$3,200	$3,400
Germany			
U.S.			
Japan			

EXHIBIT 4. A Two-at-a-Time Factor Evaluation Procedure

Marketing Strategy Simulations

We have described several applications of conjoint measurement, and still others, some in conjunction with the other techniques outlined in the Appendix, could be mentioned.[4] What has not yet been discussed, and is more important, is the role that utility measurement can play in the design of strategic marketing simulators. This type of application is one of the principal uses of conjoint measurement.

As a case in point, a large-scale study of consumer evaluations of airline services was conducted in which consumer utilities were developed for some 25 different service factors such as on-ground services, in-flight services, decor of cabins and seats, scheduling, routing, and price. Moreover, each utility function was developed on a route (city-pair) and purpose-of-trip basis.

As might be expected, the utility function for each of the various types of airline service differed according to the length and purpose of the flight.

However, in addition to obtaining consumers' evaluations of service profiles, the researchers also obtained information concerning their *perceptions* of each airline (that is, for the ones they were familiar with) on each of the service factors for which the consumers were given a choice.

These two major pieces of information provided the principal basis for developing a simulation of airline services over all major traffic routes. The purpose of the simulation was to estimate the effect on market share that a change in the service configuration of the sponsor's services would have, route by route, if competitors did not follow suit. Later, the sponsor used the simulator to examine the effect of assumed retaliatory actions by its competitors. It also was able to use it to see what might happen to market share if the utility functions themselves were to change.

Each new service configuration was evaluated against the base-period configuration. In addition, the simulator showed which competing airlines would lose business and which ones would gain business under various changes in perceived service levels. Thus, in addition to single, ad hoc studies, conjoint measurement can be used in the ongoing monitoring (via simulation) of consumer imagery and evaluations over time.

Prospects and Limitations

Conjoint measurement faces the same kinds of limitations that confront any type of survey, or laboratory-like, technique. First, while some successes have been reported in using conjoint measurement to predict actual sales and market share, the number of applications is still too small to establish a convincing track record at the present time.

Second, some products or services may involve utility functions and decision rules that are not adequately captured by the models of conjoint measurement. While the current emphasis on additive models (absence of interactions) can be shifted to more complex, interactive models, the number of combinations required to estimate the interactions rapidly mounts. Still, little is known about how good an approximation the simpler models are to the more elaborate ones·

Third, the essence of some products and services may just not be well captured by a decomposition approach that assumes that the researcher can describe an alternative in terms of its component parts. Television personalities, hit records, movies, or even styling aspects of cars may not lend themselves to this type of reductionist approach.

While the limitations of conjoint measurement are not inconsequential, early experience suggests some interesting prospects for measuring consumer trade-offs among various product or service characteristics. Perhaps what is most interesting about the technique is its flexibility in coping with a wide variety of management's understanding of consumers' problems that ultimately hinge on evaluations of complex alternatives that a choice among products presents them with.

APPENDIX
Other Techniquesfor Quantifying Consumers' Judgments

Conjoint measurement is the latest in an increasing family of techniques developed to measure persons' perceptions and preferences. Conjoint measurement can often be profitably used with one or more of the following:

Factor Analysis. Factor analysis in marketing research has been around since the 1940s. However, like all the techniques to be (briefly) described here, factor analysis did not reach any degree of sophistication or practicality until the advent of the computer made the extensive computations easy to carry out. A typical input to factor analysis consists of respondents' subjective ratings of brands or services on each of a set of attributes *provided*

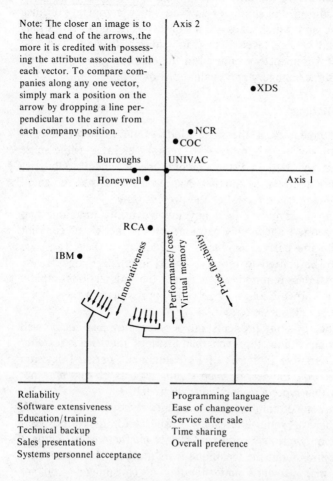

Note: The closer an image is to the head end of the arrows, the more it is credited with possessing the attribute associated with each vector. To compare companies along any one vector, simply mark a position on the arrow by dropping a line perpendicular to the arrow from each company position.

Axis 2

•XDS

•NCR
•COC

Burroughs   UNIVAC

Honeywell •   Axis 1

RCA •

IBM •

Innovativeness

Performance/cost
Virtual memory

Price flexibility

Reliability
Software extensiveness
Education/training
Technical backup
Sales presentations
Systems personnel acceptance

Programming language
Ease of changeover
Service after sale
Time sharing
Overall preference

EXHIBIT 5.   Factor Analysis of Average Respondent Ratings of Eight Computer Manufacturers' Images on Each of 15 Attributes

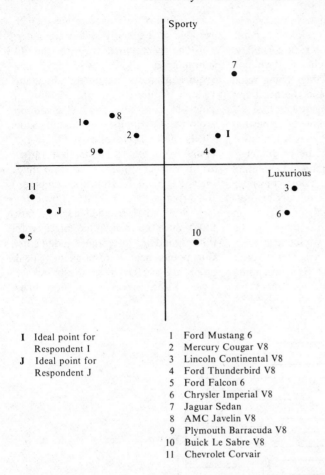

I Ideal point for Respondent I	1 Ford Mustang 6
	2 Mercury Cougar V8
J Ideal point for Respondent J	3 Lincoln Continental V8
	4 Ford Thunderbird V8
	5 Ford Falcon 6
	6 Chrysler Imperial V8
	7 Jaguar Sedan
	8 AMC Javelin V8
	9 Plymouth Barracuda V8
	10 Buick Le Sabre V8
	11 Chevrolet Corvair

EXHIBIT 6.   Perceptual Mapping of Respondents' Judgments of the Relative Similarity of 11 Cars and Two Respondents' Preference Orderings

by the researcher. For example, a sample of computer systems personnel were asked to rate various computer manufacturers' equipment and services on each of the 15 attributes shown in Exhibit 5.

The objective of factor analysis is to examine the commonality across the various rating scales and find a geometric representation, or picture, of the objects (computers), as well as the attributes used in the rating task. As noted in Exhibit 5, International Business Machines (IBM) was ranked highest on virtually all attributes while Xerox (XDS), a comparatively new entrant at the time of the study, National Cash Register (NCR), and Central Data Corporation (CDC) were not perceived as highly as the others with regard to the various attributes of interest to computer users.

The tight grouping of the attribute vectors also suggests a strong "halo" effect in favor of IBM. Only in the case of price flexibility does IBM receive less than the highest rating, and even here it is rated a close second. Thus as Exhibit 5 shows, factor analysis enables the researcher to develop a picture of both the things being rated (the manufacturers) and the attributes along which the ratings take place.

Perceptual Mapping. A somewhat more recent technique—also abetted by the availability of the computer—is perceptual mapping. Perceptual mapping techniques take consumer judgments of *overall* similarity or preference and find literally a picture in which objects that are judged to be similar psychologically plot near each other in geometric space (see Exhibit 6). However, in perceptual mapping the respondent is free to choose *his*

own frame of reference rather than to respond to explicitly stated attributes.

The perceptual map of the 11 automobiles shown was developed from consumers' judgments about the relative similarity of the 55 distinct pairs of cars that can be made up from the 11 cars listed. The dimension labels of *luxurious* and *sporty* do *not* come from the technique but rather from further analysis of the map, once it is obtained from the computer. Ideal points I and J are shown for two illustrative respondents and are fitted into the perceptual map from the respondents' preference judgments. Car points near a respondent's ideal point are preferred to those farther away. Thus respondent I most likes

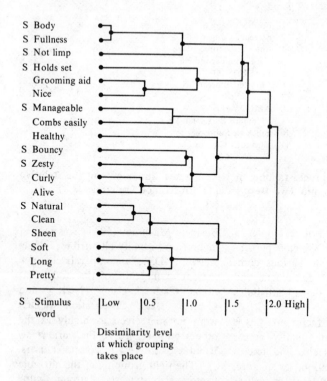

EXHIBIT 7. Hierarchical Cluster Analysis of 19 Phrases Evoked in a Free Association Task Involving Women's Hair Shampoos

Ford Thunderbird, while respondent J most likes Chevrolet Corvair. In practice, data for several hundred respondents might be used to find regions of high density for ideal points.

Cluster Analysis. Still another way to portray consumers' judgments is in terms of a hierarchical tree structure in which the more similar a set of objects is perceived to be, the more quickly the objects group together as one moves from left to right in the tree diagram. Thus the words *body* and *fullness* are perceived to be the two most closely associated of all of the descriptions appearing in Exhibit 7 that characterize hair. Note further that smaller clusters become embedded in larger ones until the last cluster on the right includes all 19 phrases. The words in this example were based on respondents' free associations to a set of 8 stimulus words. The researchers assumed that the more a stimulus evoked another word, the more similar they were.

Relationship to Conjoint Measurement. These three methods are best noted for their complementarities —both with each other and with conjoint measurement. Factor analysis and perceptual mapping can be used to measure consumers' perceptions of various products or services, while conjoint measurement can be used to quantify how consumers trade off some of one attribute to get more of another. Cluster analysis can be used in a variety of ways, either as a comparison technique for portraying the similarities of various objects or as a basis for grouping people with common perceptions or preferences. In short, all these techniques can—and frequently are—applied in the *same* study. As such, their combined use can heighten different aspects of the same general types of input data.

23. Technological Forecasting

Steven C. Wheelwright and Spyros Makridakis

Technological forecasting is far from a science, but just as there is no way to avoid forecasting the economic future—explicitly or implicitly —so there is no way to avoid forecasting the technological future. The authors survey the methods available for this purpose.

IN THIS CHAPTER we consider a number of forecasting methods that can be used when no set of historical data is available. These forecasting methods are used primarily in two types of situations. First is to forecast *when* a given new process or product becomes widely adopted; for example, consider the development of laser technology and the problem of forecasting the point at which that technology will gain widespread industrial application. This would be of interest to companies who feel that there is a tremendous market for that technology and who have the ability to exploit it, but are concerned with timing their own products and marketing efforts to coincide with the demand.

The second situation that might require a qualitative approach to forecasting would be one aimed at predicting *what* new developments and discoveries will be made in a specific area; for example, the corporation would like to forecast new processes and technologies that will be developed in their industry over the next 15 or 20 years. This would help them in planning their plant expansion program and their long-range market development.

Reprinted in abridged form from *Forecasting Methods for Management,* 3rd Edition (New York: Wiley–Interscience, 1980), pp. 267–288. © 1980 John Wiley & Sons, Inc. Used by permission.

Steven Wheelwright is a professor in the Graduate School of Business at Stanford University. Spyros Makridakis is a professor in the Department of Statistics and Operations Research at the European Institute of Business Administration (INSEAD).

The basis of all the qualitative forecasting techniques is the employment of experts to help in preparing the forecasts. The various techniques simply present alternative procedures for helping these experts to express their subjective judgments of the future. It is this dependence on the judgments of experts that makes qualitative approaches to forecasting less attractive than quantitative methods when we have a choice between the two. These experts not only vary considerably in their judgments, thus making the forecast dependent on the specific expert concerned, but their employment is generally quite expensive, particularly when reliability is considered.

Qualitative methods of forecasting, or *technological methods* as they are often called, do *not* provide a detailed procedure or a single point forecast as do most quantitative forecasting techniques. Rather qualitative methods must be flexible and their use must always be adapted to the situation in question. In these approaches man, rather than a mathematical model, is the primary processor of facts, knowledge, and information. Experts must arrive at the "best" forecast by the application of mental processes rather than by the use of formulas as in quantitative approaches.

Recent studies indicate that the motivation for adopting qualitative methods of forecasting is the increased rate of technological change and the reduced length of time between the discovery of a new technology or process and its commercial application.

These tremendously shorter lead times mean that plant and investment decisions which generally have a physical life of 20 to 30 years must be made without complete knowledge of what the industry will be like even in a decade. It is in such an area that qualitative forecasting methods can aid the company by helping them to identify *what* changes will take place and *when* they are most likely to occur.

Writers who have sought to describe specific methods of qualitative forecasting have generally distinguished two subclasses—exploratory and normative. Exploratory methods start with today's knowledge and its orientation and trends and seek to predict what will happen in the future and when. Normative methods, on the other hand, seek first to assess the organization's goals and objectives and then work backward to identify the new technologies and developments that will be most likely to lead to the achievement of those goals. Thus exploratory methods seek only to describe what may happen, whereas normative methods put the organization in a leadership role in effecting the developments that will occur.

We shall examine five methods of qualitative forecasting. The first two —logistic or S-curves and time independent technological comparisons— are exploratory methods. The next two approaches—morphological research and the Delphi method—can be exploratory or normative because the experts concerned can consider either evolutionary developments or

projects aimed at specific goals. The final approach to be examined—
the PATTERN type of relevance tree—is normative in nature.

Logistic and S-Curve Approaches

Earlier we described a number of quantitative forecasting methods that
were basically curve-fitting approaches. They sought to identify an underlying pattern in the historical data and then fit a curve to that pattern. A
similar principle is the basis of a qualitative forecasting method. In the
latter approach, however, little historical data is used directly and expert
judgment takes its place.

As an example of a qualitative curve-fitting approach, suppose that we
are interested in predicting the efficiency of man-made illumination and
we have only six data points available, a number not nearly adequate
for any form of quantitative prediction.[1] Furthermore, we cannot extrap-
olate the curve indefinitely because it is not possible to exceed the
theoretical efficiency of light. This means that the trend line will have to
bend (see figure 1) at the level of theoretical efficiency of white light, a
fact that indicates the free interpretation of the results.

One of the most applicable and frequently used curves by technological
forecasters is the S-type. An S-curve (see figure 2) implies a slow start,
a steep growth, and then a plateau. This curve is a characteristic form of
many technological developments and the sales of several products.

The use of an S-curve in representing growth can be applied not only
to a given product but also to a given technology or even more broadly to

FIGURE 1.   Curve-fitting Approach to Forecasting Man-made Illumination

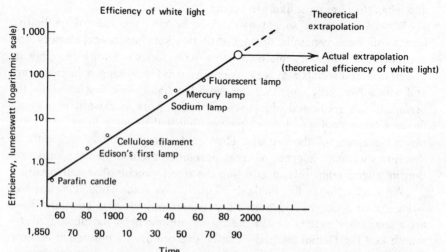

[1] Cetron, Marvin J., 1969. *Technological Forecasting*, Gordon and Breech, New
York, p. 58.

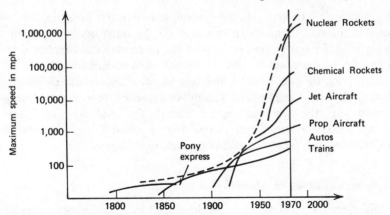

FIGURE 2.   Trend Fitting with S-curves

a given parameter; for example, Ayres[2] (1969) has applied this approach in qualitative forecasting to such things as the maximum speed of transportation. Figure 2 shows his results for the time period from the pony express to the nuclear rocket.

By connecting the tangents of each of the individual growth curves an envelope S-curve can be developed. In this particular case the upper limit of the curve can be recognized as the absolute or natural limits on transportation speed, such as the velocity of light or the exhaustion of some fixed resource. In most instances, however, predicting the point at which one finds himself on such an envelope S-curve may be extremely difficult. Thus in the business setting the S-curve approach may be of limited usefulness.

Another problem in the use of S-curves is finding the most appropriate type. It depends on the technology or the product we want to forecast. Thus by previous experience we must know the approximate S-type form in order to use this method of forecasting, and here expert judgment must be applied. Other functional forms of curves such as exponential, logarithmic, or double exponential can be used to fit the data, but the problem as always is to know what form or curve to assume is the correct one. This can be as difficult as the prediction itself. It is obvious that the choice of curve will influence the forecast significantly.

Time-independent Technological Comparisons

In many quantitative methods of forecasting it is necessary to identify a trend or pattern and extend it into the future. As pointed out earlier, with many technical or cultural changes such an approach is difficult to

[2] Ayres, Robert U., 1969. *Technological Forecasting and Long Range Planning*, McGraw-Hill, New York.

apply because of its complex relationships. It is often possible, however, to predict the developments in one area on the basis of developments in another area. In many areas of interest the forecaster can identify a trend in one part of the area that he thinks will lead to new developments in another. Thus he can forecast the second area and its development by following the trend in the first. The difficulty arises, however, in trying to determine how the two subareas are related. The qualitative approach of time-independent comparisons assigns the responsibilities of representing this interrelationship between the two trends to the forecaster.

Morphological Research Method

The morphological method was developed by Fritz Zwicky in his work in the field of jet engines. Zwicky claims more than 30 industrial applications of this approach in addition to a large number of purely theoretical uses in the area of technological possibilities.

Morphological research "concerns itself with the development and the practical application of basic methods which will allow us to discover and analyze the structural or morphological interrelations among objects, phenomena and concepts, and to explore the results gained for the construction of a sound world."[3] We shall discuss morphological research as a forecasting method.

Zwicky distinguishes five essential steps that constitute the morphological method.

STEP 1. The problem must be explicitly formulated and defined.

STEP 2. All parameters that may enter into the solution must be identified and characterized.

STEP 3. A multidimensional matrix (the morphological box) containing all parameters identified in Step 2 must be constructed. This matrix will contain all possible solutions.

STEP 4. All solutions of the morphological box should be examined for their feasibility and analyzed and evaluated with respect to the purposes to be achieved.

STEP 5. The best solutions identified in Step 3 should be analyzed, possibly in an additional morphological study, according to their feasibility and the resources and means available.

As an example of this approach Zwicky describes his attempts in the late thirties to identify possible propulsive powerplants that can be activated by chemical energy. He distinguishes six parameters that define all possible jet engines that can be activated by chemical energy.

[3] Zwicky, Fritz, 1967. "Morphology of Propulsive Power," *Monographs on Morphological Research No. 1,* Society for Morphological Research, Pasadena, California, p. 275.

P_1: The medium through which the jet engine moves:

P_{11}, moves through a vacuum,

P_{12}, moves in the atmosphere,

P_{13}, moves in large bodies of water,

P_{14}, moves in the solid surface strata of the earth.

P_2: The type of motion of the propellant in relation to the jet engine:

P_{21}, at rest,

P_{22}, translatory motion,

P_{23}, oscillatory motion,

P_{24}, rotary motion.

P_3: The physical state of the propellant:

P_{31}, a gaseous physical state,

P_{32}, a liquid physical state,

P_{33}, a solid physical state.

P_4: The type of thrust augmentation:

P_{41}, no thrust augmentation,

P_{42}, no internal thrust augmentation,

P_{43}, no external thrust augmentation.

P_5: The type of ignition:

P_{51}, a self-igniting engine,

P_{52}, an external ignited engine.

P_6: The sequence of operations:

P_{61}, continuous operation,

P_{62}, intermittent operation.

From this morphological box of six parameters we can identify 576 combinations of parameters ($4 \times 4 \times 3 \times 3 \times 2 \times 2 = 576$) which might represent different jet engines. Each would have to be studied for its feasibility and analyzed and evaluated with respect to its ability to achieve a specific set of objectives. The large number of alternatives makes impossible the examination of all of them (Step 4); therefore Zwicky had to pick some of them at random and start studying them or discover some principle that would relate a number of possible alternatives so that he could study them as a group. Thus the aim is to reduce as far as possible the number of alternatives to be evaluated. Even after that Zwicky was still faced with a large number of engines which had to be carefully studied to determine their characteristics, desirability, feasibility with existing or developing technologies, and costs. If we can solve the problem related to the huge amount of work required, we can then utilize the morphological method successfully. Zwicky, for example, was able with the above analysis, to suggest several radical new inventions that were sound, at least conceptually, and many of which were later developed successfully.

Morphological research can be viewed as a kind of checklist which in a systematic manner enumerates all combinations of technological possibilities. Its major advantage is that it allows the user to identify "hidden," missed, or rare opportunities of technological factors that can be profitably developed. It is from this checklist, or morphological box, that both the search for new technologies and their chances of being materialized are calculated.

The Delphi Method

This approach to forecasting is perhaps the most common of the qualitative methods and has been developed extensively by Olaf Helmer at the RAND Corporation.[4] In this technique the experts doing the forecasting form a panel and then deal with a specific question, such as when will a new process gain widespread acceptance or what new developments will take place in a given field of study. Rather than meeting physically to debate the question however, these experts are kept apart so that their judgments will not be influenced by social pressure or by other aspects of small group behavior. An example of how this approach has been used should demonstrate its procedural characteristics.

PHASE 1. The experts on the panel (numbering five) were asked in a letter to name inventions and scientific breakthroughs that they thought were both urgently needed and could be achieved in the next 50 years. Each expert was asked to send his list back to the coordinator of the panel. From these lists a general list of 50 items were compiled.

PHASE 2. The experts were then sent the list of 50 items and asked to place each of them in one of the five-year time periods into which the next 50 years had been divided, on the basis of a 50-50 probability that it would take a longer or shorter period of time for the breakthroughs to occur. Again experts were asked to send their responses to the panel coordinator.

PHASE 3. Letters were again sent to the experts which told them on which items there was a general consensus and asking those who did not agree with the majority to state their reasons. On those items on which there was no general agreement the experts were also asked to state their reasons for their widely divergent estimates. As a result, several of the experts re-evaluated their time estimates and a narrower range for each breakthrough was determined.

[4] Helmer, Olaf, 1966. *The Use of the Delphi Technique—Problems of Educational Innovations,* The RAND Corporation, Santa Monica, California, December, pp. 2–3.

PHASE 4. To narrow the range of time estimates still further the Phase 3 procedure was repeated. At the end of this phase 31 of the original 49 items on the list could be grouped together as breakthroughs for which a relatively narrow time estimate of their occurrence has been obtained.

The Delphi method is by no means without disadvantages. The general complaints against it have been insufficient reliability, oversensitivity of results to ambiguity of questions, difficulty in assessing the degree of expertise, and the impossibility of taking into account the unexpected.[5] These complaints are only relative, and the Delphi method should be judged in terms of the available alternatives. The same objections apply even more critically to the less systematic methods of forecasting.

The Delphi method, unlike many forecasting methods, does not have to produce a single answer as its output. Instead of reaching a consensus, the Delphi approach can leave a spread of opinions, since there is no particular attempt to get unanimity. The objective is to narrow down the quartile range as much as possible without pressuring the respondent.

PATTERN: A Relevance Tree Method

The relevance tree method uses the ideas of decision theory to assess the desirability of future goals and to select those areas of technology whose development is necessary to the achievement of those goals. The technologies can then be singled out for further development by the appropriate allocation of resources.

The initial and best-known application of relevance trees is PATTERN (Planning Assistance Through Technical Evaluation or Relevance Numbers), an approach that has been developed and used by Honeywell Corporation.[6] The aim of the approach is to aid planners in identifying the long-run developments that are most important to the accomplishment of specific objectives.

As an example, consider the situation faced by a country that has set preeminence in the areas of science and the military as its long-range goals. As a starting point a scenario is prepared. This is a brief description of the future and what the situation may be like surrounding military and scientific developments. Such a scenario could be developed by some expert or long-range planner in the government. It serves mainly as a starting point

---

[5] Gordon, T. J., 1964. *Report on a Long-Range Forecasting Study.* The RAND Corporation, Santa Monica, California, September, p. vi.

[6] Sigford, J. V., and R. H. Parvin, 1965. "Project PATTERN: A Methodology for Determining Relevance in Complex Decision-Making," IEEE Transactions on Engineering Management, *12,* No. 1 9–13 (March).

for a panel of experts and thus need not be extremely accurate in all its details but rather should suggest the types of problem that must be considered.

Based on this scenario, a panel of experts develops a relevance tree (see figure 7) to show the relation between the objective and subobjectives. They break down those subobjectives until a level is reached at which specific technological deficiencies are identified. In the relevance tree shown in figure 7 eight levels have been developed. The elements of the final level represent some of the nation's critical areas in which breakthroughs are required to achieve the long-run objective given on the first level.

By the development of the relevance tree the experts, who have met to develop it, become familiar with the various aspects of achieving that objective. In the next phase relevance numbers are assigned to each element of the tree. This is done by having the experts vote (individually on a secret ballot), according to their own judgment of the relevance and importance of each element of the tree. Once the voting has been completed, the results can be tallied and an average of some kind can be determined for each of the elements. At this point the experts are allowed to discuss among themselves how they think the relevance numbers should be determined.

Following this phase, a set of computations must be made that will give the total relevance for each element in the tree. To compute the total relevance number the individual relevance number for that element is multiplied by the relevance number of each element in the line above.

FIGURE 7.   A Sample Relevance Tree (PATTERN)

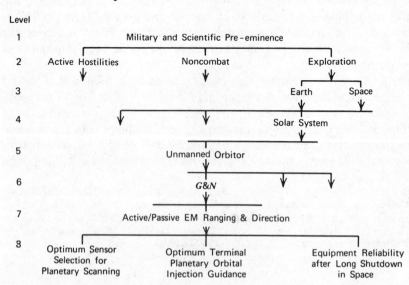

Thus a high relevance for something like "active hostilities" would be reflected in the total relevance of all elements below it in the tree.

The final result is that the experts have developed a tree that not only indicates the breakthroughs needed to achieve a long-run objective but also tells those who will use the forecast in planning just what the relative importance is of each of these breakthroughs.

The PATTERN method of qualitative forecasting is actually interactive with the planning it will affect. As critical areas are identified, the planner can make modifications in his long-range decisions and have the experts determine the additional breakthroughs that may be needed for the plan to be completed successfully.

24. The Creative Organization Summary

Gary A. Steiner

Steiner analyzes the challenge of fostering creativity within an organization. He indicates what kind of environment will enhance individual creativity but points out that such an environment is not without its limitations.

Definitions

FIRST, a few words about what the key terms in this summary mean: "Creativity" has been defined in a number of ways. We make this general distinction: *Creativity* has to do with the development, proposal, and implementation of *new* and *better* solutions; *productivity,* with the efficient application of *current* "solutions." Many studies distinguish "high-creative" from "low-" or "average-creative" groups. It should be clear that "high" and "low" are relative, and not absolute, designators. In most investigations, both "high" and "low" groups would qualify as highly creative within the population at large. It would therefore not have been euphemistic—just too clumsy—to use the designations "more highly" and "less highly" creative. However, this is what the shorthand distinction between "high" and "low" means.

I. The Raw Material: Individual Creativity

Do individual differences in creativity exist? Or is personal creativity, like fathering twins, mostly a matter of being in the right place at the right time?

Reprinted from *The Creative Organization* (Chicago: The University of Chicago Press, 1965), pp. 4–24. Used by permission.

The late Dr. Steiner was a professor in the Graduate School of Business of the University of Chicago at the time of writing.

As important as circumstances are in determining who will create what and when, it seems that there are consistent and persistent differences in individual creativity. Holding conditions constant, some people are likely to be more creative than others; and these differences are likely to show up in other situations and at other times.

Are these differences in personal creativity specific to particular areas of endeavor, or is there such a thing as general creativity?

That issue involves the distinction between *capacity* and *performance*. Except for a few outstanding historical examples, the most creative people in one field are not likely at the same time to be the most creative in another. But this may be largely a matter of specialization in training and effort.

The results of various testing programs suggest that the qualities and capacities that distinguish more from less creative practitioners of given fields *do* extend beyond the specific area of professional competence. Creative architects, for instance, differ not only in the way they approach architecture but also in the way they approach any number of situations and tasks, some unrelated to the specific demands of their profession.

What is more, there seems to be at least some differences that hold across diverse fields; for example, some of the same personality characteristics that distinguish between architects of high and average creativity have been observed in studies of creativity not only in industrial research chemists, but even among high school children differing in general creativity.

Granted that people differ in "creativity," are we really talking about anything more than general intelligence?

Yes. General intelligence seems to bear about the same relationship to on-the-job creativity at the professional level as weight does to ability in football. You have to have a lot of it to be in the game at all; but among those on the team—all of whom have a great deal of weight to begin with—differences in performance are only slightly, if at all, related to weight.

What, then, are the characteristics of the creative individual, especially those that might be subject to measurement before the fact so as to make prediction possible?

Intellectual Characteristics

Although measures of general intelligence fail to predict creativity, highs, as a group, typically outscore lows in tests of the following mental abilities:

Conceptual Fluency. The ability to generate a large number of ideas rapidly: List tools beginning with the letter *t;* novel uses for a brick; categories into which the names of a thousand great men can be sorted—to name just a few of the tasks that have actually been used.

Conceptual Flexibility. The ability to shift gears, to discard one frame of reference for another; the tendency to change approaches spontaneously.

Originality. The ability and/or tendency to give unusual, atypical (therefore more probably new) answers to questions, responses to situations, interpretations of events. Highs, for instance, are more apt to give rare—as well as more—uses of bricks.

Preference for Complexity. Highs often exhibit a preference for the complex, and to them intriguing, as against the simple and easily understood. The usual interpretation is that highs take complexity as a challenge; that they enjoy the attempt to integrate and resolve it.

Personality

Several closely related personality characteristics distinguish highs and lows in a number of studies:

Independence of Judgment. Highs are more apt to stick to their guns when they find themselves in disagreement with others. In a situation where an artificially induced group consensus contradicts the evidence of their own senses, lows more often yield in their expressed judgment.

Attitudes toward Authority. The difference between highs and lows is a matter of degree, but to make the point we describe the extremes.

Lows are more apt to view authority as final and absolute; to offer unquestioning obedience, allegiance, or belief (as the case may be); and to accept present authority as "given" and more or less permanent. Highs are more likely to think of authority as conventional or arbitrary, contingent on continued and demonstrable superiority; to accept dependence on authority as a matter of expedience rather than personal allegiance or moral obligation; to view present authority as temporary.

Attitudes toward subordinates are related in the appropriate direction; those who pay unquestioned allegiance tend to expect it, and vice versa.

Similarly, and in general, highs are more apt to separate source from content in their evaluation of communications; to judge and reach conclusions on the basis of the information itself. Lows are more prone to accept or reject, believe or disbelieve messages on the basis of their attitudes toward the sender.

"Impulse Acceptance." Highs are more willing to entertain and express personal whims and impulses; lows stick closer to "realistic," expected behavior. Highs pay more heed to inner voices, while lows suppress them in favor of external demands.

Approach to Problems

We briefly note three distinctions among creative problem solvers; all are especially significant in the management of creativity.

Motivation. Highs are more perceptive to, and more motivated by, the interest inherent in the problem and its solution. Accordingly, they get more involved in the task, work harder and longer in the absence of external pressures or incentive, and generally place *relatively* greater value on "job interest" versus such extrinsic rewards as salary or status. There is no evidence, however, that the *absolute* importance of external incentives is any less for highs than for lows.

Orientation. Along somewhat the same lines:

Lows are more likely to see their future largely within the boundaries of one organization, to be concerned chiefly with its problems and with their own rise within it, and to develop extensive ties and associations within the community; in short, to be "local" in their loyalties and aspirations.

Highs are more apt to think in terms of a larger community, both residential and professional; to view themselves more as members of the profession than as members of Company X; to take their cues from the larger professional community and attempt to rise within it; to be more mobile, hence less "loyal" to any specific organization; in short, to be cosmopolitan in orientation and aspiration.

The local is more willing to change assignments, even professions (for example, from chemistry to administration), in the interests of the organization and his own career within it. The cosmopolitan is more likely to change organizations to pursue *his* interests and career within the larger profession. In short, highs change jobs to pursue their interests, not their interests to pursue their jobs.

Pace. Highs often spend more time in the initial stages of problem formulation, in broad scanning of alternatives. Lows are more apt to "get on with it."

For example, in problems divisible into analytic and synthetic stages, highs spend more time on the former, in absolute as well as relative terms. As a result, they often leave lows behind in the later stages of the solution process, having disposed of more blind alleys and being able to make more comprehensive integrations as a result of more thorough analysis.

Can such differences be measured reliably enough to be of use in selection programs?

Many of these qualities can be measured. But the instruments are far from perfect and, more seriously, the correlation between each of these distinguishing characteristics and on-the-job creativity is limited. The characteristics "distinguish" highs from lows only in the sense that highs, on the average, have more of, or more often exhibit, the particular quality. And that is far from saying that all highs have more of each than all lows.

The procedure becomes more useful as the number of cases to be predicted increases. If many people are to be selected and it is important that some of them will turn out to be highs, a testing program can improve the odds. This would apply, for instance, in the selection of college or graduate students, or chemists in a major industrial laboratory. But if few people are being selected and it is important that almost all of them turn out to be highly creative (the top management team; or the scientists to head a project), it is doubtful that, at present, a testing program will improve the odds beyond those of careful personal appraisal and judgment. There is the interesting suggestion (not documented) that highs may themselves be better judges of creativity in others; that it "takes one to tell one."

As the examples suggest, testing to predict creativity is perhaps least effective where needed most: where the importance of the individual cases is the greatest.

What are the observable characteristics of the creative process; how does it look to an outsider while it is going on?

The appearance of the creative process, especially in its early stages, poses a problem to administrators. Up to a point, it may be hard to distinguish from totally nonproductive behavior: undisciplined disorder, aimless rambling, even total inactivity.

Irregular Progress. Creativity is rarely a matter of gradual, step-by-step progress; it is more often a pattern of large and largely unpredictable leaps after relatively long periods of no apparent progress. The extreme example is the sudden insight that occurs after a difficult problem is put aside, and at a time of no conscious concern with the matter. Many anecdotes support the film cliché where the great man cries "Eureka!" in the middle of the night or while shaving.

The administrative enigma, then, is to distinguish, before the fact, incubation from laziness; suspended judgment from indecision, "boundary expansion" from simple drinking; undisciplined thinking as a deliberate exploratory step from undisciplined thinking as a permanent characteristic; brain-storming from gibberish by committee. In short, how can one tell the temporarily fallow mind—open and receptive, working subconsciously, and just on the threshold of the brilliant flash—from the permanently idle one? There may not be an answer. But for the moment, tolerance for high-risk gambles on creativity is probably one of the prerequisites or costs of playing for the higher stakes creativity provides when it does pay off.

What are the characteristics of the psychological state optimal for creative production?

Motivation. How much should be at stake; how hard should a man be trying, in order to maximize his chances of being creative? There is an apparent paradox:

First, we often hear that the creative process is characterized by a tremendous sense of commitment, a feeling of urgency, even of mission, that results in enormous preoccupation with the problem and perseverance. On the other hand, there is evidence that extremely high motivation narrows the focus and produces rigidity, perseveration rather than perseverance, which not only precludes creativity but reduces productivity (freezing up in the clutch). Some go so far as to say that the absence of pressure is a common denominator in situations conducive to creativity. There are two suggested resolutions: One is that the relationship is curvilinear; that creativity first rises, then falls, with motivation—you need enough to maintain effort at high levels but not so much as to produce panic attempts at immediate solution.

The other possible resolution involves a distinction in quality of motivation—between "inner" and "outer," "involvement" and "pressure," "drive" and "stress"—related to the earlier observation that highs are more driven by interest and involvement in the task itself than by external incentives. Perhaps external pressure impedes creativity, while inner drive and task-involvement are prerequisites. In short, it may very well be that "Genius is 90 percent hard work" but that inducing hard work is unlikely to produce genius.

Open-Mindedness versus Conviction. What intellectual attitude toward one's ideas and suggestions is optimal: how much conviction versus continual reappraisal; self-involvement versus objective detachment? Again, both tendencies appear, and in the extreme.

On the one hand, creativity is characterized by a willingness to seek and accept relevant information from any and all sources, to suspend judgment, defer commitment, remain aloof in the face of pressures to take a stand. On the other hand, creators in the process of creating are often described as having conviction approaching zeal.

There may in fact be a sort of simultaneous "antimony" or interaction between "passion and decorum," "commitment and detachment," domination *by* a problem and yet a view of it as objective and external. The process may involve the continual and conflicting presence of both components. Or it may be a matter of stages. Perhaps the creative process is characterized by open-mindedness in the early, idea-getting phases; then by a bull-headed conviction at the point of dissemination and execution.

There could be at least two reasons. A more open mind, that initially examines more alternatives, is more likely to be convinced of the one it finally selects. An early commitment to a less carefully analyzed approach may be more vulnerable in the face of attack; beliefs developed through more painful and agonizing appraisal are more apt to stand the test of time.

In addition, creators almost always find themselves on the defensive in the period after the idea has been developed but before it has been "sold." There is an inevitable effrontery to the status quo and those responsible for it, that usually leads to some rejection of the maverick, especially if the innovation is not immediately, demonstrably superior. And people on the defensive are apt to overstate their case. In short, open-minded probers may become fervent proselytizers.

The characteristics of creative individuals suggest a number of rather direct translations or counterparts at the organizational level; and many of the characteristics independently attributed to creative organizations seem to match items in our description of individual highs.

Here is a brief summary:

The Creative Individual	The Creative Organization
Conceptual fluency . . . is able to produce a large number of ideas quickly	Has idea men
	Open channels of communication

	Ad hoc devices:
	  Suggestion systems
	  Brainstorming
	  Idea units absolved of other
	    responsibilities
	Encourages contact with outside
	    sources

Originality . . . generates unusual ideas	Heterogeneous personnel policy
	Includes marginal, unusual types Assigns nonspecialists to problems Allows eccentricity
Separates source from content in evaluating information . . . is motivated by interest in problem . . . follows wherever it leads	Has an objective, fact-founded approach Ideas evaluated on their merits, not status of originator

	Ad hoc approaches:
	  Anonymous communications
	  Blind votes
	Selects and promotes on merit only

Suspends judgment . . . avoids early commitment . . . spends more time in analysis, exploration	Lack of financial, material commitment to products, policies
	Invests in basic research; flexible, long-range planning Experiments with new ideas rather than prejudging on "rational" grounds; everything gets a chance
Less authoritarian . . . has relativistic view of life	More decentralized; diversified
	Administrative slack; time and resources to absorb errors Risk-taking ethos . . . tolerates and expects taking chances
Accepts own impulses . . . playful, undisciplined exploration	Not run as "tight ship"
	Employees have fun Allows freedom to choose and pursue problems

	Freedom to discuss ideas
Independence of judg- ment, less conformity	Organizationally autonomous
Deviant, sees self as different	Original and different objectives, not trying to be another "X"
Rich, "bizarre" fantasy life *and* superior reality orientation; controls	Security of routine . . . *allows* inno- vation. . . , "philistines" provide stable, secure environment that allows "creators" to roam Has separate units or occasions for generating vs. evaluating ideas . . . separates creative from pro- ductive functions

This analogizing has serious limitations and it may be misleading. But the table does serve as an organized index to some of the major characteristics attributed to creative organizations, and many of them sound like the distinguishing characteristics of individual highs.

What, specifically, can management do—beyond selecting creative participants—to foster creativity within and on the part of the organization?

Values and Rewards. What explicit and implicit goals and values characterize the creative organization? What system of rewards and incentives maximizes creativity?

First the creative organization in fact prizes and rewards creativity. A management philosophy that stresses creativity as an organizational goal, that encourages and expects it at all levels, will increase the chances of its occurrence.

But it is one thing to call for creativity, another to mean it, and still another to reward it adequately and consistently when it occurs. More specifically, creativity as a value should find expression in the following:

Compensation. In most areas of day-to-day functioning, productivity rather than creativity is and should be the principal objective; thus, general reward policies tend to measure and stress regular output. But even where creativity is truly desired and encouraged in good faith, activities that are potentially more creative may be subordinated to those more visibly and closely tied to reward policies. A familiar academic illustration is the "pressure to publish."

In the business enterprise, one grievance centers on discrepancies in reward between the sowing and reaping aspects of the operation; with the greater rewards for work that shows immediate, measurable results (e.g., sales) as against that which may pay off in the longer run (such as basic research). It is probably this simple: Where creativity and not productivity is in fact the goal, then creativity and not productivity should in fact be measured and rewarded. And if creativity is harder to measure and takes longer periods to assess, then this probably requires some speculative investment on the part of the firm that wants to keep and nurture the few men and the few activities that will eventually be worth it. If creativity is to be fostered, not impeded, by material incentives, they will have to be applied by a different yardstick.

"Freedom." Within rather broad limits, creativity is increased by giving creators freedom in choice of problem and method of pursuit. In line with the high's greater interest and involvement in his work, greater freedom is necessary, to maximize those satisfactions that are important to him and that channel his efforts into avenues most likely to prove creative. But such freedom often puts the appropriate objectives of the organization at odds with the demands of maximum creativity.

This, then, is one of the principal costs in the nurture of creativity: Except in the rare and fortunate case where a creative individual's interests exactly match the day-to-day operating objectives of his organization, and continue to do so over time, the organization pays a price, at least in the short run, for giving him his head. What he returns to the organization may or may not compensate it many-fold.

Communication. Many observations point to the importance of free and open channels of communication, both vertical and horizontal. On the one hand, potential creators need and seek relevant information whatever its source, within or without the organization; on the other hand, they are stimulated by diverse and complex input.

Equally important, ideas wither for lack of a grapevine. A possible approach, a feasible but half-baked notion, or even a well worked-out solution must be communicated to those with the power to evaluate, authorize, and implement.

The presence of formal channels is not enough. People must feel free to use them, and channels must not be clogged by routine paperflow that ties up time with "programmed trivia," and creates an air of apathy and neglect toward incoming messages because it is so unlikely that they will contain anything of value. Since highs tend toward cosmopolitan, professional orientation, the organization must at least provide for and perhaps encourage contact and communication with colleagues and associations on the outside. As a special case, there is the matter of scientific and professional publication in the appropriate journals, which is often of great personal importance to creators.

There may be problems of corporate secrets and employee loyalties. But in many cases, these are unrealistic or exaggerated, given the high rate of horizontal mobility, the discretion of the professional, and the fact that most "secrets" are not. At any rate, there may be no reason to think that the balance of payments will be "out"; there should be at least as much information gained as given away in most external contacts. And in many cases the net gain in satisfaction, creativity, and perhaps tenure of highs will probably offset the time and trade secrets lost to the outside.

What, specifically, are the costs of creativity? What must an organization be prepared to give up or tolerate if it wants to increase its creativity?

Answers were scattered throughout the preceding, but it may help to pull them together.

First, creativity, by definition, is a high-risk enterprise for any given unit that attempts it. The greater the departure from present practice, the less likelihood that the innovation will work; the greater the potential payoff, the less the odds of its occurring. Conversely, the larger the number of workers or units independently pursuing any problem, the better the chances that one or more of them will succeed.

Second, within the unit under consideration, fostering creativity assesses costs in assured productivity. To the extent that energy is consumed in investigation and exploration, it does not go into work known to be productive.

Finally, depending on the personal tastes and preferences of management, there may or may not be costs in "security," "comfort," and "congeniality" of the environment: (*a*) Highs are not as deferent, obedient, flattering, easy to control, flexible to *external* demands and changes, conventional, predictable, and so on, through a long list of desiderata in "good" employees. (*b*) In addition, highs are more mobile, less "loyal"—harder to hold by ordinary extrinsic rewards—but easier to acquire by the offer of interesting opportunities. At any rate, they make for a less stable and secure, more challenging but perhaps more disturbing environment. (*c*) A creative organization itself is more committed to change; operates on a faster track; has a less certain or predictable future than the efficient, me-too operation.

In short, maximizing creativity is not the principal objective of any organization at all times, or even of all organizations at some times. When it is, there are some rough guidelines to how it may be fostered—but not, it is suggested, at no cost.

B.

Analysis of New Product Proposals

NEW PRODUCT IDEAS are generally developed into written proposals so that their full implications can be more clearly identified and more systematically considered by senior management. This process normally proceeds in two steps, preliminary analysis of "short-form" proposals and full consideration of more detailed "requests." This is a process of elimination: Only those proposals which pass the first stage proceed to the second phase of analysis, and only those that pass this second stage go on to become development projects.

In this section, Montgomery and Urban discuss the popular weighted checklist approach to screening new product proposals, while Souder reviews and compares this and seven other approaches to project selection. McDonald looks into the estimation of market potential for the new offering, and Kotler discusses the financial implications—in break-even terms—of using different marketing mixes in conjunction with the new product. Herbert and Bisio and Edelman and Greenberg take somewhat more sophisticated points of view insofar as proposal preparation and evaluation are concerned. The first pair of authors propose a discounted cash flow approach (with some interesting twists) to integrate the marketing and financial aspects of the proposal itself, and the second set of authors advocate a risk analysis approach for determining which proposals should be put into development.

25. Screening New Product Possibilities

David B. Montgomery and Glen L. Urban

Montgomery and Urban discuss the elimination of obviously unsuitable ideas from the new product development process.

AFTER A SET of potential products has been identified, the next step in the analysis is to screen out the obviously unsuitable ideas. This screening is intended to identify those ideas that are not compatible with the company's goals, do not match the company's capabilities, or do not appear to have enough market potential.

These criteria are elimination criteria for the product idea. For example, if the company has decided to restrict itself to durable consumer products, all nondurable consumer products would be removed from the set of ideas because of incompatibility with the firm's goal structure, even though they might show great profit potential. The next elimination factor reflects the technical, financial, and managerial capabilities of the firm. If the firm cannot produce the product or does not have the technical or managerial abilities necessary for the product, the idea would be rejected. Similarly, the product must have sufficient market potential to justify further investment of the firm's resources.

After the products have passed through these rough elimination screens, the remaining ideas are ranked to determine the most suitable ideas. The purpose of the more detailed phase of the screening process is to reduce the total set of product proposals to a set that will be manageable at the more costly and time-consuming analysis stage.

The basic factors and subfactors relating to the suitability of a new

From *Management Science in Marketing*, © 1969. Pp. 303–312. Reprinted by permission of Prentice-Hall, Inc., Englewood Cliffs, New Jersey.

David Montgomery is a professor in the Graduate School of Business, Stanford University. Glen Urban is a professor in the Sloan School of Management, Massachusetts Institute of Technology.

product idea are listed in figure 1.[1] The first factor, marketability, is concerned with the relation of the new product to the firm's present product line and its distribution channels. It also relates to the compatibility of the product with the firm's merchandising strengths, its quantity-price comparison to competing products, and the inventory and production cost implications of the number of sizes and grades that will be necessary. The durability factor relates to the extent: (1) to which there is a broad, lasting demand for the product, (2) to which the product's design is protected, and (3) to which the product is resistant to seasonal and cyclical fluctuations which might prove costly and increase the risk inherent in the product. The productive ability factor is concerned that the firm has sufficient production knowledge, personnel, and equipment to produce the product and that there is a viable source of the necessary raw materials. The final factor, growth potential, raises the issues of the expected growth of uses, the growth of competition, and the product's over-all place in the market.

Now that many of the relevant considerations in the screening of new products have been outlined, it seems appropriate to focus attention on

---

  I. Marketability
      A. Relation to present distribution channels
      B. Relation to present product lines
      C. Quality-price relationship
      D. Number of sizes and grades
      E. Merchandisability
      F. Effects on sales of present products
 II. Durability
      A. Stability
      B. Breadth of market
      C. Resistance to cyclical fluctuations
      D. Resistance to seasonal fluctuations
      E. Exclusiveness of design
III. Productive Ability
      A. Equipment necessary
      B. Production knowledge and personnel necessary
      C. Raw materials availability
 IV. Growth Potential
      A. Place in Market
      B. Expected competitive situation—value added
      C. Expected availability of end users

FIGURE 1.   Factors and Subfactors in New Product Desirability

[1] This outline is based upon J. T. O'Meara, "Selecting Profitable Products," *Harvard Business Review* (Jan.–Feb., 1961), pp. 83–89.

alternative approaches that have been taken to the screening of new products. Three alternatives can be identified: break-even analysis, preliminary financial return analysis, and product profile procedures. Break-even concepts are considered elsewhere and will not be repeated here. Pessemier's use of a cutoff rate of return in his simulation approach to the allocation of search resources illustrates the use of financial return analysis.[2] This type of analysis generally sets a cutoff rate of return on investment for a new product. If the estimated return is greater than the cutoff (which is usually the firm's opportunity cost of capital), the product then proceeds to the analysis stage. The third approach, product profile procedures, is discussed below.

In product profile analysis, knowledgeable managers and experts are asked to rate the new product in terms of how well it is expected to perform on each of a number of dimensions. For example, they might be asked to rate a new product in terms of its compatibility with the present product line on a scale such as:

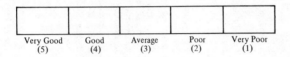

Very Good	Good	Average	Poor	Very Poor
(5)	(4)	(3)	(2)	(1)

In this case the score of the product on the product line factor F_j will be a number between 1 and 5. If more than one person has ranked each factor, the factor score for the product F_j could be determined by an average of the score each person gives the product for that factor. An alternate averaging procedure would be to weight each person's score by the confidence he has in that score.

The individuals called upon to rate a new product will generally find their task somewhat easier if the scale categories of very good to very poor are defined somewhat more explicitly for each dimension. O'Meara has provided such definitions for the subfactors. His definitions are reproduced in figure 2 as an example of how the score on each factor may be further specified.

In order to facilitate the comparison of potential new products, the firm generally finds it convenient to develop a system for combining a product's scores on each subfactor into a single index of the proposed product's quality. For example, the firm may form a score for product proposal i as

2 For further elaboration of this approach, see P. Kotler, "Computer Simulation in the Analysis of New Product Decisions," in F. Bass, C. King, E. Pessemier, eds., *Applications of the Sciences in Marketing* (New York: John Wiley & Sons, Inc., 1968).

FIGURE 2.   Factor and Subfactor Ratings for a New Product

	Very Good	Good	Average	Poor	Very Poor
I. Marketability					
A. Relation to present distribution channels	Can reach major markets by distributing through present channels.	Can reach major markets by distributing mostly through present channels, partly through new channels.	Will have to distribute equally between new and present channels, in order to reach major markets.	Will have to distribute mostly through new channels in order to reach major markets.	Will have to distribute entirely through new channels in order to reach major markets.
B. Relation to present product lines	Complements a present line which needs more products to fill it.	Complements a present line that does not need, but can handle, another product.	Can be fitted into a present line.	Can be fitted into a present line but does not fit entirely.	Does not fit in with any present product line.
C. Quality/price relationship	Priced below all competing products of similar quality.	Priced below most competing products of similar quality.	Approximately the same price as competing products of similar quality.	Priced above many competing products of similar quality.	Priced above all competing products of similar quality.
D. Number of sizes and grades	Few staple sizes and grades.	Several sizes and grades, but customers will be satisfied with few staples.	Several sizes and grades, each of which can satisfy customer wants with small inventory of nonstaples.	Several sizes and grades, each of which will have to be stocked in equal amounts.	Many sizes and grades which will necessitate heavy inventories.
E. Merchandisability	Has product characteristics over and above those of competing products that lend themselves to the kind of promotion, advertising, and display that the given company does best.	Has promotable characteristics that will compare favorably with the characteristics of competing products.	Has promotable characteristics that are equal to those of other products.	Has a few characteristics that are promotable, but generally does not measure up to characteristics of competing products.	Has no characteristics at all that are equal to competitors' or that lend themselves to imaginative promotion.
F. Effects on sales of present products	Should aid in sales of present products.	May help sales of present products; definitely will not be harmful to present sales.	Should have no effect on present sales.	May hinder present sales some; definitely will not aid present sales.	Will reduce sales of presently profitable

II. Durability					
A. Stability	Basic product which can always expect to have uses.	Product which will have uses long enough to earn back initial investment, plus at least 10 years of additional profits.	Product which will have uses long enough to earn back initial investment, plus several (from 5 to 10) years of additional profits.	Product which will have uses long enough to earn back initial investment, plus 1 to 5 years of additional profits.	Product which will probably be obsolete in near future.
B. Breadth of market	A national market, a wide variety of consumers, and a potential foreign market.	A national market and a wide variety of consumers.	Either a national market or a wide variety of consumers.	A regional market and a restricted variety of consumers.	A specialized market in a small marketing area.
C. Resistance to cyclical fluctuations	Will sell readily inflation or depression.	Effects of cyclical changes will be *moderate*, and will be felt *after* changes in economic outlook.	Sales will rise and fall with the economy.	Effects of cyclical changes will be *heavy*, and will be felt *before* changes in economic outlook.	Cyclical changes will cause extreme fluctuations in demand.
D. Resistance to seasonal fluctuations	Steady sales throughout the year.	Steady sales—except under unusual circumstances.	Seasonal fluctuations, but inventory and personnel problems can be absorbed.	Heavy seasonal fluctuations that will cause considerable inventory and personnel problems.	Severe seasonal fluctuations that will necessitate layoffs and heavy inventories.
E. Exclusiveness of design	Can be protected by a patent with no loopholes.	Can be patented, but the patent might be circumvented.	Cannot be patented, but has certain salient characteristics that cannot be copied very well.	Cannot be patented, and can be copied by larger, more knowledgeable companies.	Cannot be patented, and can be copied by anyone.
III. Productive Ability					
A. Equipment necessary	Can be produced with equipment that is presently idle.	Can be produced with present equipment, but production will have to be scheduled with other products.	Can be produced largely with present equipment, but the company will have to purchase some additional equipment.	Company will have to buy a good deal of new equipment, but some present equipment can be used.	Company will have to buy all new equipment.

317

FIGURE 2 (Continued)

	Very Good	Good	Average	Poor	Very Poor
B. Production knowledge and personnel necessary	Present knowledge and personnel will be able to produce new product.	With very few minor exceptions, present knowledge and personnel will be able to produce new product.	With some exceptions, present knowledge and personnel will be able to produce new product.	A ratio of approximately 50-50 will prevail between the needs for new knowledge and personnel and for present knowledge and personnel.	Mostly new knowledge and personnel are needed to produce the new product.
C. Raw materials' availability	Company can purchase raw materials from its best supplier(s) exclusively.	Company can purchase major portion of raw materials from its best supplier(s), and remainder from any one of a number of companies.	Company can purchase approximately half of raw materials from its best supplier(s), and other half from any one of a number of companies.	Company must purchase most of raw materials from any one of a number of companies other than its best supplier(s).	Company must purchase most or all of raw materials from a certain few companies other than its best supplier(s).
IV. Growth Potential					
A. Place in market	New type of product that will fill a need presently not being filled.	Product that will substantially improve on products presently on the market.	Product that will have certain new characteristics that will appeal to a substantial segment of the market.	Product that will have minor improvements over products presently on the market.	Product similar to those presently on the market and which adds nothing new.
B. Expected competitive situation—value added	Very high value added so as to substantially restrict number of competitors.	High enough value added so that, unless product is extremely well suited to other firms, they will not want to invest in additional facilities.	High enough value added so that, unless other companies are as strong in market as this firm, it will not be profitable for them to compete.	Lower value added so as to allow large, medium, and some smaller companies to compete.	Very low value added so that all companies can profitably enter
C. Expected availability of end users	Number of end users will increase substantially.	Number of end users will increase moderately.	Number of end users will increase slightly, if at all.	Number of end users will decrease moderately.	Number of end users will decrease substantially.

(1)

$$S_i = \sum_{j=1}^{f} W_j F_{ji}$$

where S_i = product i's total score,

W_j = weight associated with subfactor j where $0 \leq W_j \leq 1$

and $\sum_{j=1}^{f} W_j = 1$,

F_{ji} = product i's score (e.g., from 1 to 5) on subfactor j.

The score S_i of each potential product serves as a rough index of its relative desirability. The establishment of a lower cutoff value for the index will help to eliminate the apparently unsuitable projects. The projects that survive this screening are then sent to the analysis stage for a detailed profitability analysis.

Use of the scoring procedure described in eq. (1) requires that the firm establish appropriate weights W_j for the various subfactors. These weights represent the relative importance of the subfactors. Dean has suggested a method for determining these weights in which the members of the firm's new product review board independently rank the factors under consideration.[3] This ordering proceeds from the most important factor to the least important factor. The rank ordering could be converted into numeric values if the increment of importance between successive ranks were assumed to be equal. One criticism which might be made of this procedure is that it treats ordinal rankings as intervally scaled data. It might be better to use paired comparisons of the factors and Thurstone's "law of comparative judgment" to get the scaled data.[4] If it is assumed that this translation of rankings to numeric values is appropriate, the factor weights are averaged across individual raters to obtain a composite weight for each factor W_j. In a sensitivity analysis of actual rating situations, Dean found the final ranking of proposals to be relatively insensitive with respect to small changes or errors in the factor weights used.

The above approaches to determining factor weights and factor scores have certain limitations. Green, for example, has criticized this analysis on the grounds that:

1. The factor weights may not be independent of a product's scores on the various factors.

---

[3] B. V. Dean, "Quantitative Methods in New Product Planning," paper presented to the 1964 joint national meeting of TIMS and ORSA, October, 1964. Also see B. V. Dean and M. J. Miskey, "Scoring and Profitability Models for Evaluating and Selecting Engineering Projects," *Operations Research*, XIII (July–Aug., 1965), pp. 550–69.

[4] See P. Green and D. Tull, *Research for Marketing Decisions* (Englewood Cliffs, N.J.: Prentice-Hall, Inc., 1966), Chap. 7, and W. Torgerson, *Theory and Methods of Scaling* (New York: John Wiley & Sons, Inc., 1958).

2. The factors themselves may not be independent, as has been implicitly assumed above.

3. The procedure assumes more knowledge on the rater's part about product characteristics than might be apparent at first glance.

With respect to the last issue, Green contends that if the rater's knowledge is sufficient to provide meaningful evaluations, this knowledge might better be turned to a more direct linking between the product characteristics and economic indices of its likely market performance.

However, it must be kept in mind that the purpose of the screening stage is to provide an economic framework for reducing the number of proposals that are to be sent to the more costly and time-consuming analysis stage. Given any new product planning situation, there is likely to be some bound to the increment in screening complexity which will be economically justifiable.

The output of the screening stage of the new product decision process is a set of new product proposals that display the most potential and should be further subjected to detailed analysis.

26. An Appraisal of Eight R&D Project Evaluation Methods

William E. Souder

Eight characteristic types of management science models for project evaluation are critically reviewed and appraised.

LITERALLY hundreds of models have been developed for R&D project evaluation (for reviews, see references 2, 3, 5, 12). With notable exceptions, most of them have never been adopted for routine use (4, 13). The needs which originally stimulated the development of these models have intensified over the past few years. Today's climate of expanded government intervention, increased risks and uncertain markets make it all the more important to carefully evaluate projects and select the "best" ones.

It would thus seem to be a great loss to both the management and the management science professions if the past twenty-five years of model building efforts remained largely unused. How can research managers make better use of these models? What can model builders do to improve their products? This paper poses some answers to both of these questions.

Project Evaluation Models

Eight characteristic types of project evaluation models have been developed: index models, portfolio models, decision theory models, risk analysis models, frontier models, scoring models, profile models, and checklists. Each of these will be critically reviewed and appraised.

Index Models. In the simplest index model, two numbers are ratioed to obtain a single index number or rating of a project's worth. Table 1

Reprinted in abridged form from *Research Management,* 21 (September, 1978), pp. 29–37. Used by permission of both the author and the publication.

William Souder is Professor of Industrial Engineering and Director of the Technology Management Studies Group at the University of Pittsburgh.

321

TABLE 1.   Examples of Index Models

Olsen's Model	Ansoff's Model
$$V = \dfrac{r \cdot d \cdot m \cdot s \cdot p \cdot n}{\text{Total Project Cost}}$$	$$\text{Figure of merit} = \dfrac{r \cdot d \cdot m \cdot (T + B) \cdot E}{\text{Total Project Cost}}$$

V = The economic value of the project.
s = The annual sales volume derived from the project (if it succeeds).
p = The per unit proft derived from the project (if it succeeds).
n = The product's life span in years (if the project succeeds).
r, d, and m are the probabilities of research, development and market success, respectively.
T and B are subjective ratings of the technical and business merits of the project.
E = the present value of the earnings expected if the project succeeds.

presents two illustrative examples of index models (1, 10). For entries into the voluminous literature here see references 2, 12. The apparent simplicity and ease of use of index models give them a quality of seductive appeal. But accurate input data are difficult to obtain. Moreover, a basic limitation of index models is their inability to analyze projects at several funding levels, e.g., at several "total project cost" levels in Olsen's model. High-ranking projects at the low cost levels may become low-ranking projects at the high cost levels, and vice versa. This results in a confusing array of numbers. More sophisticated models, such as portfolio models, are required when multiple funding levels are involved.

Portfolio Models vs. Index Models. In a portfolio model, candidate projects are implicitly prioritized by the amount of funds allocated to them. The essence of a portfolio model is easily demonstrated by reference to Table 2. Projects A, B and C each have three alternative funding levels: $100,000, $200,000, and $300,000. The expected profits from the projects vary with these funding levels as shown in Table 2. The higher funding

TABLE 2.   Illustration of a Portfolio Model
             (Available Budget = $300,000)

Alternative Funding Levels for Each Project	Expected Profits		
	Project A	*Project B*	*Project C*
$100,000	$100 M	$ 75 M	$ 10 M
200,000	250 M	265 M	220 M
300,000	300 M	350 M	360 M
Maximum Total Expected Profit = $100M + $265M = $365M			

levels result in improved products, which yield higher expected profits. The "best" allocation of the available budget in this case would be to select and fund project A at its lowest level (fund it at $100,000) and project B at its middle level (fund it at $200,000). Project C is not selected and not funded under these conditions. No other allocation of the available budget among the three candidates, that is, no other portfolio, yields a larger total expected profit.

Three things should carefully be noted in this illustration. First of all, suppose the index model W = Project Expected Profit/Funding Level had been used here. And suppose that like most index models, only the maximum project funding level ($300,000) had been considered. Then only project C would have been selected, since this is the best single use of the available budget (it gives the largest W value). But, as Table 2 illustrates, a larger total expected profit can be achieved if one thinks in terms of a portfolio. Secondly, it is clear from this illustration that it may be fruitful to purposely fund some projects at their lowest levels (project A) or to completely reject other projects (project C), in order to marshal funds for yet more productive uses (project B). Finally, note that the portfolio model approach provides diversification, while the index model approach concentrates all the manager's resources in one project. This is a fundamental difference between these two types of models.

As the number of candidate projects increases, computerized math models become necessary in order to handle all the combinations. These math models can include various constraints which insure that the portfolio is balanced for risk, and that exploratory projects will not be disadvantaged in their competition with other projects. For entries into the literature on portfolio models see references 3, 5, 12.

More testing is needed before any final conclusions can be drawn about their effectiveness. There is an emerging position that portfolio models should not be used strictly for their analytical capabilities. Rather, the models should be used for their organization behavioral impacts, and to facilitate improved organizational decision making. In two studies in particular (13, 14), the major benefits of the models were seen in terms of improved interdepartmental involvement and improved systematic decision making. The actual outputs from the models were never implemented. Used in this way, the models served as a management decision laboratory for testing and trialing decisions, for asking what-if questions, and for stimulating inter-group discussions. Both model builders and model users should be more alert to these possibilities in the future.

Decision Theory Models. Decision theory models are based on the statistical concept that rational decision makers will select those projects having the highest expected value scores. Table 3 provides an illustration of this concept for two competing projects. A pay-off matrix is constructed, by arraying the relative worths of the candidate projects under the assump-

TABLE 3. Illustration of a Decision Theory Model

Payoff Matrix of Project Worths (in $000,000):

	Mother Nature is:		Expected Value Analysis:
	Adverse (A)	Benign (B)	$V_1 = -100 \times p(A) + 500 \times p(B)$
			$V_2 = -50 \times p(A) + 400 \times p(B)$
Project 1	−100	+500	Project with higher score would be
Project 2	− 50	+400	preferred.

Indifference Point Analysis:

Equation (1): $-100 \times p(A) + 500 \times p(B) = -50 \times p(A) + 400 \times p(B)$
Equation (2): $p(A) + p(B) = 1.0$
Conclusion: If $p(B) > .33$, then Project 1 would be preferred; if $p(B) \leqslant .33$, then Project 2 would be preferred.

tions that mother nature is either adverse or benign. The relative worth numbers in Table 3 are expected profit dollars. Note that the output data from an index model, etc., could also be used as worth numbers here. Negative numbers in the payoff matrix in Table 3 indicate "regrets", e.g., the project fails and the worth then becomes the sunk cost of the project.

In the simplest case, the probability of nature being adverse, $p(A)$, and the probability of nature being benign, $p(B)$, can be estimated. Then the expected value scores of each project, V_1 and V_2, can be calculated as illustrated in the right side of Table 3. The project with the higher expected value score would be preferred. In the more realistic case, the probabilities are unknown, and the choice of project 1 vs project 2 will depend on the decision maker's willingness to gamble.

Given the data in Table 3, a rational decision maker would be indifferent between projects 1 and 2 when $V_1 = V_2$. This occurs when $p(B) = .33$, as determined from the simultaneous solution to equations (1) and (2) at the bottom of Table 3. If the decision maker perceives that mother nature will be benign more than one-third of the time, then V_1 will be larger than V_2 and he should select project 1. Otherwise, V_2 will be larger than V_1 and project 2 should be selected. If these perceptions are wrong, then the decision maker has gambled away a better opportunity. If he selects project 1 when nature is actually adverse, then he incurs an additional regret of $50,000,000 more ($-100,000,000 as opposed to $-50,000,000) than project 2 would have given him. If he selects project 2 when nature is actually benign, then he has foregone the opportunity to receive $100,000,000 more ($+500,000,000 as opposed to $+400,000,000) with project 1.

In short, project 1 represents a bullish strategy with the potential for relatively high gains and regrets; project 2 represents a more conservative strategy. The choice of one strategy over the other cannot be determined on the basis of the payoff matrix alone. It will depend upon the decision maker's willingness to trade off the risk of the $50,000,000 additional regret for the chance at an additional $100,000,000 gain. This trade-off will be influenced by the context in which the decision is being made e.g., the perceived organizational rewards and penalties for risk-taking, the ability to afford the regret if it actually occurs, etc.

Decision theory models are attractive because they help to clarify the available strategies and the potential risks, regrets and trade-offs. They have thus been found to be particularly useful for interdepartmental design making, where natural differences in the risk propensities of the departments may get in the way of consensus. (See, e.g., 15.)

Risk Analysis Models. Figure 1 is an illustration of the enlarged perspective that a risk analysis model can provide. Projects 1 and 2 exhibit most likely lifetime profits of $100,000,000 and $150,000,000, respectively. Thus project 2 might be chosen as superior. It is not unusual for some managers to stop their analyses at this very superficial stage. But a much larger look should be taken at the whole picture. As Figure 1 shows, project 2 has a .10 probability of returning zero expected profits, and only a .40 probability of hitting its most likely $150,000,000 level. Or, looked at another way, there is a .30 probability that project 2 will yield lower expected profits than project 1. This is the relative downside risk if one chooses project 2 over project 1. Given these data, a risk averter would be inclined to select project 1. This project has a high chance of achieving a moderate profit, with very little chance of anything less or greater. A

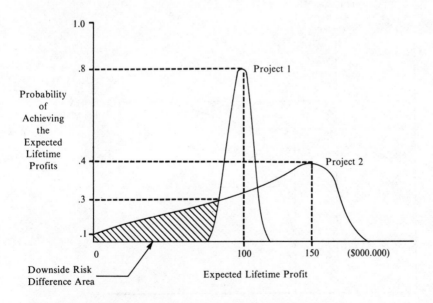

FIGURE 1. Illustration of a Risk Analysis Model

gambler would be inclined to opt for project 2, which has a small chance at a large profit. Thus, risk analysis models make the risk-averter and gambler strategies more visible, thereby permitting a decision maker to consciously select decisions consistent with one of these chosen strategies.

Risk analysis methods may be combined with other models, e.g., the s, p, etc., variables in Olsen's model (Table 1) could be specified as distributions like those in Figure 1. The output would then be a distribution for the V value in Olsen's model. For more on risk analysis models and their uses see references 7 and 8.

Frontier Models. Figure 2 illustrates a typical frontier model for a set of ten projects. Although the definitions can vary with the particular model, *risk* usually expresses the project's chances of failure and *return* expresses its expected profitability. In Figure 2, the "efficient frontier" traces the path of the dominant projects. For instance, project 9 (denoted as X_9 in Figure 2) is dominant over project 5 (denoted as X_5). Project 9 has the same risk level as project 5, but it has a higher return. Similarly, project 1 is dominant over project 2 on return, and project 9 is dominant over project 2 on risk. The maximum desired risk and the minimum desired return levels established by the organization are also depicted in Figure 2. Acceptable projects must fall in the region formed by these boundaries. Thus, Figure 2 shows that a decision maker would accept projects, 1, 6, 8, 9 and 10.

Frontier models are especially useful for weeding out unacceptable projects, and for examining risk/return trade-offs and organizational ob-

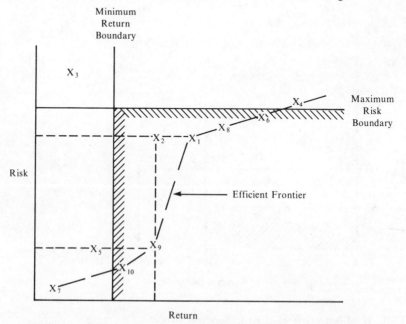

FIGURE 2.   Illustration of a Frontier Model

TABLE 4. Illustration of a Scoring Model for a Hypothetical Project

Model: $T = \sum_i W_i s_i$

Criteria (i)	Criterion Weight (W_i) $\times$	Project Score $(s_i)*$ =	Criterion Score $(W_i \times s)$
Probability of Success	4	5	20
Profitability	3	10	30
Cost	2	6	12
Patentability			
Rating	1	3	3
			$T = 65$

* Scoring scale: Excellent = 10, Poor = 1

jectives. For instance, Figure 2 shows that the high-risk, high-return project 4 (denoted as X_4) is ruled out. On the other hand, its risk/return ratio is the same as the acceptable projects 1, 8 and 6 (all four projects lie along the same straight line). This latter point suggests that the organization may want to make an exception and include project 4.

Frontier models often point out the need for greater diversification in idea generation and project proposals. For instance, Figure 2 shows that the acceptable projects are either of the low-risk variety (projects 9 and 10) or the high-risk variety (projects 1, 6 and 8). It seems reasonable that there ought to be some medium risk projects in this portfolio. For more on frontier models, see 11.

Scoring Models. A scoring model consists of a set of criteria and related scales for scoring candidate projects. A simple additive type of scoring model is illustrated in Table 4. The variable W_i is the importance weight for each criterion, and T is the total score for the project. This total project score can be used in the same way as the output from an index model, e.g., candidate projects may be prioritized on the basis of their T scores. For other literature on scoring models, see reference 9.

Scoring models are appealing because they permit one to combine quantitative (e.g., Cost) and qualitative (e.g., Patentability Rating) assessments into one convenient overall score, T. Scoring models also provide a fully visible tableau of weights, project scores and criterion scores. These tableaus perimt one to fully examine the profiles of the projects, and to analyze how and why some projects are inferior to others.

Profile and Checklist Models. An illustration of a typical profile model is shown in Table 5. Candidate projects are subjectively rated on a series of criteria. The results are visually displayed in such a way that the projects are readily compared. In a checklist model, candidate projects are checked against each criterion and simply rated as acceptable or unacceptable on each. Profile and checklist models thus possess the virtues of simplicity and ease of use, but they suffer from many of the same deficiencies as index

TABLE 5.   Illustration of a Profile Model for Two Hypothetical Projects

	Profiles for Two Hypothetical Projects A and B				
	Undesirable Region			*Desirable Region*	
Criteria	−2	−1	0	+1	+2

Patentability
Technical Feasibility
Cost
Marketability
Profitability

Profile for Project B

Profile for Project A

models. However, they have achieved some appeal in the chemical processing industries (2, 6). Users have found that these types of models introduce a desired level of formality in screening candidate projects, without demanding more data and specification than are readily available (2, 13).

Inadequacies of the Models

Table 6 compares the real world environment of project selection and evaluation with the viewpoint that is expressed in most of the models. Most models appear to be constructed largely for the single decision maker, rather than for organizational decision making. They assume that the decision maker has complete information about project risks, costs, values, manpower availabilities and resource trade-offs, and that the organizational goals and constraints are stable and well-known. The decision maker is presumed to have all the decision information at his finger-tips, along with the infinite wisdom to accurately forecast and articulate the project's success probabilities. Projects are generally treated as independent entities, to be evaluated individually, ignoring any technical or economic interdependencies between them.

Thus, the real world complexities of multiple objectives and constraints are usually glossed over, and the models are formulated around single objectives and single constraints. The models seek the economically best decision, while in reality there may be many satisfactory decisions which meet various non-economic criteria. Management science models reflect only the analytical aspects of project evaluation. But in real world project evaualtion, decisions are often profoundly influenced by a multitude of organizational and human behavioral factors. Emotions, departmental loyalties, conflicts in desires, coalitions, and divergencies in viewpoints, are some of the important aspects often not accounted for in management science models. In short, the models are especially weak in their organization behavioral content.

TABLE 6. The Real World Environment vs. The Management Science View

The Viewpoint that Management Science Models Seem to Take	The Real World Environment
1. A single decision maker, in a well-behaved environment.	1. Many decision makers and many decision influencers, in a dynamic organizational environment.
2. Perfect information about candidate projects and their characteristics; outputs, values and risks of candidates known and quantifiable.	2. Imperfect information about candidate projects and their characteristics; outputs and values of projects are difficult to specify; uncertainty accompanies all estimates.
3. Well-known, invariant goals.	3. Ever-changing, fuzzy goals.
4. Decision making information is concentrated in the hands of the decision maker, so that he has all the information he needs to make a decision.	4. Decision making information is highly splintered and scattered piecemeal throughout the organization, with no one part of the organization having all the information needed for decision making.
5. The decision maker is able to articulate all consequences.	5. The decision maker is often unable or unwilling to state outcomes and consequences.
6. Candidate projects are viewed as independent entities, to be individually evaluated on their own merits.	6. Candidate projects are often technically and economically interdependent.
7. A single objective, usually expected value maximization or profit maximization, is assumed and the constraints are primarily budgetary in nature.	7. There are sometimes conflicting multiple objectives and multiple constraints, and these are often non-economic in nature.
8. The best portfolio of projects is determined on economic grounds.	8. Satisfactory portfolios may possess many non-economic characteristics.
9. The budget is "optimized" in a single decision.	9. An iterative, re-cycling budget determination process is used.
10. One single, economically "best," overall decision is sought.	10. What seems to be the "best" decision for the total organization may not be seen as best by each department or party, so that many conflicts may arise.

329

Three important organization behavioral needs must be satisfied before any project evaluation model can be used effectively. First of all, organizational goals and constraints at all levels of the organization must be clearly-defined and agreed upon. They are the ultimate standards for killing some projects and accepting others. Parties who agree to the goals will necessarily also understand what types of projects are acceptable and how their proposals will be judged.

Second, most project evaluation data are necessarily subjective in nature. Unless a spirit of trust and openness is felt by the parties, it is not likely that such data will be fully and openly exchanged. Each person who is involved, either as a project proposer, a decider, or a supplier of information, must appreciate the larger needs of the organization vis-à-vis his own. Ideally, all parties should be able to comprehend, empathize with and come to consensus with each other.

Third, for successful project evaluation a minimum level of personal awareness is needed. The involved parties must know and truly comprehend the nature of the projects they are proposing or deliberating. This means two things. It means they must have a depth of factual knowledge. And it also means that they must have a complete awareness of their own feelings, since much of the decision data are highly personal. Many decision settings fail because the participant's feelings are not crystallized and the parties do not literally know how they feel about a particular project.

Thus there is a need for a structured process that fulfills these organization behavioral needs. Though research is still proceeding, a process which has come to be known as the QS/NI process appears to meet this need.

> *This section of the article is omitted for reasons of space. Basically, the author proposes that projects first be rank-ordered by individual evaluators using a Q-sort technique followed by organized group discussions (nominal-interacting) concerning discrepancies in individual rank-orders. For further information the reader is urged to consult the original paper.*

References

1. ANSOFF, H. I., "Evaluation of Applied R&D in a Firm," in *Technological Planning at the Corporate Level,* J. R. Bright, ed., Cambridge: Harvard University Press, 1964, pp. 12–19.

2. AUGOOD, DEREK, "A Review of R&D Evaluation Methods," *IEEE Transactions on Engineering Management,* Vol. EM-20, No. 4 (November), 1973, pp. 114–120.

3. BAKER, N. R. and FREELAND, J. R., "Recent Advances in R&D Benefit Measurement and Project Selection Methods," *Management Science,* Vol. 21, No. 10 (June), 1975, pp. 1164–1175.

4. COCHRAN, M. A.; E. B. PYLE; L. G. GREENE; H. A. CLYMER and A D. BENDER, "Investment Model for R&D Project Evaluation and Selection," *IEEE Transactions on Engineering Management,* Vol. EM-18, No. 4 (August), 1971, pp. 89–100.

5. GEAR, A. E.; A. G. LOCKETT; A. W PEARSON, "Analysis of Some Portfolio Selection Models for R&D," *IEEE Transactions on Engineering Management,* Vol. EM-18, No. 2 (May), 1971, pp. 66–76.

6. HARRIS, J. S., "Evaluating New Project Proposals," *Chemical and Engineering News,* Vol. 15, No. 8 (April 17), 1961, pp. 14–18.

7. HERTZ, D. B., "Risk Analysis in Capital Investment," *Harvard Business Review,* Vol. 42, No. 1 (January), 1964, pp. 95–106.

8. MALLOY, J. B., "Risk Analysis of Chemical Plants," *Chemical Engineering Progress,* Vol. 67, No. 10 (October), 1971, pp. 68–71.

9. MOORE, J. R. and N. R. BAKER, "An Analytical Approach to Scoring Model Design—Application to Research and Development Project Selection," *IEEE Transactions on Engineering Management,* Vol. EM-16, No. 3 (August), 1969, pp. 90–98.

10. OLSEN, F., "The Control of Research Funds, in *Coordinating, Control and Financing of Industrial Research,* A. H. Rubenstein, ed., Kings Crown Press, Columbia University: New York, 1955, pp. 95–101.

11. SHARPE, W. F., "A Simplified Model for Portfolio Analysis," *Management Science,* Vol. 9, No. 1 (January), 1963, pp. 277–293.

12. SOUDER, WM. E., "Comparative Analysis of R&D Investment Models," *AIIE Transactions,* Vol. 1, No. 2 (March), 1972, pp. 57–64.

13. SOUDER, WM. E., "Selecting and Staffing R&D Projects Via Operations Research," *Chemical Engineering Progress,* Vol. 63, No. 11 (November), 1967, pp. 27–37.

14. SOUDER, WM. E.; P. M. MAHER; and A. H. RUBENSTEIN, "Two Successful Experiments in Project Selection," *Research Management,* Vol. 15, No. 5 (September), 1972, pp. 44–54.

15. SOUDER, WM. E., "Effectiveness of Nominal and Interacting Group Decision Processes for Integrating R&D and Marketing," *Management Science,* Vol. 23, No. 6 (February), 1977, pp. 595–605.

27. Estimating Market Potential

Morgan B. McDonald, Jr.

Market potential means different things to different people. This article examines the concept in detail and shows how it can be estimated for new industrial products.

ONE OF THE FIRST things management naturally wants to know, when deciding whether to proceed with the development and marketing of a new product, is how much of the product the company can expect to sell.

All management may need to justify its approval, in some instances, is merely reasonable assurance that the company could sell a certain minimum quantity of the product. This might be the case, for example, if the product would always be manufactured to order, and if offering it for sale would draw primarily on the company's engineering skills and entail little or no investment in new facilities. In fact, the size of the *total* market may not be a crucial consideration—at least at the outset—in a number of situations where the element of risk is small. Later, if the market should prove to be a substantial one, the company would likely want more complete market data before making plans to expand its participation.

In contrast to situations of this kind, there are a great many others in which companies deem it unwise to proceed without first determining whether the size of the total market—or some segment(s) of it—would be large enough to support the new entry. Determining the short- or long-term dimensions of the market, of course, is only part of the problem. What management ultimately needs to know as well are the rate and degree of penetration the company might realistically hope to achieve in

Reprinted from *Appraising the Market for New Industrial Products* (New York: The Conference Board, SBP No. 123, 1967), pp. 38–62. Used by permission.

Morgan McDonald, at the time of writing, was a member of the research staff of The Conference Board.

the market over a given period of time. It can then appraise the company's potential sales volume in the light of profit, cost, breakeven, payout, strategy, and other goals set for the product.

Magnitude of the Job

As in the case of other marketing research on new products, the amount of effort devoted to developing sharply defined measures of market potential depends on how much the company has at stake in the project. Experienced planners tend to weigh the cost of obtaining refined estimates against the possible consequences of taking action on the basis of limited or unreliable information as to market size.

Just how complex and time-consuming a job it is to gauge the market potential for a new industrial product is generally determined by a number of factors, such as:

- Availability of existing market data for the product in question.
- Degree of precision required or obtainable.
- Structure of the market in which the product would be sold.
- Nature of the product, especially its relative "newness."

Availability of Market Data

If the researcher is very lucky, he may have access to detailed market data (and perhaps even to future projections) which are reliable, relate directly to the product in question, and are in a form ideally suited for his purposes. Frequently, however, good, relevant data are not so easy to come by.

Lacking ready information relating to the size of the specific market under consideration, companies sometimes find it advantageous to use a less direct approach and to look first at least one stage beyond for indicators of the size and activity of their customers' markets or, occasionally, of their customers' customers' markets.

Degree of Precision

It is hard enough for most companies to measure the *current* demand for *existing* products and to project future market trends for such products with precision. But the difficulties—and possibilities for inaccuracy—tend to be magnified, of course, in estimating even the short-term market potential for new products, especially when there is little current market evidence or experience to go on. Furthermore, estimates based on a polling of buying intentions are subject to sampling error and many other limitations of surveys of this kind. And the range of possible error is increased further when dealing with longer-range forecasts, which necessarily rest on a more tenuous combination of judgments and assumptions.

Market Situation and Structure

The complexity of the market structure can also affect the estimating problem. For example, companies say they often find it easier to take the measure of clear-cut markets that consist of relatively few users whose identity can be readily established; the task is apt to be harder if, say, there are a number of different submarkets, user types, classes of trade, or channels of distribution, each of which perhaps has its own special set of requirements.

All else being equal, companies note that it is usually less difficult to measure the potential of markets that are stable or growing at a fairly uniform rate. A market in an early stage of development, or one that is undergoing rapid change in size or composition, can pose serious problems for the researcher seeking an accurate reading of the current situation, let alone realistic projections for the future.

Another complicating factor is that the introduction of a new product into a market already in existence does not always mean that the new entry will simply capture some portion of aggregate current demand at the expense of the present sellers. It may be, for example, that other producers are not fully exploiting the true potential of the market.

Product Situation

If similar or identical products (or products serving essentially the same function) are already being sold by other manufacturers or by the company itself, this will sometimes facilitate the determination of market potential for a product that is still new to the company. Even if it is necessary to undertake special research or field investigations to get the necessary data, there may at least be an identifiable, existing market which can be studied.

The researcher frequently has a harder job in measuring the market for a product that performs a series of functions in some new way, possibly replacing several existing products. In such a case, he will usually try somehow to relate probable demand for the new product to the function that it will perform or to the product(s) it will replace. In any event, there remains the additional problem of determining the rate at which acceptance or substitution of the product can be expected to occur.

The truly new product—representing an entirely new departure in concept which creates a new market—is a rarity. A few companies with some experience in developing and marketing such products confirm that gauging their market is hardest of all, and requires the most skill.

Data Sources

Researchers often have to draw on several sources for information needed to estimate demand for a new product. The most common of these include:

- Public and commercial sources, such as government publications, trade associations, and the trade press.
- The company's internally developed sales and market data.
- The company's sales personnel and distributors.
- Prospective users of the product, other specifying influences, and authoritative experts.

It is considered good practice to develop and compare measures of market potential based on information from a number of different sources, if possible.

Public and Commercial Sources

In piecing together information for use in defining and measuring markets for new industrial products, experienced researchers routinely check public and commercial sources for any data that might be helpful for that purpose.

These outside sources will often include publications of the U.S. Bureau of the Census (such as the *Census of Manufacturers*); other statistical reports published by agencies of the Federal Government; reports of industry trade associations; trade periodicals; various directories and reports of state agencies and university bureaus of business research; and appropriate material from other commercial or private sources.

Company Sales and Market Data

Some companies regularly maintain highly developed sales and market information systems. For analytical purposes present customers, prospects, and/or markets may be identified as to type of business, Standard Industrial Classification code, kind and quantity of products purchased, end use, markets served, number of production workers, etc.

Sales and market data of this kind are generally oriented toward the company's existing markets. Therefore, if the new item would not be sold in these markets, or if its purchase or use would have no particular relation to those of products the firm was presently selling in such markets, then the company's routine records and analyses may not be very helpful in revealing the dimensions of demand for the item.

Company Sales Personnel and Distributors

Since it is the field representative's job to be well-informed as to the requirements of customers and prospects in his territory, some manufacturers survey their salesmen and/or distributors periodically about the market potential for new products. However, a drawback to relying strictly on sales force opinion, mentioned by several companies, is that salesmen are not always able to provide an objective evaluation of the actual needs for a new product. As a result, salesmen in many cases are asked not to give their own opinions, but to poll prospective users and to report their findings; in others, the judgment of salesmen is sought but further checked with information obtained from other sources.

Users and Other Specifiers

There are reported to be a number of instances when the best—and sometimes the only—source of reliable clues to the size of the market is a representative cross-section of those individuals who would most likely make or influence decisions to purchase the product.

In certain kinds of markets, it is sometimes feasible for the manufacturer to conduct a virtual census of all the prospective users. In others, a limited survey of probable large-volume users of the product is said to provide a fairly good basis for an estimate of total market potential. Within a prospective user's organization, researchers may gather pertinent market information from several points of contact, such as purchasing, engineering, technical development, and marketing research.

Not all user surveys are conducted solely for the purpose of getting clues to the dimensions of the market. Nor do they all take the form of special investigations. For example, users may be polled during regular contacts by the company's field personnel. Such is the practice of an equipment producer which relies on product teams for this purpose. The company explains:

> We have encountered substantial difficulty in estimating the probable demand for new products. The most serious problem for us probably lies in the nature of our product, which is a low-unit-volume, high-dollar-value item. Consequently, it is not susceptible to consumer-product market research techniques.
>
> We try to overcome such problems by intimate contacts with our markets. For each major line of products, we have established product teams consisting of representatives from engineering, sales, and service. Through the activities of these teams, which are close to their respective markets, it has become possible to reduce our market estimating problems. However, this approach is far from infallible.

Another method sometimes employed to identify various types of possible users and applications for the new product is an analysis of inquiries that have been stimulated by means of advertisements, publicity releases, exposure of the product or samples at trade shows, or even by means of limited marketing of the product. One reported difficulty with this approach to appraising markets is that it is not always easy to distinguish between the serious and the casual inquiry. However, the title of the individual making the inquiry may offer some evidence for judging this.

When parties other than those who would actually use the product are potentially influential in some way in specifying its use in various applications, they may be in a position to judge its market prospects. For example, architects, engineering firms, and governmental agencies are said to be helpful to companies that are trying to develop realistic estimates of future demand for certain kinds of products.

Still another common practice is to relate probable usage of the new product, not to expected purchases of the product by potential customers, but to the output or end product of such customers. This can lead to surveys for the measurement of customers' markets. A steel company following this practice explains:

> One way in which we have overcome the problems involved in gauging the potential demand for a new product is to survey the users of the ultimate product (i.e., the product that would be produced by our customers with our product). This provides us with the opportunity to gauge the demand as stated by our customers against a survey of the demand for their product.

Calculating Market Potential

Estimating the market potential for a new product most generally involves determining both the current and the future capacity of the market to absorb the product under consideration. If a market already exists for the product, companies will usually try first to identify the major applications and prospective users or user-types for the product, the factors influencing the utility and value of the product to its users, and the amount of the product presently required by its users. Projecting the future potential of any market requires an understanding of such things as: how the product will probably be used in the performance of those functions for which it was designed (taking into account the possibility of obsolescence); the continued need for such functions to be performed; and replacement market considerations, if any.

There is, of course, no "best" method of measuring the potential market for new products, due to dissimilarities in product and market situations. Nevertheless, many of the basic problems and the steps involved in their solution are to some extent similar from one project to the next.

A composite of a good many approaches described by participants in this study amounts to the following:

- Identify specific end-use situations for the product.
- Identify the major market segments in which these end-use situations will exist.
- Estimate the potential market for the product within each segment. (The total market potential is simply the sum of these).

In carrying out this third step, researchers generally look for some projectable measure, of size or activity for each segment that relates logically to its probable usage of the product.

Identifying Uses and User Types

A common starting point is to identify the kinds of companies that might be purchasers of the product—or the kinds of situations, installations, etc., in which the product would likely be used. The next step then is to classify these into appropriate, relatively homogeneous groups (*market segments*) having common, identifiable demand characteristics.

For market measurement purposes, major segments may be broken down still further. For example, a company may find it advantageous to divide the automotive segment of the market for bearings into two parts—one made up of original equipment manufacturers (i.e., the large automotive producers, in this case), and another embracing the aftermarket.

Logical market segments are sometimes obvious and well known to the manufacturer—or at least fairly easy to identify. In other cases, however, companies have to do a great deal of investigating in order to determine the kinds of user groups, applications, and the like, that make up the market for a new product (e.g., see discussion of such efforts made by the Weyerhaeuser Company). One purpose of early-stage surveys of potential users, intermediate field research, and even of late-stage product and market tests often is to determine the nature and requirements of various market segments.

Estimating the Potential for Market Segments

Based on practices employed by the companies studied, estimating the market potential for a given market segment frequently calls for determination of the following:

- Current and projected size, activity, end-product output, etc., of the market segment related to its use of the product.
- Current and projected usage (input) of the product per unit of size, activity, output, etc., of the market segment. The ratios of

product usage-to-market segment activity thus arrived at—i.e., the rate of incorporation of the product per unit of end product, economic activity, or other measure for the segment to which use of the product can be meaningfully related—are often referred to as usage factors.

How One Company Calculates Total Market Potential for New Products

The following is a highly simplified illustration of the calculations commonly performed by the marketing research department of one company in estimating the total market potential for proposed new products. The procedure is applied in the case of new products to be incorporated in other products whose total current and projected output is determined—in the absence of reliable published data—by surveys of companies manufacturing them. The new item may be either: (a) one that is new to the company but is already being marketed by others, or (b) one that is new to the market—possibly replacing one or more existing products, or being proposed as an added element or ingredient for use in the buyer's product.

First, the company's marketing research unit carries out investigations to determine:

• The degree to which the proposed product is (or would be) incorporated in each of the end products of which it will be a part. The mathematical expression of this is called the weighted average usage factor. An attempt is made to calculate the current and the probable future rate of usage of the product per unit of each end product.

WEIGHTED AVERAGE USAGE FACTOR

A key element in the company's approach is the calculation of a weighted average usage factor—the average amount of proposed product [K] incorporated by all producers in a unit of end product [X].[1] This calculation is carried out in two steps which are illustrated in table 1.

Step 1. The first step consists of multiplying, for each producer of end product [X], its reported market share of product [X] by its average usage rate of [K]. The company forms an estimate of the market share held by each producer of end product [X] by asking, during interviews with these producers, the following kinds of questions: "Leaving yourself out, who's who in this industry anyway? What share do they have?" The company has found through experience that by the time all producers have been interviewed, a market share profile emerges. The market share estimates thus developed are shown in column (2) of table 1.

[1] If product [K] were not yet on the market, then the investigation would seek to determine the usage of product(s) which would be replaced by or used in conjunction with the new product [K].

TABLE 1: Computation of Weighted Average Usage Factor for Proposed Product [K] in End Product [X]

| Manufacturers of End Product [X] | Reported Market Share | Reported Use of [K] (lbs. of [K] per 100 lbs. of [X]) | | | Weighted Average Use [K] Σ (Market Share $\times$ Use) | | |
| | | Actual | | Estimated | | | |
Company (1)	(2)	1960 (3)	1965 (4)	1970 (5)	1960 (6) (2)$\times$(3)	1965 (7) (2)$\times$(4)	1970 (8) (2)$\times$(5)
X_1	50%	1.0	1.5	1.5	.50	.75	.75
X_2	30%	1.5	2.0	2.5	.45	.60	.75
$X_3 \ldots X_5$	20%	1.3	1.0	1.0	.26	.20	.20
Weight Average Usage of [K] per 100 lbs. of End Product [X]					1.21	1.55	1.70

The company obtains data showing the average usage of [K] per unit of output of product [X] from the producers of [X] during interviews or, in instances where interviewing is considered to be impractical or unnecessary, by mail survey. The usage estimates thus obtained from each producer are shown in columns (3), (4), and (5) of table 1.

A hypothetical example of the calculation of the weighted average usage factor of [K] for end product [X] is shown in columns (6), (7), and (8). In this example, three years (1960, 1965, and 1970) are used for illustrative purposes. In actual practice, however, an attempt is made to gather historical data for a series of years so that trends may be computed.

Step 2. The second step is a summation. Thus, for all producers in the example (companies X_1 through X_5) a computed average of 1.21 pounds of [K] was used per 100 pounds of product [X] in 1960, and 1.55 pounds in 1965. It is estimated that usage will increase to 1.70 pounds by 1970.

TOTAL USAGE

In order to estimate total usage of proposed product [K], the computed usage factors (development of which is shown in table 1) are applied to historical, current, and future estimates of total output of the end products in which [K] is used. Continuing with the example, table 2 (opposite) shows for the years 1960, 1965, and 1970:

• *Weighted average usage of [K] in three end products: [X], [Y], and [Z] (column 2).* The weighted average usage of [K] per 100 pounds of product [X] is taken from table 1; usage of [K] in products [Y] and [Z] would have been similarly computed in that previous step; however, the calculations are not shown.

• *Estimated total output of end products [X], [Y], and [Z] (column 3).* Data showing total historical and current output of the end product may sometimes be derived from published sources. However, in the absence of published data, it may be necessary for the company to estimate historical and current —as well as future—output of the end products in which [K] will be incorporated. Such estimates may be based on information elicited from the end-product producers themselves. Since estimates of future total end-product output are likely to vary from respondent to respondent, an average estimate is calculated. Thus, the 1,500,000 pounds of output of end product [X] projected for the year 1970

represents an average or "most likely" estimate, and is based on the individual estimates elicited from producers $X_1 \ldots X_5$. In some cases, it has been found feasible to express estimated future output in terms of a range of possibilities.

• *Estimated total usage of [K] in end products [X], [Y], and [Z], respectively (column 4).* In some cases, estimates of future total usage are expressed in terms of a range.

An example of the actual calculation is shown below. Thus, in 1960 a total of 1,000,000 pounds of [X] were produced, requiring an average input of 1.21 pounds of [K] for every 100 pounds produced. Total estimated usage of [K] in the output of product [X] for that year was therefore 12,100 pounds.

$$\frac{1,000,000}{100} \times 1.21 = 12,100 \text{ lbs. [K]}$$

The final calculation is a summation, illustrated in table 3. Thus, the grand total market for [K] is

TABLE 2: Calculation of Total Usage of Proposed Product [K] in End Products [X], [Y], and [Z]

Year (1)	Weighted Average Usage Factor [K] (lbs. of [K] per 100 lbs. of End Product) (2)	Estimated Total Production of End Product (lbs.) (3)	Usage of [K] (lbs.) (4)
	End Product [X]		
1960	1.21	1,000,000	12,100
1965	1.55	1,250,000	19,375
1970	1.70	1,500,000	25,500
	End Product [Y]		
1960	2.13	3,000,000	63,900
1965	2.13	2,500,000	53,250
1970	2.63	2,250,000	59,175
	End Product [Z]		
1960	3.25	5,000,000	162,500
1965	3.15	6,000,000	189,000
1970	3.00	6,500,000	195,000

estimated in this example to be pounds in 1965, and 279,675 238,500 pounds in 1960, 261,625 pounds in 1970.

TABLE 3: Computed Total Market for [K] (Pounds)

End Product	1960	1965	1970
[X]	12,100	19,375	25,500
[Y]	63,900	53,250	59,175
[Z]	162,500	189,000	195,000
Estimated Total Usage of [K]	238,500	261,625	279,675

Usage Factors

Once the researcher has established that a measurable relationship exists between use of the product and some relevant statistical measure that either is known or can be reliably estimated, he can, say, expand sample findings into an estimate of the total market. (See, for example, procedure followed by Weyerhaeuser Company.) Or he may be able to project the related statistical measure and, by applying the projected usage factor, obtain an estimate of total market usage of the product in some future period.

If the manufacturer's new product is to be incorporated as a component or as a raw material in an end product whose production can be reliably measured, it may be possible to estimate the rate or degree of incorporation of the new product in the end product of which it is (or would be) a part. If the new product is a capital equipment or an operating supply item, the task might be, first, to identify the type or types of manufacturing establishments in which the product would likely be used, and then to estimate how demand for the product would relate to, say, the number, size, or end products of such establishments.

Another possibility is that the new product can be shown to be related either to the production, shipment, sale, or usage of some other given product, or else to some available measure of economic activity. For example, if the product were a new kind of road-building equipment, an attempt might be made to determine how demand for this equipment would relate to the volume of highway construction on a dollar or perhaps mileage basis.

In one instance, when a company wished to measure the market potential for a new log-handling device, it was first necessary to determine the productive capacity of lumber mills that could afford to use one or more of the units. Having done this, the company then obtained from various lumber mill associations complete listings of the mills and the board-foot output for the areas in which it was interested. From this, the company was able to gauge with some accuracy the total potential for log handlers.

Estimating Company Sales Potential

Almost invariably, a forecast of the company's own sales of a new product is necessarily more tentative, more liable to error, and is arrived at more subjectively than a projection of the total market.

Even if a company develops a truly new product, and can accurately gauge the new market, it must generally accept the fact that—unless it is assured of some unusual proprietary advantage in the market, or is promoting a dud—it will sooner or later be sharing the market with other suppliers.

In the absence of a track record for the new product, the forecaster seldom feels confident in applying an estimated market-share ratio to the total market projection, and therefore usually tries to build up his company sales forecast in some other way.

Sales force estimates and surveys of prospective users—are both widely used in estimating a company's own future sales of such products. And a third possibility for obtaining evidence of ultimate sales volume in advance of full-scale marketing is through limited marketing of the product.

Apart from the fact that there may be no other handy way of developing a forecast for a particular new product, there are certain other advantages—and also some disadvantages—to the sales force composite and the user survey methods of sales forecasting. As described in the Conference Board's report on "Forecasting Sales," companies have found these to be the principal advantages and disadvantages of the sales force composite method:

Advantages:

1. It uses specialized knowledge of men closest to the market.
2. Responsibility for the forecast is placed in the hands of those who must produce the results.
3. The sales force gains greater confidence in quotas developed from forecasts.
4. Results tend to attain greater stability because of the magnitude of the sample.
5. It lends itself to the easy development of product, territory, customer, or salesmen breakdowns.

How Events Altered The Potential For One Product

An equipment manufacturer developed a machine to insert the components in the printed wiring (PW) boards used in the manufacture of television sets. The company recognized at the outset that, aside from considerations of cost and technical feasibility, the market potential for the machine depended on three factors:

- The number of television sets produced.
- The number of PW boards per set.
- The number of components which needed to be inserted per PW board. (For example, for an assembly operation in which a single component was inserted per PW board, one machine would be required. If, however, ten components were inserted per PW board, a multimachine installation comprising ten units would be required.)

The company's first attempt to assess the merits of the product idea was by means of internal analysis examining its past experience in selling production equipment to the electronic industry, as well as information reported by trade associations and in trade publications. This preliminary investigation was followed by discussions with the principal manufacturers of television sets. As a result, the company was able to develop a body of factual data and logical assumptions regarding the marketability of the proposed product.

For instance, the company learned how many television sets had been produced historically (both black-and-white and color); the number of printed circuits in the average set; the average number of components inserted in each printed circuit; and the then-current costs of labor, components, and printed circuit boards.

Company planners then made a number of assumptions concerning the underlying market opportunity for the product, and the product's feasibility from a technical standpoint. Specifically, these assumptions concerned:

- Probable future growth patterns in television production (both black-and-white and color).
- The likelihood that television circuits and components would remain essentially the same in the future.
- Probability that the industry would continue to use printed circuits.
- Performance characteristics required of the proposed product.
- Estimated costs of printed circuit components when packaged for automatic assembly. (It was believed that certain components would have to be packaged in a special manner that would allow them to be fed into the machine and that in some cases would increase the cost of such components.)
- Ability of the company to design and produce equipment that would meet the perceived requirements of television set manufacturers.

From its market facts and assumptions, the company was able to prepare forecasts of the future size of the market for the product; the company's probable sales volume in that market; its probable gross income; its probable manufacturing, marketing, and development costs; and its anticipated net income.

The new machine was eventually developed and marketed. However, as a result of several unforeseen developments, the company had to reduce its earlier sales estimates. For one thing, its projections of television set output proved to be too high because of the failure of color television to develop as rapidly as had been expected. For another, two machines competitive with that being developed by the company unexpectedly appeared on the market, although these were later withdrawn. Also, it turned out to be impractical to use the company's machine to insert certain components because of the expense and difficulties encountered in packaging them for feeding into the machine.

Finally, technological obsolescence set in at a more rapid rate than had been anticipated. This was partly due to the fact that television set manufacturers made such frequent changes in the designs of their PW boards that the company was unable to modify its machine fast enough to keep pace with changing requirements. Another reason was that some components were later miniaturized, making it impractical to insert them in PW boards by means of the machine. In the end, the company was forced to lower its sights, and was able to sell only a small portion of the machines it had originally planned.

Disadvantages:

1. Salesmen are poor estimators, often being either more optimistic or more pessimistic than conditions warrant.
2. If estimates are used as a basis for setting quotas, salesmen are inclined to understate the demand in order to make the goal easier to achieve.
3. Salesmen are often unaware of the broad economic patterns shaping future sales and are thus incapable of forecasting trends for extended periods.
4. Since sales forecasting is a subsidiary function of the sales force, sufficient time may not be made available for it.
5. It requires an extensive expenditure of time by executives and sales force.
6. Elaborate schemes are sometimes necessary to keep estimates realistic and free from bias.

The same report describes these advantages and disadvantages to basing sales forecasts on users' expectations:

Advantages:

1. The forecast is based on information obtained directly from product users, whose buying actions will actually determine sales.
2. The forecaster gets a subjective feel of the market and of the thinking behind users' buying intentions.

3. It bypasses published or other indirect sources, enabling the company to obtain its information in the form and detail required.

Disadvantages:

1. It is difficult to employ in markets where users are numerous or not easily located.
2. It depends on the judgment and cooperation of product users, some of whom may be ill-informed or uncooperative.
3. The forecast is based on expectations, which are subject to subsequent change.
4. Considerable expenditure of time and manpower is required.

Reasonableness of Forecast

If independent forecasts can be obtained by two or more methods, this gives the forecaster a possible check on the reasonableness of his results. The company's own past experience with other new products may offer some basis for judging how quickly it can expect to gain acceptance for the proposed product.

When the product is already being sold by other producers, one consideration is whether the market can support another supplier—and what the reaction of present suppliers to the new entry is likely to be.

Inherent in any sales forecast is a number of other assumptions. Some have to do with the size and nature of the market as a whole; others with the company's ability and willingness to compete in that market—i.e., to make, promote, price, sell, distribute, and service the product effectively. The final forecast is very often a "negotiated" estimate, reflecting the judgment of various company units and of management as to the nature of the market opportunity and the capabilities and interests of the company.

A New-product Study by Weyerhaeuser Company

Weyerhaeuser Company recently carried out a series of market studies to determine if it should produce and market a line of movable wood partitions. This, the company felt, would be a logical extension of its timber-based product lines which include lumber, plywood, paper, and containers. A preliminary market survey of the movable partition industry had confirmed the existence of a substantial, growing market for movable partitions. Subsequently, Weyerhaeuser's research and development department reported that it would be technically feasible for the company to manufacture a movable partition system using wood or hardboard panels, sandwich construction with a paper honeycomb core, and wood mullions.

To gain practical market knowledge and field experience based on the actual product, it was decided that several prototype systems should be assembled at the company's Los Angeles fabrication plant for sale and installation in the Los Angeles metropolitan area.

However, before proceeding with pilot plant production and marketing of the prototype systems, a number of studies of the market situation in the Los Angeles metropolitan area were carried out. These included:

- A study of partition usage for the purpose of developing usage factors that might serve as a base for estimating demand.
- A field survey of buyers, suppliers, and specifiers of commercial movable partition systems in the Los Angeles area.
- A study of the installed prices of competitive partition systems.

In addition, follow-up research was conducted after the Los Angeles pilot operation had been under way for some time, to determine reaction to the product.

Usage Factors

Prior investigation of the movable partition industry had shown that movable partitions are used in the following types of buildings: offices and banks, public administration, hospitals, educational and science, manufacturing, stores and mercantile. Movable partitions were known to be used in both new construction (the largest portion of the market) and in remodeling work.

Regularly published data on construction contract awards—including floor area of new buildings, broken down by type of building and geographic region—were available to the company. By themselves, however, the floor area figures told company researchers nothing about the usage of movable partitions in new construction.

Therefore, one of the primary tasks in estimating the market potential for movable partitions was to develop projectable usage rate data—that is, a numerical relationship between partition usage and building floor area. Once usage factors were established for each major type of building, these could then be applied to published floor area figures found in the statistical reports of building activity, and estimates of the total market potential for movable partitions thereby derived.

To find out what these relationships were for buildings in the Los Angeles metropolitan area, Weyerhaeuser examined the plans of between 275 and 300 specific buildings for which construction permits had been issued, noting in each case the amount of movable partitions called for in the plans, and relating this amount to the building's floor area. Average relationships were then computed for the various major types of buildings included in the sample. The usage factors thus arrived at were expressed in terms of the average number of linear feet of movable partitions per 1,000 square feet of floor area for each specific type of building.

Research Problems. The company found that this research presented three principal problems: cost, accuracy, and obsolescence.

COST. Normally, one to one-and-a-half hours are required to take off the information covering three to five items (movable partitions being one item) from the plans of an average building. This made the research relatively expensive and limited the size of the sample.

ACCURACY. The company believed that the usage factors developed in this way could be used effectively to estimate the demand for movable partitions in the cases of hospitals, schools, and those commercial buildings built for known tenants. However, it was found that the approach does not work particularly well for buildings built on speculation, since movable partitions are not always shown in the plans for such buildings, but are installed later.

OBSOLESCENCE. Another problem was obsolescence. It was recognized that the usage factors thus obtained were static—that is, a given ratio of partition-to-floor space represented the usage rate at a given time only, and therefore did not of itself indicate trends in usage rates. It was felt, however, that this would not necessarily impair the usefulness of the computed factors since a $\pm 30\%$ error believed inherent in the data could be tolerated by the company in this instance in any projections of future demand obtained by applying the factors to forecasts of building floor space.

Field Survey

A draft of the research proposal for this survey submitted to management by Weyerhaeuser's marketing research department, indicates how this step of the research was to be carried out.

The field survey was carried out substantially in accordance with the proposal shown, and a report of survey findings was prepared covering the following major points. Highlights of the report's findings are summarized below to illustrate the kind of information obtained in the survey:

Size of Available Market. The survey revealed that a market did indeed exist in the Los Angeles metropolitan area, and that it was of sufficient size to make the proposed pilot operation worthwhile.

Current Partition Prices. It was found that the movable partition market had three distinct segments, based on installed prices. The major producers and partition systems dominant in each segment were identified.

In addition, crossover tendencies between the market segments were determined. It was found that while an individual user or specifier generally stayed in one segment, he would under special circumstances move from upper to middle, or vice versa. For example, researchers reported, "A system with clear use advantages can interest a mid-price user in an upper-price partition. Also, an upper-price user who sees the increasing quality of the mid-price partition may move himself downward, at least on a try-out basis."

Product Characteristics. Major product characteristics considered by users and specifiers, and those which they tended to weigh against installed costs, were ascertained. Needs, preferences, requirements, and the like, were noted with regard to: module, on-site flexibility, height, sound transmission, fire retardance, surface variability, partition movability, wiring, parts interchangeability, and extra parts.

Marketing Requirements. The following, a direct quotation from the survey report, covers findings with respect to marketing requirements:

> Partition purchasing is done in two ways: direct prospects who do their own specifying and control their own purchasing, and installations which are architecturally specified and purchased.
>
> The general rule is that the purchaser wants the manufacturer to take responsibility for the end result, regardless of who installs it. The actual installation can be done by the customer staff, by a subcontractor, or by the manufacturer's personnel. The ultimate responsibility is the manufacturer's.
>
> The selling procedure is handled by an architectural representative or special salesman who knows partitions and can provide the technical consultation and advice required. It seems doubtful that a nonspecialist could sell very successfully in a field accustomed to specialists.
>
> The general marketing requirements, then, are covered below. The actual importance of each, or others, cannot be judged without a test situation.
>
> - A specialized sales force (or individual) to sell a specialized product against specialized buyers and competition.
> - Availability of an erection crew, either a Weyerhaeuser crew or a reliable subcontractor to handle installation where it is not done by the purchaser.
> - Supervision of installation regardless of who handles the job so that final responsibility can rest with Weyerhaeuser.
> - A small inventory of replacement parts maintained at the fabricating location to take care of the rapid service requirement.
>
> Due to the availability of the Weyerhaeuser fabricating plant, the special sales staff, and size of the market, Los Angeles is an excellent testing ground for the Weyerhaeuser partition system, in both its product ability and marketing phases.

Price Research

Since most partition systems are sold on an installed basis, it was felt that competitors' published price lists (which usually applied only to partition components) were an inadequate guide to industry price levels. Therefore, an attempt was made to compare the prices of competitive systems with the Weyerhaeuser prototype system on an installed basis.

EXHIBIT 1

ROUGH DRAFT   WEYERHAEUSER COMPANY
                           Wood Products Division
                       Marketing Research Department

PRELIMINARY OR SCREENING AUTHORIZATION

SUBJECT   Project No. _____

Program Area: Research and Development —   Date   _____
                       Light Construction Research
                                                     Submitted by _____
Requested by:

Job Title: Opportunity for Weyerhaeuser
                       Partition Systems in the
                       Los Angeles Market

Job Description: A field survey of buyers, suppliers
                       and specifiers of partition systems
                       in the Los Angeles metropolitan area.

OBJECTIVE

1. To determine the size and kind of market opportunity for partition systems in the
   Los Angeles metropolitan area.

2. To determine the probable acceptance of the Weyerhaeuser candidate partition system.

BACKGROUND

The Light Construction Research Department of the Research Division has developed a
demountable partition system primarily based on forest products. One variation of this
system has been installed in the Seattle Laboratory. While estimates have been developed
on cost of materials and installation based on laboratory findings and the Seattle experience, and while some installation problems have been resolved, it is recognized that
more work remains in the area of better defining product line standards, material and
installation costs, fabrication and installation problems, and product acceptability.
It is planned that several proto-type systems be assembled at the Los Angeles fabrication plant for sale and installation in the Los Angeles metropolitan area as a means of
obtaining better answers to these questions. Preliminary to such pilot manufacture of
partition systems proto-types, a local marketing survey is planned to identify the
market opportunity, the competitor factors in the local market and the criteria of product performance and cost which will influence product acceptability.

A recent marketing research survey indicated that the total market at the present time
on an installed cost basis is about [$x million] annually, of which about [$x million]
represents price to manufacturers for framing and panel materials. Half of the total
market is presently supplied by integrated systems, primarily steel panel, while the
other half is supplied by many small concerns offering either frame systems or panels,
or firms which erect other manufacturers' partition systems.

Of the four major systems, integrated systems comprise [x%]; post and panel systems, [x%]; runner and slide systems, [x%]; and concealed stud systems comprise [x%] of the total market. Four large firms dominate the industry, sharing about half of the total market.

The marketing opportunity itself is primarily in office buildings which account for [x%] of the total. [x%] of the market is in new construction; [x%] in remodeling (of which [x%], again, is in office buildings). It is anticipated that the market will increase by about [x amount] in the next five years.

PLAN

Based on a listing of all architects, general contractors; corporation building departments and partition suppliers and manufacturers in the area, a series of field interviews are planned divided approximately as follows: architects, 20/25; contractors, 15; installers for partition suppliers, 10; code and other public authorities, 5; large users, 10/15. This represents three to four-man weeks in the field. The interviewers will be provided with samples, topic outline guides, and specification material. The information thus obtained will be evaluated and presented in a report.

SCOPE

The scope of this study is limited to obtaining information from field calls conducted within the Los Angeles area and the analysis of that information.

METHOD

1. General marketing questions to be answered are:

   a. How do suppliers market?
   b. What is their product line (catalogs, price, etc.)?
   c. What is the market importance of patented features?
   d. How is the partition market divided?
      1. By type of building?
      2. By code?
      3. By the decision maker?
      4. By channel of distribution?
      5. By size of commodity?
      6. By kind of partition (fixed, demountable, etc.)?

2. General technical questions to be answered are:

   a. In each office installation there can be several layers of "class" separation reflected by the partition used. Most companies supply entirely different systems to meet this requirement. Could the same effect be achieved by variations in material only, assuming the system used is constant?

   b. What are the critical factors governing width of panel?

   c. If the company supplying the system allowed modifications of shapes in order to allow the architect a certain amount of design freedom, would this be a desirable thing?

EXHIBIT 1 (cont'd.)

d. Would a non-modular system using standard parts be desirable?

e. In what instance have you sued a sound rated wall?

f. Do you know your requirements as to desirable "sound transmission class"?

g. Do you have conditions where special sound control walls are needed?

h. What S.T.C., "Sound Transmission Class", do you normally require in your partition work?

i. For what types of installations have you been required to use a fire rated wall?

j. What fire classification do you find is most normally required?

k. Have you found it impossible to get a 3/4 hr. rated panel in the standard line of metal partitions?

l. Would it be desirable to have a rated wall unit?

m. Do you normally order extra parts at the time of initial order for changes, etc., at a later date?

n. If a job has been specified for movable partitions, how often have they been moved after completion?

o. Would a system that can be easily modified in the field be an advantage?

p. How often are movable partitions refinished?

q. Rank in order of importance —

    1. Movability
    2. Good sound characteristics
    3. Wide range of surface finish
    4. Complete modular versatility
    5. Reusability of parts
    6. Interchangeable units
    7. Speed of erection
    8. Use of standard electrical outlets and switches
    9. Convenience of installing wiring
    10. Completely hidden wiring
    11. 1-hr. fire rating
    12. Installation requiring no surface damage to flooring material

This was done by soliciting bids from a number of installing firms for actual partitioning of the office of the company's Los Angeles fabricating plant.

Since most of the bids received were higher than the amount for which the Weyerhaeuser partition system could be installed, it was concluded that the proposed Weyerhaeuser partition system could hold its own in a competitive market. Judgment regarding price was qualified, however, as it seemed likely that the competitive bids contained a certain amount of fat not present in the Weyerhaeuser estimate. It was not known how much lower competitive bids might drop under pressure.

Follow-up Research

After the pilot operation in the Los Angeles metropolitan area had been under way for some time, the company interviewed a number of users and specifiers of movable partitions who had been contacted by the Weyerhaeuser sales force. These included architectural firms, the real estate management division of the County of Los Angeles, and corporations that had purchased partition systems on their own account. Some of these had installed or specified the Weyerhaeuser system, while others had rejected it for one reason or another. Information obtained in these interviews dealt with such points as appearance, price, adequacy of line, maintenance and repair, movability, electrical raceways, fire retardance, sound attenuation, delivery, and installation.

From this follow-up study, the company learned a great deal more about the prospects and requirements of the market.

28. Marketing Mix Decisions
for New Products

Philip Kotler

*Different conceptions of the marketing mix will yield different estimates
of profit potential. Kotler shows how the "best" mix can be found
under conditions of limited information.*

SUPPOSE A NEW product has been screened and found to be compatible
with the company's objectives and resources. The next task is to evaluate
the profit potential of the product. In practice, this evaluation tends to be
conducted in the following manner. On the basis of inspiration or previous
research, management develops a particular conception of product attributes and a marketing program for the new product. Based on this specific
conception of the marketing mix, management develops two different
estimates. One is an estimate of the required sales volume to break even.
The other is an estimate of the sales volume which is likely to be stimulated by the marketing mix. If the sales potential estimate comfortably
exceeds the break-even volume estimate, the product idea is judged to be
profitable. If profits promise to be large in relation to the required investment, the product idea is likely to pass to the fourth stage, that of product
development.

Yet a more refined model for the analysis of new product profit potential is both desirable and practical. Instead of considering only one
marketing mix and whether break-even volume is likely to be achieved
under it, the more refined model provides for a simultaneous evaluation
of the profit potential of several marketing mixes. The refined model can
be illustrated by the following example:

Reprinted from the *Journal of Marketing Research,* published by the American Marketing Association, 1 (February, 1964), pp. 43–49.

*Philip Kotler is Harold T. Martin Professor of Marketing at Northwestern
University.*

The ABC Electronics Company is a small manufacturer of transistors and clock radios and is presently engaged in reviewing other electronic products for possible addition to the product line. One of these is a small portable tape recorder. Small novelty tape recorders have appeared recently on the market, and they retail at prices between $20–$50. The company's marketing research department has surveyed the market and found that interest in this type of unit is substantial and growing.

An executive committee is appointed to examine the potential profitability of this product. The production department estimates that $60,000 would have to be invested in specific new equipment and facilities and that this investment would have an estimated life of five years. The accounting department submits that the product would have to absorb $26,000 a year of general overhead to cover the value of supporting facilities, rent, taxes, executive salaries, cost of capital, etc. The marketing department advises that the product be supported initially with an advertising budget of approximately $20,000 and a personal selling budget of approximately $30,000 and furthermore that it should be priced at approximately $18 F.O.B. factory with no quantity discounts. Finally, the various operating departments estimate that the new product would involve a direct material and labor cost of $10 a unit.

What Is the Break-Even Volume?

The first step in the business analysis of a new product idea is to estimate how many units would have to be sold in order to cover costs. This break-even volume is found by analyzing how total revenue and total cost vary at different sales volumes.

Total revenue at any particular sales volume is that volume times the unit price adjusted by allowances for early payment, quantity purchases, and freight. The adjustments are fairly straightforward and total revenue as a function of sales volume is generally simple to estimate.

The total cost function is more difficult to estimate. Total costs often bear a nonlinear relationship to output. It is difficult enough to establish the shape of the total cost function for existing products because the statistical data are impure; the total cost function for a new product is even more difficult to estimate because the statistical data are nonexistent. But as a practical matter, the break-even analyst usually assumes a linear total cost function. This assumption may be faulty for very low and very high levels of output but may be sufficiently accurate for intermediate levels, according to some recent statistical cost studies.

The total cost function is composed of variable and fixed cost elements. In the example, variable costs are assumed to be constant at $10 a unit. The following fixed costs are found in the example. The tape recorder requires additional fixed investment of $60,000 with an estimated life of five years. On a straight line basis, this amounts to an annual depreciation cost of $12,000. The new product is also charged $26,000 a year for its share of general overhead. This figure presumably represents a long-run estimate of the opportunity value of the corporate resources required to support this new product. In addition, the company is considering an annual expenditure of $20,000 on advertising and $30,000 on personal selling. Fixed costs therefore add up to $88,000 ($12,000 + $26,000 + $20,000 + $30,000).

The break-even volume can now be estimated. At the break-even volume (Q_B), total revenue (TR) equals total cost (TC). But total revenue is price (P) times the break-even volume and total cost is fixed cost (F) plus the product of unit variable cost (V) and break-even volume. In symbols:

$$TR = TC$$
$$P \cdot Q_B = F + V \cdot Q_B$$

Combining similar terms, and solving for Q_B, we find that

$$Q_B = \frac{F}{P - V}$$

$P - V$ is the difference between price and unit variable cost and is called the unit contribution to fixed cost. It is $8 in the example. The company would have to sell 11,000 units ($88,000 ÷ $8) to cover fixed costs.

At this point it would be useful to express the break-even volume (Q_B) not as a constant but rather as a function of the elements in the marketing mix. The break-even volume will vary with the product price and the amount of marketing effort devoted to the new product:

$$Q_B = \frac{\$12,000 + \$26,000 + A + S}{P - \$10} = \frac{\$38,000 + A + S}{P - \$10}$$

where A = advertising budget
S = sales budget
P = unit selling price to wholesaler

In table 1, eight alternative marketing programs are listed for this product along with the implied break-even volumes. In the case of mix #5, the company could sell as few as 4,143 tape recorders to break even; while in the case of mix #4, the company would have to sell as many as 23,000. This high sensitivity of the break-even volume to the marketing mix decision is often overlooked in profit analysis.

The eight marketing mixes in table 1 are a small sample from the very large number of mixes which could be used to market the new tape recorder. They were formed by assuming a high and low level for each of the marketing variables and elaborating all the combinations. Suppose executive opinion held that $16 is a price on the low side while $24 is a price on the high side; and that $10,000 is a low budget for advertising

TABLE I. Minimum Volume Requirements as a Function of Marketing Mix

	Some possible marketing mixes			Break-even volume Q_B
	Price	*Advertising*	*Sales budget*	
1.	$16	$10,000	$10,000	9,667
2.	16	10,000	50,000	16,333
3.	16	50,000	10,000	16,333
4.	16	50,000	50,000	23,000
5.	24	10,000	10,000	4,143
6.	24	10,000	50,000	7,000
7.	24	50,000	10,000	7,000
8.	24	50,000	50,000	9,857

and personal selling respectively, and $50,000 is a high budget. This yields eight strategy combinations ($2 \cdot 2 \cdot 2 = 2^3$) and makes the marketing mix problem manageable.

Each mix is a polar case. For example, mix #1 represents the common strategy of setting a low price and spending very little for promotion. This works well when the market is highly price conscious, possesses good information about available brands, and is not easily swayed by psychological appeals. Mix #4 represents a strategy of low price and heavy promotion. The interesting thing about this mix is that it produces a high sales volume but also requires a high sales volume to break even. Mix #5 consists of a high price and low promotion and is used typically in a seller's market where the firm wants to maximize short-run profits. Mix #8 consists of a high price supported by high promotion; this strategy is often used in a market where buyers are sensitive to psychological appeals and to quality. The other mixes (#2, 3, 6, 7) are variations on the same themes.

Different marketing mixes not ony imply different break-even volumes, but also differences in the sensitivity of profits to *deviations* from the break-even volume. For example, the break-even volume is approximately the same for mixes #1 and #8. Yet the high price, high promotion character of #8 promises greater losses or greater profits for deviations from the break-even volume. This is because there are higher fixed costs under mix #8 but once they are covered, additional volume is very profitable because of the high price.

Break-even analysis is necessary, but not sufficient by itself to identify the optimal marketing mix. It indicates what volumes have to be achieved but does not indicate what volumes are likely to be achieved. Missing is an account of how various elements in the marketing mix will affect the actual volume of sales.

Ideally the company requires a demand equation showing sales volume as a function of price, advertising, personal selling, and other important marketing mix elements. Such equations are difficult enough to derive for established products where there are historical data, let alone for new product ideas where there are none. Yet though the product is only an idea at this stage, there are some research procedures which can yield useful information for estimating sales. A survey could be made of the attitudes and interests of various consumers toward alternative product features and prices. It might help to develop some prototypes of the tape recorder in order to get firsthand reactions. The survey may indicate what socio-economic groups constitute major prospects for this product. The approximate number of persons in each prospect group can be estimated from census data. In addition, an analysis can be made of the relative strength of competitors in different segments of the market. Since information is expensive to collect, a Bayesian analysis of the value of specified types of additional information should be performed at each juncture.

Through this type of research and analysis, the executives will have a better idea of what sales volumes are likely to be achieved with different marketing mixes. For each particular mix, the executives can develop a subjective probability distribution of possible sales volumes. The mean of this probability distribution shows the expected sales volume for this marketing mix. Let the expected sales volume be denoted by Q. The fourth column in table 2 shows an (hypothetical) expected sales volume for each of the eight marketing mixes. It should be noted that sales are expected to move inversely with price and directly with the amounts spent on advertising and personal selling. However, increased promotion is expected to increase sales at a diminishing rate.

What Is the Best Marketing Mix and the Implied Profit Level?

At this point, the expected volume (Q) and the break-even volume (Q_B) can be compared for each mix. The results are shown in column 6 of table 2. The greatest extra volume ($Q - Q_B$) is achieved with mix #1. But extra volume is not a sufficient indicator of the best mix. The extra volume must be multiplied by the unit value ($P - V$). A high price mix delivering a small extra volume may be superior to a low price mix delivering a large extra volume. Therefore $Z = (P - V) \cdot (Q - Q_B)$ has to be calculated for each marketing mix. These results are shown in column 7 of table 2.

Z is a measure of the absolute profits expected from different marketing mixes. Of the mixes shown in table 2, mix #5 appears to promise the largest amount of profit. This mix calls for the product to be sold at a high price with little promotional support. This strategy is often used when a company believes its product has been smartly designed and essentially sells itself. But before ABC Electronics can be sure that it has found the best marketing mix, or that the product should be produced at all, it must examine some additional issues.

1. *The profit estimates for the eight marketing mixes may not be equally reliable.* The profit estimates were derived from prior cost and sales estimates. Management may have a varying amount of confidence in these

TABLE 2. A Comparison of Expected Volume (Q) and Break-even Volume (Q_1) for Various Marketing Mixes

	(1) P	(2) Marketing Mix A	(3) S	(4) Q	(5) Q_1	(6) Volume above Break-even $Q - Q_1$	(7) Absolute Profits $Z = (P - V)(Q - Q_1)$
1.	$16	$10,000	$10,000	12,400	9,667	2,733	$16,398
2.	16	10,000	50,000	18,500	16,333	2,167	13,002
3.	16	50,000	10,000	15,100	16,333	-1,233	-7,398
4.	16	50,000	50,000	22,600	23,000	-400	-2,400
5.	24	10,000	10,000	5,500	4,143	1,357	18,998
6.	24	10,000	50,000	8,200	7,000	1,200	16,800
7.	24	50,000	10,000	6,700	7,000	-300	-4,200
8.	24	50,000	50,000	10,000	9,857	143	2,002

359

different estimates. Suppose management has much more confidence in its sales estimate for marketing mix #6 than #5. This greater confidence may arise because the executives have more experience in using strategy #6. The choice they face is between a highly uncertain profit expectation of $18,998 and a more certain profit expectation of $16,800. Most managements have a risk aversion and are willing to accept a strategy with a lower expected profit if the accompanying risk is *sufficiently* less. However the specific amount of trade-off of expected profits for risk reduction will vary among managements.

How can management's taste for risk be measured and introduced into the formal analysis? There are at least two different ways to accomplish this. One is through the preparation of an indifference map in which management expresses its preferences between different combinations of expected profit and risk. Let us recall that in considering each marketing mix, management developed a subjective probability distribution of possible sales outcomes. Only the mean, Q, of the distribution was used. Now assume that the standard deviation of this distribution is used as a measure of risk. A low standard deviation means that management is fairly sure of the sales outcome and a high standard deviation means that management is very unsure. The standard deviation of the profit estimate can be calculated from the standard deviation of the sales estimate.[1] Let us use σ_z to denote the standard deviation of estimated profit. Let $(Z, \sigma_z)*$ represent the expected profit and standard deviation of profit, respectively, of the marketing mix with the highest Z; in our example, this is mix #5 and assume it is ($18,998, $12,000). Then management can be asked to list other (Z, σ_z) such that it is indifferent between them and $(Z, \sigma_z)*$. For example, management may be indifferent to ($18,998, $12,000), ($16,000, $6,800), ($13,000, $4,200), ($10,000, $2,000), and ($7,000, $0). An indifference curve has been fitted through these sample points in figure 1. The region to the left of this curve consists of inferior profit situations while the region to the right of this curve consists of superior profit situations. Then the (Z, σ_z) for the other marketing mixes can be plotted. If these points all plot in the inferior region, then mix #5 remains the best mix, subject to further qualifications. If any points plot in the superior region, the foregoing procedure can be repeated to establish a new indifference curve to the right of the old one and the remaining contending points can be tested again.

[1] Expected profit is given by $Z = (P - V)(Q - Q_B)$. Suppose both Q and Q_B are estimated with some uncertainty. The uncertainty of Q reflects the difficulty of estimating sales; and the uncertainty of Q_B, the break-even volume, reflects the difficulty of estimating costs. Suppose further that the degree of uncertainty in estimating sales is independent of the degree of uncertainty in estimating costs. Let σ_Q and σ_{QB}, the standard deviations, represent the respective degrees of uncertainty. Then σ_z, the standard deviation of profit, can be derived by applying elementary theorems on variances. Specifically, $\sigma^2_{ax} - a^2\sigma^2_x$ and $\sigma^2_{x+y} + \sigma^2_y$. Applying these theorems to $Z = (P - V)(Q - Q_B)$, $\sigma_z = (P - V)\sqrt{\sigma^2_Q + \sigma^2_{QB}}$.

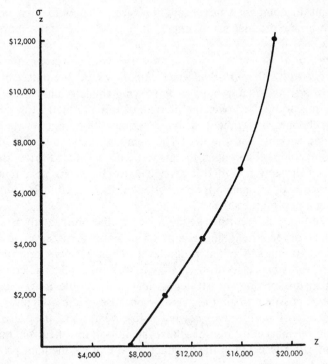

FIGURE 1. Company Indifference Curve for Expected Profit (Z) and Risk (σ_z)

If management has difficulty in thinking of risk in terms of standard deviations, an alternative procedure can be used instead. Management can be asked to express its preferences between various gambles where the risks are stated. The preferences become the basis for preparing a corporate utility scale for various money sums. For a management with risk aversion, the chance to earn twice the profit tends to carry *less* than twice the utility. For each marketing mix, the possible profit outcomes are restated as utility outcomes. Then the probabilities are used to find the expected utility for that marketing mix. The best marketing mix can be defined as the one with the maximum expected utility.

2. *The absolute profit estimates for the eight marketing mixes must be converted into rates of return on investment in order to choose the best marketing mix and to decide whether to develop the new product at all.* For example, management estimates that 5,500 units will be sold in the first year with marketing mix #5 and 8,200 units will be sold with marketing mix #6. But mix #6 will tie up more dollars than mix #5 because production, inventory, and marketing are carried out on a larger scale. For each mix, Z should be expressed as a ratio to the required investment. Mix #5 is still likely to stand out as the best choice in the example. But now a second question also can be answered: is the expected rate of return

greater than the company's target rate of return? The company is not likely to develop a new product whose expected rate of return falls short of the target rate.

3. *The use of expected profits ignores the variability and duration of profits implied by different initial marketing mixes.* At the outset, it should be emphasized that management is *not* trying to determine a permanent marketing mix to be used over the lifetime of this product. Both costs and sales will change over time because of competition, market saturation, business fluctuations, and the like. The company may start with mix #5 and if strong competition enters the market with a reduced price, the ABC Electronics Company may find it expedient to change its mix. It may reduce its price and/or change its promotion. Either reaction is tantamount to adopting a new marketing mix.

By examining different marketing mixes in the profit analysis stage of new product development, the company is trying to ascertain an initial strategy and its implied initial profit level. Thus $18,998 represents the amount of profits expected in the first year with mix #5. The company is interested in discovering the strategy which will enable it to recover as much cost as possible as soon as possible because of the difficulty of foretelling the fate of the product beyond a few years. Yet it is also a fact that the initial marketing mix can have an important effect on the company's long-run success with this product. A low price, medium promotion mix like #2, in creating a high initial sales volume, tends to bring about an earlier saturation of the market and hence a shorter period of profits. Mix #5, because it employs a high price and brings high profits, is likely to induce an early influx of competition which also tends to shorten the period of good profits. The long-run implications of the initial mixes must be considered. The solution ultimately may lie in simulating on a computer different time sequences of mix decisions under alternative assumptions and events to derive some indication of alternative profit possibilities.

4. *The previous analysis assumes that no marketing mix has been overlooked which might yield a higher expected profit than the eight listed mixes.* The sales estimates (Q) in table 2 can be viewed as a sample from a larger universe of executive opinion concerning the functional relationship $Q = f(P, A, S)$. It may be possible to find an equation which closely describes these estimates. The equation could then be solved to estimate expected sales, and ultimately profits, for marketing mixes which were not explicitly considered by the executives. For example, a plausible mathematical form for demand functions is the multiple exponential:

$$Q = kP^a A^b S^c$$
$$\text{where } k = \text{a scale factor}$$
$$a = \text{the price elasticity}$$
$$b = \text{the advertising elasticity}$$
$$c = \text{the personal selling elasticity}$$

The multiple exponential equation has provided a useful fit in several demand situations. This form fits quite well the sample values of (Q) in table 2. This is more by design than by accident. The least squares equation is

$$Q = 100{,}000\ P^{-2}A^{1/8}S^{1/4}$$

Price has an elasticity of -2, that is, a one percent reduction in price, other things equal, tends to increase unit sales by 2 percent. Advertising has an elasticity of $1/8$ and the sales budget has an elasticity of $1/4$. The coefficient 100,000 is a scale factor which translates the dollar magnitudes into the appropriate physical volume effects.

Several of the preceding equations can now be drawn together:

$$
\begin{aligned}
&Z = (P - 10)\ (Q - Q_B) &&(1)\ \text{profit equation}\\
&Q = 100{,}000\ P^{-2}A^{1/8}S^{1/4} &&(2)\ \text{demand equation}\\
&Q_B = \frac{38{,}000 + A + S}{P - 10} &&(3)\ \text{break-even volume}\\
& && \quad\ \ \text{equation}
\end{aligned}
$$

The best marketing mix was defined initially as the one which maximized Z, that is, profits. Solving equation (1) in terms of (2) and (3), Z can be rewritten as:

$$
\begin{aligned}
Z &= (P - 10)\ \left(100{,}000\ P^{-2}A^{1/8}S^{1/4} - \frac{38{,}000 + A + S}{P - 10}\right)\\
Z &= (P - 10)\ (100{,}000\ P^{-2}A^{1/8}S^{1/4}) - 38{,}000 - A - S\\
Z &= 100{,}000\ P^{-1}A^{1/8}S^{1/4} - 1{,}000{,}000\\
&\qquad P^{-2}A^{1/8}S^{1/4} - 38{,}000 - A - S \qquad (4)
\end{aligned}
$$

Thus Z is a function of three marketing variables.

The next step is to find that unique set of values of P, A, and S which maximizes Z in equation (4). This is a problem in differential calculus. The work is carried out in the . . . [calculus, which yields]:

$$
\begin{aligned}
P &= \$20\\
A &= \$12{,}947\\
S &= \$25{,}894\\
Z &= \$26{,}735
\end{aligned}
$$

It is interesting to compare this mix with mix #5 which yielded the highest Z of the eight mixes considered in table 2. Mix #5 called for a price of $24 and an advertising and sales budget of $10,000 each. The new calculation calls attention to the possibility that a somewhat lower price, a slight increase in advertising expenditure, and a substantial increase in personal selling expenditure might boost profits by several thousand dollars. Thus it may be possible to employ mathematical analysis to overcome the limitations of considering only a small set of marketing mixes. Though we have illustrated this in terms of Z, a more complicated mathematical analysis can be prepared for finding the best marketing mix under conditions of uncertainty, different investment requirements, and more than three marketing variables.[2]

---

[2] It possesses a number of plausible properties. First, it provides that the effect of a specific marketing variable depends not only upon its own level but also on the levels of the other marketing variables. Thus a price of $16 will have one demand effect if advertising and selling are each set at $10,000 and another if advertising and selling are each set at $50,000. This interdependency does not exist with linear equations. Second, the exponential equation shows diminishing marginal returns to increases in the advertising and sales budgets and this accords with intuitive expectations. Finally, the exponents represent the respective elasticities of the marketing variables, provided there is no intercorrelation between the independent variables. [Note: The Appendix has been omitted from this reading for reasons of space.]

29. Proposal Development: Analyzing the Risks and the Benefits

V. D. Herbert, Jr., and Attilio Bisio

Using a petrochemical industry example, the authors show how a discounted cash flow analysis, sensitivity analysis, and investment exposure profile can be used effectively in the preparation of a formal project proposal.

ALL OF US COME UP, at one time or another, with ideas on how our businesses can be improved. Some of these ideas may even be good. Many, however, die in their infancy because we don't launch them properly. This article describes the process of economic analysis from an idea to a venture analysis.

Let's assume you are working in your company's exploratory plastics group. Your job is to come up with product modifications that will extend your company's product line or, happy day, to discover a new plastic.

In the course of your work, let's assume, you have come up with a new plastic resin, as a result of having put together some combination of raw materials, catalysts, and process operating conditions. Your laboratory results indicate a set of physical properties that are rather interesting compared to those of the commercially available products you are aware of. You visualize that the availability of a plastics resin with these properties will enable several fabricated products to be switched over *if the price is right.*

Small laboratory-scale samples sent out selectively to the fabrication industry have elicited enthusiastic response from several companies repre-

Reprinted from *Chemtech* magazine, 6 (July, 1976), pp. 422–429. Used by permission.

Attilio Bisio serves as an Engineering Advisor and Venture Team Leader in the Technology Feasibility Center of Exxon Corporate Research. V. D. Herbert, Jr., a former manager with Exxon Chemical, is now a petrochemical industry consultant specializing in economic analysis and related work.

senting a spectrum of different end-use applications. These could become potential customers. The total feedback, both external and internal, suggests that you have a "winner" on your hands and you are getting excited.

You are aware that there are a multitude of technical and marketing aspects requiring further investigation. Processing refinements and optimizations need to be worked on. The sensitivity of product properties to process changes will have to be explored. The potential sales volumes and prices will have to be restudied often, and at a later stage marketing strategies and tactics will be evolved. Ultimately process designs and estimates of investments and production costs will be required for the prototype and, subsequently, commercial plants.

But, before all these efforts are put in motion, now is the time for the beginning of serious economic analysis to take place. Before too many dollars are spent on the presumption that you have a "winner", you must convince yourself and those who run your company that a "winner" is what you have.

Commercial implementation of your idea will have to meet some minimum financial criteria, and additionally, your idea and its potential will compete with those of others in your organization. Therefore, like it or not, there is going to be a demand that information about your project be put in economic terms.

What, then, are you going to have to create? In earlier days, the economic concepts were simple and much easier to live with for most people. One used to get by with showing management that the project would cost so many dollars to build the plant and that the plant would produce "X" pounds of product annually. The product would cost "Y" cents per pound and would be sold at "Z" cents per pound. When this plant was producing all out, the profits after taxes would generate a "conventional return" ratio of net income to investment of "such and such" percent. Your more sophisticated colleagues might have even added the bonus of having calculated the "payout period," or the time required to get the investment back.

Nowadays, managements are more demanding if only because of past mistakes. They are interested in knowing about the total capital resource requirements of the project, which will include working capital in addition to the fixed capital cost of the plant itself. They know that the *Discounted Cash Flow (DCF) return calculation* is superior since it recognizes the time value of money and allows one to make better choices among alternative courses of action.

They also will want to see a *Cash Impairment Profile* which establishes the size and timing of the funds at risk. Not only will they require these details about the specific project you have in mind, but they will also want to know about the expanding picture you foresee beyond the initial project. This, then, will cause you to come to grips with creating a *Venture*

Analysis. Unquestionably, not everyone is going to agree totally with every assumption you are going to have to build into your calculations. However, you must be perceptive enough to anticipate those areas where challenges are most likely to occur and to have prepared beforehand a *Sensitivity Analysis.* In doing this, you must be able to cope with questions on how things would change if different prices or sales volumes or investments were to prevail.

Since you are going to have to learn how to do a DCF return eventually, learn how to do it now. Do it enough times that the exercise teaches you how different assumptions about such items as price, investments, costs, and capacity utilizations influence your return levels. Conversely, preselect a given level of desired DCF return (e.g., your company's "hurdle rate") and back-calculate to see what the price has to be (or costs, or investment) for you to reach that DCF return level.

These calculations, based as they will be on such limited information, won't prove your case. However, they should be sufficient to throw out a "no go" situation—that is, one where it is impossible to achieve economic viability. More importantly, they will show you where and how the project must be improved.

The DCF Return Calculation

To understand a DCF return calculation you must first appreciate the concept of the time value of money. A dollar of today's money invested in a facility has a different (higher) value than a dollar you receive, say, five years from now.

The DCF return is that interest rate which brings the *Present Worth* value of the cash inflows (profit, depreciation, tax effects, etc.) for a project exactly equal to the Present Worth values of the cash outlays (investments, research programs, engineering studies, etc.). A decision whether to accept or reject the proposal will be influenced by whether the DCF return is greater, or less than, the investor's minimum acceptable return standard for this investment opportunity.

Let's assume a very simple situation to illustrate how a DCF return is calculated. Your cash outlay is $100 in year one. You anticipate achieving a cash inflow over the life of the project (say four years) as follows:

	$
Year 2	45
Year 3	40
Year 4	35
Year 5	30
Total cash inflow	150

Go to a handbook which has tables of present value factors.

Year	Current Year Cash Flow $	Present Value of Cash Flow @ 10%		Present Value of Cash Flow @ 20%	
		Factor	Discounted Cash Flow	Factor	Discounted Cash Flow
Cash Outlay					
1	−100	1.000	−100	1.000	−100
Cash Inflow					
2	45	0.9091	40.9	0.8333	37.5
3	40	0.8264	33.1	0.6944	27.8
4	35	0.7513	26.3	0.5787	20.3
5	30	0.6830	20.5	0.4823	14.4
	150		120.8		100.0
Net cash flow	50		20.8		0

In this simple example, the interest rate, at which the Present Value of the cash inflow exactly equals the Present Value of the cash outlay, is 20%.

The Project

Now, let's get on to examining what goes into making up the cash outflow and cash inflow. The outflow would consist of your fixed capital plant investment, investment tax credit and working capital (inventories and receivables). Your cash inflow normally is just the sum of profits after income taxes and depreciation. In some exceptional cases, making the investment you have an interest in could avoid having to make an additional investment somewhere else. In such a case, the "saved" investment could be a "credit" in the cash inflow picture. Be very careful in your analysis of such cases.

Generally one chooses to look at a period of years in a project that reflects an approximation to the useful life of the facility under consideration and also permits recovery of plant investment through depreciation. (The concept of depreciation is a tricky one; we are handling it in a rather mechanical way. Consult references for clarification.)

The zero year generally begins when you commit your first investment. If, for example, your facilities were thought to have a 10-year useful life and it was going to take two years to bring the plant on-stream, your project would cover 12 years. Your working capital would be debited year-by-year as the need for it grew. At the end of the final year of the project, you would credit back the total amount of working capital that you had debited in the intervening years.

Terminal Value in a DCF calculation sometimes includes elements other than just recovery of working capital. If, for example, the time span encompassed by your economic model is shorter than that required to fully recover the plant investment through depreciation, the residual book value of the undepreciated plant investment can be taken as a terminal value credit. Also you may believe that your company will be getting out of the business at the end of your evaluation period. Rather than undepreciated plant investment, the terminal value can be salvage scrap value for a plant that would be dismantled or a "sales value as an on-going business" value for an operation sold at that point to another company.

If sale of the operation is contemplated, a "times after-tax earnings" is used to establish this latter type of terminal value. Say the plant had averaged $500,000/year profit after taxes in its last three years of operation and that a buyer could be found to pay 10 times earnings. Under these assumptions, you would be thinking in terms of a $5 million terminal value. In using this approach, if the $5 million terminal value exceeded booked undepreciated investment, *a capital gains tax* on the excess would be included when calculating the terminal value.

While the concept of terminal value is important, don't let it cloud your thinking. Find out how it is handled in your company. Only rarely is it going to make or break your project.

So much for the cash outflow part of the DCF calculation. Now let's get to the cash inflow components. These consist of profits after income taxes plus depreciation. Profits, of course, are determined by subtracting total costs from revenues. (We shall have more to say about costs later.) Table 1 illustrates a typical setup for accumulating the elements that make up an undiscounted cash flow picture. Table 2 shows how the DCF return rate is calculated to be 10.0% for this undiscounted cash flow example.

With the mechanics of how to do a DCF calculation now firmly in place, let's now return and elaborate on the input components of the DCF cash flow picture, which consists of the sum of depreciation and profits after taxes.

To determine profits, we have to come to grips with operating costs. These are the expenditures, exclusive of capital investments, associated with the steps in the sequence of converting raw stocks into finished products and then storing, transporting, and selling these finished products to customers. In Table 3 are presented a typical breakdown of the costs to be accounted for in an economic study.

When the time comes for a definitive assessment of a project, each of these elements will have to be examined detail and estimated as accurately as possible. In earlier stages of project development, where only rough approximations are being sought, it is not unreasonable to estimate costs by applying standard rules of thumb to the various elements of cost.

TABLE 1. Accumulating the Undiscounted Cash Flow Picture (Thousand dollars)

Year	Investment	7% investment credit	Working capital	Depreciation at 10%/yr	Profit after 50% income taxes	Undiscounted cash flow
0	(5,000)	350	—	—	—	(4,650)
1	(5,000)	350	—	—	—	(4,650)
2	—	—	(1,000)	1,000	250	250
3	—	—	(500)	1,000	500	1,000
4	—	—	—	1,000	500	1,500
5	—	—	(1,000)	1,000	1,000	1,000
6	—	—	—	1,000	1,000	2,000
7	—	—	—	1,000	1,000	2,000
8	—	—	—	1,000	1,000	2,000
9	—	—	—	1,000	1,000	2,000
10	—	—	—	1,000	1,000	2,000
11[a]	—	—	—	1,000	1,000	2,000
11[b]	—	—	2,500	—	—	2,500
Totals	(10,000)	700	0	10,000	8,250	8,950

[a] Operating results. [b] Terminal value.

TABLE 2. Calculating the DCF Return
(Thousand dollars)

Year	Undiscounted Cash Flow	Present Value @ 10% Interest		Present Value @ 11% Interest	
		Factor	Discounted Cash Flow	Factor	Discounted Cash Flow
0	(4,650)	1.000	(4,650)	1.000	(4,650)
1	(4,650)	0.909	(4,227)	0.901	(4,190)
2	250	0.826	207	0.812	203
3	1,000	0.751	751	0.731	731
4	1,500	0.683	1,025	0.659	989
5	1,000	0.621	621	0.593	593
6	2,000	0.565	1,130	0.535	1,070
7	2,000	0.513	1,026	0.482	964
8	2,000	0.467	934	0.434	868
9	2,000	0.424	848	0.391	782
10	2,000	0.386	772	0.352	704
11 [a]	2,000	0.351	702	0.317	634
11 [b]	2,500	0.351	878	0.317	793
Totals	8,950		17		(509)

$$\% \text{ DCF} = 10.0 + \frac{17}{17 + 509}$$

$$\% \text{ DCF} = 10.0$$

[a] Operating results.   [b] Terminal value.

TABLE 3. Operating Cost Elements

A. Feedstock costs
B. Manufacturing costs
   • Utilities and fuel
   • Regular operating labor
   • Administrative, Clerical, and contract labor (if any)
   • Employee benefits
   • Maintenance materials
   • Contract maintenance (if any)
   • Chemicals and supplies
   • Plant services (labs, general facilities, etc.)
   • Burdens (plant management charges, services, mechanical shops, material procurement, technical costs, etc.)
   • Ad valorem taxes
   • Depreciation
C. Other costs
   • Marketing and distribution costs
   • Research costs
   • Corporate overheads

Investment Estimates by Analogy

There is general agreement that there is no completely satisfactory method of making investment estimates. All known methods are either too expensive, too slow, require too much computer time, or are too crude. However, people have learned to live with the problem and many techniques (all compromises of one sort or other) have been developed.

Of course, the most accurate evaluation of investment requirements for a new process is a detailed estimate based upon firm engineering studies. In the early stages of new processes when many development decisions are made, the available data are simply inadequate to prepare this type of estimate. Moreover, some cynics have suggested that regardless of the state of the technology, the actual investment will only be known after the plant has been built.

Lower cost, more rapid methods where one deals with equipment grouping/systems are based upon the application of factors to the purchase price of major equipment. These range all the way from the traditional Lang method with a single factor depending on whether solids, liquids, or gases, or a combination of these is being handled to a rather detailed factoring system such as described by Waddell and Allen. Our experience has been that the methods suggested by Waddell and Allen provide investment estimates acceptable for the venture studies we have in mind.

But what if one has even less than that, then Figure 1, which is based upon our recent experience, may be of value to you. Unfortunately, as cost escalation continues, the curve will have to be updated with the data available from your own experience. Simple corrections of the curves by prorations with a cost index are not sufficient.

What does the single complexity factor: low, medium, high, mean?

- Low. Batch processing plants and simple synthesis (NH_3, MeOH)
- Medium. Continuous processes involving only gases and liquids at modest temperatures and pressures
- High. Processes involving significant solids handling polymer units, high pressure and/or high temperature operations

Obviously, the curve is only a crude approximation, but it's a starting point. (Its two-sigma, 95% confidence, limits are ±30–40%.)

Example of a Venture

It's time now to begin to put a "first-pass" handle on your situation. The plastic resin you are interested in is a relatively sophisticated one requiring uncommon and rather costly raw materials. It probably will be consumed in rather narrow segments of the market having a need for its unique properties. You do not see it competing directly with the billion plus pounds per year volumes of thermoplastic resins. Nor do you see it being moved at the low prices of these tremendous volume products.

From your knowledge of the competitive environment, you feel that a market of 50 million lb per year could be created in a few years if the product could be offered for sale in the range of $1.00/lb. You use Figure 1 or reason by analogy and come up with a $50-million rough estimate of plant investment. Using that investment estimate and the upper limits of the approximate total operating cost range would result in an operating cost of about 45¢/lb.

Obviously, these estimates of price, investment costs, and volume are very crude approximations at this point. Nevertheless, it is worthwhile, and desirable, to put these factors together into a DCF economic model and see what kind of story they tell you. What you want to find out by doing so is:

- Does my project have a chance to meet profitability targets or should I drop it now?
- Is it worthwhile to go to the effort and expense to develop good estimates of the various economic components?

If we use the above data and combine with them the assumptions of a two-year construction period, a 10-year operating period, an investment credit of 7%, and a working capital requirement equivalent to 25% of sales, the DCF return would be 27%. This assumes the plant always ran at capacity.

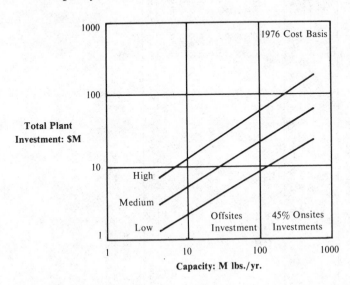

FIGURE 1. Chemical Plant Investment

TABLE 4. Calculation of Sales Price Required to Give 20% DCF Return (Thousand dollars)

	(1)	(2)	(3)	(4)	(5)	(6)	(7)	(8)	(9)	(10)
		7%		Working	*Sales*	*Sales*	Oper-			
		invest-	Depre-	Capital			ating	Profit Before	Profit After	Undiscounted
Year	Invest-ment	ment Credit	ciation @ 10%	@ 25% of Sales	M lb/yr	$ @ "X" $/lb	Cost @ $0.45/lb	Income Tax	50% Income Taxes	Cash Flow
0	(25,000)	1,750	—	—	—	—	—	—	—	(23,250)
1	(25,000)	1,750	—	—	—	—	—	—	—	(23,250)
2	—	—	5,000	(12,500)X	50,000	50,000X	(22,500)	50,000X + (22,500)	25,000X + (11,250)	12,500X + (6,250)
3	—	—	5,000	—	50,000	50,000X	(22,500)	50,000X + (22,500)	25,000X + (11,250)	25,000X + (6,250)
4	—	—	5,000	—	50,000	50,000X	(22,500)	50,000X + (22,500)	25,000X + (11,250)	25,000X + (6,250)
5	—	—	5,000	—	50,000	50,000X	(22,500)	50,000X + (22,500)	25,000X + (11,250)	25,000X + (6,250)
6	—	—	5,000	—	50,000	50,000X	(22,500)	50,000X + (22,500)	25,000X + (11,250)	25,000X + (6,250)
7	—	—	5,000	—	50,000	50,000X	(22,500)	50,000X + (22,500)	25,000X + (11,250)	25,000X + (6,250)
8	—	—	5,000	—	50,000	50,000X	(22,500)	50,000X + (22,500)	25,000X + (11,250)	25,000X + (6,250)
9	—	—	5,000	—	50,000	50,000X	(22,500)	50,000X + (22,500)	25,000X + (11,250)	25,000X + (6,250)
10	—	—	5,000	—	50,000	50,000X	(22,500)	50,000X + (22,500)	25,000X + (11,250)	25,000X + (6,250)
11 a	—	—	5,000	—	50,000	50,000X	(22,500)	50,000X + (22,500)	25,000X + (11,250)	25,000X + (6,250)
11 b	—	—		12,500X						12,500X
Totals	(50,000)	3,500	50,000	0	500,000	500,000X	(225,000)	500,000X + (225,000)	250,000X + (112,500)	250,000X + (109,000)

Notes
Col. 8 = cols. 6 + 7
Col. 10 = cols. 1 + 2 + 3 + 4 + 9
a Operating results.   b Terminal value.

You should be pleased and encouraged by this finding. You can be sure that the rate of return will not be that high when you go forward with your final project. But, at least you have some room to maneuver. You have passed your first checkpoint.

Knowing the inadequacies of the estimates you have made at this point about price, costs, and investments, you use this same economic model framework to calculate DCF returns over a wide range of changes in these variables. Because it is simpler than calculating individual DCF returns, figure out (and plot a resulting curve) what sales prices would be required to give you 0, 10, 20, and 30% DCF returns. Do the same for the operating costs and the investments that would result in these levels of return.

Tables 4 and 5 show how to carry out these calculations, the specific example being illustrative of the price required to produce a 20% DCF return. To do this, the unknown sales price is set at "X" $/lb. Since, by definition, the DCF rate of return is that percentage at which the Present Value of the cash outflow exactly balances that of the cash inflow, if you put the sum of the discounted cash flow equal to zero, you can thus solve for your unknown quantity—the sales price required.

TABLE 5.   Calculation of Sales Price Required to Give 20% DCF Return

Year	Undiscounted Cash Flow	Present Value Factors @ 20%	Discounted Cash Flow
0	(23,250)	1.000	(23,250)
1	(23,250)	0.833	(19,367)
2	$12,500 \times + (6,250)$	0.694	$8,675 \times + (4,338)$
3	$25,000 \times + (6,250)$	0.579	$14,475 \times + (3,619)$
4	$25,000 \times + (6,250)$	0.482	$12,050 \times + (3,013)$
5	$25,000 \times + (6,250)$	0.402	$10,050 \times + (2,513)$
6	$25,000 \times + (6,250)$	0.335	$8,375 \times + (2,094)$
7	$25,000 \times + (6,250)$	0.279	$6,975 \times + (1,744)$
8	$25,000 \times + (6,250)$	0.233	$5,825 \times + (1,456)$
9	$25,000 \times + (6,250)$	0.194	$4,850 \times + (1,213)$
10	$25,000 \times + (6,250)$	0.162	$4,050 \times + (1,013)$
11 [a]	$25,000 \times + (6,250)$	0.135	$3,375 \times + (844)$
11 [b]	$12,500 \times$	0.135	$1,688 \times$
Totals	$250,000 \times + (109,000)$		$80,388 \times + (64,464)$

Sales price for 20% DCF return
$$80,388 \times + (64,464) = 0$$
$$80,388 \times = 64,464$$
$$\times = 80¢/lb$$

[a] Operating results.   [b] Terminal value.

If you carry out similar calculations for 0, 10, and 30% returns, the curve shown in Figure 2 results. This curve gives you a visual picture of how sensitive your project return will be to different levels of price. Similar curves, calculated for changes in other significant variables, are helpful in orienting your understanding of the impact of different conditions from the ones you have built into your base economic model.

You have been looking, up to this point, at the best case possible, that of a plant that comes on stream at full capacity utilization and continues to operate that way throughout its useful life. This, of course, is not reality. In your particular case involving a brand new product, you certainly are not going to jump right from a laboratory stage of involvement into an immediately developed market filling up a 50-million-lb plant. It is going to take some time to grow into full use of your ultimate capacity.

Let's look at two (of many) possible paths of growth into full capacity utilization and compare those DCF returns with the 27% return that results from full capacity operation. To do this, you need to build one more basic assumption into your model—that total operating costs are 50% fixed and 50% variable.

Overall Capacity Utilization	Alternate Growth Patterns		
	78%	85%	100%
	Sales in Operating Year, MM#		
1	10	10	50
2	15	25	50
3	25	40	50
4	40	50	50
5	50	50	50
6	50	50	50
7	50	50	50
8	50	50	50
9	50	50	50
10	50	50	50
Total sales	390	425	500

Figure 3 presents the DCF returns for the 75 and 85% cases in comparison with the full-scale output case calculated originally. It is evident that the level of capacity utilization over the life of a project is critical to the attainment of satisfactory return. You can see from Figure 2 that the price/cost/investment relationships that give a 27% DCF return at full capacity lose about five of those DCF percentage points if sales average only 90% of capacity and lose much more than that as capacity utilization levels trend downward.

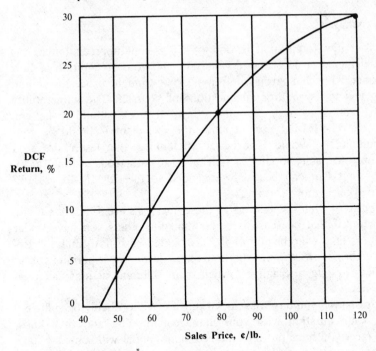

FIGURE 2.   DCF Returns at Different Sales Prices

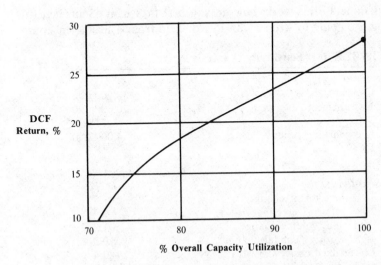

FIGURE 3.   Project DCF Return at Different Overall Capacity Utilization

Sensitivity Analysis

With your new-found skill in doing DCF's, your appreciation of the important elements of an economic analysis, and your recognition of how results change with changing assumptions, your thought processes should be leading you to ask additional questions of yourself. The vulnerability of the DCF return to undercapacity utilization levels should make you wonder, "Is a 50-MM-lb/yr plant really the size plant I should be considering building?" "Would I be better off looking at a lesser size so I could get up to capacity sooner?" "Is it more advantageous to build a 20-MM-lb/yr plant that can be easily expanded to the 50-MM-lb/yr level when the market is more certain?"

Don't guess at what the answers to these questions are. Calculate them. Prove to yourself that one case is better than the others you have under consideration. That's the beauty of the discounted cash flow analysis. Because it does bring into account the time value of money, it permits you to make choices among alternatives which span different actions taken at different times.

The information you have developed thus far will probably be sufficient to discuss your situation with your management. You and they know that every facet you have put into the economic model will someday have to be studied in depth and the assumptions validated or replaced by more accurate estimates.

Where Do We Go?

Having done all this work, how do you best present it? Someday, it is hoped, you are going to write (with lots of help from a team) an appro-

TABLE 6. Sensitivity Analysis

Base Project	
Capacity, lb/yr	30,000,000
Investment, $	20,000,000
Sales, price, ¢/lb	75
max working capital, $	4,000,000
DCF, %	16.3

Sensitivities	*Impact on % DCF*
10% investment change	±1.7
10% sales price change	±3.3
5% sales volume change	±1.3
10% working capital change	±0.3
Lower fixed costs $0.5 MM lb/yr	+0.4
50% lower sales in first two years	−4.7
Assume 110% capability output attainable	+2.1

priation request for a new facility. Start thinking about your project that way now.

Summarize your studies (and the repeats you will make) in an appropriation request format. A good general format is:

Body of the Report

Summary. Very brief presentation of the opportunity. Description of the project and/or the venture. Investment potential. Capacity potential. DCF returns. Management action requested. (Obviously not the plant.)

Background. Background information needed to understand developments that make you regard this as an opportunity, the characteristics of the market you will serve, the competitive situation, prices.

Venture. How you became interested. What you have done thus far. Results achieved to date. How this project relates to previous concepts. Specific information about this project and its major underlying assumptions.

Relationship to Business Plan. Specifically, how does this project relate to your company's corporate outlook and its business plans. Is it reflected in those plans? Is it new?

Timing. Why do it now? Schedule for the next phase.

Description of Proposed Work. Description of proposed work. Status of technology (including assessment of competitive technology position).

Manpower and Organizational Implications. If any.

Legal Aspects. Potential patent position. Other aspects if pertinent.

Economics. Has DCF been calculated? Pricing assumptions, market projections, allowances for cost escalation, raw material considerations, discussion of economic alternatives, sensitivities.

Risk Management and Environmental Considerations. Assessment of fire, employee injury, public liability, ecological impacts, product risks, known safety problems, etc., if any.

Supporting Data

Pseudo Appropriation Request Sheet. A one-page summary of salient information about the project, its investment, assumptions, economics.

Market Information Table(s). Total market projections. Assumed market share. Competitive products' market shares.

Investment Table(s). Investment details.

Working Capital Requirements. Working capital requirements. Raw materials, in-process and finished product inventories. Accounts receivable.

Cash Profile. Project and venture details of net cash flow, P/L results, DCF returns, payouts.

TABLE 7.   Cash Impairment Profile
(Thousand dollars)

Year	Capital Invest- ment	Invest- ment Credit	Working Capital	Depre- ciation	Profit After Income Taxes	Cumu- lative Total
0	(5,000)	350	—	—	—	(4,650)
1	(5,000)	350	—	—	—	(9,300)
2	—	—	(1,000)	1,000	250	(9,050)
3	—	—	(500)	1,000	500	(8,050)
4	—	—	—	1,000	500	(6,550)
5	—	—	(1,000)	1,000	1,000	(5,550)
6	—	—	—	1,000	1,000	(3,550)
7	—	—	—	1,000	1,000	(1,550)
8	—	—	—	1,000	1,000	450
9	—	—	—	1,000	1,000	2,450
10	—	—	—	1,000	1,000	4,450
11 [a]	—	—	—	1,000	1,000	6,450
11 [b]	—	—	2,500	—	—	8,950
Totals	(10,000)	700	0	10,000	8,250	

[a] Operating results.   [b] Terminal value.

Sensitivity Analysis. A table showing impact on base case DCF returns resulting from changes in assumptions about major variables taken one at a time (see Table 6, for example).

Cash Impairment Profile. Table (or plot) of maximum amount company has at risk at any time (see Table 7, for example).

There you have it. The key to going down any new road successfully is to have an idea beforehand of what to expect. It is hoped you have become acquainted with what is needed to travel more securely down future highways of economic analysis.

30. Venture Analysis: The Assessment of Uncertainty and Risk

Franz Edelman and Joel S. Greenberg

Venture (or risk) analysis considers the probabilistic nature of the critical variables affecting future costs and revenues for different ventures and develops overall measures of the risk for each investment alternative.

OUR PURPOSE is to describe a method which has been developed to assist management with the task of evaluating new investment opportunities. The method, which develops quantitative measures of the risk associated with new ventures, provides management with quantitative data indicating the likelihood that various key performance measures will achieve or exceed various levels. Thus management's comparison of investment alternatives will be greatly facilitated.

The present analysis is, in general, limited to establishing the risk of individual ventures and not the risk associated with ventures in combination. The *risk analysis* considers the probabilistic nature of the key variables which determine future costs and revenues. That is, the uncertainty of future events is recognized, and an attempt is made to take this uncertainty into account.

Venture

A basic premise underlying the evaluation of a venture is that the venture can be separated from the company; all pertinent revenues and expenses associated with the venture must be separately identified.

Reprinted from *Financial Executive*, 37 (August, 1969), pp. 56–62. Used by permission.

Franz Edelman is Director of Business Systems and Analysis for RCA Corporation. Joel Greenberg is on the faculty of the Aeronautical and Mechanical Sciences Department of Princeton University.

The term "venture" is used in a very broad sense. In general, it is *any project which involves the outlay of funds in return for an anticipated flow of future benefits*. The addition of a new product or product line, the establishment of a new business area, the purchase or lease of a new piece of equipment, make vs. buy and lease vs. buy alternatives, etc., are examples of typical ventures.

Conventional Analysis

The conventional approach to evaluation of investment alternatives considers only two fundamental dimensions—the *magnitude* of the particular measure in question (i.e., sales, profit, cash flow, etc.) and *time*. Traditional analysis is based upon expressing assumptions about key variables affecting future costs, revenues, and investment requirements, in terms of *single-point estimates*.

It is evident that single-point estimates of key input variables will in turn result in single-point estimates of key performance measures. In other words, the results of the "best guesses" are normally expressed in terms of most likely profit, cash flow, etc., as a function of time.

Management may consider the venture to be acceptable if the performance measures exceed specified criteria (or group of criteria)—if the return on assets exceeds a minimum specified value, the payback period is less than a maximum specified value, etc.—and the non-monetary objectives of the company are met. If a venture is considered particularly risky, management may raise the basic requirements to counterbalance the greater level of risk.

Another method frequently used is to evaluate the venture in terms of optimistic and pessimistic estimates (or upper and lower bounds) in an effort to provide some insight into the possible variations of results. The shortcoming of this method is that usually no estimates are made of the likelihood that the optimistic and pessimistic results will be achieved.

Frequently a sensitivity analysis is performed. Key variables are changed individually or in groups, and the resulting effects on profit, cash flow, etc., are evaluated. This technique provides insight into what would happen if the key variables deviated from their expected values. However, the likelihood of occurrence of each deviation is usually not specified. Thus, the basic shortcoming of this approach is that the decision makers are not made aware of the *likelihood of any given outcome*.

Uncertainty Assessment

The analysis of risk requires the addition of a third dimension to those of magnitude and time—the *dimension of uncertainty*. This means that a major input assumption must be described, not just by a single estimate, but by an entire range of possible values, each of which must be accompanied by an indication of the likelihood of its falling into various sectors within the range.

The super-position of the *uncertainty dimension* is shown in figure 1, which has, as its base, the *magnitude/time* plane of a sales projection. The curves rising above this plane, one for each year, represent the "uncertainty profiles" of the input variable as a function of time. The curves are derived from subjective management estimates of the variability of the sales projection, which represent the best information available at the time.

The narrow uncertainty profile in Year 1 of figure 1 indicates that Year 1 sales can be estimated more reliably than Year 5 sales, represented by a much broader uncertainty profile.

Thus, the width of a profile is one of two important properties indicating degree of uncertainty. The other property, which is not readily evident on figure 1, but which will be discussed more fully later, is *skewness*, indicating degree of bias (toward high or low values) of the uncertainty assessment.

Risk Analysis

Risk analysis involves translating input variables, including uncertainty assessments pertaining to the variables, into performance measures incorporating an analysis of the risk associated with each such performance measure. As a result, the computed quantities—profit, cash flow, return on assets, present worth, etc.—will all be probabilistic variables having computed "uncertainty profiles." The computed uncertainty profiles (henceforth referred to as *risk profiles*) indicate to management the range of probable outcomes as well as the likelihood of specific levels of the outcomes.

FIGURE 1. Typical Sales Projection Analysis with Uncertainty

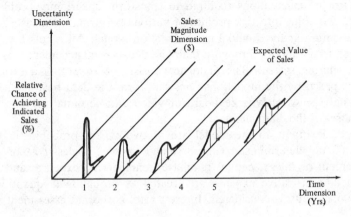

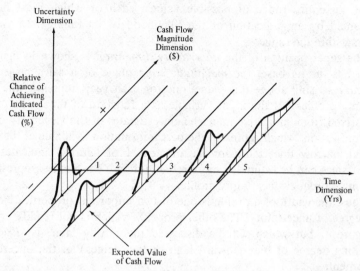

FIGURE 2.   Typical Cash Flow Projection Analysis with Uncertainty

Again, the super-position of the *uncertainty dimension* is shown in figure 2, and has, as its base, the magnitude/time plane of a conventional cash flow projection. The computed uncertainty profiles rising above this plane indicate and quantify the variability of each particular outcome, year by year. The width and skewness of the risk profiles contain information about the performance measure which is of paramount importance to the decision maker.

Simulation Model

A mathematical model called the venture analysis model has been developed and implemented on the RCA Time-Sharing System (BTSS-II) to perform the calculations required to transform uncertainty profiles of key input variables into risk profiles of various performance measures.

The venture analysis model is a simulation model. All inputs are communicated to the model through a dialogue between management-user and the time-sharing system. The dialogue consists of answering a series of questions posed by the model. The answers form the data base for a particular analysis. A teletype keyboard or video data terminal may be used for purposes of the dialogue.

The basic inputs to the model are of two types: probabilistic (i.e., uncertain) and deterministic (i.e., assumed known). Sales, cost of sales (as a percent of sales), capital purchases, engineering expense, and general and administrative expense are treated as probabilistic quantities—that is, uncertainty is considered. Interest rate, corporate assessment rate, number of years to be considered, depreciation life, depreciation type (no depreciation, straight-line, sum-of-the-years digits, double declining balance), etc., are considered to be deterministic, or known precisely.

The probabilistic data convey to the model management's assessment of the uncertainty associated with each of the key variables. They consist of management's subjective estimates of the likelihood that the variables will attain specified values.

A set of standard financial computations are performed and values of profit, cash flow, return on assets, etc., determined. These computations are repeated a large number of times utilizing different combinations of values of the key variables, as described by management's uncertainty assessments. Each time the computations are repeated, new values of profit, cash flow, etc., are obtained. This information is used to establish the risk profiles of the performance measures. The risk profiles—the model outputs—are printed out on the same teletype keyboard used to supply the input data. The outputs are available within a few minutes of inserting the data. Upon management review and evaluation, necessary input changes can be made and the computations repeated.

The values of key input variables and their uncertainty profiles are functions of many factors. For example, revenue is a function of selling price, total market, market share, etc. In turn, these factors may be inter-related; for example, market share is a function of relative selling price, total market is a function of selling price, selling price may be related to manufacturing cost, manufacturing cost may be a function of quantity manufactured, which is related to market size, etc. No attempt has been made to define these complex interrelationships within the model. Instead, it is assumed that meaningful estimates, based upon a *detailed analysis performed outside* of the venture analysis model, can be made for all pertinent data.

General Information

The venture analysis model is, in essence, a management laboratory in which management can experiment, before the fact, with a variety of investment alternatives. This experimental capability considers *explicitly* the effects of uncertainty by simulating the real-world process a large number of times, each time sampling the uncertainty profile of each key input variable. The sampling procedure is that which would be used to determine the chance of rolling a "seven" on any throw of the dice. Obviously, this involves rolling the dice a large number of times and determining the frequency of "seven." Each roll would be one experiment.

In the venture analysis model, one experiment consists of choosing a set of specific values for the key input variables, then utilizing these values to compute after-tax profit, cash flow, indebtedness (negative of cash flow summed to date), payback period, return on assets, and present worth (discounted cash flow) in the accepted financial manner. In each experiment the choice of values for key variables is based upon random sampling of the variables' probability distribution; i.e., the uncertainty profiles. The experiment is then repeated a large number of times, each time choosing, from the specified uncertainty profiles, a new set of values for the key variables and computing after-tax profit, etc. In this manner, frequency distributions—the number of times the computed results fall within specific intervals—are created for each of the computed quantities. The risk profiles are obtained directly from these frequency distributions and represent the chance that the computed quantity will exceed various specified values.

Uncertainty Profiles

The uncertainty profiles represent management's assessment of the variability or uncertainty associated with key variables. These estimates may be made as follows: *The first step* is to estimate the range of uncertainty. For example, assume that management estimates revenue will be greater than $9.0 million but less than $45.0 million.

Once this has been establised, *the second step* divides the range of uncertainty into five intervals. These five intervals may then be ranked according to the relative likelihood that the actual revenue will be in each interval. In terms of our example, actual revenue will most likely be in the range of $16.2 to $23.4 million; the next most likely range is $9.0 to $16.2 million; the third most likely, $23.4 to $30.6; the fourth, from $30.6 to $37.8; and the fifth, from $37.8 to $45.0.

The third step is to associate a quantitative measure with the relative ranking, using the ranking as a guide. The quantitative measure indicates the likelihood, or chance, that the actual revenue will fall in each of the five intervals. In the hypothetical uncertainty profile, there is a 35 percent chance that the actual revenue will be between $9.0 and $16.2 million; there is a 40 percent chance that the actual revenue will be between $16.2 and $23.4 million; a 15 percent chance that revenue will be between $23.4 and $30.6; a 7 percent chance that it will be between $30.6 to $37.8; and a 3 percent chance that it will be $37.8 to $45.0.

The minimum, maximum, and uncertainty data must be provided for each key variable for each year under consideration. To simplify the task of the evaluator and reduce the quantity of data which must be supplied to the model, a profile library consisting of up to 24 representative uncertainty profiles is stored in the computer. Several of these are illustrated in figure 3. Therefore, the evaluator need only specify, in addition to the maximum and minimum values, the numerical index of that uncertainty profile which most closely approximates his "feelings" regarding the width

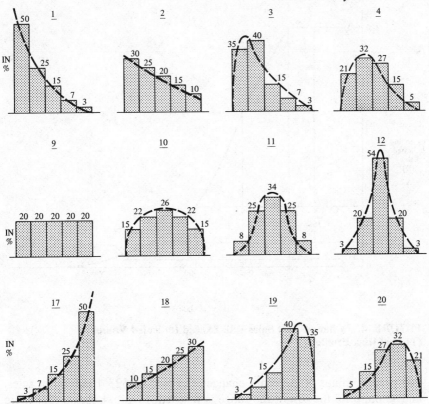

FIGURE 3.   Typical Uncertainty Profiles

and skewness of the distribution associated with each of the variables. If the profile library does not include one which approximates management's feelings closely enough, new uncertainty profiles can easily be added to the library by utilizing the dialogue.

Risk Profiles

The risk profiles indicate the chance that the variable will exceed various levels. They indicate the chance of bonanza and of catastrophe. To illustrate this, consider the uncertainty profile described above. First of all, it has been judged that there is no chance of sales falling below $9.0 million. Therefore, figure 4 shows that there is a 100 percent chance (i.e., certainty) that sales will *exceed* $9.0 million. Second, since it has been estimated that there is a 35 percent chance of sales between $9.0 and $16.2 million, there is a 65 percent (100 percent minus 35 percent) chance of *exceeding* $16.2 million in sales. Similarly, there is a 25 percent

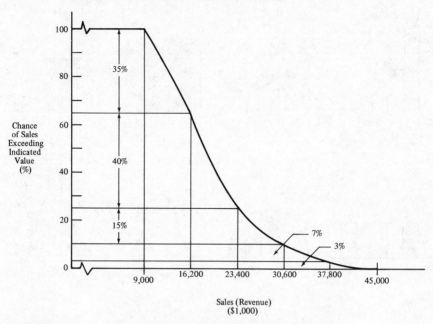

FIGURE 4.   Chance That Sales Will Exceed Indicated Values (Typical Risk Profile)

(65 percent minus 40 percent) chance of exceeding $23.4 million in sales, and so on, until the top of the range is reached. Figure 4 shows that there is no chance of sales exceeding $45.0 million, which is in accordance with the uncertainty profile. In other words, figure 4 shows the chance that sales will exceed the indicated values. It should be noted that figure 4 is based on information from the hypothetical uncertainty profile described earlier. The model computes risk profiles for both input and output variables.

Venture Comparison

The risk profile contains much of the crucial information required for informed judgments on the relative merits of different investment opportunities competing for capital resources of the firm. Figure 5 shows typical risk profiles of present worth for two hypothetical ventures. Note that Ventures A and B have the same "median" value of present worth. Median value is usually defined as that value which has an "even-money" (50 percent) chance of being exceeded. In this case, the median value for both ventures is $11.3 million.

It is most important to note that conventional analysis, which can recognize only a single-point estimate, cannot distinguish between these two ventures. Yet Venture A offers a chance of relatively large rewards

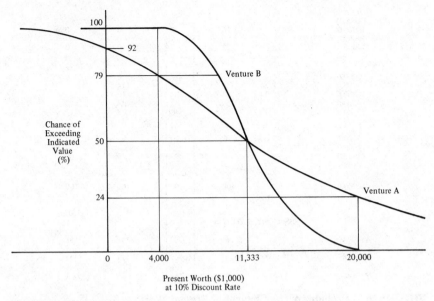

Chance of
Exceeding
Indicated
Value
(%)

Present Worth ($1,000)
at 10% Discount Rate

FIGURE 5. Risk Comparison

with the possibility, even though small, of relatively large losses. Therefore, in the "risk sense," these two ventures are far from equivalent—a
factor completely ignored by conventional analysis.

If a choice were to be made between A and B,[1] the normal tendency
of a conservative management would be to accept B and reject A, all other
things being equal. In other words, the tendency often is to maximize the
expected value and minimize the risk of the company. This, however, is
not always most appropriate since risk preference depends upon the objectives of the company and the degree of dependence of the new venture
on other activities already underway. Diversification into new areas, although in themselves risky, may reduce the total risk of the company.

The risk profiles have been shown in graphic form in this article. Since
at present the computer output is limited to alphanumerics, however, the
risk profiles are produced in tabular form by the computer model. Examples of risk profile data as computer output are shown in figures 6
and 7.

In general, the tabular data indicate the probability or chance that the
variable (present worth, profit, etc.) will exceed the value on the left-
hand scale. For example, referring to figure 6 (discount rate column of
10 percent), there is a 79 percent chance that present worth will be in
excess of $4.0 million, a 48 percent chance that it will be in excess of
$12.0 million, etc. This data is plotted as Venture A in Figure 5.

[1] Assuming that the expected cash flow patterns of A and B are similar.

DOLLARS (X1000)					
38000.0	34	16	2	0	0
36000.0	36	20	2	0	0
34000.0	41	22	2	0	0
20000.0	64	45	24	8	0
18000.0	67	50	28	14	2
16000.0	71	53	34	19	3
14000.0	74	59	42	24	6
12000.0	79	65	48	28	14
10000.0	83	70	54	37	21
8000.0	86	76	74	47	29
6000.0	88	83	70	55	40
4000.0	90	87	79	68	54
2000.0	93	90	86	78	68
−10000.0	98	100	100	100	100
	5.0	7.5	10.0	12.5	15.0
	DISCOUNT RATE (%)				
AVERAGE	31371	20083	13000	8345	5181
STD. DEV.	22947	15233	10509	7473	5449
SCALE	1K$	1K$	1K$	1K$	1K$

FIGURE 6.   Probability (% Chance) of Present Worth Exceeding Indicated Value

Figure 7 illustrates the chance that net profit will exceed the values indicated in the left-hand column. For example, in the seventh year, there is a 100 percent chance of being in the "black" by $1.0 million, an 85 percent chance of profit exceeding $2.5 million, a 28 percent chance of profit exceeding $5.0 million, etc. There is a 57 percent chance (85 percent—28 percent) that profit will be in the range of $2.5 million to $5.0 million. The average or expected profit in the seventh year is $4.16 million, as indicated in the row marked "AVERAGE."

The number of intervals, the minimum value of concern, and the interval size for each variable are specified by the input data. Thus, by changing the input data, finer or coarser looks can be taken where appropriate.

Summary

Conventional analysis of new ventures provides management with little or no insight into the risk associated with the venture. In order to evaluate such risk, it is necessary to consider explicitly the uncertainty of future sales, cost of sales, etc. Only when this is done can the risk associated with new ventures be evaluated quantitatively.

A mathematical model has been developed to assist management with the evaluation of the risk associated with new ventures. This model has been programmed and is currently operational on the RCA time-sharing

DOLLARS (X1000)									
10000.0	0	0	0	0	0	0	0	4	4	8
9500.0	0	0	0	0	0	0	0	5	6	8
9000.0	0	0	0	0	0	0	2	6	9	12
5000.0	0	0	0	0	3	15	28	42	46	50
4500.0	0	0	0	0	4	22	37	50	54	60
4000.0	0	0	0	0	7	28	47	62	61	74
3500.0	0	0	0	0	14	42	58	72	73	84
3000.0	0	0	0	2	26	55	70	81	86	95
2500.0	0	0	0	10	41	70	85	91	95	99
2000.0	0	0	0	26	56	78	0	96	100	100
-1500.0	100	100	100	100	100	100	100	100	100	100
-2000.0	100	100	100	100	100	100	100	100	100	100
YEAR	1	2	3	4	5	6	7	8	9	10
AVERAGE	-547	928	-400	1219	2255	3325	4158	4945	5277	5712
STD. DEV	37	110	284	983	1165	1548	1796	2225	2323	2400
SCALE	1K$	1K$	1K$	1K$	1K$	1K$	1K$	1K$	1K$	1K$

FIGURE 7. Probability (% Chance) of Net Profit Exceeding Indicated Value

system. A user-oriented "dialogue" facilitates the communication of pertinent data to the model. The model evaluates the likelihood that key performance measures (such as profit, cash flow, ROA, etc.) will achieve or exceed various levels. Thus, a quantitative measure of the risk associated with new investment opportunities is established, facilitating the systematic comparison of available alternatives. Providing a quantitative measure of risk will enhance management's ability to make appropriate tradeoffs between the goals of maximization of profit and minimization of risk.

Typically, the risk associated with ventures concerned with diversification into new business areas, addition of new products, addition of new facilities, etc., may be evaluated. When performing a risk analysis of diversification into new business areas or the addition of new products, care must be taken to include all pertinent effects on existing business areas and products. Estimates of revenues and expenses should include these effects.

Bibliography

1. "Risk Analysis in Capital Investment," DAVID B. HERTZ, *Harvard Business Review,* January–February, 1964.

2. "Investment Policies That Pay Off," DAVID B. HERTZ, *Harvard Business Review,* January–February, 1968.

3. *Portfolio Selection: Efficient Diversification of Investments,* HARRY M. MARKOWITZ, John Wiley & Sons, Inc., 1959.

4. "Capital-Budgeting Decisions Involving Combinations of Risky Investments," JAMES VAN HORNE, *Management Science,* Volume 13, Number 2, October, 1966.

5. "Inter-Temporal Portfolio Analysis Based on Simulation of Joint Returns," K. J. COHEN and E. J. ELTON, *Management Science,* Volume 14, Number 1, September, 1967.

6. "Utility Theory," PETER C. FISHBURN, *Management Science,* Volume 14, Number 5, January, 1968.

7. "Utility Theory-Insights Into Risk Taking," RALPH O. SWALM, *Harvard Business Review,* November–December, 1966.

8. "Better Decisions with Preference Theory," JOHN S. HAMMOND, III, *Harvard Business Review,* November–December, 1967.

9. "Improving Estimates That Involve Uncertainty," DONALD H. WOODS, *Harvard Business Review,* July–August, 1966.

10. "The Derivation of Probabilistic Information for the Evaluation of Risky Investments," Frederick S. Hillier, *Management Science,* April, 1963.

IV

DEVELOPMENT, TESTING, AND COMMERCIALIZATION

A.

Developing and Testing

DEVELOPMENT REFERS TO the stage at which a new product proposal is developed into a physical entity and tentative plans are established for its production and introduction to the marketplace. Testing can refer to the performance characteristics of the product in prototype form, to production methods in pilot plant operations, and/or to the pricing and promotion activities in a test market context. In many situations, as one might surmise, the line between development and testing activity is all but nonexistent.

Quinn and Mueller analyze the process of transferring research results across the development/testing bridge to operations in considerable detail. The extracts used here are drawn from their classic article on the subject. Mansfield and his associates also offer some revealing insights in this process, reporting, among other things, the nature of the time/money tradeoff when project development is accelerated, and the relative likelihood of commercial as opposed to technical reasons when a development project fails or is otherwise canceled. Abernathy and Utterback take a somewhat broader view, examining how the character of innovative effort changes as a company evolves from a small technology-based enterprise to a major high-volume producer. They offer some important advice to firms interested in maintaining their innovative thrust as they grow and mature.

Achenbaum and Green are particularly interested in the testing aspects of this process. Achenbaum reviews functions served by market testing with special reference to its use for controlled experiments. Green, in his classic article on the subject, shows how Bayesian decision theory can be used to weigh the cost and value of gathering additional information on a marketing issue as opposed to making a go/no-go decision now on the basis of information already in hand.

31. Extracts from "Transferring Research Results to Operations"

James Brian Quinn and James A. Mueller

Every company needs its own unique organizational and procedural system for transferring technology from the group that has originated it to the group that is going to use it. This is the classic article on the subject.

- What can top management do to ensure that the company receives maximum commercial benefit from its research dollar?
- What factors tend to inhibit the transfer of technology from research to operations?
- How can management overcome these barrier problems and stimulate technological progress in the organization?

The key problem in research management today is getting research results effectively transferred into operations. Comments like the following are increasingly common:

> From the first gasp on, research is the process of reducing an idea to practice. Anyone who thinks otherwise is only misleading himself and his company.

> Five years ago the only problem faced by our research management was that of attracting top-flight scientists. Now the problem is how to get the ideas generated by these people used in the operating departments.

The embryonic research centers of five to ten years ago have mushroomed into enormous multimillion-dollar enterprises capable of produc-

Condensed from "Transferring Research Results to Operations," *Harvard Business Review*, 41 (January–February, 1963), pp. 49–66. © 1963 by the President and Fellows of Harvard College.

James Brian Quinn is Nathaniel Leverone Professor of Management in the Amos Tuck School of Business Administration, Dartmouth College. James Mueller, at the time of writing, was a staff analyst with W. R. Grace & Company.

ing technology at fantastic rates. Simultaneously, rising wage levels and increasingly complex technologies have sent the unit costs of doing research soaring. Meanwhile, competitors, through their research efforts, have made it ever harder to obtain protected positions based on technology. Pressures like these have forced managements to seek vastly improved techniques for targeting research efforts and for converting research results into company profits. As one director of research said, "The dollar sign has appeared over the door of research."

Many technologically based companies have faced the problem of moving research results effectively into operations. Certain management actions can actively stimulate the flow of technology from research to all elements of the operation. Synthesized in this article, these actions form this four-step program:

> I. *Examine resistances at critical technological transfer points.*
> II. *Provide the information to target research toward company goals.*
> III. *Foster a positive motivational environment.*
> IV. *Plan and control the exploitation of R&D results.*

I. Technological Transfer Points

Technology is knowledge about the physical and life sciences as applied to practical purposes. In any given company several technical activities may contribute to the development of this knowledge in specific ways:

- *Fundamental research* seeks the principles and relationships underlying this knowledge.
- *Applied research* further crystallizes the true nature of the knowledge and demonstrates its potential utility through use of bench-scale apparatus.
- *Development* reduces the knowledge to practice in workable prototype form.
- *Engineering* refines the knowledge for commercial exploitation, or other practical end uses.
- *Operations* such as production and sales put the technology finally into use.

Of course, the specific cutoff points between these activities are not as precise as these definitions imply. Nevertheless, a different level of technical skill and business orientation is needed for each. Hence, each is normally performed by a different group within the company. And the interfaces between these groups are the most common points across which the technology must pass to be effectively utilized.

But there are a complex of other technology flows in the typical large company. There are lateral flows between similar technical groups in different divisions. There are diagonal flows of technology between technical groups at different levels in separate divisions. Many decentralized companies lose much high-value technical work because they do not recognize the potential value of these more subtle technological flows and provide adequately for their use.

The place where managements fail most dramatically is in the handling of new technologies not quite fitting into any of the company's existing operating units, yet falling within the broad areas of the company's interest. These would include technologies—new to the company—which could produce royalty income or which the company could exploit only if it sets up a new entrepreneuring organization. Proper handling of this problem is, of course, critical to any company seeking to diversify through research or to exploit its patent estate.

Resistance to Change

To move new technology effectively across each flow point in the organization requires the transfer of three things: (1) *information* about the technology, (2) *enthusiasm* for the technology, and (3) the *authority* to use the technology. Losses occur if any one of these components is not passed from one group to the next. Thus:

> As one vice president of research said, "A new product is like a baby. You can't just bring it into the world and expect it to grow up and be a success. It needs a mother (enthusiasm) to love it and keep it going when things are tough. It needs a pediatrician (expert information and technical skills) to solve the problems the mother can't cope with alone. And it needs a father (authority with resources) to feed it and house it. Without any one of these the baby may still turn out all right, but its chances of survival are a lot lower."

Transferring information, enthusiasm, and authority from one group to another always requires a change in the activity patterns of both groups. Hence—human beings being what they are—there tend to be resistances to these changes at each transfer point. Consequently, the first rules of thumb for technology transfers are these:

1. Keep the number of transfer points in any given flow to a minimum.
2. Maintain as much continuity as possible in the personnel carrying the technology forward.
3. Give the people involved in the change enough information about the technology's consequences to keep irrational reactions to a minimum.

Even so, as a technology moves through the organization, new skills—and generally new people—will be needed to handle it effectively at various phases. To break down the resistances which show up at transition points we must first have a clear picture of the causes.

Information Problems

Some of the resistances are caused simply by lack of information about the technology and/or its potential consequences. Two examples will pinpoint some common causes of resistance:

Purposeful Isolation of Research. In a consumer products company the research director—with the tacit consent of the top management—shielded his researchers from "commercial pressures" so effectively that researchers did not understand the company's technological needs and could not direct themselves toward problems of commercial significance. Operating groups did not hear about significant technical results until those in research were "sure they would work." Consequently, no significant research results moved to operations for three years.

Lack of Market Knowledge. A company selling almost exclusively to the government tried to diversify. But it had no marketing department with skills in nongovernment areas. To date, research has been unable to obtain information about potential new market opportunities toward which it should target its efforts. Nor has the company a marketing research group competent to evaluate research-generated new technologies which might fit into nongovernment markets. No nongovernment technologies have been successful to date.

Other frequent causes of information problems that, perhaps, do not need elaboration are:

- Too many people being involved in a transfer.
- Physical decentralization of research facilities.
- The sheer size of a large company.
- Lack of special skills and knowledge to cope with new markets and technologies.
- Operating people's failure to understand the language and utility of basic science.
- The unwillingness or inability of scientific people to communicate their ideas in terms operating people can understand.
- The sheer complexity of a market or a new technology.
- The cost of getting the information about a market.

Some of these are beyond the control of management. But more often information restraints appear simply because managements have provided neither the organizations necessary to generate required information nor the procedures to effectively bring this information before the right people. We will later show how these information barriers can be attacked.

Motivational Restraints

Many of the most serious restraints to technological progress come from an entirely different source—improper motivation. The following are important—and tragically common—examples of motivational factors inhibiting optimum production and use of industrial technology:

- Short-term management incentives.
- Lack of a sense of urgency in research.
- Entrenched ideas and vested interests.
- Aging of key management and operating personnel.
- Overly long lines of formal authority.

Similar inhibiting factors include: fear of risk taking, distrust or jealousy of ideas conceived elsewhere (the NIH—"not invented here"—complex), inadequate delegation of authority to carry the project forward, and so forth. Management can substantially reduce all of these motivational restraints by establishing the kinds of policy framework, management attitudes, and long-term controls we recommend in a later section.

"Noncontrollable" Restraints

Some factors inhibiting technological progress are, to an extent, beyond management's control. These include such things as: the rigidity and complexity of the market; the strength and actions of competitors; general economic conditions; legal, government, or competitive restrictions on access to or use of pertinent technologies; the flexibility and capacities of suppliers of materials, equipment, and components; the strength of labor unions opposing the change; large minimal investments in commercial-scale facilities; and so forth.

But few conditions are truly noncontrollable in the long run. As the following example shows, careful long-term planning often can mitigate the effects of "outside" inhibiting factors:

> A large electrical manufacturer found that the primary bottleneck to its introduction of new technologies was the inflexibility of its suppliers—particularly manufacturers of production equipment. The company had many new electrical products proved out with bench-scale techniques. But it could not manufacture them—despite a waiting market—because equipment suppliers could not keep up with the rapidly changing needs of the company. To help overcome this the company developed a program to provide closer technical liaison between R & D and the company's suppliers. It also established a manufacturing laboratory to develop advanced manufacturing techniques and began to organize its own equipment-making capacities.

While these lists of factors restraining technological progress do not pretend to be exhaustive, they do demonstrate the types of barriers management must assault. But where should this attack begin?

II. Targeting Research Toward Corporate Goals

The second step in transferring technology efficiently from research into operations is to make sure that the R&D program is specifically designed to support the company's goals and fulfill its technological needs. This "targeting" of R&D involves two essential activities: (1) developing a company-wide long-range plan into which R&D activities are properly integrated, and (2) providing adequate commercial information to rank and balance R&D programs to meet company goals.

Long-Range Planning

Effective long-range technical planning must include several major activities: (a) establishing over-all company objectives in light of expected future economic, sociological, and technological developments; (b) determining the particular technical strategy the company will use in effecting these objectives; (c) defining the specific mission of each major research and operating group in supporting the company's goals and strategies; (d) seeing that research projects are ranked and balanced to best meet the company's anticipated technological threats and opportunities.

Planning provides two key elements necessary to overcome constraints to technological progress.

First, long-range planning serves as a systematic means for bringing to bear information that targets research toward company goals.

Technological forecasting, a part of the planning process, provides analyses of future technological threats and opportunities in time for management to cope with them in an orderly way. The planning process, coordinated with R&D budget reviews, forces a periodic exchange of information to keep R&D aware of the specific technological needs of the company. Further, it defines the responsibility of individual research groups, assigns them to work on these problems, and thus assures that they are giving attention to problems of significance to the company rather than tearing off on tangents of their own choosing. When this assurance is present, there is a much greater likelihood that operating groups will actively support their work and seek out their results. And experience shows that researchers themselves are more enthusiastic and productive when they are working in areas where they know their results will be appreciated and used.

Secondly, long-range planning helps smooth the way for anticipated technological changes in operations.

It forces operating and top managers to think ahead about technological changes and predisposes them toward changes which they can agree to and support financially. It commits certain operating managers to implement technological changes in their areas of the business and indicates where new organizations are needed to exploit technologies or markets which are new to the company. Thus, long-range planning makes sure that research, development, and exploitation efforts are balanced to meet the company's present and future technological needs.

Information Infeeds

Perhaps the weakest link in most companies' technological planning is the inadequacy of the business-technical information they use to target R&D efforts. In addition to technological forecasts associated with long-range planning, three major types of information-generating functions are needed for optimum targeting: that is, opportunity-seeking, commercial-intelligence, and economic-evaluation functions. Let us see what each of these functions involves and the kinds of organizations specific companies have developed to fulfill them.

Opportunity-Seeking Functions. These activities creatively identify new opportunities for the use of technology and reduce these to specifications which serve as meaningful targets for scientists and engineers. To be successful, opportunity-seeking groups need highly original people with both marketing and technical knowledge. Yet these people must not be of the "idea a minute" variety. They must organize their efforts into a systematic screening procedure which first identifies broad fields of potential interest to the company and then determines specific technological opportunities feasible within these fields. Even then a successful unit may only come up with a few positive new opportunities out of perhaps hundreds screened each year.

This activity is an extremely demanding one, and few companies perform it well. The following cases illustrate some approaches that have proved successful in certain organizations:

> A glass company has a technical-marketing research group which considers those properties of glass which are unique to it (i.e., exceptional tensile strength, chemical resistance, translucency, ductility, and so on). It then seeks to identify present and potential markets in which consideration of one or more of these properties is a dominant factor. Its applied program then seeks glasses with intensified properties necessary to meet recognized market needs. Its fundamental program seeks primarily to further isolate and understand the properties of various glasses for which market opportunities are then sought out.
>
> A major metal fabricating company used an analysis group to investigate a large number of four-digit S.I.C. industries. This group ranked each

industry in terms of: (1) preselected desirability criteria such as size, growth potential, revenue vs. capital ratios, and market stability; and (2) similarity to the present lines of business (in terms of raw materials used, market compatibility, and technical fit). The industries with the greatest potential and closest fit were studied in detail to pick out companies and product opportunities for possible acquisition or internal development. The study formed the basis for this company's successful diversification from a single-product to a multiproduct operation.

Commercial–Intelligence Functions. These activities obtain timely information about present and potential competitors' commercial and technical activities in order to make strategic adjustments in technical and commercialization programs. Such activities can provide (entirely ethically and legally) valuable information for targeting R&D.

Economic-Evaluation Functions. Here groups are needed to assess the potential business impact of new ventures suggested by opportunity-seeking and operating groups, or new technologies produced by R&D. Effective economic evaluations contain two parts: (a) a careful "range forecast" of the cash flows which the program, if successful, will call for—from its inception until its anticipated results are finally obsolete (for later stage R&D these cash flows can also be converted into return-on-investment estimates); (b) qualitative information about the program's potential implications for manufacturing, marketing, personnel, legal relationships, and so on.

The early-stage information can be extremely broad. But it should be more focused as the project approaches commercialization. Fortunately, most early-stage research is fairly inexpensive; consequently, decisions can be made on less certain information.

Problems Involved

While the need for these three kinds of infeed information might seem obvious, many companies fail miserably in their efforts to obtain required knowledge. There are several major reasons why:

- The burden of such analyses is normally thrown onto market research groups that are so overwhelmed with pressing problems concerning today's products and profits that they "don't have time" to do adequate analyses on problems not immediately associated with the company's near-term profitability.
- Many market research groups are essentially statistical analysis groups with neither interest nor competence in seeking out new market opportunities or in making the needed types of market evaluations—which, incidentally, are not easily adapted to familiar statistical techniques.

Many marketing and market research groups do not have technically trained people who can communicate well enough with R&D either to understand the potential significance of R&D results or to specify market opportunities in technical terms researchers can appreciate.

In spite of these problems, some companies have found useful ways to provide infeed information to research. Consider the example below:

One major chemical company, with infeed groups at three levels, has a corporate development staff whose function is to seek out and evaluate new markets for the company and to coordinate new-product work on a corporate-wide basis. Until development was established, products new to the company did not receive adequate attention from central research or the operating divisions.

Secondly, each operating division has market research groups to analyze the needs of present product lines and to report them to the divisional R&D units.

Finally, central research has its own evaluation group: (a) to keep in touch with the needs foreseen by the corporate development group and operating divisions, (b) to estimate the potential economic impact of technologies first produced in central research. One of the evaluation group's primary functions is to demonstrate the potential worth of new technologies so that operating units can be convinced to use them.

In summary, then, there are several key considerations in developing and using infeed information to target R&D efforts:

1. Management must assign the responsibility for providing opportunity-seeking, commercial-intelligence, and economic-evaluation information to specific competent groups.
2. The company must develop a procedure which forces periodic evaluation of each R&D program in terms of the best available information concerning its commercial implications and technical feasibility.
3. The information must actually be used by top technical and business managers—not as rigid bench marks, but as guides in the exercise of mature judgment—to determine which R&D programs should be further emphasized, cut back, or eliminated.
4. Infeed information must be presented in a way which researchers can understand and which motivates them to work on problems significant to the company.

If any one of these considerations is ignored, the attempt to target R&D will inevitably fail.

III. Motivational Environment

The third phase of any program designed to move research effectively into operations requires the creation of a *positive management environment* which encourages technological progress throughout the organization. This is a critical—and often most inexpensive—point of attack.

But how can management establish a motivational environment favorable to technological progress? What actions are essential? And how can they be specifically implemented? Our study revealed that, to answer these questions satisfactorily, management must:

- *Establish a policy framework and a "management attitude"* which encourage flexibility, reward those responsible for successful changes, and promote cooperation between organizational units.
- *Control the organization toward long-term goals* so that its members are not overwhelmed by short-sighted, quick-profit opportunities.

Management Policies

Policies are the relatively permanent guides which an organization perceives as the rules governing its important actions. They come into being in a variety of ways. Some may be "enunciated" by higher levels of management (either in written or oral form). Others are "imposed" upon the organization by an outside group, such as a regulatory body or a trade union.

A third important source of policies deserves special attention. Policies frequently originate when a pattern of management decisions—consciously or unconsciously—results in an unwritten law which the organization interprets as the accepted code of behavior.

What kinds of policies and attitudes most significantly affect a company's environment for technological change? Some policies tend to improve the environment. Others normally have a detrimental effect. A few examples drawn from specific company experiences will demonstrate *beneficial influences:*

Risk-Taking. The chairman of the board of a very successful diversified company is the entrepreneur who gave the company its initial growth stimulus. His attitudes have led to the unwritten policy that risks should be taken and occasional failures should be expected, but not repeated.

Involvement in the Technical Program. In a pharmaceutical company the vice presidents and the president visit the central research laboratories monthly. Top management's research interest and understanding have created an environment in which research executives know they must stay attuned to commercial needs and operating managers know they must remain knowledgeable about research progress and be prepared to exploit research results.

Interchange of Personnel. In a large chemical company no man reaches the division manager level without experience in research, production, and marketing. All promising management people are purposely rotated through the various functions. This policy results in a technological orientation throughout the organization and an appreciation of all aspects of the operation at critical management levels.

Reward for Change. A very successful, diversified company stresses the executive and employment growth opportunities created by technological innovation. Its management rewards most highly those responsible for sponsoring and implementing technological change.

Absorption of Displaced People. A large electronics company says it has never laid off a single person because of technological change. Through careful planning, it has timed major changes so its growth and normal personnel turnover would absorb displaced people. It has met no organized labor resistance to technological change.

There are also many instances where poorly conceived policies and attitudes produce *detrimental results.* As examples:

Appraisal of Research Performance. A large chemical company has a written policy "to keep research free from commercial domination." Because of an overly broad interpretation of this policy there has been no corporate attempt to evaluate research results or to guide the research program. Research has felt no pressure to get rid of ineffective people or to terminate unpromising projects. Operating groups resent the "lack of urgency" in research and have resisted supporting the program or using its results. Few technologies have moved from research to operations.

Turnover of Key Personnel. Management must be careful not to change men in key transfer positions too often. For example: A packaging company found its managers strongly resisted technical innovations whose payback period exceeded the length of time the company's rotation policy would normally keep them in their present jobs.

Competition Between Operating Units. A large decentralized company makes its operating units compete against each other in somewhat overlapping markets. Because of this competition, little technology flows laterally between divisions, and technical efforts in several divisions are highly duplicative. Each operating division wants "proprietary technology" and hence opposes the support or use of the central research group in favor of its own "in house" research. The company has thus lost many of the technological advantages its large size could offer.

These examples—both the good and the bad—illustrate only the *kinds* of policies influencing the technological environment. Too often when managements do not adequately assess the potential effects of their attitudes on technological advance, the result is an environment of conservatism, shortsightedness, suspicion, and complacency, which causes the outright waste of much of the money spent on research and development today.

Long-Term Controls

Perhaps the most significant single factor contributing to negativistic motivational environments is the overuse of short-term control techniques. Unfortunately, most companies use accounting, budgeting, and statistical control devices which evaluate management actions over relatively short time periods. As a result, managers at all levels frequently try to make their performance look best in light of these short-term evaluations, regardless of the long-term impact of their actions. This "short-term orientation" can be disastrous to the technical program—and to the company's future.

Recognizing the need for a longer term viewpoint to make effective use of R&D, several companies have come up with interesting approaches to long-term control. To illustrate:

> The chairman of the operating board of a multiproduct company said: "Any damn fool can make a profit for a month—or even a year—by gutting the organization's future. Top management's job is to keep the company 'future oriented.' We try to do this by using a complex of long-term management controls. We play down the use of current profit and return standards in any rigid sense. Instead, we purposely use intuitive judgments concerning how well each operating unit is building its organization and technology to meet future demands."
>
> A large oil company regards the long-term future as the primary responsibility of corporate management. Corporate management thus supports the long-term technical program; sets major financial, legal, personnel, and public relations policy; and coordinates the plans of operating divisions into a unified corporate long-term plan. Operating division managers are primarily responsible for current profits, but must submit long-term plans every six months and support approved plans. Corporate management says its primary long-term controls are through reins on capital expenditures and through the right to remove top-level division managers. Each member of the operating board maintains constant informal contact with an assigned group of operating divisions "in order to look beyond the figures we receive in reports."

A long-term control system is a major factor in creating an environment favorable to technological progress. It normally takes two to ten years for technology to run the long road from research to exploitation. If the organization is allowed to become short-term oriented, it will inevitably—and often foolishly—respond to short-term competitive pressures and resist at every step technology which is related to longer term needs.

IV. Exploiting R&D Results

The final step in getting technology into operations is the careful planning and control of the exploitation process. Many companies have found, despite serious attempts on their part to target R&D and to create a positive motivational environment, that research results do not move easily across the various interfaces in the formal organization. These difficulties are especially serious when technologies and products are totally new to the company. For, here, entirely new skills may be needed at each technical stage, i.e., scientific inquiry, reduction to practice, entrepreneuring a new enterprise, and operating a full-scale facility. Synchronizing these skills to successfully exploit a new technology requires—in all cases—a strong coordinating authority which cuts across the usual formal lines of research, development, engineering, marketing, and manufacturing. Without such an authority, each functional group will tend to look after only its own interests.

Because of such problems we feel that in addition to having competent people throughout the company and a bit of luck—three specific actions contribute heavily to successful exploitation of R&D in large companies:

1. *Creation of specific informal organizations* (a) with explicit responsibility in riding a given new technology through to successful commercialization; and (b) with the authority and resources to motivate existing line organizations to give the technology the attention it deserves.
2. *Establishment of thorough procedures* to plan and monitor the effort, dollar flows, and timing of all phases in the exploitation of a new technology.
3. The integration of these organizations and procedures to *implement the critical strategy* which determines the success or failure of each specific technological exploitation.

Formal Organizations

A variety of organization forms have been used to exploit new technologies successfully. The following examples demonstrate specific organization forms that some companies have found useful:

Task-force Groups. These usually are made up of a small group of personnel from research, development, marketing, and manufacturing who are often given total responsibility for exploiting a new technology. The composition of the group is heavily weighted toward R&D people at first, but it shifts toward operating people as full-scale operations are approached.

Corporate Development Units. These, having their own marketing staff and flexible pilot-scale facilities, pick up new research technologies and exploit them. The unit can be a profit center, deriving profits from sale of new products. As the products prove profitable, operating groups want to take them on. Thus, development is constantly forced to seek new technologies from research, and operating resistances are eliminated.

Outside Companies. At times, these are used to entrepreneur new products in specific cases. The research laboratory may take 49% ownership in the new concern formed to exploit the technology. Or it may simply take license revenues.

Staff Groups at Corporate Level. These units serve to coordinate the introduction of new technologies through existing divisional and functional organizations. They are most effective when they either have functional authority over key aspects of line operations or have a budget with which to buy time from line units. Product managers perform this service successfully in some companies.

An Entrepreneurial Group at Corporate Level. Used by several of the companies most successfully diversifying through research-produced new products, these groups introduce technologies which are new to the company and which do not logically fit into the organizations of established operating groups. Where they are successful, these entrepreneuring units are headed by a commercially oriented dynamo with a technical background. He has at his disposal a technical group which reduces research ideas to practice, a special budget to build small-scale facilities and underwrite product introduction losses, and a small nucleus of commercially oriented technical men who simultaneously "ride two or three products into the market."

Major difficulties with this approach are (1) finding people with the complex of skills and attitudes necessary to entrepreneur new products; (2) replacing these people as they become committed to products they have "ridden into successful division status;" (3) developing the top-management attitude toward the risk taking such operations must involve.

While each of the above organizations has proved useful in specific situations, no single approach offers the optimum solution for all companies. But one significant generalization on this point must be made here.

We are convinced that if a large company wants to effectively diversify through research or to make radical technical advances, the stimulus must come from the top corporate level. Top management must be willing to underwrite long-term fundamental and new product research. There must be corporate-level, opportunity-seeking, and economic-evaluation groups to help target research activities and refine the commercial potential of research results. And there must be some corporate-level activity with the authority and the budget to exploit promising technologies new to the company.

These activities must, of course, be balanced with the rest of the technical program in support of company objectives. But without top-level interest and organization backing, the technical program will only be successful in areas which support or supplement present businesses.

Transfer Procedures

Regardless of the form of its transfer organization, each company should develop a procedure which efficiently links together the series of sequential steps leading from initial technical inquiries to the eventual goal of exploitation. This procedure must do two things:

1. *It must ensure that the program is adequately planned from research to exploitation.* The procedure must provide the commercial and technical information required for decisions between each important step in an exploitation program. And it must automatically and periodically force the proper authorities to consider the factors relevant to the program's success, to plan each major sequential step prior to its inception, and to evaluate the over-all sequence of steps needed to carry a technology through to commercialization. Finally, it must provide for the automatic assignment and transfer of program responsibility for each step.

2. *It must provide a basis for controlling the transfer throughout its cycle.* The procedure must monitor three factors related to technical progress: (a) technical and commercial effort versus results, (b) dollar costs and returns, (c) time elapsed. In terms of these parameters, it must assess each important technical program after each of its major steps to help determine whether to continue, increase, decrease, or stop planned efforts on succeeding steps. The procedure must provide for an automatic review of the program whenever it is critical. And it must force periodic reviews of the total system of programs to rank them for needed emphasis and balance to meet company goals.

Without a careful procedure to *force* planning and control of program progress, systematic planning never really gets accomplished.

Types of Procedures

Many industrial and government operations have done much detailed work on procedures to plan and control R&D progress through to successful exploitation. The following are successful examples of several of the main streams of such analysis:

PERT Networks. These are being widely used to plan and control activities toward known commercial end products. The PERT network provides an excellent model for planning, tracking, and evaluating a series of applied and development activities which need to be coordinated over time.

Budget Reviews. These are by far the most common procedures for planning and controlling program progress. To be truly effective they must analyze individual programs—

- . . . whenever these programs approach or exceed the expenditures planned for the current phase of work.
- . . . on a preset time cycle to ensure that each program receives at least periodic attention and is running on plan.
- . . . when long-range plans are set, to see that the total program's size and emphasis support long-term company goals.

Venture Analyses. These are used by several companies to plan and evaluate technical and commercial progress on new products. For example: A consumer products company draws up a venture analysis for each new technological venture whenever its annual expenditure level begins to exceed $50,000 per year. A corporate-level analysis group assembles data from marketing, manufacturing, finance, and R&D groups. Each source of information must approve (and initial) the data he generates for the analysis. Financial estimates are presented on a year-by-year basis. Present-value and return-on-investment calculations are made for each program. But, in addition, qualitative information concerning marketing, production, and technical plans for the program are included in verbal form. Key elements of the program are laid out in Gantt Chart form. Financial estimates, if approved, are tied into these and into formal program budgets. Ventures are then reviewed (a) when key phases of the program are complete, (b) whenever funds limits for a given phase are reached, and (c) periodically as a portion of budget reviews.

Decision Plans. Several companies have devised these to assist in planning and tracking each technical program through its cycle. For example: A chemical company has developed a "five-phase decision plan." This plan provides for technical and economic reviews during five critical "phases" of a program's cycle: (1) idea searching, (2) definitive research, (3) laboratory development, (4) design development, and (5) commercial development. The plan describes (a) a definite cutoff point for each "phase" of the program, (b) what information is needed to make a realistic decision to move the program to the next phase, (c) precisely who makes the decision, and (d) who assumes responsibility for the next phase of the program.

Planning and controlling technical projects toward commercialization is much like playing stud poker. The issue is always whether to buy one more card (undertake the next phase of research) in order to obtain the added information it contains, or to get out. But the player cannot win unless he sticks the whole way to commercialization. As each card appears, the player has a better idea of the total pot he is playing for and his chances of taking the pot. Before buying a card, his past cards give him general information about the worth of his hand and the relevance of the next card. He can decide whether to risk more (or less) on his next card. But *his investment in previous cards is irrelevant.* The issue is always: Should he pay an increment of money for an incremental bit of information which may lead him closer to a reward whose value may be gauged only in a limited way?

Like stud poker hands, R&D programs must be appraised in step-by-step increments. Each phase of technical work should give a better idea of the probability that the program will pay off and the size of the payoff if it occurs. But until exploitation is complete, no one can say whether there actually will be a payoff.

Using Critical Strategies

We have emphasized throughout that no single transfer system is best for all companies or even for all components of the same company. The "best transfer system" for a given situation will be the one that best implements the critical strategy in that transfer. This critical strategy will depend on the particular objectives, organization, and relative strengths of each individual company. A few examples will show how different critical strategies can be, and how substantially these affect the design of the transfer organization and procedure:

Short Cycle Time. Consider a drug company that has calculated the sizable losses caused by late introduction of a product (a) because nonrepeat sales never made are gone forever, and (b) because the percentage-of-market eventually held by a company strongly correlates with the time its product was introduced relative to competition. For each product the company must weigh these risks against two critical factors—product efficacy and product safety. The company, therefore, has a new-products group which has responsibility for all aspects of product testing and introduction. The company carefully programs all aspects of laboratory and early clinical tests until it is satisfied with the drug's effectiveness and safety. As the product begins the required government testing cycle, various steps in commercialization begin to overlap the testing process on a calculated-risk basis. As the product passes early tests, distribution and advertising plans are drawn up. Later, announcements are printed and a plant site is chosen. Later still, construction of facilities begins on a limited scale. Then, in final testing stages, actual inventories are built up and distributed. The target of such planning is "to go national, safely" the day after the drug receives FDA approval.

High Reliability and Long-term Low Cost. For example: A large utility company requires an extremely long life in its facilities. Facilities' cost is also very high relative to R&D cost. Consequently, obsolescence of facilities would be prohibitively expensive. And, furthermore, reliability of operation is most important to its customers. Therefore, the company (a) has a large group making long-term analyses of customer demands, (b) introduces parallel technical programs to get the "best available technology" before it invests in a new system, (c) spends large amounts of time and money to evaluate carefully the technical and economic implications of new technologies. It purposely sacrifices time in order "to be sure that the system operates reliably, at low cost, over the longest possible time."

Maximum Short-term Commercial Impact. For a consumer products company this is the critical consideration. Its products' success depends more on marketing appeal than on technical performance. Quality judgments are based on subjective consumer tastes, and, as a result, most product life cycles are extremely short. Therefore, the company cuts back technical effort as soon as its process will turn out a product at an acceptable quality level and in needed quantities. If the product proves successful and has a more permanent demand, the company will later back it with short-term support programs guided primarily by comparison tests of its products against those of competitors.

A Continuous Flow of Small Impact Technologies. This objective is the life blood of some companies. For example: A widely diversified mechanical products company develops a group of products with small initial sales but expanding long-term potential into strong successful "lines." It has built its product line primarily on a unique blend of applied chemical, electrical, and mechanical skills. Initially, it did not rely heavily on its fundamental research for new product ideas, but formally sought ideas of inventors outside the company.

Consequently, the company developed elaborate procedures for screening outside ideas. It established large corporate-level technical development and commercial development groups reporting, with research, to a vice president of research and development. These groups have "entrepreneurial skills" to develop ideas on the same basis as would a small new enterprise. When the new products are successful profit centers, operating divisions can take them over if they fit established lines. If not, several products may eventually be blended into a new line—and a new division.

Development of a Few Products with Massive Technical and Financial Requirements. For some large companies, this is the critical strategy. For example: A large chemical company grows by developing major "offbeat" technologies where it has unique skills or access to raw materials. Such opportunities occur only once every few years and make "order of magnitude" changes in the size and scope of the company's operations. Each requires major capital commitments and, hence, top-level corporate support. The company feels that this approach enables it to establish major new-product lines without facing heavy competition from a number of small companies.

Advanced Scientific Research. A large chemical company uses fundamental research—rather than targeted applied research—as its primary means of providing protected proprietary positions. Therefore, the company has established a broad product base, great depth in fundamental and early applied research, a large active patent department, and high technical orientation of all top-level executives. Development groups primarily seek uses for concepts evolved in early-stage research. The company strategy has been conservative—to "underbuild capacity" and to take its risks in research rather than fixed plant. It must, therefore, rely on technical know-how rather than marketing skills or timing to propel its products into new markets.

Obviously, each company should build its strategy around its particular strengths and weaknesses. Hence, it should have its own unique organizational and procedural approach to the transfer problem. Even within a given company different strategies may dominate various transfers. For example, a continuous flow of technology may be the primary consideration from fundamental to applied stages, while the rapid development of products may critically affect the flow from applied research to commercialization. There are cases where different projects—even at the same interface in the same company—require separate strategies because they go into different markets in which the company's relative technical, financial, and market strengths differ substantially vis-à-vis competition.

However, the permanent transfer organization and procedure at each transfer point should be designed to emphasize the most common, or important, strategic consideration at that point. Then, as each major program comes through, management can assess what changes need to be made so that the program's particular strategy can be implemented most successfully.

32. Research and Innovation in the Modern Corporation: Conclusions

Edwin Mansfield, John Rapoport, Jerome Schnee,
Samuel Wagner, and Michael Hamburger

This paper summarizes the findings of a series of original empirical stud-
ies dealing with the firm and its attempts to develop and apply new
technology.

IN THIS CHAPTER, we bring together many of our results and discuss their implications for model-builders and policy-makers. These results have implications for scientists interested in public policy-making concerning science and technology, and for managers, industrial scientists, and operations researchers interested in helping firms to utilize science and technology more effectively.

1. Technical Risks in Industrial Research and Development

The first point that should be made is that the technical risks involved in the bulk of industrial research and development—outside military and other government-financed areas—seem quite modest. For example, among the 19 laboratories in the petroleum, chemical, electronics, and drug industries, the average probability of technical completion for a project was better than 50-50. This was true as well of the average estimated probability of technical success among our sample of 21 large chemical and

Reprinted from *Research and Innovation in the Modern Corporation*, Edwin Mansfield, *et al.*, pp. 206–227. By permission of W. W. Norton & Co., and MacMillan, London and Basingstoke, Ltd. © 1971 by W. W. Norton & Co., Inc.

Edwin Mansfield is Professor of Economics at the Wharton School of the University of Pennsylvania. His co-authors, at the time of writing, were doctoral candidates working under his direction.

petroleum firms. This seems to be due to the fact that the bulk of the R and D projects are aimed at fairly modest advances in the state of the art. According to the directors of three laboratories in the sample, about 70 percent of the projects in their laboratories were aimed at only small advances in the state of the art.

This conclusion has several implications, one being that some of the models that are used to characterize private research and development in the civilian sector—models that suppose that the bulk of this work is very risky, far-out work aimed at really major inventions—are misconceived and perhaps misleading. For example, models based on the presumption that there are large technical risks indicate that certain types of decision rules concerning R and D are optimal, whereas these decision rules may be quite inappropriate since the technical risks are in fact quite limited. Moreover, to the extent that policy-makers and others believe that the bulk of industry's investment in research and development is aimed at bigger advances than in fact is the case, they may be formulating policy concerning the nation's investment in research and development on the basis of a misconception. If, as some say,[1] it is important that the investment in more far-reaching R and D be increased, this misconception could be dangerous.

Of course, we are not saying that all industrial laboratories doing civilian work are concerned mainly with projects entailing relatively small technical risks. On the contrary, as our results show, there is a great deal of variation. What we are saying is that the bulk of the R and D money spent by the firms in our sample—taken as a whole—seems to be devoted to projects that involve relatively small technical risks.

2. Causes of Technical Noncompletion of Projects

In the previous section we stated, that in the firms in our sample, the probability that a research and development project would achieve its technical objectives was generally greater than 50-50. By itself, this tells only part of the story. What is not evident from this statement is that many of the R and D projects that do not achieve their technical objectives are terminated before completion because new information concerning the market for the new product or process indicates that it would not be profitable to continue the project. In other words, poor commercial prospects rather than unanticipated or insoluble technical problems are responsible for their termination.

Specifically, in the three laboratories for which we have data on this score, about 60 percent of the projects that did not achieve their technical

[1] Richard Nelson *et al.*, *Technology, Economic Growth, and Public Policy* (Washington, D.C.: The Brookings Institution, 1967). See also Edwin Mansfield, *The Economics of Technological Change* (New York: W. W. Norton, 1968).

objectives were terminated before completion because of poor commercial prospects. Only about 40 percent were unsuccessful because of technical problems. Of course, the proportion of projects unsuccessful due to technical difficulties (rather than poor commercial prospects) was greater among those seeking larger advances in the state of the art. But even among projects that the laboratory administrators regarded as attempts at relatively large advances in the state of art, over 40 precent that did not achieve their technical objectives were terminated before completion because of poor commercial prospects, not technical difficulties.

These results are of importance for at least two reasons. First, if most projects that do not achieve technical success are terminated before completion because of poor commercial prospects, the proportion that would have achieved technical success if they had not been stopped for this (good) reason must be considerably greater than the proportion actually achieving technical success. In fact, of the projects in the three laboratories that were not terminated for commercial reasons, about 75 percent achieved their technical objectives.

Second, these results suggest that some research and development projects may be begun with inadequate attention having been paid to the commercial prospects of the new product or process and the ability of the firm to exploit them. Of course, even with the best coordination between the marketing department (and other parts of the firm) and the R and D department, we would expect that many R and D projects would be dropped before completion for commercial reasons. After all, a new product that seems profitable today may have little appeal tomorrow because a competitor may have introduced a better product, prices may have changed, better information may have become available concerning the size of the potential market, and so on. But one cannot help wondering whether the seemingly large number of projects that were terminated before completion for commercial reasons could not have been reduced by better coordination between marketing and R and D.[2] According to some accounts, this coordination has sometimes been less than ideal in some of these firms.[3]

3. Commercial versus Technical Risks

The risk of technical failure—discussed in the previous two sections— is not the only risk involved in industrial research and development. In

---

[2] In all, about 53 percent of the R and D projects that were begun were stopped because of poor commercial prospects (27 percent being terminated prior to technical completion for nontechnical reasons and 45 percent of the technically completed projects being terminated without being commercialized).

[3] For some examples of this lack of coordination in other firms, see A. Gerstenfeld, *Effective Management of Research and Development* (Reading, Mass.: Addison Wesley, 1970).

addition, there is the risk of commercial failure. Judging from the three laboratories for which we have data, the risk of commercial failure is considerable. Indeed, the probability of commercial failure, generally seems much greater than the probability of technical failure.

In our three laboratories 220 R&D projects were examined in detail. We found that about 40 percent of the projects that were begun were not technically completed. Of those projects that were technically completed, 45 percent were not commercialized, presumably because commercialization did not seem profitable. Of those projects that were commercialized, about 60 percent did not earn an economic profit. Thus, it is much more likely that a project will achieve its technical aims (this probability being about 0.60) than that, if it achieves these aims, it will earn an economic profit (this probability being about 0.20). In other words, it is much more likely that the laboratory can solve the technical problems involved in developing the new or improved product or process than that it will be economically worthwhile to solve these problems.

These results seem to imply that a great deal of the risk involved in industrial research and development stems from potential difficulties faced by a new product or process in the marketplace, not from the purely technical uncertainties. Moreover, these results, like those in the previous section, make one wonder whether better coordination between marketing and R and D people could not reduce the large percentage of technically successful projects that are commercial failures. It is difficult, of course, to estimate the extent to which this large percentage is due to the laboratories' choosing projects without paying sufficient attention to their commercial prospects, or the extent to which it is caused by an inability of the marketing people to exploit the laboratories' results properly. But in either event, one wonders whether the percentage could not be reduced by better coordination—and incentives for pursuing policies benefiting the entire firm, not just particular departments. In this connection, it is worth noting that the commercial risks were considerably lower at laboratory X—*where marketing inputs were injected earlier into the decision-making process*—than at laboratories Y and Z.

It is also important to note that a trade-off seems to exist between technical risk and commercial risk. The probability of technical success tends, of course, to be lower among projects aimed at larger advances in the state of the art. To compensate for the higher technical risks involved in such projects, firms apparently screen these projects carefully to make sure that the commercial risks involved are relatively low. In each of the laboratories for which we have data, the probability of commercial success (given technical completion) is higher for the projects attempting large or medium advances in the state of the art than for those attempting small advances in the state of the art. Indeed, the probability of commercial success (given technical completion) is so much greater for projects attempting large or medium advances in the state of the art that the probability that a project of this sort will be a commerical success (once a project is begun) is higher than for a project attempting a small advance in the state of the art. It would be interesting to find out more about the extent to which firms take proper account of *both* types of risk. In some cases, one suspects that laboratories—more aware of, and responsive to, technical risks than commercial risks—tend to shy away from projects where lower commercial risks are attained by incurring higher technical risks, even though the acceptance of such projects might, on balance, result in an R and D portfolio better constituted to meet the firm's overall objectives. To a considerable extent, this problem, like others cited above, is due in considerable measure to difficulties in coordinating R and D with marketing. The importance of properly coupling R and D with marketing (and production) cannot be overemphasized: It lies at the heart of any successful system for product innovation.

4. Accuracy of Predictions of Technical Success

A relatively large percentage of the research and development projects carried out by the industrial laboratories in our sample are technically successful. Does this mean that a laboratory's personnel can predict reasonably well whether a particular R and D project will be technically successful or not? Judging by the experience during the sixties of a major proprietary drug firm, it appears that a laboratory's estimates of the probability of technical success are of some use in predicting whether a particular project will be technically completed.

However, these estimates do not seem to be of much use in predicting which projects will be technically completed and which ones will not. Even if they are employed in such a way that the probability of an incorrect prediction is minimized, they predict incorrectly in about 30 percent of the cases. It is possible that the usefulness of the estimates may be increased by combining them with information concerning the extent of the technical advance sought by the project, there being some apparent tendency for the estimates to overstate the risk of failure for projects attempting small technical advances and to understate the risk of failure for projects attempting large technical advances. But further work is needed to test this possibility.

Used without some modification of this sort, it does not appear that the firm's estimates of the probability of technical success are very accurate predictors—although they are of some use. Apparently, despite the fact that the bulk of the firm's R and D projects will turn out to be technically successful, the firm is not able—or, at any rate, its formal estimates are not able—to predict with much accuracy which ones will not be technically successful. The situation seems somewhat similar to the old story of the advertising manager who said that he knew that one-quarter of his expenditures would be a waste—but that he didn't know which quarter.

5. Cost and Time Overruns

Until the cost overruns on the Lockheed C-5A made the headlines, the subject of cost and time overruns seldom came up in polite conversation. In contrast to military research and development, practically nothing has been determined in previous studies about cost and time overruns in civilian R and D.

To help fill this gap, we studied the cost and time overruns in a major ethical drug firm and a major proprietary drug firm, the results being as follows: First, there are large cost and time overruns in these drug firms, the average ratio of actual to expected cost being 1.78 (in the ethical drug firm) and 2.11 (in the proprietary drug firm), and the average ratio of actual to expected time being 1.61 (in the ethical drug firm) and 2.95 (in the proprietary drug firm). Thus, if these firms are at all representative, large overruns are not confined to military work; they are typical of civilian research and development as well.

A comparison of the overruns in these drug firms with the overruns is a dozen major military projects indicates that the cost overruns tend to be larger and the time overruns tend to be smaller in military work than in the drug industry. The reasons for this are not difficult to find: In the military projects, more importance undoubtedly is attached to time, and less importance is attached to cost, than in the drug industry. It is well known that the military services have placed much greater emphasis on time and quality than on cost.

It is somewhat unfair to compare the cost overruns for the military projects with the cost overruns for all drug projects, since the military projects generally attempt much greater advances in the state of the art than the drug projects. If we compare the cost overruns for the military projects with the cost overruns for the more ambitious drug projects— new chemical entities in the ethical drug firm and new products in the proprietary drug firm—we find that the cost overruns tend to be closer to the size of the military cost overruns.

The factors that seem to influence the size of a project's cost overrun are much the same in the drug industry as in military work. In both cases, the extent of the attempted advance of the state of the art is important, more ambitious projects having greater overruns than less ambitious projects. Also, in both cases, the length of the project affects its cost overrun. However, in the drug industry—unlike military work—there is no evidence that cost overruns have tended to decrease over time. This is probably due in part to the fact that cost overruns in recent years have tended to increase in response to changes in drug-development procedures.

Although cost and time overruns are partly due to the uncertainty inherent in research and development, it is important that the reader recognize that they also stem from deliberate underestimations of time and cost. Low estimates are frequently used to marshal support for particular projects. This tendency toward downward adjustment of estimates seems to exist in the drug industry, and it has frequently been noted in military R and D. So long as there are incentives to shade estimates in this way—and little or no penalty for doing so—this tendency is bound to continue.

6. Quantitative Project-Selection Techniques: Uses and Limitations

In recent years researchers have spent a considerable amount of time and effort attempting to devise techniques to select research and development projects. Many articles have appeared in the professional and business journals describing methods that a firm might use to help determine which project proposals it should accept and which it should turn down. Most of these suggested techniques are adaptations of capital-budgeting techniques, such as the use of pay-out periods and rates of return. Some of the more elaborate suggestions involve the use of linear and dynamic programming.

To what extent are firms making use of these quantitative project-selection techniques? Judging from our sample of nineteen industrial laboratories in the chemical, drug, petroleum, and electronics industries, about three-quarters of the laboratories use such techniques to allocate funds. However, it is important to note that many of these firms use these techniques in only a limited way: Intuition and hunch continue to play an important role. The probability of a quantitative technique being used is directly related to the size of the laboratory. Although a few laboratories began using these techniques in the early and middle fifties, the bulk of the laboratories have begun using them since 1960. The employment of these project-selection techniques is itself an innovation. Compared with major innovations in the steel, railroad, brewing, and coal industries, quantitative project-selection techniques have spread relatively slowly, despite the relatively small investment required to introduce them. This may well have been due to skepticism concerning their usefulness.

Our own results do little to dispel such skepticism. In general, these quantitative project-selection techniques are based on estimates of the probability of technical success, the development time, and the development cost. As we stressed in the previous two sections, these estimates are subject to errors that are large and variable. In addition, these techniques usually are based on estimates of the probability of commercial success, the size of the market, and the capital-facility requirements of the project. According to laboratory administrators, these estimates are even less accurate than the ones discussed in the previous two sections.

Thus, if the laboratories in our sample are at all representative, these techniques rely heavily on estimates that, by practically any standard, are very poor.

Unfortunately, some laboratory administrators do not seem to realize how bad these estimates are. About one-half or more of the laboratory directors in our sample feel that estimates of a project's manpower requirements, its development cost, its capital requirements, its research cost, its probability of technical success, and its development time are good or excellent. Only about 10–20 percent of the laboratory directors in our sample regard these estimates as poor or untrustworthy. Given our findings concerning the size of the errors in estimates of development cost, time, and technical outcome, it appears that laboratory directors may be unduly optimistic.

Needless to say, we are not condemning the use of quantitative project-selection techniques. The employment of such techniques does force people to think about the relevant factors. Moreover, it is useful for people to make their assumptions explicit. What we are saying is that these techniques should be viewed with more caution and applied with more flexibility than is sometimes the case. It is particularly important that sensitivity analyses be carried out to show the effects on the results of large errors in the estimates that are used. A great deal of harm can be done by an enthusiastic and well-meaning operations researcher who takes these techniques too seriously—or by a laboratory manager who takes the operations researcher too seriously.

7. The Role of Research and Development in the Innovative Process

Thus far in this chapter, we have focused almost entirely on research and development. Despite R and D's obvious importance, it must be recognized that R and D is only part of the process leading to the introduction of a new product or process. Some idea of the relative importance of R and D in the total set of activities leading to a new product is provided by our findings concerning the percentage of total innovation costs accounted for by R and D in three product groups—chemicals, electronics, and machinery: The results indicate that, in each of these areas, R and D accounted for about half of the total innovation costs for the new products in our sample.

Besides research and development, what are the other major types of expenditures involved in product innovation? Our results indicate that the largest percentage of the total cost of product innovation generally occurs in the stage of the innovation process during which tooling occurs and the manufacturing facilities are designed and constructed. For our sample of innovations, this stage accounted, on the average, for almost 40 percent of the total costs. Also, costs associated with manufacturing start-up and marketing start-up accounted, on the average, for almost 15 percent of the total costs. The non-R and D stages of the innovation process also accounted for a large portion of the time involved. Tooling and construction of manufacturing facilities went on for about 30 percent, on the average, of the total elapsed time. Manufacturing start-up went on for about 10 percent of the total elapsed time.

These findings are important in at least three respects. First, they show that the amount of resources devoted to innovative activity in the United States—and other countries—is considerably greater than is indicated by the statistics on R and D expenditure. Second, to the extent that the ratio of R and D expenditures to the total costs of innovation varies among industries, firms of various sizes, countries, or periods of time, it shows that differences among industries, firms of various sizes, countries, or periods of time in R and D expenditure may be an inadequate measure of differences in the costs of innovation. Third, it shows that a firm, when it sets out to innovate, must be willing to risk a great deal more than its R and D expenditure alone, the result being that the difficulties and risks involved, particularly for smaller firms, are that much greater.

8. The Nature and Determinants of the Time-Cost Trade-off Function

A product often can be developed and brought to market more quickly if more money is spent during the course of the innovation process. Although economists have recognized the importance of this time-cost trade-off, no attempt has been made in previous studies to estimate the time-cost trade-off function for particular innovations. To help fill this gap, we estimated the time-cost trade-off functions for twenty-nine innovations in chemicals, electronics, and machinery, on the basis of a series of interviews with the managers who had the principal responsibility for the innovations. The data suggest that a downward-sloping convex function will usually be a reasonable approximation to the time-cost trade-off function (in the relevant range). The empirical support for the hypothesis that the slope is negative is very strong. There is somewhat more question about the hypothesis of convexity, but in our sample at least, a convex shape is strongly suggested in a large proportion of the cases.

Judging by our sample of innovations, it is possible to represent the time-cost trade-off function by a simple equation, the parameters of which vary from innovation to innovation. This equation has three parameters, one being the minimum expected cost of the project, another being the minimum expected duration of the project, and the third determining the elasticity of cost with respect to time. In general, this equation fits the data for the twenty-nine innovations quite well, the coefficient of correlation usually being 0.9 or more. In our sample of projects, the minimum expected cost of a project is directly related to the size of the technical advance and the size of the firm carrying out the project. The minimum expected duration of a project is also directly related to these variables. In large part, the relationship between firm size and a project's minimum expected cost or minimum expected duration reflects the fact that bigger firms carry out bigger projects.

The elasticity of cost with respect to time is the expected percentage increase in cost due to an expected 1-percent reduction in the duration of the project. The elasticity becomes greater as the duration of the project is pushed closer and closer to its minimum value. When the duration of the project is less than 30 percent above its minimum value, this elasticity averages about 1.6 in our sample of innovations. When the duration of the project is about 30–80 percent above its minimum value, this elasticity averages about 0.5. According to our data, a project's elasticity of cost with respect to time depends on the extent to which the project advances the state of the art and on the size of the firm carrying out the project: Projects that attempt greater advances in the state of the art and that are carried out by larger firms tend to be more costly than others to speed up.

9. The Important Role of Overlap

Our results emphasize that overlap—the beginning of one stage of the innovation process before a previous stage is completed—may be a major reason for the increased expected costs associated with a decrease in expected time. In our sample of innovations, the amount of overlap tended to increase as an innovation's time to completion was pushed closer and closer to the minimum time to completion. Moreover, there was a tendency for bigger firms to overlap stages to a greater extent than smaller ones. In general, it was felt by the managers we interviewed that increased overlap between two stages would tend to increase the cost of the later stage. The most commonly mentioned reason for this was characterized by one manager as the increased likelihood of "engineering-change notices." The problem arises when work in the later stage is critically dependent on information or results obtained in the earlier stage. When there is considerable overlap, the later stage must be started before the results of the work in the earlier stage are known. Estimates or tentative results must be used as the basis for the later work. If these estimates prove to be incorrect, the expense of correcting mistakes and redoing work may be considerable.

According to the managers, the effect of overlap on costs may be particularly great in the case of overlap between the prototype or pilot-plant stage and the tooling and construction stage. If tooling and the construction of the production facilities are begun before all prototype engineering problems are solved, the tooling may have to be modified or even scrapped when the prototype stage is finally completed. Our results are quite consistent with this hypothesis: The proportion of total costs incurred in the tooling and construction stage is directly related to the extent of the overlap between the prototype or pilot-plant stage and the tooling and construction stage.

10. The Importance of External Sources of Technology

Even in research-intensive industries like chemicals and drugs, innovations are often based to a large extent on technology derived from organizations other than the innovating firm. Our results emphasize the importance of external sources of technology. With regard to the innovations studied in Chapter 6 [of *Research and Innovation in the Modern Corporation*], about one-third were based to some extent on specific technology derived from outside the innovating firm. With regard to the pharmaceutical industry, about one-half of the major innovations during 1935–1962 were based on discoveries made outside of the innovating firm. With regard to numerical control, it is clear that the makers of the first commercial numerically controlled machine tools were heavily dependent for the basic technology on organizations and firms outside the machine-tool industry.

If it is true that a large proportion of significant innovations are based on inventions made outside the innovating firm, it would seem to be extremely important for a firm to look outward for ideas and to avoid focusing too much attention exclusively on its own inventions. There is sometimes a tendency for R and D managers to devote too large a part of their resources to developments arising from their own laboratories and to neglect developments in other firms and industries. If something is "not invented here," it may be neglected or resisted.

11. Implications for Technological Forecasting

Technological forecasting is presently a fashionable topic in industry and government. But even the most enthusiastic practitioners of technological forecasting admit that it is far from being a science: The sophistication of its methods and the reliability of its results seem low even when judged against the standards of the social sciences. However, despite the obvious difficulties in technological forecasting, it is a necessary part of decision-making by firms and government agencies. Just as there is no way to avoid forecasting the economic future—explicitly or implicitly—so there is no way to avoid forecasting the technological future.

Our findings seem to have at least two important implications for technological forecasting. First, it appears that major innovations generally take quite a long time to go from conceptualization to commercial introduction to widespread adoption. For example, the average time interval between the discovery of a new drug and its first commercial introduction seems to have been about five years—and this lag appears to be shorter than the lag in other industries. Moreover, in most cases for which we have data, it took a decade or more before the bulk of the firms in an industry began using a new technique. The implication for technological forecasting seems clear: If one is interested in forecasting the impact of major innovations at the point when they are widely diffused, the inventions that have already occurred—or are well along toward completion— are all that really matter in the short—and often the intermediate—run.

Second, the model of the diffusion process outlined in Chapter 9 [of *Research and Innovation in the Modern Corporation*] seems to be of some help in forecasting the rate at which a new technique will displace an old one. This model was employed to make short-run forecasts for a government agency of the rate of diffusion of numerical control in the tool-and-die industry.[4] It has also been used by firms to forecast the rate of market penetration of innovations. In general, the results have seemed useful. Of course, this model cannot be employed indiscriminately to make such forecasts; the assumptions underlying it are discussed elsewhere in detail.[5] But where these assumptions hold reasonably well, it may be a valuable tool for technological forecasters.

12. Limitations of the Studies

Finally, it may be worthwhile to remind the reader of some of the limitations of the studies reported. For one thing, the basic information underlying our results pertains to only a small number of industries— chemicals, petroleum, drugs, electronics, machinery, and machine tools. For another, some of our models are relatively simple, and some of our data are rough. What is important for present purposes is that the reader recognize that many of our findings must be viewed as tentative.

At the same time, it is appropriate to add that although the data used are not as precise or as plentiful as we would like, these data are a great deal better than anything heretofore available. Indeed, with regard to a great many of the questions taken up practically no data at all existed in the past. The studies reported here are part of a continuing investigation of the economics of technological change. We hope to extend and build on these studies—as well as their predecessors—in the years ahead.

---

[4] See Edwin Mansfield, "Determinants of the Speed of Application of New Technology," paper presented at the 1971 Conference of the International Economic Association at St. Anton, Austria.

[5] E. Mansfield, *op. cit.*

33. Patterns of Industrial Innovation

William J. Abernathy and James M. Utterback

A new model suggests how the character of its innovation changes as a successful enterprise matures; and how other companies may change themselves to foster innovation as they grow and prosper.

How DOES A COMPANY'S INNOVATION—and its response to innovative ideas—change as the company grows and matures?

Are there circumstances in which a pattern generally associated with successful innovation is in fact more likely to be associated with failure?

Under what circumstances will newly available technology, rather than the market, be the critical stimulus for change?

When is concentration on incremental innovation and productivity gains likely to be of minimum value to a firm? In what situations does this strategy instead cause instability and potential for crisis in an organization?

Intrigued by questions such as these, we have examined how the kinds of innovations attempted by productive units apparently change as these units evolve. Our goal was a model relating patterns of innovation within a unit to that unit's competitive strategy, production capabilities, and organizational characteristics.

This article summarizes our work and presents the basic characteristics of the model to which it has led us. We conclude that a productive unit's capacity for and methods of innovation depend critically on its stage of evolution from a small technology-based enterprise to a major high-volume

Reprinted from *Technology Review*, 80 (June/July, 1978), pp. 41–47. © 1978 by The Alumni Association, M.I.T. Used by permission. The original monograph source is William J. Abernathy and James M. Utterback, "A General Model," Chapter 4 in W. J. Abernathy, *The Productivity Dilemma* (Baltimore: Johns Hopkins Press, 1978), pp. 68–84.

William Abernathy is Professor of Business Administration and coordinator of the Harvard Business School's doctoral program on the management of technology. James Utterback is a Professor in both the Sloan School and the School of Engineering at M.I.T. He also directs research on the process of technological change at M.I.T.'s Center for Policy Alternatives.

The changing character of innovation, and its changing role in corporate advance. Seeking to understand the variables that determine successful strategies for innovation, the authors focus on three stages in the evolution of a successful enterprise: its period of flexibility, in which the enterprise seeks to capitalize on its advantages where they offer greatest advantages; its intermediate years, in which major products are used more widely; and its full maturity, when prosperity is assured by leadership in several principal products and technologies.

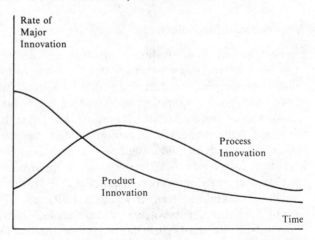

	Fluid pattern	Transitional pattern	Specific pattern
Competitive emphasis on	Functional product performance	Product variation	Cost reduction
Innovation stimulated by	Information on users' needs and users' technical inputs	Opportunities created by expanding internal technical capability	Pressure to reduce cost and improve quality
Predominant type of innovation	Frequent major changes in products	Major process changes required by rising volume	Incremental for product and process, with cumulative improvement in productivity and quality
Product line	Diverse, often including custom designs	Includes at least one product design stable enough to have significant production volume	Mostly undifferentiated standard products
Production processes	Flexible and inefficient; major changes easily accommodated	Becoming more rigid, with changes occurring in major steps	Efficient, capital-intensive, and rigid; cost of change is high
Equipment	General-purpose, requiring highly skilled labor	Some subprocesses automated, creating "islands of automation"	Special-purpose, mostly automatic with labor tasks mainly monitoring and control
Materials	Inputs are limited to generally-available materials	Specialized materials may be demanded from some suppliers	Specialized materials will be demanded; if not available, vertical integration will be extensive
Plant	Small-scale, located near user or source of technology	General-purpose with specialized sections	Large-scale, highly specific to particular products
Organizational control is	Informal and entrepreneurial	Through liaison relationships, project and task groups	Through emphasis on structure, goals, and rules

producer. Many characteristics of innovation and the innovative process correlate with such an historical analysis; and on the basis of our model we can now attempt answers to questions such as those above.

A Spectrum of Innovators

Past studies of innovation imply that any innovating unit sees most of its innovations as new products. But that observation masks an essential difference: what is a product innovation by a small, technology-based unit is often the process equipment adopted by a large unit to improve its high-volume production of a standard product. We argue that these two units—the small, entrepreneurial organization and the larger unit producing standard products in high volume—are at opposite ends of a spectrum, in a sense forming boundary conditions in the evolution of a unit and in the character of its innovation of product and process technologies.

One distinctive pattern of technological innovation is evident in the case of established, high-volume products such as incandescent light bulbs, paper, steel, standard chemicals, and internal-combustion engines, for examples.

The markets for such goods are well defined; the product characteristics are well understood and often standardized; unit profit margins are typically low; production technology is efficient, equipment-intensive, and specialized to a particular product; and competition is primarily on the basis of price. Change is costly in such highly integrated systems because an alteration in any one attribute or process has ramifications for many others.

In this environment innovation is typically incremental in nature, and it has a gradual, cumulative effect on productivity. For example, Samuel Hollander has shown that more than half of the reduction in the cost of producing rayon in plants of E. I. du Pont de Nemours and Co. has been the result of gradual process improvements which could not be identified as formal projects or changes.

In many instances, major systems innovations have been followed by countless minor product and systems improvements, and the latter account for more than half of the total ultimate economic gain due to their much greater number. While cost reduction seems to have been the major incentive for most of these innovations, major advances in performance have also resulted from such small engineering and production adjustments.

Such incremental innovation typically results in an increasingly specialized system in which economies of scale in production and the development of mass markets are extremely important. The productive unit loses its flexibility, becoming increasingly dependent on high-volume production to cover its fixed costs and increasingly vulnerable to changed demand and technical obsolescence.

Major new products do not seem to be consistent with this pattern of incremental change. New products which require reorientation of corporate goals or production facilities tend to originate outside organizations devoted to a "specific" production system; or, if originated within, to be rejected by them.

A more fluid pattern of product change is associated with the identification of an emerging need or a new way to meet an existing need; it is an entrepreneurial act. Many studies suggest that such new product innovations share common traits. They occur in disproportionate numbers in companies and units located in or near affluent markets with strong science-based universities or other research institutions and entrepreneurially oriented financial institutions. Their competitive advantage over predecessor products is based on superior functional performance rather than lower initial cost, and so these radical innovations tend to offer higher unit profit margins.

When a major product innovation first appears, performance criteria are typically vague and little understood. Because they have a more intimate understanding of performance requirements, users may play a major role in suggesting the ultimate form of the innovation as well as the need.

It is reasonable that the diversity and uncertainty of performance requirements for new products give an advantage in their innovation to small, adaptable organizations with flexible technical approaches and good external communications, and historical evidence supports that hypothesis. For example, John Tilton argues that new enterprises led in the application of semiconductor technology, often transferring into practice technology from more established firms and laboratories. He argues that economies of scale have not been of prime importance because products have changed so rapidly that production technology designed for a particular product is rapidly made obsolete.

A Transition from Radical to Evolutionary Innovation

These two patterns of innovation may be taken to represent extreme types—in one case involving incremental change to a rigid, efficient production system specifically designed to produce a standardized product, and in the other case involving radical innovation with product characteristics in flux. They are not in fact rigid, independent categories. Several examples will make it clear that organizations currently considered in the "specific" category—where incremental innovation is now motivated by cost reduction—were at their origin small, "fluid" units intent on new product innovation.

John Tilton's study of developments in the semiconductor industry from 1950 through 1968 indicates that the rate of major innovation has decreased and that the type of innovation shifted. Eight of the 13 product innovations he considers to have been most important during that period occurred within the first seven years, while the industry was making less than 5 per cent of its total 18-year sales. Two types of enterprise can be identified in this early period of the new industry—established units that

The Unit of Analysis

As we show in this article, innovation within an established industry is often limited to incremental improvements of both products and processes. Major product change is often introduced from outside an established industry and is viewed as disruptive; its source is typically the start-up of a new, small firm, invasion of markets by leading firms in other industries, or government sponsorship of change either as an initial purchaser or through direct regulation.

These circumstances mean that the standard units of analysis of industry—firm and product type—are of little use in understanding innovation. Technological change causes these terms to change their meaning, and the very shape of the production process is altered.

Thus the questions raised in this article require that a product line and its associated production process be taken together as the unit of analysis. This we term a "productive unit." For a simple firm or a firm devoted to a single product, the productive unit and the firm would be one and the same. In the case of a diversified firm, a productive unit would usually report to a single operating manager and normally be a separate operating division. The extreme of a highly fragmented production process might mean that several separate firms taken together would be a productive unit.

For example, analysis of change in the textile industry requires that productive units in the chemical, plastics, paper, and equipment industries be included. . . . Major change at one level works its way up and down the chain, because of the interdependence of product and process change within and among productive units. Knowledge of the production process as a system of linked productive units is a prerequisite to understanding innovation in an industrial context.—*W.J.A., J.M.U.*

came into semiconductors from vested positions in vacuum tube markets, and new entries such as Fairchild Semiconductor, I.B.M., and Texas Instruments, Inc. The established units responded to competition from the newcomers by emphasizing process innovations. Meanwhile, the latter sought entry and strength through product innovation. The three very successful new entrants just listed were responsible for half of the major product innovations and only one of the nine process innovations which Dr. Tilton identified in that 18-year period, while three principal established units (divisions of General Electric, Philco, and R.C.A.) made only one-quarter of the product innovations but three of the nine major process innovations in the same period. In this case process innovation did not prove to be an effective competitive stance; by 1966 the three established units together held only 18 per cent of the market while the three new units held 42 per cent. Since 1968, however, the basis of competition in the industry has changed; as costs and productivity have become more important, the rate of major product innovation has decreased, and effective process innovation has become an important factor in competitive success.

Product and process evolved in a similar fashion in the automobile industry. During a four-year period before Henry Ford produced the renowned Model T, his company developed, produced, and sold five different engines, ranging from two to six cylinders. These were made in a factory that was flexibly organized much as a job shop, relying on trade craftsmen working with general-purpose machine tools not nearly so advanced as the best then available. Each engine tested a new concept. Out of this experience came a dominant design—the Model T; and within 15 years 2 million engines of this single basic design were being produced each year (about 15 million all told) in a facility then recognized as the most efficient and highly integrated in the world. During that 15-year period there were incremental—but no fundamental—innovations in the Ford product.

In yet another case, Robert Buzzell and Robert Nourse, tracing innovations in processed foods, show that new products such as soluble coffees, frozen vegetables, dry pet foods, cold breakfast cereals, canned foods, and precooked rice came first from individuals and small organizations where research was in progress or which relied heavily upon information from users. As each product won acceptance, its productive unit increased in size and concentrated its innovation on improving manufacturing, marketing, and distribution methods which extended rather than replaced the basic technologies. The major source of the latter ideas is now each firm's own research and development organization.

The shift from radical to evolutionary product innovation is a common thread in these examples. It is related to the development of a dominant product design, and it is accompanied by heightened price competition and increased emphasis on process innovation. Small-scale units that are flexible and highly reliant on manual labor and craft skills utilizing general-purpose equipment develop into units that rely on automated, equipment-intensive, high-volume processes. We conclude that changes in innovative pattern, production process, and scale and kind of production capacity all occur together in a consistent, predictable way.

Though many observers emphasize new-product innovation, process and incremental innovations may have equal or even greater commercial importance. A high rate of productivity improvement is associated with process improvement in every case we have studied. Semiconductor prices have been falling by 20 to 30 per cent with each doubling of cumulative production. The introduction of the Model T Ford resulted in a price reduction from $3,000 to less than $1,000 (in 1958 dollars). Similar dramatic reductions have been achieved in the costs of computer core memory and television picture tubes.

Managing Technological Innovation

If it is true that the nature and goals of an industrial unit's innovations change as that unit matures from pioneering to large-scale producer, what does this imply for the management of technology?

We believe that some significant managerial concepts emerge from our analysis—or model, if you will—of the characteristics of innovation as production processes and primary competitive issues differ. As a unit moves toward large-scale production, the goals of its innovations change from ill-defined and uncertain targets to well-articulated design objectives. In the early stages there is a proliferation of product performance requirements and design criteria which frequently cannot be stated quantitatively, and their relative importance or ranking may be quite unstable. It is precisely under such conditions, where performance requirements are ambiguous, that users are most likely to produce an innovation and where manufacturers are least likely to do so.

The stimulus for innovation changes as a unit matures. In the initial fluid stage, market needs are ill-defined and can be stated only with broad uncertainty; and the relevant technologies are as yet little explored. So there are two sources of ambiguity about the relevance of any particular program of research and development—target uncertainty and technical uncertainty. Confronted with both types of uncertainty, the decision-maker has little incentive for major investments in formal research and development.

As the enterprise develops, however, uncertainty about markets and appropriate targets is reduced, and larger research and development investments are justified. At some point before the increasing specialization of the unit makes the cost of implementing technological innovations prohibitively high and before increasing cost competition erodes profits with which to fund large indirect expenses, the benefits of research and development efforts would reach a maximum. Technological opportunities for improvements and additions to existing product lines will then be clear, and a strong commitment to research and development will be characteristic of productive units in the middle stages of development. Such firms will be seen as "science based" because they invest heavily in formal research and engineering departments, with emphasis on process innovation and product differentiation through functional improvements.

Although data on research and development expenditures are not readily available on the basis of productive units, divisions, or lines of business, an informal review of the activities of corporations with large investments in research and development shows that they tend to support business lines that fall neither near the fluid nor the specific conditions but are in the technologically-active middle range. Such productive units tend to be large, to be integrated, and to have a large share of their markets.

A small, fluid entrepreneurial unit requires general-purpose process equipment which is typically purchased. As it develops, such a unit is expected to originate some process-equipment innovations for its own use; and when it is fully matured its entire processes are likely to be designed as integrated systems specific to particular products. Since the mature firm is now fully specialized, all its major process innovations are likely to originate outside the unit. But note that the supplier companies will now see themselves as making product—not process—innovations.

The organization's methods of coordination and control change with the increasing standardization of its products and production processes. As task uncertainty confronts a productive unit early in its development, the unit must emphasize its capacity to process information by investing in vertical and lateral information systems and in liaison and project groups. Later, these may be extended to the creation of formal planning groups, organizational manifestations of movement from a product-oriented to a transitional state; controls for regulating process functions and management controls such as job procedures, job descriptions, and systems analyses are also extended to become a more pervasive feature of the production network.

As a productive unit achieves standardized products and confronts only incremental change, one would expect it to deal with complexity by reducing the need for information processing. The level at which technological change takes place helps to determine the extent to which organizational dislocations take place. Each of these hypotheses helps to explain the firm's impetus to divide into homogeneous productive units as its products and process technology evolve.

The hypothesized changes in control and coordination imply that the structure of the organization will also change as it matures, becoming more formal and having a greater number of levels of authority. The evidence is strong that such structural change is a characteristic of many enterprises and of units within them.

Fostering Innovation by Understanding Transition

Assuming the validity of this model for the development of the innovative capacities of a productive unit, how can it be applied to further our capacity for new products and to improve our productivity?

We predict that units in different stages of evolution will respond to differing stimuli and undertake different types of innovation. This idea can readily be extended to the question of barriers to innovation; and probably to patterns of success and failure in innovation for units in different situations. The unmet conditions for transition can be viewed as specific barriers which must be overcome if transition is to take place.

We would expect new, fluid units to view as barriers any factors that impede product standardization and market aggregation, while firms in the opposite category tend to rank uncertainty over government regulation or vulnerability of existing investments as more important disruptive factors.

We believe the most useful insights provided by the model apply to production processes in which features of the products can be varied. The most interesting applications are to situations where product innovation is competitively important and difficult to manage; the model helps to identify the full range of other issues with which the firm is simultaneously confronted in a period of growth and change.

Consistency of Management Action

Many examples of unsuccessful innovations point to a common explanation of failure: certain conditions necessary to support a sought-after technical advance were not present. In such cases our model may be helpful because it describes conditions that normally support advances at each stage of development; accordingly, if we can compare existing conditions with those prescribed by the model we may discover how to increase innovative success. For example, we may ask of the model such questions as these about different, apparently independent, managerial actions:

- Can a firm increase the variety and diversity of its product line while simultaneously realizing the highest possible level of efficiency?
- Is a high rate of product innovation consistent with an effort to substantially reduce costs through extensive backward integration?
- Is government policy to maintain diversified markets for technologically active industries consistent with a policy that seeks a high rate of effective product innovation?
- Would a firm's action to restructure its work environment for employees so that tasks are more challenging and less repetitive be compatible with a policy of mechanization designed to reduce the need for labor?
- Can the government stimulate productivity by forcing a young industry to standardize its products before a dominant design has been realized?

The model prompts an answer of "no" to each of these questions; each question suggests actions which the model tells us are mutually inconsistent. We believe that as these ideas are further developed they can be equally effective in helping to answer many far more subtle questions about the environment for innovation, productivity, and growth.

34. Market Testing: Using the Marketplace as a Laboratory

Alvin A. Achenbaum

Test marketing means different things to managers and researchers. The author examines the worth of market tests as controlled experiments.

To THE RESEARCH-ORIENTED PERSON, the term *market test* has a rather precise meaning. To him, *it is a controlled experiment, done in a limited but carefully selected part of the marketplace, whose aim is to predict the sales or profit consequences, either in absolute or relative terms, of one or more proposed marketing actions.* It is essentially the use of the marketplace as a laboratory and of a direct sales measurement which differentiates this test from other types of market research.

At the other extreme, *market testing* has the very loose meaning of merely *trying something out* in the marketplace. This meaning is commonly held by, although hardly limited to, the self-made businessman.

Of course, between the two extremes of *scientific testing* and *trying something out,* there is room for many different degrees of experimentation. Often, the choice of a market test design between the two extremes is largely governed by the purse strings. Yet, no matter what choice is made, one thing is common to all such tests: the results are used as if they were predictive. Unfortunately, evidence keeps popping up which reveals that market tests done in a traditional manner have another thing in common: predictively, they are not working very well.

No matter which kind of market test is used—the more precise scientific test or the looser, pragmatic trial-and-error one—we can distinguish two fundamental types, each type serving a more or less unique function:

Reprinted in abridged form from the *Handbook of Marketing Research,* Robert Ferber (ed.), pp. 4:31–4:54. © 1974 McGraw-Hill Book Co., Inc. Used by permission.

Alvin A. Achenbaum is Chairman of Canter, Achenbaum, Heekin, Inc., a marketing counseling firm involved in giving advice on a wide diversity of marketing problems, including market testing.

1. The first serves what we might call the *managerial control function*. It permits a company to gain needed information or experience before going into something on a large scale.
2. The second serves what we might call the *predictive research function*. This, like any other decision-oriented method, is supposed to indicate whether an action should or should not be taken.

Market Testing as a Managerial Control Tool

Many managements, faced with a new product or a new process, are often apprehensive—as they should be—about converting their operation to it on a full scale. Everyone recognizes the risks of doing so. For one thing, it is difficult to anticipate all the problems associated with a change. Things occur which cannot be visualized in advance. Then there is the matter of training. Rarely can one be effective or efficient without some experience. And finally, there is the question of being sure that it (if not the whole operation, then at least some of its more important individual parts) will work. Considerations such as these make some kind of experimentation or exploration worth doing. The analogy in manufacturing would be to the establishment of a pilot-plant operation.

Very often, if a market test does nothing else, it can more than justify its cost by merely *serving as a pilot operation for the large-scale marketing activity*. This is particularly true for marketing new products and new brands. Certainly where completely new products are concerned—ones not familiar to consumers—there is reason for management apprehension. But even with new brands in established categories, where innovations may be slight or where the product is new only to the company, there is reason for caution. National marketing is a risky business. There are, for example, many physical problems—of handling, shelf life, breakage, storage, stocking, and shipping—which can turn into costly mistakes if not carefully worked out in advance. Take the case of the prominent manufacturer who tested facial tissue in a smaller, more compact box than his regular one. Fortunately, one of his test markets was in the South. After being on the shelf for one month, many of these boxes exploded at the seams because the tissues absorbed more moisture than the box would allow.

Think of the cost if the marketer went directly national with the new box. Or think what would have happened if it were only product tested and not permitted to sit on shelves for a month or so. Yet until the product is actually sold in the marketplace in a normal manner, it is difficult to anticipate such problems.

Then there are the marketing problems of alternative executions in packaging, in product form, in advertising, in promotion, and in price. Often, without being in the market, research on these elements cannot be done effectively. Frozen food is a good case in point. Because of the way retailers handle this product, *blind* product tests would not be fair unless all the products involved were stored similarly. This would not be possible unless the product were put on the market.

There also is the problem of simply learning the ropes—of finding out firsthand the difficulties of getting distribution, of learning from experience the real price structure, of producing a new commercial, of seeing the actual operation in action. Until one enters the market, such problems cannot be attacked with any degree of confidence.

Finally, there is the matter of not having enough merchandise to supply more than a limited introduction. Under such circumstances, it makes sense to go from market to market, checking progress along the way.

But let us not be under any illusions about market testing used in this manner. Its purpose is to help improve the *mechanics* of the marketing operation, to find out if unanticipated problems in fact exist, to constantly improve one's approach while doing the job on a limited scale. Its purpose is *not* to predict whether a product will be a success or a failure nationally.

Thus when market testing is used for managerial control purposes, we need not worry about developing elaborate experimental designs and conducting store audits for projecting sales. Instead, we should use these pilot introductions to gain experience, to ferret out problems that need correction, and to do the kind of research that will help develop a sound marketing program. The choice of markets is more a matter of convenience than scientific selection. At most, one wants more than one market and considerable geographic dispersal to be sure of testing under the varying circumstances eventually faced in national marketing.

Market Testing as a Predictive Research Tool

While market testing may be both a useful and a desirable managerial control tool, most tests are treated as though they were designed for prediction. The fact that market testing has failed to live up to its potential as a predictive tool has not deterred many from using it in this fashion.

Essentially, market testing has been used as a predictive device in two broad and quite dissimilar situations, (1) the introduction of a new product or brand and (2) the evaluation of alternative marketing variables.

Actually, the methodological requirements for both uses of test marketing are almost identical, with one major exception—testing alternative variables requires a control group. Yet there are other distinctions which should be covered before we get into method.

Market Testing New Products or Brands

In its most widely accepted use, market testing *is considered the predictive aspect of a new product or new brand introduction,* where management not only expects to learn something about how its new product or brand will perform in the marketplace but also hopes to predict the outcome of a national introduction by first testing the introduction in a small area. Different new product situations call for different testing procedures.

The New-Product Category Where There Are No Direct Substitutes. In this case, not only is the company devoid of experience with the product category but it is difficult to rely on the experience of others even if available.

In the consumer goods area, there are very few such situations.

Obviously, for new-product categories, particularly where substitutes are not that similar, the key to product success is consumer acceptability— will it satisfy an overt or latent need better than what is currently available? While product tests and consumer surveys have been used to determine this, they are not predictive since there usually are no standards against which to measure the results. For this reason market testing is usually required. Not only can it serve as a pilot operation but, if done properly, it can permit other forms of research as well as attempt to yield a predictive market result.

The New Brand of an Existing Product Category. This is the most common situation. Here there are a number of different possibilities.

On one continuum, there is the matter of differentiation; some brands are real innovations, that is, quite different from others in the category, either in the way they are made, in the way they are used, or in the needs they can gratify. Others can be "me-toos," identical in almost every way except perhaps for the way they are positioned competitively or the way they are sold. Since close substitutes of the new brand are available, much valuable product research can be done prior to market introduction. Certainly some form of blind product testing is desirable to ascertain if the innovation is more acceptable than or at least on a parity with competitive brands. Too often, marketers use market testing to do what can be done better and cheaper with consumer product testing.

Even with so-called parity brands, where positioning may be crucial, market testing may not be called for immediately. Certainly much can be learned from copy testing to see whether a position is being clearly communicated and whether it has persuasive leverage with the consumer before going to the expense of a market test. But when all this is done and the results are still favorable, a market test may eventually be called for, particularly if the innovation requires a higher price or some different method of shelving, packaging, or distribution.

The other continuum is experience with the product category. Obviously, a marketer with great experience with the brand would be foolish to test market if he is sure from product tests and copy tests that his product is at least on a parity with competition and his copy is understood and persuasive. Yet a situation in this case may call for a market test.

Many times, a marketer has no way of knowing whether his new proposition will pay in terms of the promotional investment he has in mind. A market test—again only if done right—will help predict the consequences. Unfortunately, most payouts for highly promoted items are set for three years. It is, therefore, difficult to make a payout prediction unless a test is run for the full three years, a highly unlikely proposition to say the least.

Recycling an Existing Brand. Some marketers consider a major repositioning or repackaging of a brand or some improvement in an existing brand a basis for market testing before going national. However, unless the change is dramatic or at least readily discernible by the consumer, there would appear little reason for market testing.

While the aforementioned situations essentially deal with market tests of an entire marketing mix, some marketers try to test more than one marketing mix in introducing a new product. In so doing, they are in essence also incorporating the design imperatives of testing alternative variables, which in one very important respect changes the ground rules—it requires some control area.

Testing Alternative Marketing Variables

Market testing's other predictive use is *to evaluate alternative individual marketing variables, strategies, or patterns.* Here we are not concerned with measuring the effect of the total marketing mix but rather a single variable of that mix or, as is often the case, one variable versus another, usually the one in use. For example, market tests are often used to determine the extent to which a new media pattern is better than an existing one, or one distribution method more effective than another, or a higher advertising budget more profitable than a lower one.

Almost any marketing variable—a broad issue of a minor one—is amenable to testing, although it may be more difficult to measure the effect of a minor variable. Most marketing variables are amenable to testing, but the real issues deal with the design of the test—how to design one that can predict a national outcome, whether it is worth the cost, and whether one is exposing oneself to other problems.

Design Methodology

As with any laboratory experiment, three methodological conditions must be met in designing a test market.

1. The experiment or test must be *representative of the whole,* at least to the degree that one wishes to quantitatively project the relationship of the small area to the larger one. This is not merely a matter of spatial representativeness. It is also a matter of choosing a repre-

sentative time period and of doing what one eventually hopes to do in the larger universe.

2. The test must be *carefully controlled.* One must do what is planned and keep extraneous variables from contaminating the test. This is particularly important in testing alternative variables where a control group against which the new element can be compared is necessary.

3. The test must be *accurately measured.* This is a much more complex issue than usually contemplated. For one thing, which type of sales measure should be used—factory shipments, wholesale sales, retail sales, usage, and so forth? Even after accepting a measurement criterion, there is the matter of projecting it to the total. There are many methods for doing this and they often yield different answers. There is also the issue of the base period against which the comparison is to be made, and again there are various approaches.

Test Representativeness

Achieving representativeness in a market test experiment is perhaps the most critical aspect of predictability, particularly in testing a new-product introduction. As indicated, there are a number of elements to representativeness.

1. There is the matter of choosing a sample of markets, both in terms of the number and their dispersion, that are truly reflective of the total universe involved—usually the continental United States. The sample must be large and random enough to reflect the heterogeneity of the universe being measured. As in any sampling problem, the more heterogeneous the population, the bigger the sample required. These differences affect consumer behavior in countless ways, and they also affect the way goods are distributed and promotion is communicated. This heterogeneity led many market tests to go awry. Before long, those with experience recognized the need to do things differently. At first, there were attempts to increase the size of the sample, either by increasing the number of markets or increasing the size of the individual test area. Typically, three or four test cities were used or some larger area, like a sales region or Nielsen area, was chosen. Some would even use an area as large as New England or the West Coast. While these larger areas were often 6 to 10 percent of the United States, they were not truly representative, so that the problem was really not eliminated.

Another approach was to match the test area with the control area. This was usually done on the basis of demographic information—income, home ownership, age distribution, share of market, and so on. Yet it soon became abundantly clear that even matching would not do.

It was in reality not a matter of which city or cities were chosen, for there is no such thing as a small group of cities or a large region being representative of the United States. Nothing has been more detrimental to the development of sound test-market design than the publication in our trade press of lists of cities widely used in market tests. It was as if use of these cities made them representative of the United States.

2. There is the question of a representative time period. The marketplace is not static. It changes not only with respect to season but also changes over time in terms of market communications, competitive responses, and so on. For example, once a competitor knows that a market is being used to test a new product or an important marketing variable, he may react in a number of ways. He can obviously ignore it until the test marketer goes national and then react. This, of course, could easily distort the prediction, particularly if his reaction is effective. Or he might try to distort the test by some immediate, gross action in the test market itself. This is often done deliberately so that the test marketer cannot make an accurate prediction, usually with the hope that the new product or test alternative will be killed. Finally, the competitor can react normally to find out for himself what to expect. In any case, unless the test is run long enough to see what will happen, it can hardly be a reflection of what is to come.

More and more marketers are realizing the necessity of covering all the situations that time will allow in a market test—seasonal fluctuations, communication cycles, and competitive reactions. They are also recognizing that unless a test is run for a substantial time, they will not be giving consumers enough time to buy the product again. Because sales efforts are not effective immediately, the sales curve at the beginning of a test market usually represents only the initial trial of a product. After a while, depending on the use rate of the product, the sales curve begins to reflect continued trial plus repeat purchases. As so many packaged goods marketers have learned to their sorrow, until they know what proportion of the consumers will buy the brand again, they do not have an accurate picture of possible future sales.

3. There is the matter of keeping the test variable representative of future reality. The purpose of a predictive test is to see if what is done in the small will work in the large. Accordingly, good test-market practice would suggest translating every anticipated national action as realistically as possible in the test market. Thus distribution should be obtained exactly as desired normally. Nothing special should be done to get the product into stores. Moreover, all promotion and advertising budgets should be economically realistic. Prices and discount structure should also be as planned nationally.

Test Control

Test control is of particular importance in testing alternative variables. Traditionally, variation has been dealt with in one of three ways: by ignoring it, by attempting to match markets, or by using the statistical principles of experimental design. None of these has proved especially effective to date, although the latter offers some hope. Obviously, ignoring the influences of the exogenous factors is ludicrous.

The second approach—matching markets—is usually impractical. Attempting to match markets on as few as 4 variables (it is easy to list 20 which might be pertinent) can exhaust a list of even 200 markets. Besides, one really does not know in advance the truly pertinent variables for matching purposes.

Even the third approach—the use of sophisticated experimental designs—is not an automatic guarantee of success. Three or four markets do not permit true randomization. As already pointed out, markets in the United States are much too different from each other for three or four to be representative of the whole. Moreover, what does one do about the truly unique ones like New York, Chicago, and Los Angeles? Thus, test results often show a high level of random variation, and statistical significance of any but tremendous differences in performance is difficult to detect. Yet, of the three approaches, randomization must remain our best hope.

Test Measurement

No matter how well one designs an experiment and controls its implementation, without a relevant and accurate measurement of the test market, one will fail to predict what will happen in the larger universe. Test-market measurement and projection present complex problems.

One problem is the measurement criterion—the so-called dependent variable. By definition, the measurement criterion is some reflection of sales, of which there are many—manufacturer sales, wholesale sales, or retail sales. The two latter measures usually must be obtained from special audits, such as Nielsen, or some tailor-made survey of retail outlets.

Sometimes share-of-market measures can be obtained from which sales can then be calculated. This approach also requires some special auditing procedure. Some advocate consumer usage data derived from consumer surveys or panels. It is only from such surveys or panels that the distinction between trial and repeat usage, about the future, can be made. Moreover, some products are sold in outlets not covered by syndicated audits. An accurate prediction requires covering their sales too, and survey data are often the only way to do so.

There are, of course, situations—particularly in testing a single marketing variable—where sales are not the most accurate criterion of the effect of a variable. For example, in testing two different media alternatives, differences in brand or advertising awareness may be more pertinent criteria of effectiveness than sales. From a diagnostic point of view, they are probably correct, but if market tests are to be truly meaningful, they must eventually be translated into sales.

Finally, a good case can be made—especially when we are concerned with the economic feasibility of a new-product introduction—for using anticipated profits as the basic criterion of test effectiveness. To do this obviously requires sales (revenue) estimates and accurate cost figures.

The second issue in measurement is the choice of base period against which the measurements are to be made. Normally there are two choices—comparing the results to the same time period one year before or to the last previous time period before the test began. Because seasonal factors are almost always present, the best practice is to use the same period of the previous year. Needless to say, this requires substantial back data. Moreover, even this practice does not take into account longer trend values. If product-category sales are tending up or down at a somewhat inordinate rate, one must almost always choose a control area to take this trend into account; the difference between the test area and the control area prior to injection of the test variable must be discounted from results during the test period.

Finally, consideration must be given to the method of projecting the measurement criterion to the larger universe. These methods of projection vary from those that are very simple to those that are quite complex. Five basic techniques have been isolated by Davis.

1. *Projection of brand share:* This method involves taking a brand-share figure in the test market and applying the same figure to the larger universe by multiplying it by the known national product category sales level.

2. *Projection of sales per head:* Here one calculates actual sales (retail) per capita and multiplies it by the known population of the larger area. It assumes that the rate of usage for the population in the test area also obtains in the larger universe.

3. *Projection of purchasing power:* Since there are many product categories whose distribution by area is not directly proportional to population, some index of purchasing power—*Sales Management* magazine's BPI (Buying Power Index) is a good example—such as disposable personal income or retail sales is used, and one multiplies the reciprocal of the proportion of purchasing power in the test area over purchasing power in the nation by absolute sales in the test area to obtain the national estimate.

4. *Projection using a known brand:* Many times a company is selling a brand similar to the one it is market testing. Rather than using the absolute figures found in the test market, it may use the ratio of test-market sales of its test brand to the test-market sales of its established brand. This ratio is then multiplied by the total factory sales of the nontest brand. This permits the manufacturer to eliminate possible errors in projection resulting from distribution chan-

nels. However, the technique makes no sense if there is no meaningful relationship between the two brands.

5. *Projection using market segments:* This is probably the most complex approach, although it offers the best hope for accuracy. Essentially, the method involves getting either brand share, per capita sales, or retail turnover rates by subunits or segments within the market for which data are also available in the larger universe.

It is difficult to say which of these different projection methods is best, since they often yield somewhat different results. Two approaches to making a choice are worth considering. The first is using as many methods as possible. If the results are similar, there is some reason to be more optimistic about the prediction. The other alternative is to "backcast" as many methods as possible to see which replicates the past best and to use that one for forecasting the future.

Cost and Other Considerations

A number of factors affect the cost of a market test. The two most important are the cost of marketing for advertising, personal selling, and promotion and the cost of measurement. Obviously, the more markets used and the greater their dispersion, the greater the cost of marketing. This is also the case with measurement, particularly where special audits and surveys are required.

There are also other costs. In new-product introductions, there is the cost of producing the merchandise—much of which may never get sold—inefficiently, and the cost of administering the test. The latter represents the opportunity costs involved in spending management's time on the market test as opposed to spending it in running the established business.

The size and scope of a market test should be determined by comparing the risk of not testing against the risk of not getting a decisive result. Davis suggests that much can be done by preanalyses of the probabilities of success and failure. In doing so, one must consider not only out-of-pocket expenditures but pull-out costs as well—the net loss if one must abort a test prematurely.

Considering how difficult and expensive it is to obtain a decisive result, would we not be better off testing fewer products more accurately than testing a great many with little chance of success? It would seem wiser to spend more money in screening products by doing situation analyses and by conducting need/satisfaction studies, product tests, and copy tests before subjecting a product to market test. Many ideas and products would never reach a market test if this were done, but when they did succeed, a company would be able to afford a larger-scale operation, one which might at least offer some probability of projectability.

With regard to alternative variables, it is a rare marketing variable other than a major change in advertising or promotion budget that is worth the cost of a well-executed market test. Yet, if one is called for, the change should at least be large enough so that the effects will overcome the "noise" in the marketplace. Again, one should consider fewer tests in the hope of doing them better.

Another major issue that usually arises in market testing is *confidentiality*—letting the competition know too far in advance what is contemplated. To some degree, if the plan is easy to copy and of great prima facie value, competition may well try to reach the marketplace first.

Any way this issue is viewed, it should not prevent market testing for fear of competitive reaction. In fact, if competitors stay out, a projectable result is less likely. Probably the silliest thing is to try to distort someone else's test. If anything, the most intelligent response is to compete in a realistic manner and to track the results.

New Approaches to Market Test Design

So far, only two truly novel approaches to market test design have been developed which meet the criteria of projectability and which may still be practical. Since they have not been widely used, it is difficult to say that they will work. Yet they do offer hope. In addition, there is a third approach which, while not predictive of the total, may still be worthy of consideration for new-product introductions because it reduces risk without a national introduction.

The Checkerboard Design Test[1]

Conceptually, this method is simple; it is in a sense a practical extension of the grid approach to sampling populations. Without going into detail here, it requires, (1) dividing the universe into two or more equal but randomly selected groups of markets; (2) injecting basically opposite or different marketing patterns in each group of markets; and (3) measuring sales results in each using special tabulations of a readily available national survey or syndicated retail auditing service. Standard television areas (there are 192 well-defined, relatively mutually exclusive ones in the United States) are the basic market areas.

On logic alone, the assets of the checkerboard test design would appear to be great; in almost every way it overcomes the basic shortcomings of traditional market tests. First, it comes as close as possible to being a representative test. Certainly with a two- or three-group test it is inconceivable that each group alone would not come extremely close to being representative of the nation. The sample is not only large but systematically dispersed in a random fashion. Moreover, it can be run for as long as

---

[1] This technique was developed jointly by the author, Harold Miller, and Lawrence Deckinger while at Grey Advertising in 1965.

necessary to cover seasonal variations. In addition, by its very size, the design requires the test variable to be used in a typical fashion.

Unlike the traditional market test, the checkerboard test is easy to control. Nothing need be done other than carefully implementing the plan. The random nature of the sample is theoretically designed to eliminate the effect of extraneous variables. With such a broad variety of markets in each test group, unique influences are unlikely to affect the results, nor could a competitor easily figure out how to distort it.

In terms of measurement, nothing could be easier for a company already receiving syndicated sales data or doing standard tracking studies. No supplemental samples are required, only special tabulations of the same random groups. Nor can it be criticized as impractical. It is flexible enough to implement broadly. It is even unlikely that marketing exigencies could upset the test. There are almost no measurement costs; only the cost of special tabulations.

A problem does, however, exist—risk—though in many cases it is more apparent than real. Obviously a test over such a broad area of the country does entail taking a big chance. Nevertheless, for many variables, this is an unreal risk. For example, consider the three-group expenditure test previously mentioned. No advertiser knows if his current level of expenditure is best. Yet if an advertiser tested the three alternatives, his sales might suffer if one of the other alternatives were unsound.

The checkerboard design has wide application. It can be used to test different creative strategies, distribution systems, promotions, prices, and personal selling approaches as long as the marketer can control these locally. It can also be used to test new-product introductions, although it is vulnerable to many of the cost and practical problems associated with large-scale, dispersed, traditional market tests.

The Marketing Model Design

A marketing model normally attempts to describe the process by which a market operates and how, by manipulating the factors which determine the process (such as advertising, price, distribution, and so on), a company can affect the final level of sales and profitability. Such a model will not merely reveal the relationship of the factors in the process but also indicate the magnitude of each factor's influence. These factors can then be expressed in some form of mathematical equation. In a sense, a model, if good, should allow one to change one variable and ascertain the net effect based on how the others will react. Knowing this permits the use of marketing models in two ways as market testing techniques. One is to obtain pretest data from the marketplace and use them in a computer simulation of the model.

Needless to say, such a prediction, if accurate, is a breakthrough in marketing experimentation. Work by Erhenberg also suggests that it works. The second approach is one developed by E. J. Davis. He suggests using a traditional test market, but instead of using the raw data as results, he injects the results into a marketing model. In doing so, the known changes in the test market on all variables in the model are also applied to the model for the industry, thereby adjusting them in accordance with the known national model. The adjusted results are then projected to national levels.

Needless to say, if either of these techniques works, many of the practical problems which have plagued market testing would be obviated. They, therefore, deserve further exploration and experimentation. They certainly offer greater hope than the traditional market tests which remain so prevalent even in the face of continued failure.

Preemptive Limited Introductions

This approach, one may quibble, is not projectable. Yet, it has experimental merit beyond the pilot-test concept for introducing a new brand. It essentially involves picking the top five markets—New York, Los Angeles, Chicago, Philadelphia, and Boston in the United States (they represent approximately 25 percent of the total population)—and introducing the new brand in them. Since they are large and broadly dispersed, they can give a strong indication whether the brand will succeed economically, for the fact is that no basic product can be a national success unless it does well in these five markets. Moreover, if it is economical, one can then expand into the next 20 markets, representing slightly more than 25 percent of the United States, and so on until national distribution is achieved.

The point is simple. The initial risk is only 25 percent of going national. While large, it is still much smaller than going national. Yet it is a preemptive move, easy to measure, and probably capable of control.

Other Approaches to Market Testing

One cannot review market testing methodology without discussing other suggested approaches, some of which do not seem very promising.

Mini-Market Tests

Perhaps the most widely heralded recent approach is the mini-market test. Essentially, a mini-market test is conducted in a very small area. Its popularity relates to new-product introduction. It is not seriously suggested for testing alternative marketing variables.

The major reason for its popularity would appear to be its low cost and the speed with which results can be obtained. There seems to be an assumption among those who use mini-market tests that the way to new-product success is to roll the dice often; in that way a winner is bound to show up sooner or later. Evidently, the theory goes, many cheaper tests are better than a few good ones, since a good product will eventually show through. Yet in light of what we have said about designing a predictive market test, one would have to consider mini-market testing unadulterated nonsense. It cannot possibly have predictive capability except by pure coincidence. It is not representative in any way, being limited to one market, nor is a mini-market test typical of reality. Although many measures are usually obtained, it is hard to see how such tests can project to the United States, considering the sample they start with.

In-Store Tests

This is almost always used for measuring an alternative marketing variable rather than a new-product introduction—usually for testing a revised package or a different price on an established brand.

When this is done well, the stores within a market are usually randomly split into two groups, with one approach put into one group and the other approach into the second group. To eliminate extraneous differences between the two groups from distorting the test, the variables are crossed over every month. To really work, tests must be carefully controlled.

Most of the time, the tests are made in one market or at most in a few markets. The assumption is that the between-city variation is less than the within-city variation. If so, the test may yield a decisive result, particularly when properly handled. It has been used effectively for checking whether a variable which does not need advertising or promotion (some action outside the store) is uneconomic. If in-store tests were done in a number of places and if similar results were obtained, one could feel more secure in moving forward on a larger scale even if the results were not perfectly projectable. Yet, because its value is only where an in-store variable is testable, its usefulness is limited.

CATV Labs

The use of CATV (Community Antenna Television) for market testing began when split cables were installed in a city in such a way that two randomly matched groups could be reached by television.

In the CATV approach, since the matching is home to home, distribution is not controlled. Measurements have to be by consumer panels or surveys. Tests can be of only two alternatives at any one time.

Like the in-store test, the assumption—particularly where only one city is involved, which has been the case so far—is that the within-city variation is greater than the between-city variation. There is a question of the validity of this assumption with respect to promotion. Evidence to date would suggest that the between-city variation is high.

In any case, it has limited value, being usable for testing advertising variables only. Yet the CATV idea should not be discarded too quickly. Someday CATV systems may cover most of the United States. When they do, representativeness may be possible. Since they offer tremendous control of media, they could be an excellent market testing vehicle.

A Few Final Points

Three additional points are worth mentioning. First, what has been discussed applies essentially to consumer products. Industrial product markets are usually not geographically dispersed or defined. Thus it is almost always impossible to use the market as a laboratory. Of course, to the degree that analogous situations might be found, the same principles of test design would still apply.

Second, it should not be inferred that the type of test one designs or uses is an either-or proposition. There may be reason to use the marketplace for pilot testing and to continue with such a test even when a bigger, predictive test is possible. Each type of use has its own design imperatives.

Finally, it is hoped that the desirability of more basic market research prior to test marketing was clearly communicated. Too much emphasis—both in time and money—is placed on market testing and too little on premarket test research. If more premarket test research were done, fewer market tests would be necessary, therefore permitting companies to do better market tests when required.

References

ACHENBAUM, A. A., "The Purpose of Market Testing," *Proceedings of the Forty-seventh National Conference of the American Marketing Association,* Chicago, June 1964.

DAVIS, E. J., *Experimental Marketing,* London: New Company, 1970.

EHRENBERG, A. S. C., "Predicting the Performance of New Brands," *Journal of Advertising Research,* vol. 11, December 1971.

GREEN, P. E., R. E. FRANK, and P. J. ROBINSON, "Cluster Analysis in Test Market Selection," *Management Science,* vol. 13, April 1967.

KROEGER, A., "Test Marketing: The Concept and How It Is Unique," *Media/ Scope,* December 1966.

35. Bayesian Statistics and Product Decisions

Paul E. Green

Bayesian decision theory can be very useful for making choices under conditions of uncertainty. This article discusses its application to new product decisions with special reference to the determination of the cost and value of additional research.

THE PURPOSE OF THIS ARTICLE is to show the relevance of the Bayesian approach to product development decision-making. More specifically, we shall illustrate how these techniques can be used to help answer two persistent questions related to each stage in the development of a new product:

1. Should we make a decision *now* (with respect to passing a product along to the next development stage vs. terminating the project), or should we *delay* this decision until some future date, pending the receipt of additional information regarding the new product's chances for commercial success?
2. Given a decision on *when* to make the decision, *what* action ("go" vs. "stop") should we take?

The power of the Bayesian approach as applied to these basic questions is described in two parts. First, we shall review the nature of the costs associated with moving too slowly vs. too quickly through the product development process. Second, an illustrative case will show how these groups of costs can be introduced within a Bayesian framework to guide both the "when to" and "what to do" classes of decisions.

Reprinted from *Business Horizons*, 5 (Fall, 1962), pp. 101–109. © 1962 by the Foundation for the School of Business at Indiana University. Used by permission.

Paul Green is S. S. Kresge Professor of Marketing at the Wharton School of the University of Pennsylvania.

Time-related Costs

The ultracautious decision maker tends to incur sizable costs when he delays each development decision until he has assembled enough information to make the choice patently clear. These costs are partly associated with time and partly associated with the cost of the information gathering activity itself (which also takes time to accomplish).

An illustration should make clear the nature of these time-related costs. Assume that a new chemical product has reached the development stage where the company must either (1) decide now whether to construct a semiworks unit or to terminate the project, or (2) delay, pending the receipt of additional information regarding the anticipated outcomes associated with the alternative to proceed. Apart from sunk costs (that is, historical costs, not relevant from an economic standpoint), termination at this point would result in a payoff of zero. The decision to proceed, however, is related to a series of future decisions up to and including commercialization before a positive payoff could be forthcoming. From the standpoint of delay, the decision maker should be concerned with how these conditional payoffs would be expected to change between now and some future time for viewing the same set of choices that he presently faces. Moreover, in multistage decisions, a present commitment does not demand that the project be continued in subsequent periods, should later information suggest termination.

If the decision maker decided to delay his choice, pending the receipt of additional information, it should be clear that at least three groups of costs can be associated with delay. First, as a function of delay time, the present value of all future revenues attendant with commercialization would be reduced as a consequence of delaying the start of the receipt of these revenues until a more distant time. This type of delay cost merely gives recognition to the time value of money.

Second, also as a function of delay time, the present value of all future revenues attendant with commercialization could be lowered as a consequence of the increased risk of competitive imitation or supersedure of the product (at the hands of competitors or conceivably of a future product of the decision maker's own research organization).

Finally, gathering the information obviously costs money and incurs time for its development. If one assumes some linear relationship of money spent for information with the period required to obtain the information, then this cost also can be associated with the time variable.

Certain implications obviously stem from the preceding listing of delay costs. If required target rates of return are low (that is, a low opportunity cost of the company's capital exists), and/or the threat of competitive retaliation is low, and/or the costs of data gathering are low, a relatively small penalty is attached to delay. Conversely, when these costs are high, a larger penalty is attached to the delay option.

On the other side of the coin, an impatient decision maker who eliminates or gives short shrift to vital steps of information gathering runs the risk of incurring sizable costs associated with acting under a high degree of uncertainty (and perhaps costs associated with "crashing" the program, that is, telescoping development steps, as well). The behavior of these groups of costs can be viewed as a function of time, which, in turn, is a function of the amount of information collected.

Thus, the decision maker must view the change in payoff associated with the go vs. no-go decision now vs. the payoff associated with delay of this decision, pending receipt of additional data. Why collect additional data at all? Additional data would be collected for the purpose of reducing the variance associated with the estimated distribution of payoffs related to acting now. A simple example should clarify this concept.

If the option to build the semiworks now is a "sure thing," that is, no matter what information that could conceivably be developed on, say, potential sales, could change the decision, then it is obvious that additional information (cost-free or not) is irrelevant. On a more realistic basis, however, some potential sales levels (say, zero sales) would obviously favor the option of no-go. The essence of this concept can be expressed in Bayesian terms as the expected cost associated with acting under uncertainty.[1] That is, the difference in payoff between taking the best act now (in the light of current uncertainties) and taking the best act under perfect information about future events represents the expected value of perfect information; and, hence, the upper limit that the decision maker should spend for additional information if it could be collected immediately and would be without error.

Other things equal, it is clear that when the costs of uncertainty are large the decision maker could suffer by moving too rapidly to the next stage of the development process. On the other hand, if the costs of wrong decisions are low, he should move rapidly.

It is thus implied that gathering additional information would at least reduce, if not eliminate, the cost of uncertainty; otherwise the information would not be gathered. It is further implied that time and money would be spent on the information gathering activity until the sum of the expected costs associated with information collection and delay and the expected costs of acting under uncertainty was minimal. Otherwise, a shorter or longer delay period would produce lower expected total costs. Figure 1 represents conceptually the behavior of the costs associated with moving too slowly vs. moving too quickly with respect to some stage in the development of a new product.

[1] The adjective "expected" is applied here in the usual statistical sense. That is, expected costs are weighted averages found by multiplying each admissible cost by the probability of incurring it and then adding these products. The weights (probabilities) sum to unity.

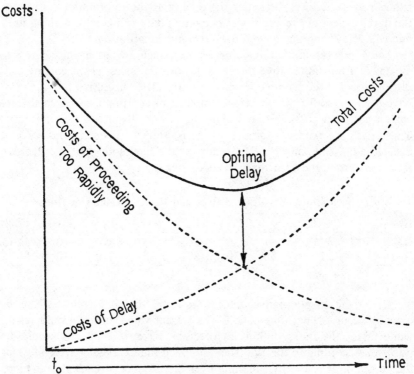

FIGURE 1. **Behavior of Total Costs: Proceeding Too Rapidly vs. Too Slowly**

Applying Bayesian Theory

While the preceding remarks have focused on the nature of the costs associated with moving too quickly vs. too slowly at any stage in the development process, we must still illustrate how Bayesian decision theory utilizes these costs to provide a rationale for answering both the "when to" and "what to do" questions. The following example is deliberately simplified to deal with the simplest of cases, a one-stage choice.

Assume that a point has been reached in the development of a new product regarding whether or not a semiworks should be constructed now vs. delaying this decision (pending receipt of further market information). To be more explicit, three options will be considered:

1. Build a semiworks vs. terminate project now
2. Delay this decision until one period (year) into the future
3. Delay this decision until two periods (years) into the future.

Options 2 and 3 imply, of course, that better marketing information than now exists could be secured over the next year or two and that the more extensive this inquiry, the better the quality of the information. However, the development of the additional marketing data will cost something itself and will delay subsequent steps toward commercialization.

Some present marketing information, which is rather imprecise, indicates that four alternative forecasts of potential sales, given commercialization, bracket the possible levels of future sales. Subjective probabilities[2] have been stated for the occurrence of each forecast and, given each forecast, it has been possible to calculate the payoff, given commercialization. These data are noted in table 1 where F_1 stands for each sales forecast deemed admissible and $P(F_1)$ stands for the likelihood that the decision maker assigns to the occurrence of each forecast.

TABLE 1. Conditional Payoffs and Expected Values (Millions of Dollars)

Acts	F_1	$P(F_1)$	F_2	$P(F_2)$	F_3	$P(F_3)$	F_4	$P(F_4)$	EP
Go	−$12	.15	−$1	.30	$5	.45	$10	.10	$1.15
No-go	$ 0	.15	$0	.30	$0	.45	$ 0	.10	$ 0

Under the go alternative, table 1 indicates that if forecasts F_1 or F_2 actually occurred, negative payoffs (in present value terms) would result, while under the more optimistic forecasts, F_3 or F_4, payoffs would be positive. According to the Bayesian approach the expected payoff (EP) of the go option is found by summing over the product of each payoff times its probability. The present value of future returns of the no-go alternative (termination) is, of course, zero.[3] In this oversimplified problem situation, the decision maker—in the absence of the opportunity to collect additional market information—would go with the project, that is, construct the semi-works. The expected payoff associated with this alternative is $1.15 million.

More realistically, however, the decision maker frequently has the option of delaying his decision pending the receipt of additional data regarding the occurrence of the alternative sales forecasts. These additional data will cost something to collect, delay construction time, and rarely, if ever, be perfectly reliable.

[2] The term subjective probability refers to the degree of belief the decision maker wishes to assign to the occurrence of each admissible event. This degree of belief is expressed numerically along a scale ranging from zero to one and reflects the experienced judgments of the decision maker. All weights are assigned so as to obey the postulates of probability theory.

[3] A project payoff of zero, on a present value basis, would imply that the project's cash flow back (over its anticipated life) would just be sufficient to pay back all cash outlays and to earn some net rate of return, say 10 percent, on the present value of those outlays. Adoption of the no-go alternative thus assumes that other projects exist that could just earn this return; an opportunity cost concept is involved here.

One-Year Delay Option

We shall first consider the one-year delay option.[4] For purposes of illustration we will assume that a delay of one year in construction would have the following results: (1) the cost of delayed revenues amounts to payoffs that are only 91 percent of the former payoff (interest rate equal to 10 percent annually); (2) the firm's market share would drop from 100 percent, under the no-delay case, to 75 percent because of the resulting greater lead time for competitive imitation; and (3) the cost of collecting additional information concerning future sales would be $150,000. However, information obtained at this early stage of development is assumed to be only 70 percent reliable. That is, if the market survey results indicate f_1 (namely, that forecast F_1 will occur), there is a 30 percent chance that this information could have been assembled if the true underlying sales potential were not F_1 but really F_2, F_3, or F_4.

All of the assumptions of our simple expository case can be summarized in figure 2, which should be examined by working from right to left. To illustrate, the upper branch (do not delay) summarizes the results of table 1. The conditional payoffs under each forecast, given go, are −$12 million, −$1 million, $5 million, and $10 million. Multiplying these payoffs by their respective probabilities and summing the results yields, of course, the expected payoff of $1.15 million. Since this is clearly higher than the $0 associated with no-go, this latter alternative is blocked off, and the best alternative, *given no delay,* is go.

However, the second main branch of the tree is still to be evaluated. The conditional payoffs, −$10.91 million, −$0.91 million, $3.41 million, and $6.82 million at the extreme right of the lower branch, reflect the penalties associated with (1) the discount penalty for delay and (2) the effect on the firm's market share due to delay if the product were successful (see author's note).

Notice that several sets of new probabilities appear along the subbranches of the lower main branch of figure 2. These probabilities are

---

[4] Although not explicitly shown above, it is relevant to note that the expected value of perfect information (EVPI) is $2.10 million. As mentioned earlier, this provides an upper limit on funds that could be spent on the collection of additional data, which could be collected immediately and would forecast perfectly which event would actually occur. To obtain EVPI, subtract the expected payoff of the best act in the light of current uncertainties from the expectation of the payoffs associated with the best acts (given the actual occurrence of each event):

EVPI = [.15 ($0 million) + .30 ($0 million) + .45 ($5 million) + .10 ($10 million)]
    −$1.15 million

The result is $3.25 million − $1.15 million, or $2.10 million.

This calculation may be interpreted as follows. If the decision maker could purchase a "perfect" forecasting device that would tell him which event would actually occur, it is clear that before the purchase he must still apply his prior probabilities as to which event the device would indicate; he would then be able to take the best act associated with the event specified.

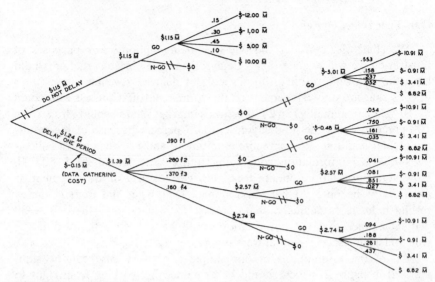

FIGURE 2. Build Semiworks: Terminate Project Now vs. One-Period Delay

derived by application of Bayes's theorem, a central tenet of this approach. We shall need to compute marginal, joint, and posterior probabilities. Their meaning will be made clear in the computations to follow.

First we consider the calculation of the *marginal* probabilities, .190, .280, .370, and .160 appearing beside the market survey results f_1, f_2, f_3, and f_4, respectively. These calculations are shown in table 2. The cell entries represent joint probabilities (the probability assigned to the joint occurrence of each survey result f_i and each underlying event F_i). For example, the joint probability of survey result f_1 and event F_1 occurring is found, under the oversimplified assumptions of our problem, by multiplying the conditional probability, $P(f_1|F_1)$, by the prior probability, $P(F_1)$, which the decision maker assigned to F_1; $.70 \times .15 = .105$. The conditional probability of observing survey result f_1, given the fact that the true underlying forecast is F_2, is assumed equal to .10. (Similarly, for sake of simplic-

TABLE 2. Marginal and Joint Probabilities Under the One-Period Delay Option

Survey Results	Joint Probabilities				Marginal Probabilities
	F_1	F_2	F_3	F_4	
f_1	.105	.030	.045	.010	.190
f_2	.015	.210	.045	.010	.280
f_3	.015	.030	.315	.010	.370
f_4	.015	.030	.045	.070	.160
	.150	.300	.450	.100	1.000

ity, the probability of obtaining the survey result f_1 if the true forecast is F_3 or F_4 is also assumed to be .10.) Hence the joint probability of survey result f_1 and event F_2 occurring is, by way of illustration, $P\ (f_1|F_2) \cdot P\ (F_2) = .10 \times .30 = .030$ as shown in the second column of row f_1. The other cell entries are computed analogously.

The *marginal probabilities* f_1, f_2, f_3, and f_4 are then found by merely summing over the column entries for each row—$P\ (f_1) = P\ (f_1$ and $F_1)$ $+ P\ (f_1$ and $F_2) + P\ (f_1$ and $F_3) + P\ (f_1$ and $F_4)$ or $.190 = .105 + .030 + .045 + .010$. Also note that the marginal probabilities, found by summing over rows for each column F_i, are simply the prior probabilities that the decision maker had originally assigned to the occurrence of these four events.

We can next proceed to the calculation of the *posterior probabilities, $P\ (F_i|f_i)$,* and to a brief description of how Bayes's theorem can be used to derive them. These calculations are shown in table 3.

Table 3 can be explained as follows: Under the assumptions of our problem it was noted that each survey result was deemed to be only 70 percent reliable in correctly "calling" the event assumed to be most strongly associated with it. Suppose, however, that we really did observe a particular survey result, say f_1. Under our assumptions it is more likely that event F_1 "caused" this specific result than events F_2, F_3, or F_4. Still, the other events could have caused this result. We would like to reason backward, so to speak, in order to determine how likely it is that F_1 was the underlying event, now to determine how likely it is that F_1 was the underlying event, now knowing that f_1 has occurred.

Given that we have observed f_1, it is clear that only the joint probabilities along row one of table 2 are now relevant. We would next wish to partition the total (marginal) probability associated with f_1 (.190) among the four events, F_1, F_2, F_3, or F_4, which could have produced this survey result. Hence the first row of table 3 is derived by merely dividing each entry in table 2 (.105, .030, .045, and .010) by the marginal probability (.190) associated with f_1. In summary, *before* observing f_1 we would have assigned the prior probabilities, .15, .30, .45, and .10 to events F_1, F_2, F_3, and F_4, respectively. *After* having observed f_1 we would then revise these probabilities to .553, .158, .237, and .052, respectively,

TABLE 3. Posterior Probabilities Under the One-Period Delay Option

Survey Results	Posterior Probabilities				
	F_1	F_2	F_3	F_4	*Total*
f_1	.553	.158	.237	.052	1.000
f_2	.054	.750	.161	.035	1.000
f_3	.041	.081	.851	.027	1.000
f_4	.094	.188	.281	.437	1.000

so as to reflect the fact that the observance of f_1 was deemed more likely under F_1 than under F_2, F_3, or F_4. Analogous considerations apply to the calculation of posterior probabilities shown in the remaining rows of table 3.

Bayes's theorem formalizes this notion in terms of the following formula:

$$P\ (F_i|f) = \frac{P\ (f|F_i) \cdot P\ (F_i)}{\sum\limits_{j=1}^{n}\ P\ (f|F_j) \cdot P\ (F_j)}$$

In terms of our problem, the posterior probability assigned to, say, event F_1, given that survey result f_1 was observed, is:

$$P\ (F_1|f_1) = \frac{.105}{.105 + .030 + .045 + .010}$$

$$= \frac{.105}{.190} = .553$$

The appropriate marginal and posterior probabilities (as derived in tables 2 and 3) appear along the subbranches of the lower main branch in the tree diagram of figure 2. We can now proceed to discuss which act we would choose, given the occurrence of each admissible survey result:

If the market survey information indicates f_1 (that forecast F_1 is the best estimate), then, as noted earlier, some probability exists that this survey information could have been developed if the true underlying sales forecast were not F_1 but F_2, F_3, F_4. If f_1 is observed however, the best action to be taken after the survey is no-go—terminate the project. Hence, the go alternative branching from f_1 is blocked off. Similar results pertain to survey results f_2. Under survey results f_3 and f_4, however, the resulting best action is to build the semiworks. On an expected payoff basis, collecting the additional information produces a gross payoff of $1.39 million. From this gross figure must be subtracted the $0.15 million cost of collecting the information, yielding an expected payoff of $1.24 million associated with the one-year delay option.

The power of this technique is found in the recursive nature of solution. That is, the two payoffs, $1.24 million and $1.15 million, *summarize completely the whole series of moves along the decision tree.* Moves have been optimally planned from this point forward by, in effect, solving the problem backward. Thus, the decision maker is assured that the best decision now (which happens to be delay one period) has been derived by considering the relationship of this decision to the future decisions that the decision maker visualizes.

Two-Year Delay Option

We now consider the third option: delaying the decision pending a two-year inquiry into the sales potential of the product, in this case we will assume that: (1) cost of deferred revenues amounts to payoffs that are only 83 percent of the payoffs under the no-delay case; (2) the anticipated market share would drop to only 50 percent of the market; (3) market survey costs increase to $300,000; but (4) the reliability of the resultant information increases to 90 percent.

Figure 3 summarizes this second analysis. The upper main branch of the decision tree, covering the no-delay case, is exactly the same as that in figure 2. All payoffs and probabilities in the lower main branch, however, are adjusted in accordance with the changed assumptions just enumerated by developing tables analogous to tables 2 and 3. Solution of the problem again proceeds from right to left, always choosing the best alternative for each subbranch of the tree.

The upshot of this analysis is that the two-year delay option produces a lower expected payoff than the no-delay option. In other words, the costs associated with delaying the venture more than outweigh the gains expected through increased reliability of the sales information. For this reason the lower branch of the tree is blocked off in figure 3.

In summary, it has been shown, via the preceding simplified examples, how costs associated with delay can be balanced against the costs associated with the higher costs of uncertainty related to moving a development along too quickly.

FIGURE 3.   Build Semiworks: Terminate Project Now vs. Two-Period Delay

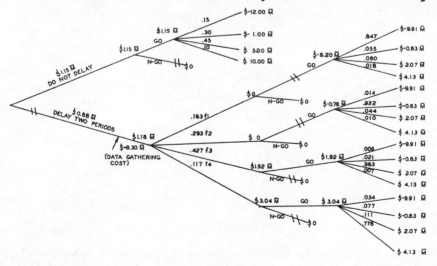

The preceding illustrative case has touched upon some aspects of Bayesian decision theory but has by no means exhausted the many facets of this approach.[5] As could be inferred from our preceding example the Bayesian approach to decision making under uncertainty provides a framework for explicitly working with the economic costs of alternative courses of action, the prior knowledge or judgments of the decision maker regarding the occurrence of states of nature affecting payoffs, and the conditional probabilities of observing specific events, given each state of nature.

[5] A full and lucid description of these features can be found in Robert Schlaifer, *Probability and Statistics for Business Decisions* (New York: McGraw-Hill, 1959).

B.

Commercialization

COMMERCIALIZATION is the last phase of the product innovation process. At this point a successfully developed and tested product is introduced on a full-scale basis to the entire market. This introduction must be carefully planned, with special reference to the response characteristics of potential buyers and competitors. Brown, in an interesting piece, makes a strong case for the use of life-cycle costing in designing as well as promoting capital goods; this approach is sure to ascend in importance as maintenance and operating costs continue to increase relative to the initial capital outlays. Engel *et al.* and Webster look at new product introductions from the other end of the telescope—i.e., how individual consumers and industrial concerns, respectively, decide whether to accept or reject new product offerings.

Most firms today, of course, weigh the prospects of introducing a new product successfully from a somewhat broader perspective than that of immediate commercial gains. Keegan looks at second-round opportunities in terms of the strategies available to the firm interested in introducing domestically successful offerings into new international markets. Bennigson addresses the vital issue of product liability, with special reference to the fundamental precautions to be observed in preventing such suits and the defenses available to the firm in the event such a suit is filed. Rothberg concludes this section and the book with a short note speculating about the future of product innovation in the face of recent economic events.

36. A New Marketing Tool: Life-Cycle Costing

Robert J. Brown

As energy and related costs of maintaining and operating capital goods increase, purchase decisions involving new products will come to be increasingly predicated on total costs over the particular product's life. The author looks at LCC as an important new marketing tool.

INDUSTRIAL PRODUCTS which find a market primarily on the basis of lowest initial cost are not necessarily those which cost the least in the long run. Costs incurred in the years after purchase may be significant, often far exceeding initial cost, and should be included in any purchase analysis. The method used to determine the total cost of a purchase over its life cycle or planning period is known as life-cycle costing. The purpose of this article is to explain the concept and use of life-cycle costing.

Life-cycle costing's most important use is in product analysis where costs expected over the asset's life are large relative to the purchase and installation costs. Factors of particular relevance are length of life and maintenance and operation costs. Initial cost will probably dominate for a short-lived asset while post-purchase costs will be more significant for long-lived assets. Where economies on maintenance and operation costs can be effected, LCC (life-cycle costing) can clearly demonstrate the savings.

Life-cycle costing is not a new concept. It has been used by the United States Department of Defense for a quarter century. What is new is the surge of interest in its use in the 1970s.

The primary cause of the increased emphasis on life-cycle costing has been inflation, in particular, the escalation of energy prices. Expected rising

Reprinted from *Industrial Marketing Management*, 8 (April, 1979), pp. 109–113. Used by permission. © 1979 by Elsevier North Holland Inc.

Robert J. Brown is a professor of finance in the School of Business Administration on the Capitol Campus of Pennsylvania State University.

costs of labor, materials, oil, and other operating and maintenance elements give greater weight to post-purchase cost estimates viz-a-viz initial cost. The result is that life-cycle costing, which allows for both categories of costs, is becoming an essential evaluative technique.

The Method

There are two basic life-cycle costing methods: present value and average annual cost. The former reduces all dollar costs and benefits of a project to present value while the latter converts then to an average annual figure. If the length of life of competing projects is identical, both methods will rank the projects in the same order. However, the information obtained from both methods may be useful. For example, the present value method may reveal that equipment A will have a life-cycle cost of $10,000 less than B, while the average annual cost method will show that the average annual difference is only $200. The buyer may hesitate to incur an additional $10,000 cost to obtain a nonquantifiable benefit associated with B, but may have a changed opinion upon realizing that the difference averages out to only $200 a year.

If competing assets have different expected lives the present value method is not appropriate without some adjustment for the difference. The average annual cost method may, however, be used for comparison. Information needed for LCC is as follows:

1. Initial cost: this will include cost of delivery and installation.
2. Length of life: number of years of life or of the planning period.
3. Terminal value: this may be a benefit if it is a salvage value or a cost if it is a removal estimate.
4. Maintenance: average annual cost of maintaining the asset as well as any periodic replacement of parts.
5. Operation: average annual cost of energy, labor, materials, supplies, insurance.
6. Relevant taxes: investment tax credit, tax benefits from depreciation.
7. Discount rate: future costs must be discounted for the time value of money to the firm.
8. Escalation rate: estimated rate at which costs will grow as attributable exclusively to inflation.

Solving by the present value method is essentially the same as described in the capital budgeting section of any basic textbook on financial management (see, for example [1]). The formula to be used for discounting a single value (e.g., the terminal value) is:

$$P = \frac{T}{(1 + r)^n},$$

where r = discount rate, T = terminal value, n = length of life in years, and P = present value of T. If tables are utilized, T may be multiplied by the present value factor.

The formula for present value of a uniform annual series (e.g., maintenance and operation) is:

$$P = \sum_{t=1}^{n} \frac{C}{(1+r)^n},$$

where C = uniform annual cost and t = the year in which the cost is incurred. Present value tables will provide the factor for a uniform annual series.

If a cost is expected to escalate at rate e, the appropriate formula is:

$$P = \frac{a(a''-1)}{a-1} C,$$

where $a = (1+e)/(1+r)$. A brief table of discount/escalation factors, developed by computer program, is provided in Table 1.

The discount rate to be used is the buyer's cost of capital. The buyer may be willing to provide the rate or the seller may estimate it.

Since expenses are tax deductible they should be multiplied by $(100\% - TR)$ where TR is the tax rate. The investment tax credit is the amount by which the Federal Income Tax is to be reduced. Depreciation is the annual amount by which the original cost is expensed and it provides a tax benefit of TR multiplied by the depreciation amount.

As an example of the use of LCC, take the case where a buyer is interested in purchase of a water chiller of 180-ton capacity. The manufacturer has two models (A and B) available, and the buyer wishes to choose between them on the basis of cost. Details on the two models and determination of the life-cycle cost of each are provided in Table 2. Al-

TABLE 1. Present Value Factors for Annual Expenses That Are Escalating: Life 20 Years

Discount Rate	Escalation Rate			
	5%	6%	7%	8%
6%	18.133620	20.000000	22.103420	24.477340
8%	15.075810	16.532210	18.165020	20.000000
10%	12.717780	13.867230	15.151140	16.588210
12%	10.874180	11.793080	12.815220	13.954010

SOURCE: Author's computer program.

TABLE 2.   Present-Value Method of Solution [a]

	Model A	Model B
Initial cost [b]	$ 28,000	$ 26,000
Annual kWh consumption [c]	150,000	165,000
Operation and maintenance		
(3,000 × 10.87418 × 0.52 =)	16,964	16,964
Power		
(150,000 × 0.03 × 12.81522 × 0.52 =)	29,988	—
(165,000 × 0.03 × 12.81522 × 0.52 =)	—	32,986
Investment tax credit	(2,800)	(2,600)
Depreciation tax benefit		
(28,000 ÷ 20 × 0.48 × 8.51355 =)	(5,721)	—
(26,000 ÷ 20 × 0.48 × 8.51355 =)	—	(5,312)
Present value of costs	66,431	68,038
Present value differential in favor of A:	$ 1,607	

[a] Benefits in parentheses.
[b] Includes sales tax, shipping, installation.
[c] Based on customer's estimated operating needs.
Customer's annual discount rate: 10%. Life cycle: 20 yr. Estimated escalation rate of power: 7%. Estimated escalation of operation and maintenance: 5%. Investment tax credit: 10%. Customer's tax rate: 48%. Annual operation and maintenance cost of each model: $3,000. Power cost ($/ kWh): $0.03. Depreciation method: straight line.

though Model A has an initial cost of $2,000 greater than B, A has a life-cycle cost $1,607 less than B.

If the present value has already been calculated, the average annual value may be found by multiplying by the Capital Recovery Factor. The formula is:

$$A = \frac{r(1+r)^n}{(1+r)^n - 1},$$

where A is the average annual value to which a present value of $1 is equivalent.

In the Compound Interest Tables the Capital Recovery Factor for 20 years at 10% is found to be 0.11746. The average annual cost of each type of equipment is:

A: $66,431 × 0.11746 = $7,803,
B: $68,038 × 0.11746 =   7,992.

If the present value has not been calculated, it may be easier to convert the costs and benefits to average annual values directly. However, escalated values must first be converted to present value (calculations are provided in Table 3).

TABLE 3.   Average Annual-Cost Method of Solution

	Model A	Model B
Initial cost ($\times$ 0.11746)	$3,289	$3,054
Operation and maintenance		
(16,964 $\times$ 0.11746)	1,993	1,993
Power		
(29,988 $\times$ 0.11746)	3,522	
(32,986 $\times$ 0.11746)		3,975
Investment tax credit		
(2800 $\times$ 0.11746)	(329)	—
(2600 $\times$ 0.11746)	—	(305)
Depreciation tax benefit		
(1400 $\times$ 0.48 =)	(672)	—
(1300 $\times$ 0.48 =)	—	(624)
Average annual cost	$7,803	$7,993
Average annual cost differential in favor of A:	$190	

The $190 average annual cost differential in favor of A leads to the same preference as the present worth method. The average annual cost method, however, provides a different perspective in quantifying the yearly cost. Whereas the $1,607 present worth differential could seem an impressive saving, it is possible that the decision maker would consider other benefits of Model B worth the additional $190 yearly difference.

Discounting

Anyone who has ever utilized the net present-value method for capital budgeting will recognize the application to LCC analysis. The only distinction is that LCC is the term generally applied to analysis of a subset of capital budgeting problems: projects that do not generate revenue. The latter may be divided into two types.

Type 1.   Projects intended to produce economic benefits, e.g., devices to reduce the cost of labor or energy.

Type 2.   Projects intended to produce benefits other than economic ones, e.g., pollution control equipment, public schools, defense installations.

The objective of LCC analysis of both Type 1 and 2 projects is cost minimization rather than revenue maximization.

The appropriate discount rate for Type 1 and Type 2 projects is the marginal cost of capital, i.e., the cost of raising the additional funds needed for the project.

Upward adjustment of the discount rate reduces the net present value of the cash flows. When applied to net cash inflows from a prospective project the procedure causes the project's benefits to be evaluated conservatively. However, such an adjustment for an LCC analysis of a Type 1 or Type 2 project, where outflows rather than inflows are involved, would reduce the present value of the periodic costs.

Payback

Payback is the period required to recover initial outlay, and has traditionally been an important consideration for revenue-producing projects. Projects with attractive prospects simply won't be accepted by many firms unless the payback period is less than a prescribed minimum. Selling to such firms by LCC analysis may require some consideration of payback.

Type 1 assets provide economic benefits in the form of reduced costs and payback may be measured as the number of years it will take to recover initial outlay from the cost savings. Although a rough approximation may be obtained by dividing the annual savings into first cost—obtaining what may be termed the base payback period—this would ignore the time value of money and could over- or understate the payback period. A more accurate figure can be obtained if the payback definition is interpreted as the period needed to recover outlay from the cost savings *discounted*. This latter period may be termed the true payback period.

The true payback period will be the same as the base payback period if the cost savings escalate at the same rate as they are being discounted. For example, a new lighting system costing $12,000 and producing operating and maintenance savings of $3,000 a year will have a base payback of four years. If the savings escalate at 8% a year and are discounted at 8% a year, the true payback will be four years (see Table 4 for calculations).

Payback analysis may also be used for both Type 1 and Type 2 projects where the initial costs of competing projects differ and where the objective is to determine the time period required to recover the difference (assuming that the one with the higher first cost has the lower life-cycle cost). The water chiller problem can be used for illustration (Table 5).

TABLE 4

Year			Annual Return	Cumulative Return
1	$\dfrac{3,000\,(1.08)}{(1.08)}$	$=$	3,000	3,000
4	$\dfrac{3,000\,(1.08)^4}{(1.08)^4}$	$=$	3,000	12,000

TABLE 5

Initial cost of A $28,000 less 10% = $25,200
Initial cost of B $26,000 less 10% = 23,400

Amount to be recovered: $ 1,800

Year			Annual Return	Cumulative Return
1	$\dfrac{450 \, (0.52) \, (1.07)}{(1.10)}$	$= \dfrac{100 \, (0.48)}{(1.10)} =$	183.98	183.98
.	.		.	.
.	.		.	.

etc.

True payback $\cong$ 10.5 yr

The buyer now has three helpful pieces of information about the water chillers: (1) model A will have a life-cycle cost $1,607 less than B; (2) the average annual cost of model A will be $190 less than B; and (3) the true payback for the additional $2,000 initial cost of model A will be 10.5 years. In the light of this lengthy payback period, the cost advantage of A may seem of little consequence. In any case, however, the three bits of information are available to the buyer and should be helpful in decision making.

The term *life-cycle costing* is not yet a part of the vocabulary of the average citizen, but as the concept becomes better understood it will have an enormous impact on the buying and selling of industrial goods and services. As buyers integrate factors such as operating and maintenance costs and length of service into their purchasing decisions through LCC analysis, suppliers will be forced to consider these factors in product development, pricing, and marketing decisions. Some firms are already fully aware of LCC and utilize it in planning, buying, and selling, but widespread use of it has yet to be realized. In a society that is becoming increasingly cost-conscious and intolerant of inflation, suppliers who choose to ignore life-cycle costing risk negative economic consequences.

References

1. PHILIPPATOS, GEORGE C., *Essentials of Financial Management*, Chap. 4, Holden-Day, San Francisco, 1974.
2. WILLIAMS, JOHN E., *Life Cycle Costing: An Overview*, Joint Conference of American Institute of Industrial Engineers and American Association of Cost Engineers, Washington, D.C., October 5–6, 1977.

37. Diffusion of Innovations

James F. Engel, David T. Kollat, and
Roger D. Blackwell

The authors review the literature dealing with consumer acceptance of innovation from the standpoint of the innovation, communications, the social system, and time.

THE DIFFUSION PROCESS has four basic elements, or analytical units. These elements or structural variables are:

(1) the *innovation,* (2) the *communication of the innovation among individuals,* (3) the *social system,* and (4) *time.*

The Innovation

An innovation can be defined in a variety of ways. The most commonly accepted definition of an innovation, however, appears to be *any idea or product perceived by the potential innovator to be new.* This may be called a subjective definition of innovation, since it is derived from the *thought structure* of a particular individual.

The operational definition of innovation that appears to have been most used by consumer researchers is *any form of a product that has recently become available in a market.* According to this definition, an example of an innovation is a brand of coffee that was not previously available in a given geographical area. Other examples are modifications of existing products, such as new features in the annual model change on

Reprinted from James F. Engel *et al., Consumer Behavior,* 3rd Edition (New York: Holt, Rinehart & Winston, Publishers, 1978), pp. 304–312; 315–322. Copyright © 1968, 1973, 1978 by Holt, Rinehart & Winston. Used by permission.

James Engel is Professor of Management in the Graduate School of Wheaton College. David Kollat is Vice President and Director of Research for Management Horizons, Inc. Roger Blackwell is Professor of Marketing at Ohio State University.

automobiles or a new package for a food. An innovation can also be, of course, a totally new product such as television, the electric toothbrush, or automobile diagnostic centers. It can also be the opening of a new retail store.

There is thus a need for a classification system to handle widely differing types of product innovations. One such classification system is based on the impact of the innovation on the social structure accepting the innovation. In this taxonomic system, innovations may be classified as (1) continuous, (2) dynamically continuous, and (3) discontinuous.

1. A *continuous* innovation has the least disrupting influence on established patterns. Alteration of a product is involved rather than the establishment of a new product. Examples: flouride toothpaste, new-model automobile changeovers, menthol cigarettes.
2. A *dynamically continuous* innovation has more disrupting effects than a continuous innovation, although it still does not generally alter established patterns. It may involve the creation of a new product or the alteration of an existing product. Examples: electric toothbrushes, the Mustang automobile, Touch-Tone telephones.
3. A *discontinuous* innovation involves the establishment of a new product and the establishment of new behavior patterns. Examples: television, computers.

Communication

Communications affecting the diffusion of innovation may be of two types, informal and formal. *Informal* communications are largely outside the influence of the marketer and consist of reference-group and family influences. There is a temptation to assume that the people who first adopt a product are the ones who influence others to purchase the product and that their communications are therefore instrumental in the diffusion process. However, the interpersonal influence relations appear to be much more complex.

Formal communications can often be influenced by marketers. They include advertising, various forms of reseller support, and personal salesmen. When control of communications is possible, questions arise such as: What types of media are most likely to transmit messages to those persons who are most likely to be the first adopters of an innovation? What media are most likely to be considered authoritative? What messages are most likely to influence new product acceptance?

The diffusion of innovations is a social phenomenon. The word "diffusion" has little meaning, except as it relates to a group of people. Acceptance or rejection of a product can apply to an individual person, but diffusion is a concentration gradient and refers to some aggregate of individuals. The individual's acceptance of a product and his relation to the rest of the group are both so important that one cannot be appropriately analyzed without considering the other. Consequently, diffusion research focuses not only on characteristics of a decision-making unit (individual or family) but also on the environment of diffusion provided by the social system.

Adoption of new products is also a temporal phenomenon and needs to be analyzed as such. The decision to adopt a new product is a *process* rather than an event. People recognize problems, search for alternatives, evaluate new products as potential alternatives, decide to purchase the new product, and perhaps eventually purchase it. The adoption process is not considered complete, however, until postpurchase evaluation and perhaps a further behavior sequence is generated, because adoption is defined to be the *decision to continue full use of an innovation*. To study the rate of diffusion in a social structure, it is necessary to evaluate the exact position of individual consumers in the *process that leads to adoption*.

The Innovation-Decision Process

The process individuals move through in adopting a new product has been conceptualized as multistage in character. These stages have been discussed thoroughly in Rogers and are described in figure 1 along with the variables that influence each stage. The stages described below are knowledge, persuasion, decision (which may lead to adoption or rejection), and confirmation.

Knowledge

The knowledge stage begins when a consumer receives physical or social stimuli that give him exposure to the innovation's existence and some understanding of how it functions. The consumer is aware of the product but has made no judgment concerning the relevance of the product to a problem or need that exists for him. His information is incomplete and the knowledge or awareness that exists is stored in the central control unit for potential future use.

Persuasion

This refers to the formation of favorable or unfavorable attitudes toward the innovation. The individual may mentally apply the new idea to his present or anticipated future situation before deciding whether to try, which might be called vicarious trial.

The persuasiveness of a *new* idea may be related to the perception of risk in the new product, with uncertainty reduction as a determinant of evaluation. When an individual considers a new product, he must weigh

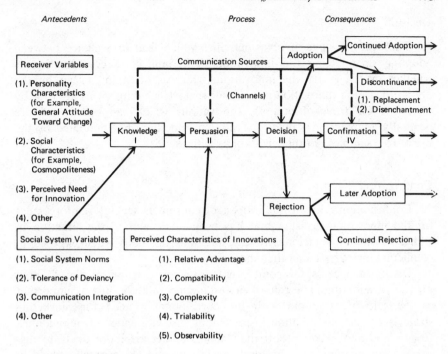

Antecedents   Process   Consequences

FIGURE 1. Paradigm of the Innovation-Decision Process. *Source: Everett M. Rogers and F. Floyd Shoemaker,* Communication of Innovations (*New York: Free Press, 1971*), p. 102.

the potential gains from adopting the product with the potential losses from switching from his present product strategy. The consumer recognizes that if he adopts the new product, it may be inferior to his present product, or the cost may be greater than the increased value. Thus, adopting the new product has a risk involved that he can avoid by postponing acceptance until the value has been clearly established. If, however, the product is designed to solve a problem that is of significant concern to the consumer, there is also the risk that he may lose value from delaying adoption of a product that is truly superior to his present product.

The consumer can reduce the risk of adopting the new product—and therefore his uncertainty about the buying situation—by acquiring additional information about the new product. He may seek out news stories, pay particular attention to advertising for the product, subscribe to product-rating services, talk with individuals who have already tried the product-rating services, talk with individuals who have already tried the product, talk with experts on the subject, or try the product on a limited basis (where possible). Each of these strategies, however, has an economic and/or psychological cost. Moreover, they are unlikely to yield information with certainty.

Decision

The decision stage involves activities which lead to a choice between adopting or rejecting the innovation. The immediate consideration is whether or not to try the innovation, which is often influenced by the ability to try the innovation on a small scale (including vicarious trial by observing the trials of others). Innovations which can be divided are generally adopted more readily. Trial can sometimes be stimulated by the use of free samples or other small units with low risk.

Confirmation

Confirmation refers to the process of consumers seeking reinforcement for the innovation decision that has been made and of the situation in which consumers sometimes reverse previous decisions when exposed to conflicting messages about the innovation.

Discontinuance is, of course, as serious a question as the original process of adoption. The rate of discontinuance may be just as important as the rate of adoption, with the corresponding need for marketing strategists to devote attention to preventing discontinuance of innovations. Rogers and Shoemaker report that later adopters are more likely to discontinue innovations than are earlier adopters and are generally likely to have the opposite characteristics (in education, social status, change agency contact, and the like) to those of the innovators. Discontinuance is most likely to occur when the innovation is not integrated into the practices and way of life of the receivers, suggesting the need for after-the-purchase activity by marketing strategists designed to ensure integration.

Correlates of New Product Adoption

Marketers are strongly motivated to determine what variables are associated with innovativeness. This is based upon a persistent belief that innovators are different in important ways from later adopters. With knowledge of such differences, it may be possible to design new products that are compatible with variables leading to innovativeness or to direct other marketing efforts toward potential innovators. There are three primary groups of variables that are examined in connection with innovativeness. These are consumer characteristics, product characteristics, and social relations within the potential market.

Consumer Characteristics

Sociodemographic Variables. A few variables emerge fairly consistently as associated with early adoption of innovations. Table 1 summarizes the results of studies relating to these consumer characteristics. The table in-

dicates that sociodemographic variables most often associated with innovativeness are education, literacy, income, and level of living. These
findings, it should be noted, and those that follow are primarily based
upon *correlational* studies. Thus they indicate only associations between
the variables and innovativeness. They should not be construed as *causa-
tion*. In many cases they only indicate to the marketer that these variables
facilitate understanding and buying new products when other reasons
exist for buying them.

   Attitudinal Variables. Some attitudinal variables emerge as consistently
associated with innovativeness, as indicated in Table 1. Many parents
apparently want to provide the latest and best products to enable their
children to compete with others. This is manifested in the consistent findings that the variable "*aspirations for children*" is associated with innovativeness. Related to this is *achievement motivation*. Both of these indicate

TABLE 1. Consumer Characteristics Related to Innovativeness

| | Number of Empirical Findings Indicating Relation to Innovativeness (%) | | | | | |
	Posi-tive	None	Nega-tive	Condi-tional	Total	Total Number of Published Findings
Sociodemographic						
(1) Education	74.6	16.1	5.2	4.1	100	193
(2) Literacy	70.4	22.2	3.7	3.7	100	27
(3) Income	80.3	10.7	6.3	2.7	100	112
(4) Level of living	82.5	10.0	2.5	5.0	100	40
(5) Age	32.3	40.5	17.7	9.5	100	158
Attitudinal						
(6) Knowledge-ability	78.8	16.7	1.5	3.0	100	66
(7) Attitude to-ward change	73.6	14.5	8.2	3.8	100	159
(8) Achievement motivation	64.7	23.5	0.0	11.8	100	17
(9) Aspirations for children	82.6	8.7	4.3	4.3	100	23
(10) Business orientation	60.0	20.0	20.0	0.0	100	5
(11) Satisfaction with life	28.6	28.6	42.8	0.0	100	7
(12) Empathy	75.0	0.0	25.0	0.0	100	4
(13) Mental rigidity	20.8	25.0	50.0	4.2	100	24

SOURCE: Modified with special permission from Everett M. Rogers and J. David Stan-
field, "Adoption and Diffusion of New Products: Emerging Generalizations and Hypotheses," in Frank Bass, *et al.* (eds.) *Application of the Sciences to Marketing Management*, (New York: John Wiley & Sons, 1967). © 1977 The Purdue Research
Foundation.

the individual's desire to better the life of his family, especially in his children's education and occupation. *Knowledge ability* refers to the awareness that an individual has of the external world and events in general that occur about him. Also associated with innovativeness is *attitude toward change. Mental rigidity* or *satisfaction with life,* conversely, lead to rejection of innovations.

Product Characteristics

The acceptance of a new product by innovators is determined to a large degree by characteristics of the product itself. It is more correct to say that the product's acceptance is determined by what consumers *perceive* the product to be. Those that have been investigated in multiple studies are presented in Table 2 and are described briefly below.

Relative advantage of the new product is an important determinant of a product's success. The product must be perceived by consumers to be superior to the product it supersedes or to offer a "benefit" recognized as more attractive than present products. Similarly, research indicates the stronger the fulfillment of felt needs is perceived by the consumer, the more readily he seeks information about a new product, maintains interest, and undertakes trial and adoption. Some evidence indicates that the more *immediate the benefit,* the more likely the consumer is to try the product.

The *compatibility* of a new product refers to the degree to which the product is consistent with existing values and past experiences of the

TABLE 2. Product Characteristics Related to Innovativeness

	Number of Empirical Findings Indicating Relation to Innovativeness (%)					
	Positive	*None*	*Negative*	*Conditional*	*Total*	*Total Number of Published Findings*
(1) Relative advantage	78.8	15.2	3.0	3.0	100	66
(2) Compatibility	86.0	14.0	0.0	0.0	100	50
(3) Fulfillment of felt needs	92.6	3.7	3.7	0.0	100	27
(4) Complexity	18.8	37.5	43.7	0.0	100	16
(5) Trialability	42.9	42.9	14.3	0.0	100	14
(6) Observability	75.0	25.0	0.0	0.0	100	8
(7) Availability	55.6	22.2	16.7	5.6	100	18
(8) Immediacy of benefit	57.1	28.6	14.3	0.0	100	7

SOURCE: See Table 1.

adopter. The norms of the relevant reference group will retard acceptance of products that are not compatible with the social system. If the consumer perceives the product to be similar to previously tried and rejected products, acceptance of the new product will also be retarded. The color and design of the package, product, and promotional material accompanying the product act as a symbol to the consumer, communicating to him the compatibility of the new product with his existing value structure.

The *observability* (or communicability) of an innovation influences its rate of acceptance. Products that are visible in social situations or that have significant impact upon the social system appear to be those that are most communicable.

Some product characteristics have been identified that appear to inhibit the rate of adoption. One such characteristic is *complexity,* or the degree to which a new product is difficult to understand and use. Products that require detailed personal explanation, for example, are unlikely to diffuse rapidly. Although the research is far from conclusive, it appears that the *trialability* (or divisibility) of a product affects the rate of acceptance. This is due to the desire of consumers to try the product in a small quantity before deciding to adopt it. When the consumer is forced to buy a large unit at one time, he is likely to perceive more risk in the purchase than if he were able to purchase a little at a time.

Social and Communication Variables

The relations between a consumer and other members and objects of the social system influence the rate of adoption of new products. The relations that affect new product acceptance are of two basic types: marketing dominated and nonmarketing dominated. The effectiveness of one is often influenced by the other.

Marketing-Dominated Influences. Intensive contact with the mass media and commercial change agents tends to produce individuals who accept innovations more readily than others. This fact is indicated in items (2) and (3) of Table 3. The majority of research on diffusions indicates that communications from the mass media affect the adoption process most strongly at the awareness stage, the most important function being to inform the public of new products or ideas. At later stages in the adoption process, personal influences become more important.

Word-of-Mouth Communications

Word-of-mouth, or personal, communications play a critical role in the adoption of new products. Numerous studies have indicated such a finding, as indicated in item (6) of Table 3. Traditionally, it has been postulated that as an individual moves through early stages and toward adoption, the

TABLE 3. Social and Communications Variables Related to Innovativeness

	Number of Empirical Findings Indicating Relation to Innovativeness (%)					Total Number of Published Findings
	Positive	None	Negative	Conditional	Total	
(1) Cosmopoliteness	80.8	11.0	2.7	5.5	100	73
(2) Mass media exposure	85.7	12.2	0.0	2.0	100	49
(3) Contact with change agencies	91.9	6.6	0.0	1.5	100	136
(4) Deviancy from norms	53.6	14.3	28.6	3.6	100	28
(5) Group partici- pation	78.8	10.3	6.4	4.5	100	156
(6) Interpersonal communication exposure	70.0	15.0	15.0	0.0	100	40
(7) Opinion leader- ship	64.3	21.4	7.1	7.1	100	14

SOURCE: See Table 1.

individual increasingly turns to other individuals for confirming information. The individual seeking information turns either to someone who has already purchased the new product or to an "expert"—someone who by reason of training or experience has superior ability to judge the product. For example, a consumer interested in buying a new model of a camera may ask a photographer or a serious camera hobbyist to help evaluate the new model.

Individuals apparently turn to personal sources of influence as the amount of perceived risk in the new product increases. Generally it has also been found that individuals turn to personal sources of information when the choice between products is ambiguous.

Word-of-mouth influence about new products is a two-way information flow. A study of adoption of a new automobile service demonstrated that word of mouth was the most important influence in the *trial* stage leading to adoption (as differentiated from *awareness* and *interest*), and that the innovators actively *sought* opinion from a variety of personal sources.

Marketing as a Change Agent

The marketing organization plays the role that is generally described as a "change agent"—stimulating the adoption of a new idea or product in a social system. The process of bringing about acceptance of a new product does not occur instantly, however. It is a process that occurs *over time*.

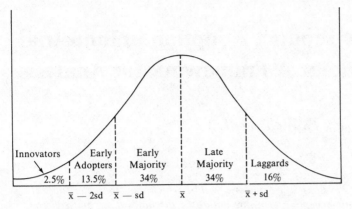

The innovativeness dimension, as measured by the time at which an individual adopts an innovation or innovations, is continuous. However, this variable may be partitioned into five adopter categories by laying off standard deviations from the average time of adoption.

FIGURE 2.   Adopter Categorization on the Basis of Innovativeness

Source: Everett M. Rogers and F. Floyd Shoemaker, *Communication of Innovations* (New York: Free Press, 1971), p. 182. Used by permission.

This is illustrated in Figure 2. Although not all products may follow this distribution, it is useful in making the point that people vary in their willingness and ability to adopt new offerings.

It should be concluded that the acceptance of new products does not occur for "one" reason or because of a "single" influence. A variety of forces are necessary to stimulate adoption. Some are marketer-dominated such as advertising, sampling, and the sales force. Effective utilization of these marketing forces depends upon knowledge of the diffusion characteristics of the product category. At the same time, other variables which are beyond the control of the marketing strategist influence the adoption process. In the latter instance, knowledge of consumer behavior can help the marketer adapt to consumer realities rather than trying to change them.

38. New Product Adoption in Industrial Markets: A Framework for Analysis

Frederick E. Webster, Jr.

This paper develops a framework within which the characteristics of the innovation-accepting firm, the nature of the innovation, and sources of information can be analyzed as an aid to understanding industrial new-product purchase decisions.

RECENT PROGRESS in developing a body of knowledge about "buyer behavior" has been heavily weighted in favor of "consumer" (i.e., individual and household) behavior. While a handful of first-rate studies of industrial buyer behavior have been reported by Cardozo, Levitt, and Wind, among others, the total available theory and empirical knowledge is meager and disjointed.[1] But the need is great. Whether one's motivation is that of the practitioner or the researcher, each new venture into industrial markets seems to pose the same dangers and to be hindered by the same blind spots.

Nowhere can the need for a more complete understanding of industrial buying be better seen than in the decision to introduce a new product or service. New products and new markets pose a real test for the depth of

Reprinted from the *Journal of Marketing*, published by the American Marketing Association, 33 (July, 1969), pp. 35–39.

Frederick Webster is a professor of business at the Amos Tuck School of Business Administration, Dartmouth College.

[1] Richard N. Cardozo, "Segmenting the Industrial Market," paper presented at the Conference of the American Marketing Association, Denver, August 1968; Theodore Levitt, *Industrial Purchasing Behavior: A Study of Communications Effects* (Boston, Division of Research, Graduate School of Business Administration, Harvard University, 1965); Yoram Wind, "Industrial Buying Behavior: Source Loyalty in the Purchase of Industrial Components," unpublished Ph.D. dissertation, Graduate School of Business, Stanford University, 1966.

the marketer's understanding of those buying processes he is trying to influence.

Anatomy of Industrial Product Failures

Analysis of several new product introductions in industrial markets that failed to meet management's expectations reveals a set of conditions which tend to be characteristic. These conditions reflect a rather basic lack of understanding of buyer behavior in industrial markets. When sales revenues fail to meet expectations, the explanation often lies in one or more of the following areas:

1. Failure to define precisely that segment of the total market where the product is likely to have greatest value for users.
2. Underestimation of the amount of marketing effort required to generate the expected revenue level.
3. Underestimation of the amount of new investment required on the part of customers and the extent to which present production technology is made obsolete.
4. Failure to anticipate the demands which the new products make on customers' technical and applications skills.
5. Inadequate understanding of the buying process and influence patterns within customer organizations leading to underestimation of the amount of time required for evaluation and trial by each customer.
6. Lack of awareness of existing relationships and influence patterns between prospective customers and their present vendors as well as relationships and influence patterns among members of the customer's industry.

The body of theory and empirical knowledge applicable to industrial buyer behavior is not as meager, however, as review of the marketing literature would indicate. The economist and the sociologist in particular have an important contribution to make.[2] The remainder of this article is concerned with drawing together several research findings from economics, sociology, and marketing in a framework that permits a useful analysis of industrial buying behavior. The discussion focuses on *new product adoption* decisions because these involve, by definition, nonrepetitive and nonroutine behavior which is more important from the point of view of increased marketing efficiency.

[2] Frederick E. Webster, Jr., "On the Applicability of Communication Theory to Industrial Markets," *Journal of Marketing Research*, Vol. V (November 1968), pp. 426–428.

The Firm as Decision Maker

For present purposes, it is useful to consider the firm as a decision making unit. Industrial marketing strategies are aimed at specific buying organizations and typically involve more than one individual decision maker or influencer within the organization. To consider only individuals in the buying organization is to overlook such critical factors as information flows and authority structures within the buying process. Furthermore, to consider the firm as a decision making unit is consistent with the assumption, discussed below, that firms have characteristics systematically related to differences in their speed of adopting innovations.

There can be no doubt that the nature of the organization and internal communication can significantly influence speed of adoption. Such factors as the extent to which purchasing is a centralized responsibility, procedures exist for coordinating purchasing and using departments, and the existence of buying committees may all have an impact.[3] However, for the purpose of analyzing response to new product offerings, these can be thought of as "neutral" factors, which operate consistently over all of the variables to be examined and are not systematically related to any of them.

The argument to be developed also assumes that the superordinate goal of the firm is long-run profit maximization. This is not to deny the validity of other formulations such as the "satisficing" postulate or, one of its corollaries, sales maximization. While uncertainty is considered in the proposed framework, it is still assumed that the firm tries more or less systematically to evaluate alternative courses of action in terms of the streams of revenues and costs which are likely outcomes from these actions.

A Description of the Adoption Decision

The following comments are intended to be an informal but reasonably complete set of assertions about the decision by a firm to adopt an innovation. Each assertion can generally be supported by at least one published research result or earlier theorizing, or both. They are based on a review of over 70 research studies on industrial marketing, buying behavior, and diffusion of innovations.[4] The framework (or "model") to be suggested for analyzing industrial markets as targets for new products considers (1) buying motivation, (2) amount of perceived risk, and (3) information handling by the buying firm. The model also examines the extent to which

[3] Frederick E. Webster, Jr., "Modeling the Industrial Buying Process," *Journal of Marketing Research,* Vol. II (November 1965), pp. 370–376.

[4] Frederick E. Webster, Jr., "Diffusion of Innovations: A Literature Review with Special Reference to Industrial Markets," unpublished working paper, Amos Tuck School of Business Administration, Dartmouth College, September 1967.

these processes are influenced by the characteristics of the firm and the innovation.

Motivation: Search for Relative Advantage

For industrial buyers, the decision to adopt an innovation is motivated by a search for relative advantage.[5] Relative advantage can be defined as the incremental profit that will be realized from the innovation, compared to the available alternatives. Incremental profit can be realized either from an increase in revenues or a decrease in costs. At least three events, or any combination of them, can lead to a positive incremental profit from the adoption of an innovation:

1. The innovation leads to a reduction in average total cost per unit.
2. The innovation leads to an increase in total revenue, due to increased demand for the finished product because of improved product quality or differentiation.
3. The innovation leads to an increase in average revenue per unit, because the innovation permits an increase in price.

Of course, the reverse is also true. An innovation is "risky" because it may also increase costs and decrease revenues. A decision to adopt an innovation requires an estimate as to which combination of events is most likely. The decision is then based on expected incremental profit, a measure of the "relative advantage" offered by the innovation.

The phrase "relative advantage" implies competition. A firm's motivation to search for relative advantage may be related to (1) its market share relative to its competitors, (2) the recent trend of changes in its market share, (3) its absolute size, and (4) its profit trend. These relationships are not clear, however. One study found that size of firm and relative advantage of the innovation together explained about half of the variation in time of adoption among firms.[6]

The notion that a firm is motivated by such variables as profitability and market share, and by changes in these variables over time, is analogous to the concept of level of aspiration in individual motivation. A specific mechanism can be hypothesized that operates to revise the firm's goals upward or downward in response to its recent success and failure experience, as measured by changes in sales volume, profitability, and market

[5] Jacob Schmookler, *Invention and Economic Growth* (Cambridge, Mass.: Harvard University Press, 1966), p. 199. See also Yale Brozen, "Invention, Innovation, and Imitation," *American Economic Review,* Vol. XLI (May 1951), pp. 239–257.

[6] Edwin Mansfield, "The Speed of Response of Firms to New Techniques," *Quarterly Journal of Economics,* Vol. LXXVII (May 1963), pp. 290–312. See also by Mansfield, "Technical Change and the Rate of Imitation," *Econometrica,* Vol. XXIX (October 1961), pp. 741–766, and "Size of Firm, Market Structure, and Innovation," *Journal of Political Economy,* Vol. LXXI (December 1963), pp. 556–576.

share. Firms with a more successful recent history are likely to be more aggressive and more innovative.[7]

Risk: The Possibility of Negative Outcomes

The adoption of an innovation is risky, by definition, since it involves uncertainty about the outcome of the innovative act, and some of the outcomes may be negative. There may be opportunity losses compared with other alternatives that were foregone (other products that could have been purchased) or with the status quo. The decision maker will act on the basis of *perceived* risk, his subjective estimate of the probability of a negative outcome, and of the loss attached to that outcome.

Firms differ in their ability to tolerate risk according to the size of the firm, its financial well-being, and the extent of diversification. These factors influence its ability to absorb the negative consequences of a wrong decision. Ability to tolerate risk may also be related to such "subjective" factors as management aggressiveness, optimism, and desire for growth.[8] The probability of a large negative payoff, however small that probability, may preclude the adoption of an innovation by the firm. There is some maximum risk which the firm can tolerate. The amount of *new* investment required is not only innovation decreases over time. As other firms adopt the innovation, additional information becomes available, reducing uncertainty about various outcomes. The range of outcomes becomes more clearly specified, as do the probabilities associated with various outcomes.

Risk is also a function of the net amount of *new* investment required for adoption. One of the possible outcomes of adoption is that the investment will prove to be valueless. Clearly, the larger the required investment, the larger the risk involved. The amount of *new* investment required is not only a function of the price of the innovation, but is also influenced by (1) the need for *other* investments to facilitate the use of the innovation and (2) the amount of additional investment that may be required if the innovation is *not* adopted. For example, a company may have to decide between investing in new equipment of the type being used (due to obsolescence or the need for additional capacity) or investing in a new type of equipment. The larger the net investment required for adoption, the more resistance there will be for adoption and diffusion. As the amount of required investment increases, the influence of the size of the firm as a determinant of time of adoption becomes greater.

[7] C. F. Carter and B. R. Williams, "The Characteristics of Technically Progressive Firms," *Journal of Industrial Economics,* Vol. VII (March 1959), pp. 87–104.

[8] Alister Sutherland, "The Diffusion of an Innovation in Cotton Spinning," *Journal of Industrial Economics,* Vol. VII (March 1959), pp. 118–135.

Information: Amount, Quality, and Use

Whether a firm adopts, and when it adopts, are determined, in part, by its awareness of the innovation and its advantages, and by its attitudes toward that innovation. Adoption can be thought of as a five-step process: (1) awareness, (2) interest, (3) evaluation, (4) trial, and (5) adoption.[9] Progress through these five stages is partly determined by the potential adopter's information processing activities. The probability that an individual firm will adopt an innovation during a given period of time is influenced by the amount, quality, and value of the information available. Stated differently, these characteristics of the information available to the firm influence the speed with which it moves from awareness through interest, evaluation, and trial to full-scale adoption.

The amount of information available to a prospective adopter will increase over time as additional firms use the innovation and "word gets around." Amount of information is also directly related to what the selling firm is doing—how much effort it is putting into promotion, and how precisely that effort is directed at particular market targets.

Information *quality* is a subjective concept. It is the capacity of the information to reduce the uncertainty in the mind of the potential customer. It is measured by the reduction in perceived risk. The capacity of the information to reduce perceived risk is related to its completeness and its accuracy, as well as to the credibility which the source of the information is perceived to have in the mind of the receiver. Credibility is a combination of competence, or expertise, and trustworthiness. For industrial marketers, credibility is a function of company reputation and the salesman's presentation.[10] Both influence the extent to which a potential customer is willing to believe what he hears about a new product.

A factor of special significance in industrial markets is the relative advantage to be gained from the information provided by potential vendors. Customer firms differ significantly in their ability and willingness to use information provided by potential vendors. Information may take the form of laboratory evaluation results, pilot test runs, technical assistance in the plant, training of personnel, and other services which result in an increase in the competence of the customer organization. For example, a company selling plastic resins for use in paper coating may also provide information on coating formulations and application techniques. This information is likely to have the greatest value for smaller firms that do not have the necessary resources to generate the information themselves. It may lead the smaller firm to adopt earlier in the product life cycle than the larger firm.

[9] Everett M. Rogers, *Diffusion of Innovations* (New York: The Free Press of Glencoe, 1962), pp. 81–86.
[10] Webster, "On the Applicability of Communication Theory to Industrial Markets."

Smaller firms can make a decision faster because the organization is less complex and because they are willing to rely upon what the vendor tells them.

This consideration of the relationship between value of information and size of firm suggests some reasons why previous research findings on the relationship between size of firm and innovativeness have been inconclusive. Four separate arguments about size of firm and time of adoption have been presented above:

1. *Larger* firms are more likely to be able to afford the net new investment required for adoption, and will therefore tend to adopt earlier.
2. *Larger* firms are more likely to be able to tolerate the risk of innovation, and will therefore tend to adopt earlier.
3. *Smaller* firms are more likely to value technical information provided by the selling firm, and will therefore tend to adopt earlier.
4. *Smaller* firms have less complex decision making structures and may therefore be able to adopt earlier.

Consequently, one cannot specify the influence of size without also specifying the investment required, the ability of the adopting firms to tolerate risk, the value of information that the seller can provide to potential buyers, and the complexity of the organization.

The sources of information which potential adopters rely upon change as the market shifts from earlier to later adopters, and as the individual adopter moves through the stages of the decision process. It was noted earlier that source credibility is an important consideration. Decision makers will resist information sources that they regard as biased, untrustworthy, or incompetent. The extent of this resistance will also increase as one gets closer to a final decision.

For these reasons, commercial sources of information such as advertising, salesmen, and direct mail, are likely to be most valuable for creating simple awareness of the product. Advertising especially is likely to be significant at the awareness stage because it can deliver a simple message to many receivers much more economically than personal selling. However, noncommercial sources of information are likely to be more convincing, and thus assume greater significance as the prospective adopter moves closer to a final decision.[11] In industrial markets, however, word-of-mouth advertising and conversations about new products with "friends and neighbors" such as purchasing agents and engineers in other companies

---

[11] E. A. Wilkening, "The Communication of Ideas on Innovation in Agriculture," in *Studies of Innovation and of Communication to the Public* (Stanford, Calif.: Stanford University Institute for Communication Research, 1962), pp. 39–60; Everett M. Rogers and George M. Beal, "The Importance of Personal Influence in the Adoption of Technological Change," *Social Forces,* Vol. XXXVI (May 1958), pp. 329–335.

appear to have little significance. Field study has failed to identify any significant amount of word-of-mouth activity in industrial markets.[12] On the other hand, it does appear that the seller can influence his prospective customer's decision about a new product by citing successful applications by other companies to somewhat similar problems. The ability to confirm the validity of these assertions probably contributes to the high credibility of such information.

Summary

It has been argued that those firms which are first to adopt an innovation are those:

1. for whom the innovation offers the largest *relative advantage,* as measured by expected incremental profit.
2. that can best tolerate the *risk* involved in adoption, as measured by the amount of investment required and the maximum possible loss. Ability to tolerate risk is a function of size, liquidity, and management's "self-confidence."
3. that have the highest *level of aspiration,* as indicated by recent trends in profitability, market share, and gross sales.
4. for whom *information* relating to the innovation, and provided by the firm selling the innovation, has the greatest value, as measured by
   a. its influence on the adopter's relative advantage from innovating, and
   b. its ability to enable the adopter to reduce perceived risk.

For the industrial marketing manager considering the likelihood of market acceptance for a new product and trying to identify firms most likely to be receptive to the innovation, this framework suggests the factors that should be considered in his analysis. These factors which are said to influence the *adoption* decision by the firm can be restated as assertions about the diffusion process among firms if one considers "time of adoption" or "probability of adopting at time t, t+1, . . ., t+n." Viewed in this manner, these observations lead logically to the following conclusions about industrial markets' response to new products:

1. For innovations requiring some net new investment or commitment of resources and involving some risk of negative outcomes, earliness of adoption is positively related to size of firm, liquidity, and the trend of profit rate, sales growth, and market share of buying firms.

---

[12] Frederick E. Webster, Jr., *Word-of-Mouth Communication and Opinion Leadership in Industrial Markets,* paper presented at the National Conference of the American Marketing Association (Denver, August 1968).

2. For innovations requiring little or no investment, little risk of negative outcomes, and no significant commitment of resources, earliness of adoption is positively related to the trend of profit rate, sales growth, and market share.

3. Earliness of adoption is positively related to the relative advantage (profitability) of the innovation for the firm.

4. Earliness and speed of adoption are negatively related to size of firm where the selling firm also provides information of value to the adopter.

39. Multinational Marketing Management: Strategic Options

Warren J. Keegan

The author outlines and discusses five strategic alternatives open to companies seeking to expand their current geographic product-market boundaries.

INTERNATIONAL COMPANIES can grow in three different ways. The traditional methods of market expansion—further penetration of existing markets to increase market share, and extension of the product line into new product–market areas in a single national market—are both available. In addition the international company can expand by extending its existing operations into new countries and areas of the world. The latter method, geographical expansion, is one of the major opportunities of international marketing. In order to effectively pursue geographic expansion, a framework for considering alternatives is required. Given any geographic product market base within a multicountry system, five strategic alternatives are available to the company seeking to extend this base into other geographic markets.

Strategy One: Product–Communications Extension

Many companies in extending their operations internationally employ product extension, which is the easiest and in many cases the most profitable marketing strategy. In every country in which they operate,

Reprinted from Warren J. Keegan, *Multinational Marketing Management,* 2nd Edition. © 1974, 1980 Prentice-Hall, Inc., pp. 273–281. Note: This article is adapted from his classic paper, "Multinational Product Planning: Strategic Alternatives," *Journal of Marketing,* January, 1969. Used by permission of both Prentice-Hall and the American Marketing Association.

Warren J. Keegan, a noted authority on International Marketing, is visiting Professor of Marketing at the Graduate School of Business Administration, New York University, on leave from the School of Government and Business Administration, The George Washington University.

491

these companies sell exactly the same product with the same advertising and promotional themes and appeals they use in the United States. One of the leading practitioners of this approach is Pepsico, whose outstanding international performance is a persuasive justification of this practice.

Unfortunately, Pepsico's approach does not work for all products. When Campbell Soup tried to sell its U.S. tomato soup formulation to the British, it discovered after considerable losses that the English prefer a more bitter taste. Another U.S. company spent several million dollars in an unsuccessful effort to capture the British cake mix market. It offered U.S.-style fancy frosting covered cake mixes only to discover that Britons consume their cake at teatime, and that the cake they prefer is dry, spongy, and suitable for being picked up with the left hand while the right manages a cup of tea. Another U.S. company, which turned to a panel of housewives and asked them to bake their favorite cake, discovered this about the British and has since acquired a major share of the British market with a dry, spongy cake mix.

Closer to home, Philip Morris attempted to take advantage of U.S. television advertising campaigns that have a sizable Canadian audience in border areas. The Canadian cigarette market is a Virginia or straight tobacco market in contrast to the U.S. market, which is a blended tobacco market. Philip Morris officials decided that they would ignore market research evidence, which indicated that Canadians would not accept a blended cigarette, and go ahead with programs that would achieve retail distribution of U.S. blended brands in the Canadian border areas served by U.S. television. Unfortunately, the Canadian preference for the straight cigarette remained unchanged. American-style cigarettes sold right up to the border but no farther. Philip Morris had to withdraw its U.S. brands.

The experience of discovering consumer preferences that do not favor a product is not confined to U.S. products in foreign markets. CPC International discovered this in an abortive attempt to popularize Knorr dry soups in the United States. Dry soups dominate the soup market in Europe and Corn Products tried to transfer some of this success to the United States. However, a faulty marketing research design led to erroneous conclusions concerning market potential for this product. CPC International based its decision to push ahead with Knorr on reports of taste panel comparisons of Knorr dry soups with popular wet soups. The results of these panel tests strongly favored the Knorr product. Unfortunately, these taste panel tests did not simulate the actual market environment for soup, which includes not only eating but also preparation. Dry soups require fifteen to twenty minutes cooking, whereas wet soups are ready to serve as soon as heated. The preparation difference is apparently a critical factor in influencing the kind of soup purchased, and it resulted in another failure of the extension strategy.

The product-communications extension strategy has an enormous appeal to most multinational companies because of the cost savings that are associated with this approach. Two sources of savings, manufacturing economies of scale and elimination of product R & D costs, are well known and understood. Less well known but still important sources of savings are the substantial economies associated with standardization of marketing communications. For a company with worldwide operations, the cost of preparing separate print and TV-cinema films for each market would be enormous. Although these cost savings are important, they should not distract executives from the more important objective of maximum profit performance, which may require the use of an adjustment or invention strategy. As we have seen above, product extension in spite of its immediate cost savings may in fact prove to be a financially disastrous undertaking.

Strategy Two: Product Extension–Communications Adaptation

When a product fills a different need or serves a different function under use conditions that are the same or similar to those in the domestic market, the only adjustment required is in marketing communications. Bicycles and motor scooters are illustrations of products that often fit this approach. They satisfy needs mainly for recreation in the United States and for basic transportation in many foreign countries. Outboard motors are usually sold to a recreation market in the United States, while the same motors in many foreign countries are sold mainly to fishing and transportation fleets.

When the approach to products fulfilling different needs is pursued (or, as is often the case, when it is stumbled upon by accident) a product transformation occurs. The same physical product ends up serving a different function or use than that for which it was originally designed. An example of a very successful transformation is provided by the U.S. farm machinery company that decided to market its U.S. line of suburban lawn and garden power equipment in less-developed countries as agricultural implements. The company's line of garden equipment was ideally suited to the farming task in many less-developed countries, and most importantly it was priced at almost a third less than competing equipment offered by various foreign manufacturers and especially designed for small acreage farming.

There are many examples of food product transformation. Many dry soup powders, for example, are sold mainly as soups in Europe and as sauces or cocktail dips in the United States. The products are identical; the only change is in marketing communications. In the soup case the main communications adjustment is in the labeling of the powder. In Europe the label illustrates and describes how to make soup out of the powder. In the United States the label illustrates and describes how to make sauce and dip as well as soup.

The appeal of the product extension-communications adaptation strategy is its relatively low cost of implementation. Since the product in this strategy is unchanged, R & D, tooling, manufacturing setup, and inventory costs associated with additions to the product line are avoided. The only costs of this approach are in identifying different product functions and reformulating marketing communications (advertising, sales promotion, point-of-sale material, etc.) around the newly identified function.

Strategy Three: Product Adaptation–Communications Extension

A third approach to international product planning is to extend without change the basic communications strategy developed for the United States or home market, and to adapt the United States or home product to local use conditions. The product adaptation-communications extension strategy assumes that the product will serve the same function in foreign markets under different use conditions.

Exxon (then Esso) followed this approach when it adapted its gasoline formulations to meet the weather conditions prevailing in market areas, and employed without change its basic communications appeal, "Put a Tiger in Your Tank." There are many other examples of products that have been adjusted to perform the same function internationally under different environmental conditions. International soap and detergent manufacturers have adjusted their product formulations to meet local water conditions and the characteristics of washing equipment with no change in their basic communications approach. Agricultural chemicals have been adjusted to meet different soil conditions and different types and levels of insect resistance. Household appliances have been scaled to sizes appropriate to different use environments, and clothing has been adapted to meet fashion criteria.

Strategy Four: Dual Adaptation

Market conditions indicate a strategy of adaptation of both the product and communications when there are differences in environmental conditions of use and in the function that a product serves. In essence, this is a combination of the market conditions of strategies two and three. U.S. greeting card manufacturers have faced this set of circumstances in Europe, where the function of a greeting card is to provide a space for the sender to write his own message in contrast to the U.S. card, which contains a prepared message, or what is known in the greeting card industry as "sentiment." The conditions under which greeting cards are purchased in Europe are also different from those in the United States. Cards are handled frequently by customers, a practice that makes it necessary to package the greeting card in European markets in cellophane. American manufacturers pursuing an adjustment strategy have changed both their product and their marketing communications in response to this set of environmental differences.

Strategy Five: Product Invention

The adaptation and adjustment strategies are effective approaches to international marketing when potential customers have the ability, or purchasing power, to buy the product. Unfortunately, this is not always the case, particularly in the less-developed countries of the world, which contain three-quarters of the world's population. When potential customers cannot afford a product, the strategy indicated is invention, or the development of an entirely new product designed to satisfy the identified need or function at a price that is within reach of the potential customer. This is a demanding but, if product development costs are not excessive, a potentially rewarding product strategy for the mass markets in the middle and less-developed countries of the world.

Although potential opportunities for the utilization of the invention strategy in international marketing are legion, the number of instances where companies have responded is small. For example, there are an estimated six hundred million women in the world who still scrub their clothes by hand. These women have been served by multinational soap and detergent companies for decades, yet until recently not one of these companies had attempted to develop an inexpensive manual washing device.

How To Choose a Strategy

Most companies seek a product strategy that optimizes company profits over the long term, or more precisely one that maximizes the present value of cash flows associated with business operations. Which strategy for international markets best achieves this goal? There is, unfortunately, no general answer to this question. Rather the answer depends upon the specific product-market-company mix.

Some products demand adaptation, others lend themselves to adaptation, and others are best left unchanged. The same is true of markets. Some are so closely similar to those in the United States as to require little adaptation. Other markets are moderately different and lend themselves to adaptation, and still others are so different as to require adaptation of the majority of products. Finally, companies differ not only in their manufacturing costs but also in their capability to identify and produce profitable product adaptions.

Product-Market Analysis

The first step in formulating international product policy is to identify the product-market relationship of each product in question. Who uses the product, when is it used, for what, and how is it used? Does it require power sources, linkage to other systems, maintenance, preparation, style matching, and so on? Examples of almost mandatory adaptation situations are products designed for 60-cycle power going into 50-cycle markets; products calibrated in inches going to metric markets; products that require maintenance going into markets where maintenance standards and practices differ from those of the original design market; and products that might be used under different conditions than those for which they were originally designed. Renault discovered this latter factor too late with the ill-fated Dauphine, which acquired a notorious reputation for breakdown frequency in the United States. Renault executives attribute the frequent mechanical failure of the Dauphine to the high-speed turnpike driving and relatively infrequent U.S. maintenance. The driving and maintenance turned out to be critical differences for a product that was designed for the roads of France and the almost daily maintenance that a Frenchman lavishes upon his car.

Even more difficult are the product adaptations that are clearly not mandatory but are of critical importance in determining whether the product will appeal to a narrow market segment rather than a broad mass market. The most frequent offender in this category is price. Too often, U.S. companies believe they have adequately adapted their international product offering when they make mandatory adaptations to the physical features of a product (for example, converting 120 volts to 220 volts) but extend its U.S. price. The effect of such practice in markets where average incomes are lower than those in the United States is to put the U.S. product in a specialty market for the relatively wealthy consumers rather than in the mass market.[1] When price constraints are considered in international marketing, the result can range from margin reduction and feature elimination to an "inventing backwards" approach that starts with price and specifications and works back to a product.

Even if product-market analysis indicates an adaption opportunity, each company must examine its own product/communication development and manufacturing costs. Clearly any product or communication adaption strategy must survive the test of profit effectiveness. The often repeated exhortation that in international marketing a company should always adapt its products, advertising, and promotion is clearly superficial because it does not take into account the cost of adjusting or adapting product and communications programs.

Adaptation costs fall under two broad categories—development and production. Development costs will vary depending on the cost effectiveness of product/communications development groups within the company. The range in costs from company to company and product to product is

---

[1] The extreme case of this occurs when the product for the foreign market is exported from the United States and undergoes the often substantial price escalation that occurs when products are sold via multilayer export channels and exposed to import duties.

great. Frequently the company with international product development facilities has a strategic cost advantage. The vice-president of a leading U.S. machinery company told recently of an example of this kind of advantage:

> We have a machinery development group both here in the States and also in Europe. I tried to get our U.S. group to develop a machine for making the elliptical cigars that dominate the European market. At first they said "who would want an elliptical cigar machine?" Then they grudgingly admitted that they could produce such a machine for $500,000. I went to our Italian product development group with the same proposal and they developed the machine I wanted for $50,000. The differences were partly relative wage costs but very importantly they were psychological. The Europeans see elliptical cigars every day, and they do not find the elliptical cigar unusual. Our American engineers were negative on elliptical cigars at the outset and I think this affected their overall response.[2]

Analysis of a company's manufacturing costs is essentially a matter of identifying potential opportunity losses. If a company is reaping economies of scale from large-scale production of a single product, then any shift to variations of the single product will raise manufacturing costs. In general, the more decentralized a company's manufacturing setup, the smaller the manufacturing cost of producing different versions of the basic product. In the company with local manufacturing facilities for each international market, the addition to marginal *manufacturing* cost of producing an adapted product for each market is relatively low.

A more fundamental form of company analysis occurs when a firm is considering whether or not to explicitly pursue a strategy of product adaptation. At this level, analysis must focus not only on the manufacturing cost structure of the firm but also on the basic capability of the firm to identify product adaptation opportunities and to convert these perceptions into profitable products. The ability to identify preferences will depend to an important degree on the creativity of people in the organization and the effectiveness of information systems in the organization. The existence of salesmen, for example, who are creative in identifying profitable product adaption opportunities is no assurance that their ideas will be translated into reality by the organization. Information in the form of their ideas and perceptions must move through the organization to those who are involved in the product development decision-making process, and this movement is not automatic.

To sum up, the choice of product and communications strategy in international marketing is a function of three key factors: (1) the product itself defined in terms of the function or need it serves; (2) the market defined in terms of the conditions under which the product is used, the

---

[2] Interview with a vice-president of a large U.S. manufacturing company.

TABLE 1. Multinational Product-Communications Mix: Strategic Alternatives

Strategy	Product Function or Need Satisfied	Conditions of Product Use	Ability to Buy Product	Recommended Product Strategy	Recommended Communications Strategy	Relative Cost of Adjustments	Product Examples
1	Same	Same	Yes	Extension	Extension	1	Soft drinks
2	Different	Same	Yes	Extension	Adaptation	2	Bicycles, motor scooters
3	Same	Different	Yes	Adaptation	Extension	3	Gasoline, Detergents
4	Different	Different	Yes	Adaptation	Adaptation	4	Clothing, Greeting cards
5	Same	—	No	Invention	Develop new communications	5	Hand-powered washing machine

preferences of potential customers, and the ability to buy the products in question; and (3) the costs of adaptation and manufacture to the company considering these product-communications approaches. Only after analysis of the product-market fit and of company capabilities and costs can executives choose the most profitable international strategy. The alternatives are outlined in Table 1.

40. Product Liability—Producers and Manufacturers Beware!

Arnold I. Bennigson

An attorney explains the current law of product liability, defines defective products, and outlines three defenses.

THE NATIONAL COMMISSION on Product Safety reported to Congress in 1970 that each year thirty thousand Americans are killed in accidents involving products, one hundred and ten thousand are permanently disabled and twenty million are injured. Based upon those statistics, by the time you have finished reading this article, two Americans will be dead, seven will be permanently disabled and one hundred and fourteen thousand will be injured.

It is from these injured people and the heirs of those that have been killed that there will be hundreds and thousands of lawsuits against the manufacturer of the involved product. The law that will be applied will be the law of products liability. No other law in the United States has changed as rapidly and as dramatically as this law. The philosophy of the law has swung from *caveat emptor,* buyer beware, to *caveat venditor,* manufacturer and seller beware. When I say, "Products liability manufacturers beware," I mean beware of those changes in the law, for your product is going to be judged by the current law.

Historical Development of Product Liability Law

In order to understand the current law of products liability and why it is as it is today, it is necessary to have an appreciation of the historical development of that law. In the 1850's, the only theory of liability avail-

Reprinted from *Research Management,* 18 (March, 1975), pp. 16–19. Used by permission.

Arnold Bennigson is a member of the law firm of Floyd A. Demanes Associates, Burlingame, California.

able to an injured consumer was based on negligence. In order to be successful in negligence, the injured consumer had to prove that the manufacturer's carelessness caused the product to become defective and that this defect caused the consumer's injuries. The courts adopted a rule that the injured consumer had to be in privity of contract with the manufacturer before he could bring his lawsuit. Privity of contract simply means that the injured consumer had to have entered into a purchase contract or a lease contract directly with the manufacturer before he could sue.

There were complicated marketing schemes in those days and very few consumers purchased their products directly from the manufacturer. Thus, there were very few lawsuits. However, several exceptions to the privity of contract requirement started appearing. The first was the inherently dangerous product exception, including such products as poisons, drug, explosives and firearms, which the courts felt killed and maimed by surprise and where the consumer has no way of physically protecting himself. The second exception applied when manufacturers put goods on the market which they knew were defective. Since this constituted an intentional act, the courts felt that they had to provide further protection to the injured consumer against the intentional acts of the manufacturer.

In 1916, the highest court in the State of New York abolished the privity of contract requirement. They did so based upon the inherently dangerous products exception. Judge Cardozo said that any product that is negligently manufactured that causes harm to an individual is in itself an inherently dangerous product. The exception then swallowed the general rule. This decision has been followed by every state in the United States since 1966.

During this same period the state legislatures felt that they had to give some help to the consumer. They started adopting the Uniform Sales Act which established implied warranty concerning goods that were sold. The implied warranties were that the products were fit for their intended use and that they were safe. In order to be successful for a lawsuit on implied warranty, the consumer no longer had to prove that the manufacturer was negligent. He only need prove that the manufacturer produced a product that was not safe, or was not fit for its intended use and that caused his injuries.

However, the Uniform Sales Act, also included defenses based on the law of sales. These defenses included disclaimer, notice, and privity of contract. Disclaimer is when the sales contract includes a statement disclaiming any of the implied warranties. Notice required that the injured consumer notify the manufacturer within a reasonable period of time after the accident so the manufacturer could have an opportunity to investigate while the facts were still fresh. And last because it was based on the law of sales, the sale required a contract between the two parties. Exceptions to the privity of contract requirement in the implied warranties started being recognized by the courts. The first involved goods that were meant or used for consumption, such as food. Another exception was goods that were used for bodily use.

Then in 1960, the highest court in the State of New Jersey, in a monumental decision, involving an automobile accident, completely abolished the privity of contract requirement concerning all products. Shortly thereafter the California Supreme Court, in the case of Greenman versus Power Products, recognized what we know today as the law of strict liability. The court said that a manufacturer will be strictly liable for any product that he puts on the market that proves to be defective, and that the doctrine of strict liability would no longer be based on the law of sales. Therefore, the defenses of disclaimer, of notice and of privity of contract were invalid. The strict liability doctrine has been followed in just about forty states today. This is not to say that ten states have not followed it, for no state has rejected it, but those ten states have not had the opportunity to accept it as yet.

What Is a Defect?

Let us look now at some of the particular aspects concerning the doctrine of strict liability. We remember that the doctrine requires that the manufacturer be proved to put a defective product on the market. What constitutes a defect? The cases that have held products defective have fallen into three classifications—defects in the manufacturing process, defects in design, and failure to give adequate instructions or warnings concerning his product.

The cases involving defect in manufacture are those where the product is adequately designed, but for some reason, during the manufacturing process, the product ends up not in conformance with the specifications, called for in the design. For example, take the case of a man standing on an aluminum ladder on the fourteenth rung, when he falls to the ground because the rung breaks. The ladder was designed for the welds on the rungs to be stressed many times the weight of a man. An x-ray analysis revealed that the welds on the fourteenth rung were stressed to fifty pounds.

The cases that involve defect in design can be sub-classified. First there are the cases where the design creates a dangerous condition. The manufacture of a large earthmoving machine, while being operated in reverse, kills a man. The earthmoving machine is designed so that the operator, while operating the machine in reverse, cannot see a distance within forty-eight feet behind him. Inexpensive sideview mirrors would have reduced this distance to ten feet. A seven-year-old boy receives third degree burns when hot water spills out of the steam vaporizer. The steam vaporizer is designed with a high center of gravity and insubstantial touching or bumping of the vaporizer causes it to tip over. Further, the top is designed so that it'll fall off. There are no securing mechanisms between the top and the body. At no extra cost to the manufacturer, the top could have been designed with a screw-on feature so it would not have easily fallen off.

The second type of design cases involve circumstances when the design fails to supply a safety device. A young girl is severely burned in bed while she is using a hand hair dryer. She falls asleep and the hair dryer overheats, setting the bed on fire. For pennies, the manufacturer could have installed an overheat cutoff switch and have prevented this accident. An eleven-year-old boy severely injured his arm in a washing machine. The washing machine finishes the spin cycle, so he opens the door to pull out the laundry. Because of a defective timer, the machine goes back into the spin cycle. For fifty cents, the manufacturer could have designed a micro-switch to be placed on the door so that anytime the door was opened, no electricity could go to the machine.

The third type of defective design cases involve those where the design calls for inadequate materials. A senior in high school football player receives a concussion when he's tackled and his head hits the ground. An analysis of the plastic football helmet that he is wearing shows that the helmet material failed under such type of impact. The manufacturers of an automobile knowingly use a gear shift knob out of a plastic that after twelve months exposure to the environment will become brittle. A twelve month old automobile is involved in an accident and the brittle knob explodes upon impact, exposing a spearlike gear shift handle which impales the driver.

The last type cases are those where the manufacturer fails to adequately give proper instructions or warnings concerning a product that cannot be made safe. Such products include an adequate warning concerning the way it can be used unsafely. Instructions must be distinguished from warnings. Instructions are intended to tell the user the most effective way to use the product. However, if there is a variation from the instruction and that variation can cause injuries, the manufacturer must provide a separate warning.

An illustrative case is charcoal briquets. There is no way to manufacture charcoal briquets so they won't give off deadly carbon monoxide fumes. A woman purchased a bag of charcoal briquets with the instructions provided, "Do not use these charcoal briquets in an unventillated room." She of course did and died of carbon monoxide fumes. The manufacturer did not provide a separate warning as to what would happen to her if she did burn the briquets in an unventillated room and, therefore, he was held responsible.

In failure to warn cases where the manufacturer knows his product to be unsafe, but fails to give any warning at all, the courts have allowed the jury to award punitive damages. Punitive damages are those that are intended to punish the defendant as compared to compensatory damages that are intended to compensate the plaintiff for his injuries. One important warning should be given concerning punitive damages. Product liability insurance coverage usually will contain an exclusion as to punitive damages. And if it doesn't, a number of States have laws under which insurance contracts for indemnification for wilful or intentional conduct are void.

Who Can Sue?

Along with the philosophy that the manufacturer is the person who is in the best position to insure against risks of injury, the courts have extended the type of people that can sue under the doctrine. The purchaser of the product can sue, and that's irrespective to whether or not he bought his product from the manufacturer; the nonpurchasing user or consumer can sue, and lastly, the bystander can sue. The bystander is the individual who is hit by the automobile that goes out of control because of a defect in the steering mechanism.

The persons that are subject to the strict liability doctrine include the manufacturer and have been extended to anyone who is in the marketing scheme, retailers, wholesalers, wholesale-retail distributors, and it's being extended further today to protect anyone who is involved with the product for a financial gain. This includes lessors of personal property, bailors of personal property and licensors of personal property.

What products are covered under the doctrine of strict liability? Generally all. There are two minor exceptions, however. Both are based on public policy considerations, for if a manufacturer did not put this particular product on the market, it would be detrimental to the public as a whole. The first include those cases where the product defect is scientifically undiscoverable. This involves such cases as blood transfusions. There is no discoverable way today that we can find hepatitis in blood transfusions. However, if we stopped having blood transfusions being made available it would be detrimental to the American public.

The second exception concerns products that are unavoidably unsafe. An example of this product is the rabies serum. An injection from the rabies serum can cause serious and severe injury, but for the same reason, if the rabies serum were taken off the market, the detriment would be substantial to the public as a whole.

Defenses Against Suit

There are three defenses that the manufacturers do have in a lawsuit based on strict liability. The first is assumption of the risk. If the user of the product discovers the defect and continues to use the product well knowing the consequences of the injuries that could be sustained by the defect, then the manufacturer will be relieved of responsibility. An example is an experienced motorcycle driver who buys a new motor bike. The first time he gets the bike up to fifty miles an hour, he experiences a shimmy in his front wheel. He immediately realized that the shimmy dampener is bad and defective. However, he continues to ride the bike for fifteen hundred more miles, at which time, while traveling over fifty miles an hour, because of the defective shimmy dampener the bike goes out of control and he is injured. In that case, he was not successful in recovering against the manufacturer. He had been considered to have assumed the risk.

The second defense is misuse of the product. This misuse must be an unforeseeable misuse. It must be a misuse that the manufacturer neither intended nor contemplated. An example of this is the case of a paper bailer that was manufactured and designed to compress and bail the paper on the downstroke of the piston. The user of this machine added a chain and a pipe to it and redesigned it so on the upstroke of the piston, it would extract the bailed paper. Because this put excessive stress on one of the bolts, the machine broke and injured the user. The jury held that this was a use of the machine that the manufacturer could have never foreseen and thus, the injured user was not successful.

The last defense is that the product is not defective. Products can still injure and not be considered to be defective. An example of a case where it was held that the product was not defective involved a man who was looking into his car from the left outside window to see if his keys were still in the ignition. The left front side window which he had left halfway open, was designed with a point on the top. When he bent over to look inside the car he inadvertantly hit his eye on the point, putting it out. In his lawsuit, the jury held that the design of that window was adequate and the product was not defective.

In conclusion, I would like to emphasize that you apprise yourselves and keep abreast of the current changes in the law of products liability, for when you find yourself involved in a products liability lawsuit, it is the current law that will be used to judge your product.

41. A Final Comment

Robert R. Rothberg

As THESE WORDS are being written, a combination of double-digit inflation and severely reduced levels of economic activity has raised serious questions about the volume and character of new product activity in the years ahead. Behind these questions is the implicit assumption that new products are a function of market growth and that the American economy is past its peak in this regard. They deserve to be answered, even if the response necessarily must contain a large element of speculation.

Survival Versus Growth

The first point to be stressed is that new products are essential for business survival as well as for business growth. Companies will actively continue to develop and commercialize new products so long as they consider it in their interest to do so, regardless of whether the economy is in a state of recession or growth. The main difference is not so much the presence or absence of opportunity as the attitudes of managers concerning uncertainty and risk. Business expectations can greatly influence both the amount and nature of new product effort. During economic downturns managers tend to be far more interested in avoiding failure than in pursuing success. This in itself may create opportunities for more venturesome companies.

Rising Costs and Product Substitutions

The current recession may be distinguished from its predecessors in two ways, the rising cost of raw materials—particularly energy—and the shortage of long-term capital for business investment purposes. Both can

506

be expected to have important effects on the character of new product activity.

Markets, of course, are always more price-conscious in times of recession than in times of prosperity. Major changes in the relative prices of raw materials should encourage the greater use of substitutes, both in terms of final products and semi-finished or raw materials. Where substitution is not feasible, equally strong efforts may be made to curb unnecessary consumption. Substitution and conservation represent opportunities as well as problems insofar as new products are concerned.

The automobile is a classic case in point. The rising costs of automobile ownership and use coupled with falling real incomes have triggered the increased use of substitutes ranging from mass transit to the telephone. Automobile sales have slumped drastically. It would seem obvious that Ford, Chrysler, and General Motors will have to abandon their traditional strategies in favor of a Japanese or European-like approach of producing smaller, more economical cars with model changes every five or six years instead of every year or two as at present. Given the interest shown by government in the automobile industry it is still not clear whether these changes will be made in response to shifting buying patterns or be mandated by new government regulations.

The important thing to remember is that goods are purchased in order to perform some important customer or user function. There is nothing particularly sacred about the manner in which these functions might be served. In times of economic change, product substitutions can offer important new product opportunities.

Investment Constraints and New Product Initiatives

The shortage of long term investment capital is a less obvious but equally serious problem affecting the development of new products. High interest rates and/or capital rationing require business to scrutinize all new product proposals more carefully, both with respect to the size of the investment and the potential return.

To be sure, the investment opportunities in different industries will continue to vary. At the present time, for example, energy-related businesses, whether in exploration, processing or conservation, look much more attractive than businesses that rely on the discretionary spending proclivities of consumers. Investment opportunities in different industries might also be strongly influenced by new and more selective forms of government intervention. For example, the federal government might elect to subsidize or guarantee investments in certain sectors of the economy deemed to be vital to the national interest, such as mass transit, electric power generation, and so on.

In general, however, business will probably try to minimize the investment required to develop promising new products, and to seek greater assurances that acceptable levels of profit can be achieved. This would seem to imply two things; a heavier reliance on proprietary product technology and proven marketing strengths and a more deliberate pace through the process of product-market expansion.

A greater reliance on proprietary technology and proven marketing strengths means that companies will tend to concentrate on what they do best and try to minimize their weaknesses by working more closely with and through other firms. Colgate-Palmolive, for example, considers itself to be a strong selling organization but recognizes its limitations insofar as the development of new product technology is concerned. This company has tried to maximize its strengths and minimize its weaknesses by entering into a variety of exclusive sales agreements with firms possessing complementary capabilities such as Johnson & Johnson (Handiwipes), Mobil Oil (Baggies), and Weetabix (Alpen cereal).

Consider also Corning Glass Works. It is a leader in a variety of technologies but it appreciates its weaknesses in the marketing area. It has long been willing to enter into licensing agreements and joint ventures of various kinds in order to obtain the marketing strengths it lacks.

The point to be made here is that new products frequently require a sizeable investment in new product technology or marketing capabilities. These investment requirements can be reduced by working with and through other firms with complementary strengths and weaknesses.

If new products can be developed and marketed without a major investment in new technology or marketing resources, the company may not elect to seek outside partners. It can avoid unnecessary risks if it proceeds more carefully through the process of market testing and commercialization. This tactic is only feasible to the extent that the company possesses some proprietary advantage that cannot be easily imitated.

Procter & Gamble, for example, frequently elects to roll out its new products region by region rather than to introduce them nationally. Not only is its total investment in these new products at any given time smaller, but it can take advantage of what it learns as these rollouts progress. It is by no means obvious that this tactic necessitates settling for a lower return on investment, despite the fact that failures, if they occur, would be less costly than would otherwise be the case.

Thus, as far as new products are concerned, the years ahead should witness a wide variety of efforts aimed at two things, lower investment requirements to bring a new offering to market, and increased assurances that it will prove to be technically and commercially successful. Opportunities as well as problems are created by changes in the relative prices of factor inputs and by the shortage of long-term investment capital. It is fruitless to speculate about the aggregate level of new product activity in this or any other economic climate. The real challenge facing business is to identify and take advantage of the opportunities presented by a changing economic environment, making best use of the resources that can be made available.

Selected Bibliography

I. The Importance of Innovation

ABERNATHY, WILLIAM J. and BALAJI S. CHAKRAVARTHY. "Government Intervention and Innovation in Industry: A Policy Framework," *Sloan Management Review*, 20 (Spring, 1979), pp. 3–18.

COOPER, ROBERT G. "The Components of Risk in New Product Development: Project Newprod, Part V," Working Paper, McGill University Faculty of Management, December, 1979.

———. "The Dimensions of Industrial New Product Success and Failure," *Journal of Marketing*, 43 (Summer, 1979), pp. 93–103.

CRAWFORD, C. MERLE. "New Product Failure Rates-Facts and Fallacies," *Research Management*, 22 (September, 1979), pp. 9–13.

DE KLUYVER, CORNELIS A. "Innovation and Industrial Product Life Cycles," *California Management Review*, 20 (Fall, 1977), pp. 21–33.

GEE, SHERMAN. "Factors Affecting the Innovation Time Period," *Research Management*, 21 (January, 1978), pp. 37–42.

HAYES, ROBERT H. and STEVEN C. WHEELWRIGHT. "Link Manufacturing Process and Product Life Cycles," *Harvard Business Review*, 57 (January–February, 1979), pp. 133–140.

HOPKINS, DAVID S. *New Product Winners and Losers*. (Conference Board Research Report No. 773) New York: The Conference Board, 1980.

HURTER, ARTHUR P. JR., ALBERT H. RUBENSTEIN, and others. "Market Penetration by New Innovations: The Technological Literature," *Technological Forecasting and Social Change*, 11 (March, 1978), pp. 197–221.

JEWKES, JOHN et al. *The Sources of Invention*. 2nd Edition. New York: W. W. Norton and Co., Inc., 1969.

KAMIEN, MORTON I. and NANCY L. SCHWARTZ. "Market Structure and Innovation: A Survey," *Journal of Economic Literature*, 13 (March, 1975), pp. 1–37.

RINK, DAVID R. and JOHN S. SWAN. "Product Life Cycle Research: A Literature Review," *Journal of Business Research*, 7 (September, 1979), pp. 219–242.

STEELE, LOWELL W. *Innovation in Big Business*. New York: American Elsevier Publishing Co., Inc., 1975.

II. Strategy and Planning

ABERNATHY, WILLIAM J. and KENNETH WAYNE. "Limits of the Learning Curve," *Harvard Business Review,* 52 (September–October, 1974), pp. 101–119.

BANKS, ROBERT L. and STEVEN C. WHEELWRIGHT. "Operations vs. Strategy: Trading Tomorrow for Today," *Harvard Business Review,* 57 (May–June, 1979), pp. 112–120.

BOYD, HARPER W. JR., and JEAN-CLAUDE LARRÉCHÉ. "The Foundations of Marketing Strategy," in G. Zaltman and T. Bonoma (eds.), *Review of Marketing, 1978.* Chicago: American Marketing Association, 1978, pp. 41–72.

DAY, GEORGE S. *et al.* "Customer-Oriented Approaches to Identifying Product-Markets," *Journal of Marketing,* 43 (Fall, 1979), pp. 8–19.

FAST, N. D. "New Venture Departments Organizing for Innovation," *Industrial Marketing Management,* 7 (April, 1978), pp. 78–88.

FOGG, C. DAVIS. "New Business Planning: The Acquisition Process," *Industrial Marketing Management,* 5 (June, 1976), pp. 95–113.

GULLANDER, STAFFAN. "Joint Ventures and Corporate Strategy," *Columbia Journal of World Business,* 11 (Spring, 1976), pp. 104–114.

HANAN, MACK. *Venture Management.* New York: McGraw-Hill Book Company, 1976.

HARWOOD, DAVID L. *et al. Sales Forecasting.* Conference Board Research Report No. 730. New York: The Conference Board, 1978.

HOFER, C. W. "Research on Strategic Planning: A Survey of Past Studies and Suggestions for Future Efforts." *Journal of Economics and Business,* 28 (Spring–Summer, 1976), pp. 261–287.

HOPKINS, DAVID S. *Options in New-Product Organization.* Conference Board Research Report No. 613. New York: The Conference Board, 1974.

HORWITCH, MEL and C. K. PRAHALAD. "Managing Technological Innovation: Three Ideal Modes," *Sloan Management Review,* 17 (Winter, 1976), pp. 77–89.

KOTLER, PHILIP *et al.* "The Marketing Audit Comes of Age," *Sloan Management Review,* 18 (Winter, 1977), pp. 25–43.

LORANGE, PETER and RICHARD F. VANCIL. *Strategic Planning Systems.* Englewood Cliffs: Prentice-Hall, 1977.

MONTGOMERY, DAVID B. and CHARLES WEINBERG. "Toward Strategic Intelligence Systems," *Journal of Marketing,* 43 (Fall, 1979), pp. 41–52.

O'CONNOR, ROCHELLE. *Planning Under Uncertainty: Multiple Scenarios and Contingency Planning.* Conference Board Research Report No. 741. New York: The Conference Board, 1978.

PESSEMIER, EDGAR A. *Product Management: Strategy and Organization.* New York: John Wiley & Sons, Inc., 1977.

PORTER, MICHAEL E. "How Competitive Forces Shape Strategy," *Harvard Business Review,* 57 (March–April, 1979), pp. 137–145.

QUINN, JAMES B. "Strategic Change: Logical Incrementalism," *Sloan Management Review,* 20 (Fall, 1978), pp. 7–21.

———. "Strategic Goals: Process and Politics," *Sloan Management Review,* 19 (Fall, 1977), pp. 21–37.

ROTHBERG, ROBERT R. and DOUGLAS W. MELLOTT, JR. *New Product Planning: Management of the Marketing/R&D Interface* [Annotated Bibliography]. Chicago: American Marketing Association, 1977.

ROTHSCHILD, WILLIAM E. *Strategic Alternatives: Selection, Development, and Implementation.* New York: Amacom, 1979.

SCHENDEL, DANE and CHARLES W. HOFER (eds.). *Strategic Management: A New View of Business Policy and Planning.* Boston: Little, Brown, 1979.

SHAPIRO, BENSON P. "Can Marketing and Manufacturing Coexist?" *Harvard Business Review,* 55 (September–October, 1977), pp. 104–114.

STEVENSON, HOWARD H. "Defining Corporate Strengths and Weaknesses," *Sloan Management Review,* 17 (Spring, 1976), pp. 51–68.

VON HIPPEL, ERIC. "Successful and Failing Internal Corporate Ventures: An Empirical Analysis," *Industrial Marketing Management,* 6 (June, 1977), pp. 163–174.

WHITE, GEORGE R. and MARGARET B. W. GRAHAM. "How to Spot a Technological Winner," *Harvard Business Review,* 56 (March–April, 1978), pp. 146–152.

WIND, YORAM and HENRY J. CLAYCAMP. "Planning Product Line Strategy: A Matrix Approach," *Journal of Marketing,* 40 (January, 1976), pp. 2–9.

WORTHING, PARKER M. "Improving Product Deletion Decision Making," *MSU Business Topics,* 23 (Summer, 1975), pp. 29–38.

ZARECOR, WILLIAM D. "High-Technology Product Planning," *Harvard Business Review,* 53 (January–February, 1975), pp. 108–115.

III. Concept Generation and Evaluation

AYERS, F. THOMAS. "The Management of Technological Risk," *Research Management,* 20 (November, 1977), pp. 24–28.

BAKER, NORMAN and JAMES FREELAND. "Recent Advances in R&D Benefit Measurement and Project Selection Methods," *Management Science,* 21 (June, 1975), pp. 1164–1175.

BILLER, ALAN D. and EDWARD S. SHANLEY. "Understanding the Conflicts Between R&D and Other Groups," *Research Management,* 18 (September, 1975), pp. 16–21.

CHOFFRAY, JEAN-MARIE and GARY L. LILIEN. "A New Approach to Industrial Market Segmentation," *Sloan Management Review,* 19 (Spring, 1978), pp. 17–29.

COZZOLINO, JOHN M. "A New Method for Risk Analysis," *Sloan Management Review,* 20 (Spring, 1979), pp. 53–66.

CRAWFORD, C. MERLE. "Unsolicited Product Ideas—Handle with Care," *Research Management,* 18 (January, 1975), pp. 19–24.

DEAN, JOEL. "Pricing Policies for New Products" [*HBR* Classic], *Harvard Business Review,* 54 (November–December, 1976), pp. 141–153.

GREEN, PAUL E. "A New Approach to Market Segmentation," *Business Horizons,* 20 (February, 1977), pp. 61–73.

———. "Marketing Applications of MDS: Assessment and Outlook," *Journal of Marketing,* 39 (January, 1975), pp. 24–31.

HARRIS, JOHN S. "New Product Profile Chart" [*Chemtech* Classic], *Chemtech* 6 (September, 1976), 554ff.

HAX, ARNOLDO C. and KARL M. WIIG. "The Use of Decision Analysis in Capital Investment Problems," *Sloan Management Review,* 17 (Winter, 1976), pp. 19–48.

HERTZ, DAVID B. "Risk Analysis in Capital Investment" [*HBR* Classic], *Harvard Business Review,* 57 (September–October, 1979), pp. 169–181.

KIRPLANI, V. H. and STANLEY J. SHAPIRO. *Marketing Effectiveness: Insights from Accounting and Finance* [Annotated Bibliography]. Chicago: American Marketing Association, 1979.

LOCANDER, WILLIAM B. and RICHARD W. SCAMELL. "Screening New Product Ideas—A Two-Phase Approach," *Research Management,* 19 (March, 1976), pp. 14–18.

MAKRIDAKIS, SPYROS and STEVEN C. WHEELWRIGHT. "Forecasting: Issues and Challenges for Marketing Management," *Journal of Marketing,* 41 (October, 1977), pp. 24–38.

McGUIRE, E. PATRICK. *Evaluating New Product Proposals.* Conference Board Research Report No. 604. New York: The Conference Board, 1973.

———. *Generating New Product Ideas.* Conference Board Research Report No. 546. New York: The Conference Board, 1972.

MYERS, JAMES H. and EDWARD TAUBER. *Market Structure Analysis* [Monograph]. Chicago: American Marketing Association, 1977.

RUBENSTEIN, A. H. and H. H. SCHRÖDER. "Managerial Differences in Assessing Probabilities of Technical Success for R&D Projects." *Management Science* 24 (October, 1977), pp. 137–148.

SHOCKER, ALLAN D. and V. SRINIVASAN. "Multiattribute Approaches for Product Concept Evaluation and Generation: A Critical Review," *Journal of Marketing Research,* 16 (May, 1979), pp. 159–180.

SOUDER, WILLIAM E. and ROBERT W. ZIEGLER. "A Review of Creativity and Problem Solving Techniques," *Research Management,* 20 (July, 1977), pp. 34–42.

TAUBER, EDWARD M. "Forecasting Sales Prior to Test Market," *Journal of Marketing,* 41 (January, 1977), pp. 80–84.

VAN HORNE, JAMES C. "Analysis of Uncertainty Resolution in Capital Budgeting for New Products," *Management Science,* 15 (April, 1969), pp. B376–B386.

VON HIPPEL, ERIC. "Successful Industrial Products from Customer Ideas," *Journal of Marketing,* 42 (January, 1978), pp. 39–49.

WEINGARTNER, H. MARTIN. "Some New Views on the Payback Period and Capital Budgeting Decisions," *Management Science,* 15 (August, 1969), pp. B594–B607.

IV. Development, Testing, and Commercialization

ALLEN, THOMAS J. *Managing the Flow of Technology.* Cambridge, Mass.: M.I.T. Press, 1977.

ASSMUS, GERT. "New Product Models," Chapter 6 in Randall L. Schultz and Andris A. Zoltners (eds.), *Marketing Decision Models.* New York: Elsevier North Holland, 1980.

CHANDRAN, RAJAN and ROBERT LINNEMAN. "Planning to Minimize Product Liability," *Sloan Management Review,* 20 (Fall, 1978), pp. 33–45.

FOGG, C. DAVIS. "The Market-Directed Product Development Process," *Research Management,* 20 (September, 1977), pp. 25–32.

GREEN, PAUL E. *et al.* "Cluster Analysis in Test Market Selection," *Management Science,* 13 (April, 1967), pp. B387–B400.

HESPOS, RICHARD F. and PAUL A. STRASSMAN. "Stochastic Decision Trees for the Analysis of Investment Decisions," *Management Science,* 11 (August, 1965), pp. 244–259.

KAMEN, JOSEPH M. "Controlling Just Noticeable Differences in Quality," *Harvard Business Review,* 55 (November–December, 1977), 15 ff.

KLOMPMAKER, JAY E. *et al.* "Test Marketing in New Product Development," *Harvard Business Review,* 54 (May–June, 1976), pp. 128–137.

LEROY, GEORGES. *Multinational Product Strategy: A Typology for Analysis of Worldwide Product Innovation and Diffusion.* New York: Praeger Publishers, 1976.

LILIEN, GARY L. "Advisor 2: Modeling the Marketing Mix Decision for Industrial Products," *Management Science,* 25 (February, 1979), pp. 191–204.

MAHAJAN, VIJAY and EITAN MULLER. "Innovation Diffusion and New Product Growth Models in Marketing," *Journal of Marketing,* 43 (Fall, 1979), pp. 55–68.

MANSFIELD, EDWIN and SAMUEL WAGNER. "Organizational and Strategic Factors Associated with Probabilities of Success in Industrial R&D," *The Journal of Business,* 48 (April, 1975), pp. 179–198.

MOORE, P. G. and H. THOMAS. "Measuring Uncertainty," *Omega,* 3 (1975), pp. 657–672.

MORSE, WAYNE J. "Probabilistic Bidding Models: A Synthesis," *Business Horizons,* 19 (April, 1975), pp. 67–74.

ROGERS, EVERETT M. and FLOYD SHOEMAKER. *Communication of Innovations.* Rev. ed. New York: The Free Press, 1971.

TERPSTRA, VERN. "International Product Policy: The Role of Foreign R&D," *Columbia Journal of World Business,* 12 (Winter, 1977), pp. 24–32.

"Test Marketing," *Advertising Age* [Special Section], 51 (February 4, 1980), pp. S1–S28.

URBAN, GLEN L. and HAUSER, JOHN R. *Design and Marketing of New Products*. Englewood Cliffs, N.J.: Prentice-Hall, 1980.

INDEX